Village Information System

Vol. Two

Innovation of Human Infrastructure

VILLAGE INFORMATION SYSTEM

VOLUME ONE: Innovation of Natural Infrastructure
VOLUME TWO: Innovation of Human Infrastructure
VOLUME THREE: Development Planning

About the Author

Hridai R. Yadav obtained degrees of M.Phil., Ph.D. from Jawaharlal Nehru University, New Delhi, worked with CSIR, Government of India as Pool Scientist for eight years, having authored 11 Books and 73 Research Papers. He has been the Member of the National Wastelands Development Board, Government of India and nominated as U.G.C. Observer for the selection of Professors in the various Universities and U.G.C. Nominee in the Board of Management of Autonomous Institute of Engineering and Technology (GBTU), Lucknow. He is also the Member, Governing Body, Madhya Pradesh Bhoj (Open) University, Bhopal. H.R. Yadav has been the member of various Government and Autonomous Institutions/Universities besides being Founder Member-Secretary-Director of the Institute of Wastelands Reclamation and Rural Development (1990) and Institute of Science and Technology for Rural Development (1994), Editor, *Amethi Sangharsh* (Hindi/Weekly Newspaper) and U.G.C. accredited RIWARD Post Graduate College, Hanumanganj, Sultanpur. Presently he is engaged in the implementation of Agro-Afforestation on the Patta Banjar Lands, allotted to Scheduled Castes Communities to promote MNREGA and Bhoomi Sena Programmes, Women Empowerment and Rural Health Mission Programmes in Amehi.

Village Information System

Vol. Two
Innovation of Human Infrastructure

[With 77 Coloured Maps]

Prof. (Dr.) Hridai R. Yadav

CONCEPT PUBLISHING COMPANY PVT. LTD.,
NEW DELHI-110059

This Study has been supported by NRDMS, Department of Science and Technology, Government of India, New Delhi.

ISBN-13: 978-81-8069-940-5 (Set)
ISBN-13: 978-81-8069-941-2 (Vol. I)
ISBN-13: 978-81-8069-981-8 (Vol. II)
ISBN-13: 978-81-8069-982-5 (Vol. III)

First Published 2014

Published and Printed by

Concept Publishing Company Pvt. Ltd.
A/15-16, Commercial Block, Mohan Garden
New Delhi-110059 (India)
T: 25351460, 25351794, *F*: 091-11-25357109
E: publishing@conceptpub.com, W: www.conceptpub.com
Editorial Office: H-13, Bali Nagar, New Delhi-110 015, India.

Cataloging in Publication Data--Courtesy: D.K. Agencies (P) Ltd. <docinfo@dkagencies.com>

Yadav, Hridai Ram, 1957-
Village information system / Hridai R. Yadav.
3 v. cm.
Includes bibliographical references and indexes.
Contents: v. 1. Innovation of natural infrastructure — v. 2. Innovation of human infrastructure — v. 3. Development planning.
ISBN 9788180699405 (set)
ISBN 9788180699412 (v. 1)
ISBN 9788180699818 (v. 2)
ISBN 9788180699825 (v. 3)

1. Rural development projects—Geographic information systems—India—Amethi. 2. Infrastructure (Economics)—Geographic information systems—India—Amethi. 3. Natural resources—Geographic information systems—India—Amethi. I. Title.

DDC 307.141209542 23

Preface

The soul of India lives in the villages, where more than 76 per cent population survives on the Natural and Human (Socio-Eecomic), infrastructure resources in the remote rural areas. Development programmes for the remote rural areas has been pursued with genuine concern for human values. The development should ensure the betterment and welfare of all the deprived resourceless multitudes living in the remote rural areas.

The existing process of development has neither been true, nor good, nor beautiful, but it does not mean that everything is wrong. Really, the development lies in the techno-scientific application for quantity and quality Agri-Horti-Forestry production for realizing the better quality of life by the village common people.

The process of development should be implemented equally, effectively, efficiently through people's participation, by the people, with the people and for the people for whom such development programmes has been formulated and planned for implementation at the grassroots level.

The formulation of the plan based on the human resources has been adopted but at the grassroots level or village level or field level the formulated and implemented plans did not yield the desired results due to inequities amongst the people mismanagement and disparities between rich and poor. Tremendous pressure on land, water and forest and natural infrastructure and its over-exploitation has led to deforestation, land degradation and environmental and socio-economic crises.

The nature has given bounty to us—land, water, forest resources, agro-climatic conditions and eco-system of the remote villages—must be utilized optimally but not exploited in an unplanned system. The village development planning process for the appropriate management and optimum utilization of available water, land, forest, Natural and Human (Socio-economic-Institutional) Infrastructural resources has always been challenges to the policy-makers and planners.

Thus, there is, an urgent need to evolve a planning strategy through evolving Village Information System and Innovation of Natural-Social-Economic-Institutional) Resources and the assessment of the ongoing development programmes and need based people participatory integrated village development planning.

In view of the above Natural (Human) Resources Data Management System (HRDMS), Department of Science and Technology, Government of India sanctioned a project on "Developing Village Information System in Amethi" which has been successfully implemented at village panchayat level in the Amethi Block.

The outcome of the implemented project has been properly documented and an effort has been made to publish the achievement of this study in the Book Form in three Volumes:

Vol. I: Innovation of Natural Infrastructure
Vol. II: Innovation of Human Infrastructure
Vol. III: Development Planning

The first Volume of this study has been related to Village Information System — Innovation of Natural Infrastructure, viz. land, water, forest and agro-climatic conditions of 44 village panchayat of Amethi Block covering 82 revenue villages and 377 purwas/ tolas/hamlet villages based on the revenue records, Economic Register and other sources of Data and direct field level survey work has been carried out. In this volume an attempt has been made to analyze the socio-economic—institutional infrastructural available resources has been studied at village panchayat level in the Amethi Block.

I hope this study will serve as useful guide for policy planners while implementing agencies for the implementation of Village Development Programmes at grassroots level. This study will also be useful for academicians, research scholars and grassroots level village development programme implementing institutions and social workers, equally to understand field level or village level people participatory development planning process and also the implementation of various integrated rural development programmes.

Prof. (Dr.) Hridai R. Yadav

Acknowledgements

Natural Resources Data Management System (NRDMS), Department of Science and Technology, Government of India, sanctioned a project entitled "Developing Village Information System in Amethi" to the Institute of Wastelands Reclamation and Rural Development (RIWARD), Payagipur, Sultanpur, U.P. An attempt has been made to document the outcome of the sanctioned project in the form of Book "Village Information System (Innovation of Human Infrastructure) Volume-II for which Techno-Scientific assistance of Dr. Bhoop Singh, Director, NRDMS, Department of Science and Technology, Government of India has been highly appreciable because without his support this study could not have been successfully implemented.

Sincere gratitudes are recorded to the revenue authorities of the Amethi and officials of the Block Development and all Village Pradhans of the Amethi Block for providing need base support for collecting the Socio-Economic-Institutional Infrastructural Information at grassroot level i.e. Village Panchayats level in the Amethi Block.

Neeraj Kumar and Dinesh Kumar deserve heartiest thanks for supporting the collection of the information at village panchayat level in Amethi.

The tedious typing of the data and manuscript and finalization of the Maps, etc. has been very carefully managed by Sri Kamlesh Chandra Verma, who deserves special thanks.

I thank to all those, who directly or indirectly supported in the completion of this study. I acknowledge my sincerely gratitude to Sri Ashok Kumar Mittal, CMD, Concept Publishing Co. (Pvt.) Ltd., New Delhi for the publication of this study within the stipulated time.

Last, but not the least, I am highly obliged, grateful and indebted to late Baba Sultan Shah Ji and Nafees Baba and my wife Reeta and lovely son Sahit Hridai, without whose support writing and completion of this study would not have been possible.

Prof. (Dr.) Hridai R. Yadav

Contents

Preface v
Acknowledgements vii
List of Maps x
List of Tables xii

1. Introduction 1
2. Social Infrastructure 31
3. Economic Infrastructure 71
4. Institutional Infrastructure 107
5. Conclusion 139

References 154
Coloured Maps 157
Index 236

List of Maps

1.1.	Blocks and Tehsils, Amethi Districts	159
1.2.	Village Panchayats, Amethi Block	160
2.3.	Houses, Amethi Block	161
2.4.	Households, Amethi Block	162
2.5.	Population, Amethi Block	163
2.6.	Male Population, Amethi Block	164
2.7.	Female Population, Amethi Block	165
2.8.	Population Density, Amethi Block	166
2.9.	Scheduled Caste, Amethi Block	167
2.10.	Kurmi, Amethi Block	168
2.11.	Yadav, Amethi Block	169
2.12.	Gupta Population, Amethi Block	170
2.13.	Carpenter, Amethi Block	171
2.14.	Other Backward Castes, Amethi Block	172
2.15.	Minorities, Amethi Block	173
2.16.	Brahmins, Amethi Block	174
2.17.	Rajput, Amethi Block	175
2.18.	Total Workers, Amethi Block	176
2.19.	Cultivators, Amethi Block	177
2.20.	Agricultural Labourers, Amethi Block	178
2.21.	Non-Skilled Workers, Amethi Block	179
2.22.	Skilled Workers, Amethi Block	180
2.23.	Literary, Amethi Block	181
2.24.	Primary Education, Amethi Block	182
2.25.	Junior Education, Amethi Block	183
2.26.	High School Education, Amethi Block	184
2.27.	Intermediate Education, Amethi Block	185
2.28.	Graduate Education, Amethi Block	186
2.29.	Post Graduate Education, Amethi Block	187
3.30.	Size of Land Holdings (Less than one hectare)	188
3.31.	Size of Land Holdings (1-2 hectares)	189
3.32.	Size of Land Holdings (2-4 hectares)	190
3.33.	Net Irrigated Area	191
3.34.	Canal Irrigated Area	192
3.35.	Government Tube-well Irrigated Area	193
3.36.	Private Tube-well Irrigated Area	194

3.37. Rice Cropped Area 195
3.38. Wheat Cropped Area 196
3.39. Peas Cropped Area 197
3.40. Mustard Cropped Area 198
3.41. Potato Cropped Area 199
3.42. Fodder Cropped Area 200
3.43. Seeds 201
3.44. High Yielding Variety Seeds 202
3.45. Use of Insecticides and Pesticides 203
3.46. Use of Nitrogen Fertilizer 204
3.47. Use of Phosphate Fertilizer 205
3.48. Use of Compost Fertilizer 206
3.49. Use of Bio-gas 207
3.50. Use of Wood Cultivator 208
3.51. Use of Iron Cultivator 209
3.52. Distribution of Cows 210
3.53. Distribution of Buffalowes 211
3.54. Distribution of Goats 212
3.55. Distribution of Hens/Cocks 213
3.56. Average Monthly Income of Cultivators 214
3.57. Average Monthly Income of Agricultural Labourers 215
3.58. Average Monthly Income of Non-Skilled Workers 216
3.59. Average Monthly Income of Skilled Workers 217
3.60. Average Monthly Income of Husbandry Workers 218
3.61. Average Monthly Income of Business Workers 219
3.62. Average Monthly Income of Transportation Workers 220
3.63. Average Monthly Income of Agro-Industries Workers 221
4.64. Water Supply 222
4.65. Hand Pump (India Mark-II) 223
4.66. Hand Pump 224
4.67. Other Sources of Drinking Water 225
4.68. Small Scale and Agro Industries 226
4.69. Low Cost Houses 227
4.70. Non-Conventional Sources of Energy 228
4.71. Household Electricity 229
4.72. Commercial Electricity 230
4.73. National Highway 231
4.74. Pucca Road 232
4.75. Kharanza Road 233
4.76. Kucha Road 234
4.77. Educational Infrastructure 235

List of Tables

TABLES

1.1 Village Panchayat/Revenue/Hamlet Villages (Amethi Block) 7
1.2 Indicators of Social Infrastructures 16
1.3 Indicators Economic Infrastructures 17
1.4 Indicators of Institutional Infrastructures 18

2.5 Village Information System 33
2.6 Sectoral Indicators 34
2.7 Village Information System 35
2.8 Village Information System 36
2.9 Village Information System 37
2.10 Village Development 38
2.11 Demography (Social Infrastructure)—Amethi Block 41
2.12 Caste Composition (Social-Infrastructure)—Amethi Block 47
2.13 Proportionate Distribution of Castes (Social-Infrastructure)—Amethi Block 50
2.14 Workers (Social-Infrastructure)—Amethi Block 54
2.15 Proportionate Distribution of Workers (Social-Infrastructure)—Amethi Block 58
2.16 Literacy (Social-Infrastructure)—Amethi Block 61
2.17 Proportionate Distribution of Literacy (Social-Infrastructure)—Amethi Block 64
2.18 Professionally Educated Persons (Social-Infrastructure)—Amethi Block 67

3.19 Land Ownership and Irrigation (Economic-Infrastructure)—Amethi Block 74
3.20 Agricultural Cropping Pattern (Economic-Infrastructure)—Amethi Block 81
3.21 Use of Seeds and Fertilizers (Economic-Infrastructure)—Amethi Block 86
3.22 Agricultural Implements (Economic-Infrastructure)—Amethi Block 91
3.23 Animal Husbandry (Economic-Infrastructure)—Amethi Block 95
3.24 Average Monthly Income (Economic-Infrastructure)—Amethi Block 100

4.25 Institutional Infrastructure—Amethi Block 114
4.26 Institutional Infrastructure—Amethi Block 126
4.27 Institutional Infrastructure (Religious, Transportation & Others)—Amethi Block 131
4.28 Institutional Infrastructure (Telecommunication)—Amethi Block 134

1

Introduction

1. INTRODUCTION

Sustained, integrated economic development has been realized and commendable advances have been made in the diverse field of rural development programmes, would in reality be incomplete, if such rural development programmes fail to translate into better and dignified life for the majority of people who live in remote rural areas, because the benefit of the development must reach to the down trodden deprived resourceless rural poor multitudes *equally, effectively* and *efficiently.*

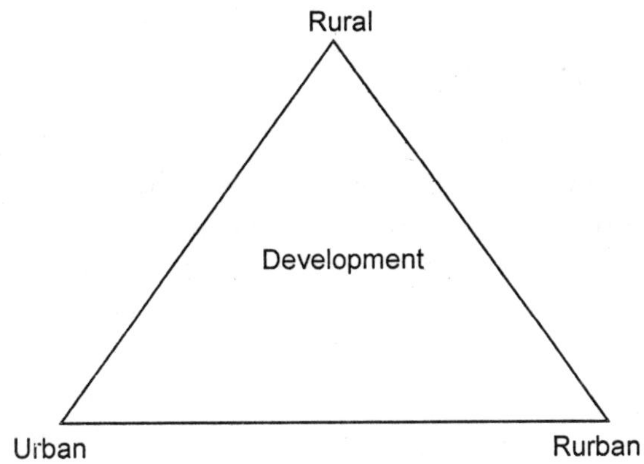

The better quality of life and integrated economic growth has been realized effectively more in the urban areas than the rural areas. The poverty and backwardness has been comparatively more in the rural areas than the urban areas. The government has formulated various policies and development planning programmes to bridge the gap between rural and urban.

It has been argued that the faster development is required to bridge the gap between rural-urban and rur-ban areas. An appropriate and faster development of rural areas are required to fulfil the ever increasing demand of growing cattle and human population, so that the disparities between rural and urban may be bridged to ensure an integrated sustainable development.

It has been felt that the development should be participatory and it should be planned according to the local needs of the deprived rural poor multitudes. The development should be planned through tapping the available village infrastructures, viz. Natural and

Human Resources, local talent, in order to ensure the proper implementation of the various need based rural development programmes self-sustainable.

The various rural development programmes are being implemented aiming at the sustainable, integrated development of the remote rural areas with the focus on enhancing the livelihood of weaker and vulnerable sections of the society, in confirmity with the commitments to accord foremost priority to the integrated village development. In this regard a number of steps has been initiated to make the implementation of ongoing rural development programmes more effective and accelerated.

The formulation and the implementation of various rural development programmes at village level is an intensive, innovative, informative and infrastructure (Natural and Human Resources) oriented activity. The Natural Resources and Human Infrastructure Information System at the grassroots level, i.e. village level are not properly arranged, but such available information needs to be integrated and innovated for village development planning. The conventional methods of collection of information, collection of data at the grassroots level and its storage are not appropriate for quick updation, retrieval and holistic analysis and several problems are existing in the conventional system of the formulation of policy planning and implementation of the integrated rural development programmes.

The human resources play an important role in the policy planning and in the formulation of need based action plans for an integrated development of the village. The human resources include the ever increasing population, caste composition, occupational structure, educational pattern, etc. are the important part of social infrastructure. The social infrastructure has been playing crucial role in the developmental planning process. The social backwardness and the backwardness of an area has positive relationship with each other.

The economic infrastructure of any region also plays an important role in the integrated development of an area. The forward and backward linkage of development and gap between urban to rural areas has been realized by the policy-makers and the planners but no positive approach has been initiated at the grassroots level and such rural development programmes have been in reality found incomplete, because such development programmes fail to translate into better and dignified meaning for the life of the majority of people who are surviving in the remote rural areas because the fruits of the development has not appropriately reached to the downtrodden deprived section of the society surviving in the remote rural areas. The sectoral economy of the rural areas has been based on primary sectoral economy which includes agricultural activity, mining, animal husbandry, forestry, etc., because more than 76 per cent of our population who lives in the rural villages and the village people are dependent on the agricultural and animal husbandary activities. The secondary and tertiary sectors of economy has been concentrated in the urban and rurban areas. The secondary and tertiary source of economy contributes major part of our economy and decides the overall income and economic growth of the area. The economic infrastructure in the remote rural villages has been found partially backward and inappropriate than the urban areas.

The institutional infrastructure has been the backbone of the development because the creation of institutional resources of an area is helpful in strengthening the implementation of economic developmental activities. The institutional infrastructure has been observed more in the urban areas in comparison to the rural areas. To fulfil the gap between rural to urban, it has been initiated to create institutional infrastructure in the remote rural areas as per the needs of the rural poor people including the education, health, water, employment avenues, communication and other amenities as per the needs of the local people, with the view to meet the increasing demand of the growing population. To strengthen the institutional infrastructure the Panchayati Raj Institutions has been given more administrative and financial powers at the village levels. The Panchayati Raj Institutions (PRIs) has been strengthened under three tier Panchayati Raj System, i.e. at Village Panchayat level, Block Panchayat level and District Panchayat level. Need based planning and implementation of the peoples participatory rural development programme has been ensured at Village Panchayat level under the supervision of the Village Panchayat peoples representatives.

It has been realized that the participatory planning and implementation of the development programmes must be initiated and launched through continued involvement of the local people starting from the plan formulation up to the final implementation of the rural development programmes at grassroots level or village level.

It has been properly indicated and mentioned in the Constitution of India that the government should evolve appropriate methods to unite and strengthen the Village Panchayat and provide such powers and rights which can be helpful to work as an unit of Self-Government.

The father of the Nation Mahatma Gandhi stated that *"In the Panchayati Raj System each village should be self-sustained and independent, the implementation of the welfare programmes of rural masses, can be implemented in a better manner in the villages of Vast Rural India."*

In view of the above as per policy of the Government of India, the State Governments established self-government to strengthen the Panchayati Raj Institutions in the rural areas. The historical and revolutionary decisions has been taken to allot the work and to allocate financial resources to implement the planned programmes and also allocated financial powers and administrative rights to provide the Self-Government of Village Panchayats, Block Panchayats and District Panchayats.

The real meaning of democracy is important to the people and Self-Government is the main soul of Rural Development, Management of Financial and Administrative Control of the Village Panchayat and continued participation, co-operation of the local people to establish Village Panchayat for Self-Government *For the People, By the People, With the People* to ensure Peoples Participatory Planning Process (PPP) and implementation of the various rural development programmes for self-sustenance.

The optimum utilization of the available Socio-Economic and Institutional Infrastructural Resources to meet the ever increasing demand of growing cattle and human population for the *Fuel wood, Fodder, Fibre, Fruits, Fisheries, Foodgrains* (F^6) and vegetables should be ensured through people participation to strengthen *Self-Government → Panchayati Raj → Lok Raj → Gram Raj → Ram Raj*, in which Scientific-Technological infrastructural facilities are procured in an innovative manner to generate employment and increase the income of deprived resourceless rural poor multitudes surviving in the remote villages and to improve the socio-economic conditions of the village people for integrated sustainable development.

In view of the above on attempt has been made in this study to analyse the available socio-economic-institutional infrastructural resources at Village Panchayat level in Amethi Block of the Tehsil and District Amethi. Attempt has been made to explain the population, caste-composition, workforce and educational profile at village panchayat level under the social infrastructure available at Village Panchayat level in Amethi.

The agricultural productivity, land ownership pattern, agricultural inputs—irrigation, animal husbandry, primary, secondary and tertiary sectoral economy at village panchayat level have been analysed under the Economic Infrastructure available at village panchayat level in Amethi Block.

The institutional infrastructure including Historical, Administrative, Communication, Water, Energy, Medical/Health, Agro-Industry, Small Scale Industry, Animal Hospitals, Banking, Educational Infrastructure, etc. has been explained at Village Panchayat level in Amethi Block.

2. HISTORICAL BACKGROUND

Archaeologically, historically and religiously Amethi has importance for the tomb of Sufi Poet Malik Mohammad Jaisi and religious temple of Nandmohar which is very famous for worship place of Yadavs. Amethi has been associated with a number of peoples, writers and learned persons some of whom were of the first rank. Malik Mohammad Jaisi (born about 1492 AD), resident of Jais, composed many famous books in Hindi and Urdu literature. Jaisi Memorial is also situated in the Jais town. There is Martyr memorials of freedom strugglers and peasants who were killed by Britishers during freedom struggle. There is no noteworthy archaeological importance of the Amethi.

The Gazetteer was published in 1903 AD which throws some light on the history and origin of the Amethi. It has been recorded that the chief land owning families of the past were the Rajputs of the various clans, who possessed 76.16 per cent of the total land area. Among them the Rajkumars alone held over one-fourth area of the Amethi, while the kinsmen of the Bachhgotis and Rajwars owned 11.4 and 3.4 per cent land respectively. The Rajkumars were the main proprietors of the Amethi and the Chief of the Rajwars were the Taluqdars of the revenue land tax collection. The next to the Bachhgotis and their kinsmen come the Bandhalgotis who owned almost the whole of the Amethi Pargana. Their head was the Raja of Amethi while the Taluqdar of Shahgarh belonged to the same clan. The other Rajputs with large properties in this area were the Bhale Sultans who owned 4.72 per cent land and Kanhpurias with 4.7 per cent and the Bais with 2.8 per cent properties. Of the Bhale Sultans half were Hindus and half Muslims. They were dwelling in Jagdishpur and Musafirkhana areas of the District. The Kanhpurias were chiefly confined to Pargana Gaura Jamo, almost the whole of which belonged to them. The Bais were scattered about in small groups in allover the district.

Manohar Singh, who had six sons, was the only son of the first of the Bandhalgotis. Six sons of the Manohar Singh divided the estate among themselves. Raj Singh, youngest of the six brothers, succeeded in adding to his share those of his brothers Ram Singh and Kunwar Singh who died childless. The fourth descendant from Raj Singh, Sri Ram Deo Singh has two brothers Shyamlal and Dharamvir who owned Barna Tikar Estate on the extreme west and the Tikeri Estate on the extreme east. Ram Sahai, the grand son of Sri Ram Deo, was given as his share of the estate Kasrawan on the northern boundary of Amethi, while his great grandson, Sultan Shah obtained Shahgarh intermediate between Kasrawan and other estates. Thus the hold of Bandhalgotis seemed to have spread over the entire Amethi.

Gurdatt Singh was the next of the Bandhalgotis, who was fined during 1743 by the local authorities and ultimately he had to flee to the neighbouring jungles of Ram Nagar. His fort of Raipur was destroyed in the seige of eighteen days and his estate was taken over. Drigpal Singh, the son of Gurdatt Singh, recovered the estate and from his time dates the present Taluqa of Amethi. The property used to be called Udaiwan. Gurdatt Singh was sometimes styled Raja and sometimes Babu. The title of the Raja was hereditary but it is not known how long it had been adopted by the head of the family. Gurdatt Singh has two sons, Harchand Singh, who obtained the bulk of his father's possessions and Jai Chand Singh, who became a seperate proprietor of Kannu Kasrawan. Hemchand Singh owned the whole of Amethi Pargana excepting Raghipur. In 1810 he was defied by Saadat Ali Khan and the Raja was left with only 48 villages. However, Dalpat Shah, his son in whose favour he abdicated recovered in 1813 all his fathers original estates. Dalpat Shah died in 1815 and was succeeded by his son, Bisheshar Singh, who died childless in 1842. He was succeeded by Madho Singh, nephew of Dalpat Shah. Madho Singh tried to expand his estate and had to face hostilities from the Nazim of Sultanpur, Maharaj Man Singh during 1845. As the result of the hostilities was indecisive, negotiations followed and Madho Singh was given the lease of the whole Pargana with the exception of a few villages. Madho Singh died in August 1891. Shortly after the death of his only son and he was succeeded by an adopted heir, Raja Bhagwan Baksh Singh, son of Babu Sheodarshan Singh, a relative of the late Raja. The estate consisted of 314 villages and four pattis, all in the Pargana of Amethi. Bal Bhaddara Singh, Mahavir Baksh Singh of Jamo who owned 17 villages of that Pargana was a descendant of Raj Shah in the tenth generation. Babu Raghuraj Singh of Baraulia who owned 13 villages in Gaura Jamo was another descendant. The Taluqdar of Bhawanshahpur, Babu Devi Baksh Singh who owned 12 villages and one Patti in the North Pargana Amethi, was the son of Tribhubhan Shah, the third son of Bal Bhaddara Singh. The whole of Kanhpuria possessions were included in the old Pargana of Jais, but it was broken up into four parganas of Jais, Mohanganj, Simrauta and Gaura Jamo during 1775.

The historical background of the Amethi indicates that the area has been extremely ruled by Rajputs, Rajwars and Taluqdars. The kingship ruled estates of Amethi had developed forward and backward linkages, and gap between poor and rich. The kings were rich and the common people of Amethi has been noticed poorer. The most of the lands were held by the kings and the common people of the estate were the service providers to the kings, which led towards poverty of the people. The land concentration among the limited households has been found very high.

The house of Shahgarh was founded by Sultan Shah, the brother of Bikram Shah of Amethi. It derived name from a fort he built and called after himself. The estate consisted of 121 villages. From 1803 to 1810 Shahgarh was with the rest of the Pargana, leased to Harchand Singh but was taken away in the latter year. Then it comprised 40 villages but had increased to 60 during 1846 when it was again given to Amethi Estate.

The Kanhpurias were descendants of Rahas, the second son of Kanh, the founder of the clan. Seventh in descent from Rahas came Prashad Singh who had three sons, Janga Singh who obtained Tiloi, Man Singh received Atheha and Madan Singh of Simrauta. The fourth descendants of Janga Singh were Udebhan of Tiloi and Gulal Shah of Shahmau. The Raja Tiloi in the beginning of the twentieth century was the descendant of Udebhan. His property consisted of Suratgarh and Naudand in the Pargana Goura Jamu of the District.

The other Kanhpurias were the descendants of Indrajit Singh, great grandson of Janga Singh. Bal Bhaddar Singh, son of Indrajit Singh had four sons. Pratap Bahadur Singh, Raja of Katari who owned 13 villages in the Pargana Gaura Jamo was the grandson of Balbhaddar Singh. Raj Shah who founded the house of Jamo was the second son of the Raja.

Thus, it has been noticed that Amethi has been found backward from the historical period, the service class people were socially and economically backward and the land rights were not given to them. The backwardness of Amethi has been historical phenomenon due to kingship ruled estate, the land ownership was concentrated to the kings and their associated people of Amethi.

3. OBJECTIVES OF THE STUDY

The main objectives of the study have been as follows:

- To study the various indicators of Social Infrastructure at Village Panchayat level.
- To analyse the available Economic Infrastructure at Village Panchayat level in Amethi.
- To explain the existing Institutional Infrastructure at Village Panchayat level in Amethi.

4. TIME PERIOD OF THE STUDY

The time period of the study has been based on 2011 as a base year. The census data for the year 2001 has also been taken as support for the study. The field level/village level, door to door survey has been carried out during the year 2011-12 as a base year of this study which has been carried out at Village Panchayat level including revenue villages and Purwas/Tolas/Hamlet villages in Amethi Block.

5. THE STUDY AREA

The study area has been based at Village Panchayat Level → Revenue Village Level → Purwas/Tolas/Hamlet Villages in the Amethi Block of the Tehsil and District of Amethi of Uttar Pradesh.

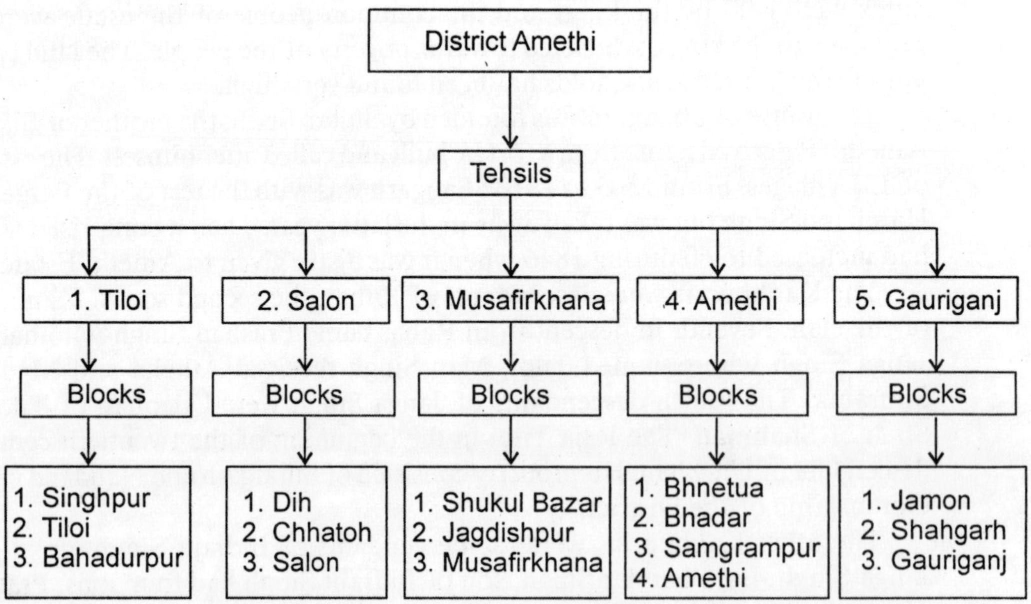

The newly created District of Amethi comprises 5 Tehsils and 16 Blocks out of which Amethi Block has been selected to study the Socio-Economic-Institutional infrastructural resources at Village Panchayat level in Amethi Block.

Tehsil level and Block level location of the Amethi District has been depicted in the location Map 1.1.

There are 44 Village Panchayats, 82 Revenue villages and 377 Purwas/Tolas/Hamlet villages in Amethi Block which have been depicted in Table 1.1. Village Panchayatwise location of Amethi Block has been shown in Map 1.2.

Table 1.1: Village Panchayat/Revenue/Hamlet Villages (Amethi Block)

Sl. No.	*Village Panchayat*	*Revenue Villages*	*Hamlet Villages/Purwa/Tola*
1.	Katra Maharani	1. Katara Maharani	1. Katara Maharani, 2. Munshiganj, 3. Chauraha, 4. Usarapur
		2. Laukipur	1. Laukipur
		3. Matiyar Baghaura	1. Matiyar Baghaura
2.	Sarai Khema	1. Sarai Khema	1. Sarai Khema Khas, 2. Munshiganj, 3. Basuapur, 4. Halapur, 5. Beni Madhavpur, 6. Kutia, 7. Ahmad Nagar
		2. Dandupur	1. Dandupur Khas, 2. Pure Kutur, 3. Jagapur
		3. Ram Nagar Mafi	1. Pure Pandit, 2. Mainapur
3.	Trilokpur	1. Trilokpur	1. Pure Subedar, 2. Pure Bhagwandin, 3. Trilokpur, 4. Pure Darshan, 5. Dubepur
		2. Teri	1. Teri, 2. Kutur Ka Purwa
4.	Ramdaipur	1. Ramdaipur	1. Ramdaipur, 2. Chhawani, 3. Punnapur
		2. Bhupatipur	1. Bhupatipur
		3. Naugnawa	1. Naugnawa
		4. Bahapur	1. Bahapur, 2. Sitarampur, 3. Rajan Ka Pura, 4. Gaudawa
5.	Jangal Ram Nagar	1. Jangal Ramnagar	1. Chhawani, 2. Pure Mannuram, 3. Pure Durga Pasi, 4. Ram Nagar, 5. Ram Nagar Pachhimi, 6. Katara, 7. Shiv Darshan Nagar, 8. Hanumat Nagar, 9. Amriti, 10. Uttari, 11. Van Satahi, 12. Pure Swayambar, 13. Pure Pathak, 14. Sitarampur Usari, 15. Pure Jhilcai, 16. Pure Pandey, 17. Dhamrawa, 18. Pure Bodhan, 19. Derkha Chhatolia, 20. Pure Gayasi, 21. Baramati, 22. Pure Parsada, 23. Pure Bhwal, 24. Pure Digarihan, 25. Pure Sheetal, 26. Pure Hira Simar, 27. Pure Pandit, 28. Pure Belaura, 29. Semsahawa, 30. Pure Bhagan Ahir, 31. Bhusupar, 32. Pure Ram Prasad Kurmi, 33. Ranbir Nagar Uttari Bhag, 34. Ranbir Nagar Dakshini Bhag, 35. Gahari, 36. Gondwa, 37. Pure Murai, 38. Pure Mistri, 39. Karbala, 40. Devi Patam, 41. Kakarahi, 42. Amriti. 43. Mahua Tali. 44. Chhiwala Tali, 45. Walada. 46. Pure Dutta, 47. Usarahia, 48. Pure Banaha.
6.	Benipur	1. Benipur	1. Benipur, 2. Benipur New
7.	Parsanwa	1. Parsanwa	1. Pure Bhatani, 2. Parsanwa, 3. Pasanwa Khalawa, 4. Parsanwa Dihwa
		2. Ram Nathpur Chhota	1. Ram Nathpur Chhota
8.	Mahmoodpur	1. Mahmoodpur	1. Mahmoodpur, 3. Ramnathpur Bada, 3. Munshiganj Road, 4. Lakharia Khera Ke Pichhe, 5. Awas Vikas Gopalpur
		2. Marafapur	1. Marafapur, 2. Mainapur
		3. Valipur	1. Valipur Khas, 2. Valipur Aam
9.	Raipur Fulwari	1. Raipur Fulwari	1. Pure Ram Prasad Pandit, 2. Baniyani, 3. Salamat Ali Ka Purwa, 4. Ojha Ka Purwa, 5. Datta Ka Purwa, 6. Kakawa Mod.
		2. Katara Raja Himmat Singh	1. Katara Raja Himmat Singh
10.	Umapur Ganapatti	1. Umapur Ganapatti	1. Bhagwanpur, 2. Pure Guru Baksh, 3. Pure Prem, 4. Hati, 5. Pure Ichha, 6. Pure Nidhi, 7. Sri Rampur.

(Contd.)

Table 1.1 (*Contd.*)

Sl. No.	Village Panchayat	Revenue Villages	Hamlet Villages/Purwa/Tola
11.	Bhaganpur	1. Bhaganpur	1. Bhaganpur, 2. Durgapur, 3. Pure Lal, 4. Pure Nand Mishra, 5. Sringarpur, 6. Pure Bhojai
		2. Jangal Tikari	1. Jangal Tikari, 2. Dhamranwa
12.	Tala	1. Tala	1. Tala, 2. Lodhani Patti, 3. Bhaisapur, 4. Pure Dina Mankata, 5 Baripur, 6. Mahadewan
13.	Kushi Tali	1. Kushi Tali	1. Patakhapur, 2. Pure Nardutt, 3. Kushı Tali, 4. Pure Ram Lal
		2. Haripur	1. Haripur
14.	Loharata	1. Loharata	1. Loharata, 2. Mali Ka Purwa
		2. Sompur Mankanth	1. Pure Shiv Gulam, 2. Lala Ka Purwa, 3. Kalu Tewari Ka Purwa, 4. Chak Belan
		3. Ahirawal.	1. Ahirawal, 2. Pure Mod
15.	Darakha	1. Darakha	1. Pure Chandika, 2. Pure Shiv Lal, 3. Pure Bariyar, 4. Pure Dutta, 5. Darakha Diti, 6. Pure Jagannath, 7. Naya Purwa, 8. Pure Shital
16.	Mochawa	1. Mochawa	1. Mochawa, 2. Maheshpur
		2. Sarai Hirmati	1. Sarai Hirmati, 2. Barsati
		3. Jhaunei	1. Jhaunei, 2. Pure Daya Mishra
		4. Sultanpur	1. Sultanpur, 2. Pure Daljit, 3. Pure Dashrath, 4. Pure Galhin, 5. Pure Daya Mishra
17.	Nuwanwa	1. Nuwanwa	1. Nuwanwa Khas, 2. Dubepur, 3. Kodari, 4. Saidapur, 5. Teliyani, 6. Pure Gopal, 7. Pure Yamati
18.	Loniapur	1. Loniapur	1. Mattha Shukul Ka Purwa, 2. Teliyani, 3. Badhai Ka Purwa, 4. Loniapur
		2. Bharathipur	1. Bharathipur
19.	Kherauna	1. Kherauna	1. Kherauna, 2. Baramati, 3. Kewalapur, 4. Hardew Nagar
		2. Sarai Raj Shah	1. Sarai Raj Shah
		3. Sarwanpur	1. Sarwanpur, 2. Keshawa Nagar, 3. Gayatri Nagar, 4. Gangaganj, 5. Sringarpur, 6. Pure Bhojai
20.	Katara Phulkunwar	1. Katara Phulkunwar	1. Katara Phulkunwar, 2. Bahorapur, 3. Tewaripur, 4. Kewalapur
		2. Jagipatti	1. Jagapatti
		3. Baghwaria	1. Baghwaria
		4. Parsauli	1. Parsauli
21.	Hathkila	1. Hathkila	1. Hathkila, 2. Dewaraka Tola, 3. Dewatar, 4. Baripur
22.	Rebha	1. Rebha	1. Rebha, 2. Pure Pothi
		2. Mandharpatti	1. Mandharpatti
23.	Raidaipur	1. Raidaipur	1. Raidaipur
		2. Chachakapur	1. Chachakapur
		3. Birahimpur	1. Birahimpur Kundwa
24.	Korari Girdhar Shah	1. Korari Girdhar Shah	1. Pure Matadin, 2. Ghatampur, 3. Pure Bhagwan, 4. Mahadewan, 5. Pure Roshani, 6. Baba Ka Purwa, 7. Pure Telin, 8. Pure Shoschiman
		2. Mangalpur	1. Mangalpur
		3. Dariyapur	1. Tewari Ka Purwa, 2. Gohanwa, 3. Bariyapur, 4. Bikham Bharpur, 5. Manharia

(*Contd.*)

Table 1.1 (*Contd.*)

Sl. No.	Village Panchayat	Revenue Villages	Hamlet Villages/Purwa/Tola
25.	Dedhpasar	1. Dedhpasar	1. Tulapur, 2. Parashuram, 3. Dedhpasar, 4. Sarai Kodha, 5. Pure Dakshin
		2. Jamalpatti	1. Pure Uttar, 2. Jamalpatti
26.	Mahaso	1. Mahaso	1. Mahaso, 2. Basupur Tola, 3. Dewatar, 4. Paripar
		2. Gyan Chandpur	1. Pandit Ka pura, 2. Banktawa, 3. Pahia
27.	Gangauli	1. Gangauli	1. Pandit Ka Purwa, 2. Subedar Ka Purwa, 3. Gangauli Matera, 4. Pure Diggaj Ka Purwa, 5. Bari Ka Pura, 6. Tulsi Pandey Ka Purwa, 7. Agaha, 8. Pure Kurai, 9. Dinaka Purwa, 10. Soiya
28.	Dhandhudhar	1. Dhandhudhar	1. Dhandhudhaı, 2. Pure Upadhyaya
		2. Pithipur	1. Pure Hanuman Tewari, 2. Pure Ojhan, 3. Pure Mishra
29.	Gaderi	1. Gaderi	1. Gaderi, 2. Sadwa, 3. Banpurwa, 4. Pure Hardatt, 5. Pure Duban, 6. Pure Kalika, 7. Pure Tularam, 8. Rampur, 9. Pure Gangu, 10. Pure Bal, 11. Pure Bidhasia, 12. Samari, 13. Pure Bhagwandin, 14. Pure Hawaldar, 15. Pure Chandra Mani, 16. Bangarwa
30.	Bhusahari	1. Bhusahari	1. Bhusahari Khas, 2. Barain Tola, 3. Pure Gaderian, 4. Karnaipur, 5. Makhdumpur, 6. Patipur, 7. Jham Singh Ka Purwa
31.	Purabgaon	1. Purabgaon	1. Purabgaon
32.	Chaturbhujpur	1. Chaturbhujpur	1. Pure Khuklan, 2. Hanumanganj, 3. Jagat Gaon, 4. Chaurbhujpur, 5. Pure Harsahai, 5. Piıepur
33.	Maharajpur	1. Maharajpur	1. Maharajpur Khas, 2. Kurmiyan Ka Purwa, 3. Khusadi
34.	Agahar	1. Agahar	1. Agahardih, 2. Pure Ram Sewak, 3. Pure Bhawani, 4. Pure Gosnai, 5. Pure Patoli
35.	Saidpur	1. Saidpur	1. Pure Shivalal, 2. Pure Dala, 3. Pure Vir Singh, 4. Saidpur
		2. Dalshahpur	1. Dalshahpur, 2. Ram Nagar Pur, 3. Sadakpur
36.	Kakawa	1. Kakawa	1. Kuwnarganj, 2. Kakawa, 3. Pure Ganesh Baksh Singh, 4. Pure Ram Sahai, 5. Pure Girdhari, 6. Shahadara, 7. Kakarahia, 8. Voda Nagar, 9. Pure Valdi Tewari
		2. Vidhasiya	1. Pure Gadarian, 2. Vidhasiya, 3. Pure Dhandauia, 4. Pure Valdu, 5. Pure Tada Tewari
37.	Saraiya Duban	1. Saraiya Duban	1. Saraiya Duban, 2. Jaggubari, 3. Pure Lal Ram Prasad, 4. Gudiyan Tola, 5. Pure Man Kunwar, 6. Pure Brahmachari, 7. Murarpur
38.	Kohara	1. Kohara	1. Harakhpur, 2. Dodhai Ka Purwa, 2. Dihawan, 4. Vishyapur, 5. Devigarh, 6. Kohara Khas, 7. Ahiranki Saraiya, 8. Aditya Nagar (Chamrauti), 9. Pure Jogdhar, 10. Ulapur, 11. Pure Shivdas, 12. Pure Hanuman Mishra, 14. Bhawani Baksh (Chaubepur), 14. Pure Jagannath. 15. Baniyan Ka Purwa, 16. Ganga Mishra Ka Purwa, 17. Pure Shiv Bhikh, 18. Malin Ka Purwa, 19. Ojha Ka Purwa, 20. Murai Ka Purwa, 21. Pure Bhadosian, 22. Mukunpur, 23. Pure Ghisiya.

(*Contd.*)

Table 1.1 (*Contd.*)

Sl. No.	*Village Panchayat*	*Revenue Villages*	*Hamlet Villages/Purwa/Tola*
39.	Mahmadpur	1. Mahmadpur	1. Mahmadpur, 2. Shankarpur, 3. Dudhai Ka Purwa, 4. Kalu Ka Purwa, 5. Sitaram Nagar, 6. Chaubepur, 7. Kurmi Ka Purwa, 8. Pure Baksh Singh, 9. Hulasi Ka Purwa, 10. Bhawani Baksh Ka Purwa, 11. Pure Pandit Ka Purwa, 12. Pure Hari Baksh
40.	Naraini	1. Naraini	1. Narainidih, 2. Pure Pachhim, 3. Pure Matlu, 4. Pure Wakta, 5. Dadi, 6. Pure Gangeran, 7. Pure Ayodhya, 8. Pure Khojhwa
41.	Nainaha	1. Nainaha	1. Nainaha Khas, 2. Pure Tewari, 3. Pure Bishen, 4. Dhanapur, 5. Pure Satya Shukul
		2. Bartali	1. Bartali Khas, 2. Dhaksahiya
		3. Rajapur Kohara	1. Pure Jangali, 2. Damgarha, 3. Rajapur, 4. Ajyab Sinda, 5. Sadarpur
42.	Ramgarh	1. Ramgarh	1. Badisoiya, 2. Chhoti Soiya, 3. Pure Bhoop, 4. Rampur, 5. Bahni, 6. Mahoka, 7. Saraiya Purwa, 8. Pure Kotwa, 9. Ramgarh Khas
43.	Himmatgarh	1. Himmatgarh	1. Pure Bhoop, 2. Madaripur, 3. Pure Ajit, 4. Jhali, 5. Visheshganj, 6. Pure Upadhyaya
44.	Dehra	1. Dehra	1. Dehra Khas, 2. Pure Darjiyan, 3. Pure Shivpal, 4. Pure Pandey, Shanichara, 6. Gulabgarh, 7. Shukla Ka Purwa
		2. Kudawa Mohamadpur	1. Daya Garha, 2. Pure Jhingur, 3. Kudwa Mohamadpur
Total	**44**	**82**	**377**

6. HUMAN INFRASTRUCTURE

The planning process for better and optimal utilization of available human resources always has been a great challenge to the policy-makers and planners. There is an urgent need to evolve a planning strategy applicable at different levels, i.e. Village level-Block level-District level especially village as lowest unit of planning to strengthen Panchayati Raj system. In this study an attempt has been made to discuss vide range of issues which are very important for Local Area Development Planning. In the present context, when efforts are being made to allocate resources at Village Panchayat level, it has become necessary to explain the human resources including Socio-Economic-Institutional and man made Infrastructural Resources at Village Panchayat level in Amethi.

The planning is an organised process by which the people achieves its developmental goals or planning is a means to achieve the development. The development means the evolution of the people in which the people acquire better perception and best control over its natural and human resources. The Macro-Level Planning process has been adopted in our country, while Micro-Level Planning did not yield the desired results. Natural and Human Resources Data Management System has been initiated by the Department of Science and Technology, Government of India during 1982, focusing on the technological and institutional capacity building, so that the people can plan their own need based development planning through tapping the available local level human infrastructural resources. Micro-level/Village Development Planning at Village Panchayat level in Amethi Block adopting various sectoral indicators at the grassroots level.

Newly created District Amethi comprises Salon and Tiloi Tehsils of the Rae Bareli District and Musafirkhana, Amethi and Gauriganj Tehsils of the Sultanpur District. There are 16 Development Blocks in the Amethi. Amethi Block has been selected for analysing Human Infrastructural resources at Village Panchayat level. There are 44 Village Panchayats in the Amethi Block.

There are very insignificant archaeological importance of the Amethi but it has religious importance including Sufi Saint Malik Mohammad Jaisi and religious temple at Village Nand Mohar which has been very famous worship place of Yadavs. Amethi has also strong historical background due to kingship rulership.

The human resources of the Amethi plays an important crucial role in its economic development. The human resources of the area includes social-economic and institutional infrastructure available at Village Panchayat level. Various sectoral indicators has been selected to analyse the availability of human infrastructure for the development planning at Village Panchayat level in Amethi Block. Various sub-indicators related to human infrastructure data have been collected at Village Panchayat level through primary field survey.

The creation and establishment of institutional infrastructure has also been alaysed at Village Panchayat level in the study area. The data related to the institutional infrastructure has been collected through door to door survey and primary field survey at Village Panchayat level. The created institutional infrastructure at village level including the community amenities also plays an important role in the policy making and formulation of the need based village development planning at Village Panchayat level to strengthen the Panchayati Raj Institutions at the grassroots level to fulfil the increasing demand of ever growing population.

6.1 Social Infrastructure

The social infrastructure at Village level or at grassroots level varies from one place to another. The social backwardness of the area affects the economy of the Amethi. It is known fact that the Amethi has been kingship ruled Estate. The Kings/Rajas ruled the Amethi. The Rajputs/Rajwars and Taluqdars ruled the Amethi as Revenue Tax Collector from the farmers. The land ownership right has been vested with the kings and his associated peoples. The service class providers in Amethi has been backward from historical period till now, because they do not have the land ownership rights and these people have been land cultivators and service providing class to the Kings. The Rajas and Maharajas exploited the social infrastructure of the area historically. The kings did not allow the common people to grow and develop due to which the common people of the area especially the service class population has been backward socially at Village level in Amethi. Most of the households of the Amethi are landless labourers and surviving under below poverty line.

The social infrastructural resources include the total population (male and female), number of households and the number of houses at Village Panchayat level. The pressure of the population and the size of land holding and the concentration of the land affects the Village development planning. Due consideration of the households and the need based planning may affect positively, for the finalization of the planning process and implementation of the people's participatory development planning at Village level or grassroots level in Amethi.

The village people are socially fabricated with each other. Historically, it is known fact that Amethi has been ruled by Kings and Taluqdars and exploited by the local land revenue tax collectors, due to which the rich people became richest and the poor people became poorest. Similarly, the large size land holders grabbed more land. The land was concentrated within the 10 per cent of the total population in Amethi. The land concentration adversely affected the socio-economic condition of the people of Amethi which led towards the socio-economic backwardness of the common people of Amethi from the historical period. Social structure of Amethi has also been different than the other parts of the district because the kings and Rajputs were basically the rulers of the Estate out of which the Brahmins were the religious service class people who were helping the Rajputs in the worship of the God while the backward class and the scheduled caste people were the service providing class to the rulers. The minorities especially the Muslims, were those people who changed their religion during the Muslim invasion in the Mughal period. The kings and service class providers changed their religion due to the interest of saving their land and properties. The kings who opted to change their religion, also forced to change the religion of the service providers as well.

The innovation of the workforce including primary, secondary and tertiary workers is important for analysing the social infrastructure of the village. The analysis of the cultivators/farmers, agricultural labourers, skilled labourers, non-skilled labourers, plantation and animal husbandry workers, transportation workers, business workers, other workers including the office workers and small scale/agro-industry workers are necessary in the process of planning through people's participatory village development planning at the grassroots level in Amethi.

The educational profile of the village also plays an important role in the plan formulation for the integrated village development. It has been realised that educationally backward villages are socially and economically backward. Therefore, the innovation of the educational profile including total literacy ratio and number of illiterates and the primary, secondary (Junior and High School), Intermediate, Graduate, Post-Graduate, Vocational Training personnel including Industrial Training, Polytechnic, Graduate Technology and Management Graduates and Undergraduate educated people and their involvement in the development and also the growth of economy may be an asset for the policy makers, village development planners and the officials of the implementing institutions at village level.

In view of the above an attempt has been made in this study to innovate the various social infrastructural resources especially the population, caste composition, workforce and educational profile at Village Panchayat level in Amethi Block which can be used as tool for the formulation of policy planning and implementation of need based integrated village development programmes in Amethi.

6.2 Economic Infrastructure

The economic infrastructure of Amethi is very poor from the historical era, due to kingship ruled estate. Proportionately the maximum land ownership was concentrated with the kings/taluqdars and land revenue tax collectors. The high concentration of land among the limited section of the society has led towards economic backwardness among the large section of the people of the Amethi. The highest land concentration has also caused very poor fertility status of the soil which could not be properly conserved for agricultural and other activities, due to the large size land holdings the farmers could not pay proper attention for its reclamation and the conservation of the land, which has led to usarization and waterlogging problem of the land. The sustained growth in the area under the wastelands has not only caused environmental crisis of the area but it has created socio-economic backwardness of the people of Amethi. Due to techno-scientific ignorance and socio-economic backwardness the wastelands could not be reclaimed sustainably. Various government and non-government organisations have been engaged in the reclamation of wastelands for the last three decades but they could not achieve the requisite targets due to non-people's participation. The reclamation of wastelands for agricultural, agro-forestry, social-forestry programmes has been implemented without people's participation and without willing consent of the local people, may have been the one of the basic reasons for such unsuccessful efforts.

It has been noticed that less than one hectare land is owned by most of the households of the Amethi. Very high size of land holding is concentrated among very nominal landholers, while very nominal land has been owned by most of the households of the Amethi. An attempt has been made in this study to analyse the land concentration at Village Panchayat level in Amethi.

The net irrigated area and the gross irrigated area has not been properly managed, because the net cultivated area and the gross cropped area at village level in Amethi varies from one village to another. The need based scientific irrigation system has been managed which has led to an increase in the area and Usar land, Banjar land and the waterlogged land in Amethi and it has also adversely affected the agricultural productivity of the area. The canal irrigation is one of the dominant source of irrigation in Amethi, followed by the private tube-well irrigation system. The irrigation through the government tube-well is being ensured among the selected villages while other sources of irrigation including pond irrigation etc. are nominally observed in this area. It has been observed that irrigation system of the area has been mis-managed. Appropriate scientific management of irrigation system including sprinkler irrigation system may be helpful in increasing the agricultural productivity of Amethi.

The wheat and paddy crops are one of the most dominant foodgrain crops of the Amethi followed by the Barley, Pea, Mustard, Sugarcane, Potato, Sanai, Green fodder and other foodgrain crops including commercial crops and pulses are grown in this area.

There is no scientific and hi-tech use of agricultural implements in Amethi. The traditional agricultural implements are still used which have also been responsible for low agricultural productivity. Mostly, the traditional wood cultivators and iron cultivators are being used by the farmers of Amethi. Proportionately very nominal high-tech cultivators are used for the agricultural activities. The traditional agricultural implements are time taking and involves much more power for its application in the field. The use of tractors for cultivation by the individual farmers and also on the hire basis are being used by most of the farmers of Amethi. The other agricultural implements including Khurpi, Hansia, Kudal, Spade and other traditional agricultural implements are used by the cultivators in the various villages of Amethi. The use of traditional agricultural implements has also been one of the major factor for the poor agricultural productivity of the area.

It has been noticed that the traditional system of seeds are procured for the agricultural cropping while very nominal cultivators prefer application of hybrid seeds. The use of insecticides and pesticides are very nominal and it's non-scientific application has adversely affected the agricultural yield per hectare in Amethi. The use of Nitrogen, Phosphate, Potash (NPK) is being used in a traditional system of agricultural cropping. The farmers have mis-conception that the increase in the NPK fertilizers in the subsequent agricultural cropping may increase the agricultural productivity of the land but it has negative results because in spite of increasing the agricultural productivity, there has been low agricultural productivity and it has led towards poor fertility status of the soil leading towards Usarization of the soil and waterlogging problem. Therefore the oganic and inorganic amendments should be applied as per the needs of the soil to maintain its fertility status to produce agricultural crops. The need based scientific use of insecticides and pesticides as per the crop requirements must be applied with the view to increase the agricultural productivity. The excessive use of insecticides-pesticides and chemical fertilizers in a non-scientific system may cause poor agricultural productivity and also adversely affect the fertility status of the soil.

The economy from the animal husbandary is also very poor. Very nominal milking economy has been recorded in Amethi. Some of the farmers have the cow and buffalowes for their household purpose while very few farmers sell the milk for the purpose of increasing their income and the middle men including very few farmers have opted for supply of the milk in the nearby market which has been their source of income.

The sheep husbandry has been vanished and very few sheep owners having very insignificant number of sheeps has been observed in various village Panchayats of Amethi. Pal/Gaderia caste is the main sheep owners in Amethi. The goat husbandry has been nominally recorded in various villages of Amethi. The goat husbandry has been done by the scheduled caste and minority people in most of the villages of the Amethi Block. The horses are not found in Amethi Block except very insignificant number of horses are found in Amethi for the use of Tanga and other purposes. The pig husbandry is found in most of the village Panchayats of Amethi. The pig husbandry has been done by the scheduled caste people. The hen/cock husbandry has been done by the Minority people and scheduled caste families of Amethi. It has been noticed that the animal husbandry has been done only for their household requirements but not for the commercial use with the view to increase the income of the villagers in Amethi.

It has been observed that approximately more than 70 per cent population of Amethi has been dependent on primary sector economy. The secondary source of economy has been found very nominal and very insignificant people of the area are dependent on the tertiary source of economy including trading and business activities because Amethi has been the agriculturally dominant area and most of the people are engaged in agricultural farming and working as agricultural labourers. The low agricultural productivity has led towards poor economy which has caused economic backwardness of the people of Amethi.

6.3 Institutional Infrastructure

The institutional infrastructure has been very nominal in comparison to the ever increasing population at village level. The rapid growth of population and increasing demand of the people could not be fulfilled based on the existing institutional infrastructure. The historical infrastructure of the Amethi has been insignificant except the Fort of the Raja Amethi and Shahgarh. The *Maqbara* of the famous Sufi Poet Malik Mohammad Jaisi and the religious Hindu Temple of Yadavs at Nand Mohar has been the most important religious infrastructure of Amethi.

The administrative infrastructure at Village Panchayat level has been found very poor in comparison to the village level government and semi-government officials working at the grassroots level. Village Panchayat Bhawan, road communication, i.e. Pucca road, Kharanza road, Chack road have been the common basic amenities infrastructure available at village level in the Amethi Block. The road, communication and telecommunication have been the basic institutional infrastructure available in most of the villages of Amethi. The drinking water through water supply, India Mark II Hand Pumps, Private Hand Pumps, Dug Wells and other sources have been the basic infrastructure at Village level in Amethi.

The non-conventional sources of energy including solar light, solar lamps have been insignificantly used at village level in Amethi. The most of the villages of the area have been well connected with electricity. The private electricity use and household use of the electricity have been very common, electricity has also been found for the small scale industries and various agro-industries at village level in Amethi.

The institutional infrastructure related to veternity hospitals and primary Medical Health Centres and medical health amenities are not properly distributed at village level in proportion to the cattle and human population in Amethi. The small scale industries and Agro-industries are not properly promoted with the view to increase the agri-processing to ensure value addition of the agricultural products. An appropriate banking infrastructure and need based low cost housing under the Indira Awas Yojana (IAY) have not been provided to the needy beneficiaries. The other institutional infrastructure related to integrated rural development programmes are insufficient at village level in Amethi.

The educational infrastructure at the village level for primary educational infrastructure has been appropriate as per the student ratio and local population but the Junior, High School and Intermediate level educational government infrastructure has been inappropriate. The higher educational infrastructure has been insignificant excepting the private/self-financing colleges established at Block level in Amethi. The professional educational infrastructure including Industrial Training Institute, Polytechnic, Engineering and Management and Medical and Health Educational institutions in Amethi has been insignificant except one polytechnic institution, Industrial Training Institute established by the government while Management, Engineering and Pharmacy colleges have been established under the Self-Financing Scheme. There is no famous tourism place in Amethi but one Tourist Rest House has been established at Munshiganj, Amethi.

The Panchayati Raj Institutional infrastructure, i.e. Village Panchayat Bhawan has been established in each Village Panchayat of Amethi Block. Panchayat Industrial centre have also been established in Amethi with the view to generate employment. Various institutional infrastructures have also been established and constructed by the Village Panchayats, Block Panchayat and District Panchayat with the objectives of fulfilling the increasing demand of the growing population. An attempt has been made in this study to analyse the social, economic and institutional infrastructure at Village Panchayat level in Amethi.

7. CHOICE OF THE INDICATORS

In this study an effort has been made to analyse the various social, economic and institutional infrastructures available at village panchayat level in Amethi. The detailed indicators related to the social, economic and institutional infrastructure are as follows:

(I) Social Infrastructural Indicators
(II) Economic Infrastructural Indicators
(III) Institutional Infrastructural Indicators

Table 1.2: Indicators of Social Infrastructures

Sl. No.	*Indicators*	*Village Panchayat*	*Revenue Villages*	*Hamlet Villages*
1.	Houses			
2.	Households			
3.	Total Population			
	i. Male			
	ii. Female			
	iii. Child			
4.	Scheduled Caste			
5.	Backward Caste			
6.	Minorities			
7.	Brahmins			
8.	Kshatriya			
9.	Other Castes			
10.	Total Workers			
11.	Farmers/Cultivators			
12.	Agricultural Labourers			
13.	Non-skilled Labourers			
14.	Skilled Labourers			
15.	Plantation and Husbandry Workers			
16.	Construction Workers			
17.	Business Workers			
18.	Transportation Workers			
19.	Others Workers including office Workers			
20.	Small Scale/Agro industries Workers			
21	Total Literates			
22.	Primary Literates			
23.	Junior School Literates			
24.	High School			
25.	Intermediate			
26.	Graduate			
27.	Post-Graduate			
28.	Industrial Training Institute			
29.	Polytechnic			
30.	Graduates of Technologies			
31.	B.B.A./M.B.A.			
32.	Others			

8. SOURCE OF DATA

The study on village information system is based on micro-level information system, i.e. grassroots level or village level data on the socio-economic-institutional infrastructure. Due attention has been given for the collection of dependent and independent data which can be used for propounding a theory. The collection and collation of the data base varies from the one theme to the another according to the nature of the problem. The source of data/information has been based on the following system:

- The land revenue records from Amethi Tehsil and Village Khasara Maps, Village level land revenue records and village khasara records have been consulted. The economic register from the Block Development Office, Amethi have also been taken as a base for the study on socio-economic-institutional infrastructure at Village Panchayat level in Amethi.
- District Statistical Hand Book of the District Amethi.
- Zila Yojana 2011-12 of the Amethi District.
- Annual Plan of the District Panchayat, Amethi.
- Most of the data have been collected through fieldwork and intensive field survey at grassroots level. Requisite questionnaires have been prepared for the collection of the needful information at village panchayat level in Amethi.

Table 1.3: Indicators Economic Infrastructures

Sl. No.	*Indicators*	*0.5 to 1.00 hect.*	*1.00 to 2.00 hect.*	*2.00 to 4.00 hect.*	*4.00 to above hect.*
	Village Panchayat Revenue Village				
1.	Land Ownership				
	1. No. of Households				
	2. Area in Hectares				
	Hamlet Villages				
2.	Source of Irrigation and Area.				
	1. Net Irrigated Area				
	2. Gross Irrigated Area				
	3 Canal Irrigated Area				
	4. Govt. Tube well Irrigated Area				
	5. Private Tube well Irrigated Area				
	6. Other Irrigated Area				
3.	Agricultural Production Area				
	1. Rice Cropped Area				
	2 Wheat Cropped Area				
	3. Barley				
	4. Pea				
	5. Mustard				
	6. Sugarcane				
	7. Potato				
	8. Sanai/Chara				
4.	Agricultural Implements				
	1. Cultivator — Wood				
	2. Cultivator — Iron				
	3. High-tech Cultivator				
	4. Agricultural Implements				
	5. Tractor				
	6. Other Agricultural Implements				
5.	Seeds				
	1. Seeds				
	2. Hybrid Seeds				
	3. Use of insecticides and pesticides				
	4. Nitrogen (N)				
	5. Phosphate (P)				
	6. Potash (K)				
	7. Other Fertilizers etc.				
6.	Biogas				
7.	Economy from Husbandry				
	1. Cow				
	2. Buffaloes				
	3. Sheep/Goat				
	4. Horse				
	5. Pig				
	6. Hen/Cock				
8.	Economy of Cultivators				
9.	Agricultural workers Economy				
10.	Non-skilled workers Economy				
11.	Skilled workers Economy				
12.	Plantation and Animal Husbandry workers Economy				
13.	Construction workers Economy				
14.	Business workers Economy				
15.	Transportation workers Economy				
16.	Office workers Economy				
17.	Small scale/Agro-Industries workers Economy				
18.	Other workers Economy				

- The Village Pradhan, Villagers, Village Land Management Committee Members, Panchayat Mitras, Panchayat Secretaries and other government officials have been consulted at field level for collection of socio-economic-institutional infrastructure data at the Village Panchayat level in Amethi. The field level survey and observations

Table 1.4: Indicators of Institutional Infrastructures

		Village Panchayat	*Revenue Village*	*Khasra Village*
1.	Historical Infrastructure.			
2.	Religious Infrastructure.			
3.	Administrative Infrastructure.			
4.	Roads - 1. National High Way, 2. Pucca Road. 3. Kuchha Road, 4. Kharanja Road. 5. Chackroads.			
5.	Communication.			
6.	Telecommunication.			
7.	Drinking water. 1-Water supply. 2- India Mark - 11 Hand Pump. 3- Private Hand Pump. 4- Other sources of drinking water.			
8.	Energy. 1- Non conventional sources of energy. 2- Electricity Private Use. 3- Electricity Commercial Use.			
9.	Animal Hospital.			
10.	Medical/Health.			
11.	Small Scale Industries.			
12.	Agro-Industries.			
13.	Low cost Housing/Indira Awas Yojana.			
14.	Banking Infrastructure.			
15.	Other Institutional Infrastructure.			
16.	Educational Infrastructure. 1- Primary & Junior. 2- High School. 3- Intermediate. 4- Graduate. 5- Post Graduate. 6- I.T.I./Polytechnic 7- Other Education etc.			
17.	Tourism.			
18.	Panchayati Raj Institutions etc.			

etc. have also been carried out for the collection of the required information system at the grassroots level.

- National Atlas for Thematic Maps Organisation (NATMO), Maps of the District Rae Barelli and Sultanpur.
- Survey of India Topo sheets: 63/100, 11, 12, 14, 15, 16, 63J/3, 4, 7, 8, 11, 12 and 63 K/5, 9.
- Primary Census Hand Book of District Rae Barelli, 2001.
- District Census Hand Book of the District Sultanpur, 2001.

9. CHOICE OF THE SAMPLES

Various socio-economic-institutional indicators have been selected for innovation of available infrastructure at Village Panchayat level including 82 revenue villages and 377 Purwas/Tolas/Hamlet villages in Amethi. The revenue villages and the hamlet villages have not been taken for the study at grassroots level because under the Panchayati Raj Institutional System. Village Panchayats have been accepted as lower level unit for the policy planning and implementation of the various rural development programmes. Therefore, in this study Village Panchayats have been taken as basic unit to innovate and

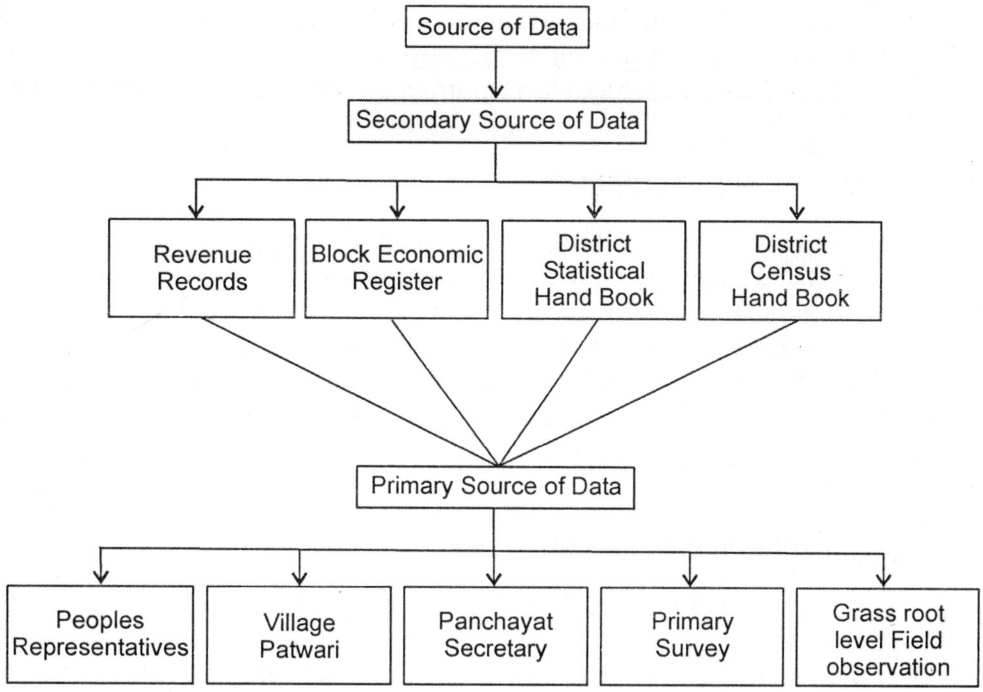

analyse the available socio-economic-institutional infrastructure at Village Panchayat level for Amethi Block, because the Village Panchayat and Block Panchayat are the important basic units at grassroots level in Panchayati Raj Institutional System. An effort have been made in this study to innovate the existing socio-economic-institutional infrastructural resources at Village Panchayat level in Amethi Block, which may be an asset for the policy-makers and planners for the formulation of grassroots level need based village development planning in Amethi.

10. EXPLANATORY SYSTEM

Various human resources data has been collected, collated and analysed at Village Panchayat level in Amethi. The population, caste composition, workforce, literacy and educational profile, infrastructural resources have been explained at Village Panchayat level with the view to analyse the social status of the people of Amethi and their need to strengthen the educational and employment generation programmes for their self-sustenance. The agricultural inputs especially the irrigation system, use of fertilizers and the application of insecticides and pesticides, the use of agricultural implements existing system has been explained and the economy from various sources have also been analysed with the view to provide appropriate formulation of planning process to increase the employment among the interested people of Amethi with the view to improve their economic conditions for self-sustenance and socio-economic upliftment at Village Panchayat level in Amethi. Various institutional infrastructures established at Village Panchayat level have been explained. An effort has also been made to analyse the development of need based infrastructural resources at Village Panchayat level in Amethi. The development of the institutional infrastructure indicates the level of the implementation of rural development programmes and also the growth of the rural development at Village Panchayat level in Amethi. It has been realized that the innovation of available socio-economic-institutional infrastructural resources information system may be helpful in the formulation of the need based People's Participatory Planning Process (PPPP) at Village Panchayat level to strengthen the Panchayati Raj Institutions in Amethi.

11. CARTOGRAPHIC TECHNIQUES

Various cartographic techniques have been adopted to represent and depict the collected and collated data in a graphic form related to socio-economic-institutional infrastructural resources at Village Panchayat level in Amethi. Choroplething Techniques have been used to show the distribution of socio-economic-institutional infrastructural data at Village Panchayat level. Geographic Information System (GIS) techniques have also been adopted for appropriate analysis of available socio-economic-institutional infrastructural information system at Village Panchayat level in Amethi.

12. SOCIO-ECONOMIC PLANNING

The planning is an organised process by which the people achieves their developmental goals or the planning is a means to achieve sustainable socio-economic-infrastructural development. But when the intention, aspiration and objectives of the development are distorted, then the planning also becomes a distorted exercise.

The planning is a systematic procedure which objects at the implementation of several specific aims and objectives. Therefore, it has become necessary to:

(1) Specify quantified socio-economic-institutional infrastructural targets.
(2) Specify potential variants of reaching such targets, i.e. variants of utilization of the various socio-economic-institutional infrastructural resources at the grassroots level.
(3) To find out the various socio-economic-institutional infrastructural resources available at the Village Panchayat level and reaching to such targets at the field level or grassroots level.
(4) Revise the targets if some of the resources are not fully utilized or proved scientifically and technically insufficient system for reaching the local level targets.
(5) To find out which variants are optimal (in the sense of allowing the "best set" of targets to be reached with the available resources, at the grassroots level.
(6) To organise the instruments which will ensure operational implementation of the variant related to socio-economic-institutional infrastructure finally chosen;
(7) To organise the instruments which will ensure operational implementation of the variant finally chosen; and
(8) To supervise the process of implementation of the planned programmes in order to find out eventual discrepancies and to set in motion adaptive achievements.

It has been noticed that the planning at the grassroots level or at the village level is being done without the willing consent of the local level village people, in some cases the planners interpret the need of the people and their aspirations for developing a plan for the people but without their participation and interest. Lastly, the planning is the task of the people in which the planners can provide the backup support to achieve their planning goals. The administrative machinery of the government is stressing hard for the involvement of the people in the policy planning and formulation of the need based planning for an integrated development, i.e. the grassroots level development planning from within.

Thus the policy planners will have to provide developmental planning and to provide techno-scientific backup support at the grassroots level, i.e. Village Panchayat level people's representatives, villagers and officials involved in the formulation of the planning process for the implementation of various rural development programmes at Village Panchayat level. The policy planners at village level should not be a technocrat to provide planning backup support and projections but they should assist villagers as a social scientist and promoters who can easily understand the basic grassroots level needs of the village people so that the requirements and needs of the local people are incorporated in the formulation of the planning process and the implementation of the planned developmental programmes at the village Panchayat level. The integrated developmental programmes and activities are carried out as per the need of the local village level people, with the involvement of the village people, for the village people and with the involvement of the local level village beneficiaries and the planned people's participatory development is achieved as per planned target at the grassroots level. In this study on effort has been made to innovate and analyse the socio-economic-institutional infrastructures available at village panchayat level which can be used as an asset for the formulation of need based village development planning at the grassroots level in Amethi.

13. VILLAGE DEVELOPMENT

The 'Development' is after all a multifaceted phenomenon. The development can neither be understood nor promoted unless it is seen from the multidisciplinary and interdisciplinary approach and holistic perspectives. Moreover, the development is basically a human enterprize and therefore, it requires the combined efforts of all the systems of knowledge which can be physical, biological, social, human, economic, institutional to comprehend and articulate the development activities at the grassroots level. It is more so with respect to planned development programmes. The plan formulation must draw upon all relevant socio-economic-institutional infrastructural disciplines including the area specific development planning according to the needs of the grassroots level people living in the remote level areas.

The 'Development', whether it is related to rural or urban or rurban areas, is one which is pursued with genuine concern for human values and sustainable growth of the particular area in an integrated manner. The development means the evolution of the people in which the people acquires better perception and best control over the human resources especially socio-economic-institutional infrastructure at the grassroots level or village level. In the process of development the sustainable growth alone does not ensure development but it requires continued people's participation and people's involvement in the policy planning, in the formulation of the need based planning and also ensuring people's participation in the implementation of planned village development programmes at the grassroots level.

The development must ensure the betterment and welfare of all the local people living in the rural areas. Thus the feel good and to fulfil the aspirations of the people for development at field level or at the village level have to be ensured through people's participation at the grassroots level perspectives. The present development planning processes are neither true, nor good, nor beautiful but it does not mean that everything is wrong. In reality the development lies in the development of the latest developed science and technology and its application by the common resourceless, deprived downtrodden people surviving the remote rural areas in the backward districts like Amethi. The progress of the people in the socio-economic-institutional infrastructural front has made more destructive than constructive approach of development for all the concerned people at the grassroots level.

Thus the village development means to fulfil the aspirations of the village people, for the betterment and welfare of the local level village people for their actions aspirations and perceptions for better quality of life and also to feel good for an integrated development. The village development should be planned according to the needs of the local village people and to strengthen the available socio-economic infrastructure available at the village level and to ensure an appropriate technique for optimum utilization of available human resources at the village level. The sustainable village development is only possible through innovation of the existing socio-economic-institutional infrastructural resources at village level. In the present scenario the progress of the village people in the socio-economic-institutional front has been made more destructive than the constructive approach of sustainable eco-friendly integrated development for all the people by the people and with the village people and to ensure people's participatory village development planning to fulfil the increasing demands of ever growing cattle and human population.

14. VILLAGE DEVELOPMENT PLANNING

It has been noticed that there is quest for evolving a model for planning. Macro level planning has been adopted in our country without ensuring people's participation. The approach of the Macro-level planning in India did not yield the desired results due to inequities amongst people and disparities between one region to the another regions. The varying agro-climatic conditions continued to degrade, leading to severe stress on the land and water resources. Around late seventies sustainable and integrated development of the specific areas has been ensured. In this regard conceptual changes in the planning process has been adopted in the Macro-level, Meso-level or Micro-level process of planning. The main objectives of the decentralized development planning process at the various levels have been as follows:

- To increase the productivity of the land.
- To increase the scope for the employment generation with the focus on creation of assets.
- Poverty alleviation.
- To provide minimum amenities and the infrastructural facilities.

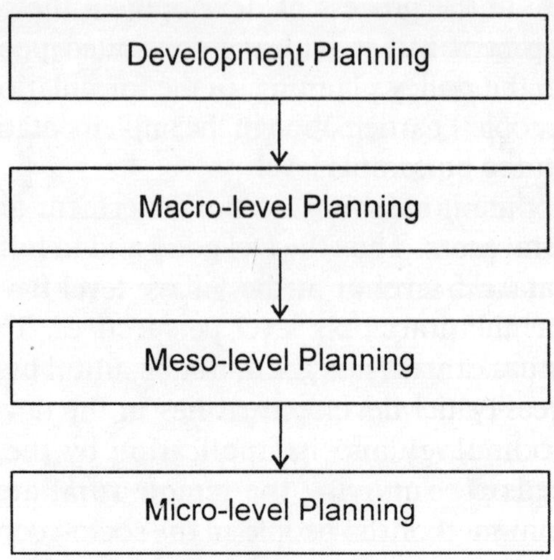

Various institutional changes were brought to implement the above strategies through thc 74th Constitutional Amendment Acts (1992 and 1993). The State Governments were empowered from the institutions of the Local Self Government right from the village level up to the district level and also within the Municipal jurisdiction, i.e. the Panchayat level and Nagar Palikas in the context of rural, urban and rur-ban development respectively.

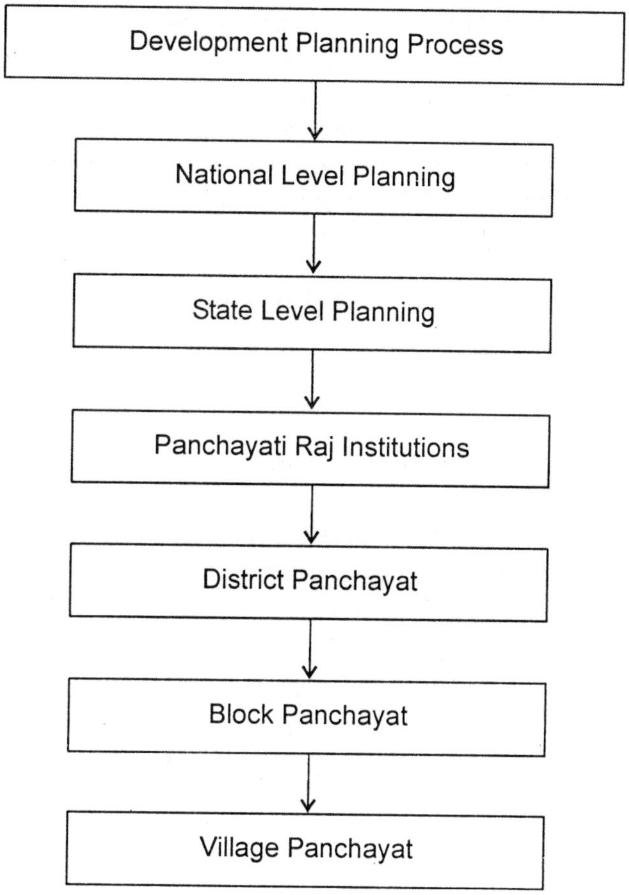

The Eleventh and the Twelfth Schedules of the Constitution while specifying the sectors for the Panchayats and Nagar Palikas, have also defined the role for the multi-level institutions of the governance in the planning process and the implementation of the various developmental programmes at different levels. The State Governments have accordingly constituted such local level bodies with definite mandates to collect the revenue, to draw up the planning and implement integrated development programmes. It requires capacity building at the institutions of the local self-governance to prepare and formulate the planning process and also to implement local level area specific integrated development programmes by assessing and utilizing the local level available socio-institutional infrastructural resources.

The plan formulation and the implementation of the developmental programmes in the urban and rural areas is an information intensive work at the grassroots level. The Human Resources Data Management Systems (HRDMS) which are existing at the village level or grassroots level are not properly arranged and updated but such available information needs to be integrated for the purpose of the development planning process. The conventional methods of the data collection, collation, storage are not amenable for quick updation, retrieval and holistic analysis and several problems, which are existing in the conventional system are as follows:

— Incompatible and non-standard data sets inhibiting integration.
— In efficient inter-sectoral data flow.
— Lack of information on quality, completeness and lineage of data.
— Integrated approach to planning process requires a detailed knowledge of the interrelations and interdependents between various sectors to resolve often conflicting demands. This leads to a requirement for the appropriate data management system and the explanation tools and techniques and large matrix of the sectoral indicators data in a digital format on the socio-economic-institutional infrastructural resources and invites for specific scientific and technological interactions in the following points:

    (i) Creation of the need base data.
    (ii) Development and improvement in the data handling and analysing tools and techniques.
    (iii) Efficient distribution of data and information to the user institutions and development planning institutions and implementing agencies.

In view of the above Human Resources Data Management System (HRDMS) have been required for the formulation of planning at the grassroots level. The development in the areas of Information and Communication Technology (ICT) and Geo-Spatial Data Management and Analysis Techniques like Geographic Information System (GIS) may be helpful in the planning process to know the existing human resources and need base formulation of the development planning at various levels. It has been observed that certain initiatives have been taken at the National level to create awareness on the usefulness of these technologies amongst policy makers and planners and decision-makers. The Human Resources Data Management System (HRDMS) has been such pioneering effort for creation of the socio-economic-institutional infrastructural resources at the grassroots level.

The Human Resources Data Management System (HRDMS) includes Socio-Economic-Institutional Infrastructural resources. The innovation of the available socio-economic-institutional infrastructures at the grassroots level may be an asset for the policy-makers, planners of the programmes for the formulation of the need base village development planning and also the implementation of the people's participating integrated rural development programmes at the village Panchayat level to strengthen the Panchayati Raj Institutions for self-governance and self-sustainance of the implemented development schemes.

15. HUMAN RESOURCES DATA MANAGEMENT SYSTEMS (HRDMS)

It has been observed that there is longest known tradition of the systematically collecting spatial data through various organisations at National level in our country. Different line departments are engaged for the collection of non-spatial data in a strong traditional system.

Hanumatha Rao Committee (1984) has emphasized on the management of the spatial data for efficient local level area specific development planning.

In view of the above requirements Department of Science and Technology, Government of India, started (during 1982) a programme on Natural Resources Data

Management System, which has been a multi-disciplinary and multi-institutional Research and Development Programme with a vision to provide appropriate scientific and technological inputs for operationalized planning. The main objectives of the programme had been to develop techno-scientific data base having an approach to support the grassroots level planning. During the end of the first decade of the National Resources Data Management System programmes, 73rd and 74th Constitutional Amendments Act came into being and with the entry of computers at the District level. The Geographic Information System (GIS) techniques have been evolved to develop spatial data management technologies for integrated rural development planning and its demonstration at the grassroots level policy decision-making institutions. In the context of Natural Resources Data Management System (NRDMS) various natural and human resources data have been collected, collated and analysed at various levels in the different districts of the country. The natural and the human resources information system has been important for local area development planning and also implementation of the various planned rural development programmes.

The Human Resources Data Management Systems (HRDMS) have always focusing on technological and institutional capacity building in a interdisciplinary and multi-institutional framework, so that the village people can utilize the local level available human resources. In this regard Human Resources Data Management Systems (HRDMS) develop and provide tools and techniques for assessing local level available human resources endowment and their utilization potential and generating alternative scenarios for the integrated rural development at the grassroots level.

Inspite of the National and State level efforts, from the two decades large segment of the end-users are yet to explore the full potential of the system and use it in most of their planning activities, due to lack of the technical institutional and organizational capacity. To reduce the impediments in the widespread use of the technologies and make it an effective tool in the process of local level area specific integrated rural development planning. The Human Resources Data Management System (HRDMS) has been focusing its efforts on simplifying the methods and techniques of data collection, collation, organisation and analysis of the data and to develop various devices and suitable strategies to transfer the techniques for adoption by the end-user institutions in their area specific grassroots level integrated rural development activities.

In view of the increasing needs of the Human Resources Data Management System (HRDMS) and considering the recent trends in the development of the spatial data technologies, the emerging changes in the system of governance of planning policies the institutionalization of the Spatial Data Infrastructure has been helpful in meeting the aspirations of the end-users and in support of the overall transformation in the concept of information sharing the development thrusts of the programmes.

- The spatial Data Management and Analysis Technologies.
- Advanced Technology Applications in the large scale spatial Data Collection and Collation.
- Human Resources Data Management System.
- Innovation of the Human resources infrastructure.
- Innovation of socio-economic-institutional infrastructure available at grassroots level.
- Transfer of technologies and capacity building.

The basic vision of the Human Resources Data Management System (HRDMS) has enabled the people, communities and the institutions of self-governance, with spatial Data Technologies, for sustained participation of the grassroots level people in the decision making process for integrated rural development of the village people.

The most important goals of the Human Resources Data Management System (HRDMS) have strengthened the Science and Technological inputs for integrated Human Resource Management through development of an appropriate tools and techniques in the collection of the Data, Collation and analysis of the generated information system at the micro-level.

Technical Capacity building at various levels of administration for enlisting the adoption of the technologies developed in an integrated area specific rural development planning.

In order to implement at least some of the activities to realise the vision of the Human Resources Data Management System (HRDMS) support from a large segment of scientists, social activists and entrepreneurs are required. Human Resources Data Management System is expected to stimulate the imagination of the research community to relate specific problems in their areas of interest and evolve suitable research proposals to persue line of investigation to arrive at meaningful solutions to the problems as well as advancing the existing knowledge in certain spheres of the activity, thereby aiding the overall integrated development at the grassroots level.

In this study an attempt has been made to analyse the various indicators related to the human resources and to develop the human resources data management at village level in Amethi. The human resources data included socio-economic-institutional resources available at the grassroots level. An effort has also been made to innovate the socio-economic-institutional infrastructural resources at the village Panchayat level in Amethi.

The Human resources data has been collected through the secondary sources of information available from the various government and non-governmental agencies but the basic source of the information has been the direct field survey and personal visits at the grassroots level. Primary field survey has been carried out to collect the socio-economic-institutional infrastructural information system at the grassroots level. The collected informations through primary field visits and field survey have been collected and compared with the already available secondary sources of information to check the authenticity of the collected human resources data at the Village Panchayat level/revenue village level/hamlet/purwas/tolas level in the Amethi Block.

The innovation of human resources along with socio-economic-institutional infrastructural resources have been created at the Village Panchayat level in Amethi which may be a base for the formulation of need base people's participatory integrated village development planning and to meet the ever increasing demand of the growing cattle and human population because the successful development planning and its implementation through peoples participation may ensure the sustenance of the various implemented integrated rural development programmes.

16. CONCLUSION

The sustained, integrated economic development has been realized and commendable advances have been made in the diverse field of rural development. The development programmes has been in reality incomplete because such rural development programmes have been failed to translate into better and dignified life for the majority of the people who live in the remote rural areas because the benefit of the development must reach to the downtrodden deprived resourceless rural poor *equally*, *effectively* and *efficiently*.

The poverty and backwardness have been recorded comparatively more in the rural areas than the urban areas. The government has formulated various policies and development planning programmes to bridge the gap between rural to urban.

It has been realized that the development should be participatory and it should be planned according to the local needs of the deprived rural multitudes. The development should be planned through tapping the available human resources including socio-economic-institutional infrastructure at Village Panchayat level, in order to ensure the proper implementation of the need based rural development programmes self-sustainable.

Various rural development schemes are being implemented aiming at the sustainable, integrated development of the remote rural areas with the focus on enhancing the livelihood of weakers and vulnerable sections of the society inconformity with the commitments to accord foremost priority to the integrated village development. In this regard a number of steps have been initiated to make the implementation of the ongoing rural development programmes more effective and accelerated. The formulation and implementation of various rural development programmes at the grassroots level is an intensive, innovative, informative and infrastructure oriented activity.

The human resources plays an important role in the policy planning and in the formulation of need based action plans for an integrated development of the remote villages. The human resources include the socio-economic-institutional infrastructure available at the grassroots level. The social infrastructure plays crucial role in the formulation of the development planning process. The available economic and institutional infrastructure at the grassroots level, must be considered before the formulation of need based people's participatory planning process. The developed institutional infrastructure at the grassroots level should be considered as an asset for the formulation of the policy planning.

In the Panchayati Raj System each village should be self-sustained and independent, the implementation of the welfare programmes of rural masses, can be implemented in a better manner when socio-economic-institutional infrastructures already available at the village level are innovated, requisite data is collected and collated for analysing the need base policy planning for the remote rural areas.

The real meaning of democracy is important to the people and Self-Government is the main soul of rural development, management of financial and administrative control of the Village Panchayats and continued participation, co-operation of the local people to establish village panchayats for Self-Government through peoples participatory planning process.

The optimum utilization of the available socio-economic institutional infrastructural resources to meet the increasing demand of the growing population and to generate employment and increase the income of the deprived resourceless poor multitudes surviving in the remote rural areas.

In view of the above an attempt has been made to analyse the available socio-economic institutional infrastructural resources available at the Village Panchayat level in Amethi Block. The innovation of the existing socio-economic-institutional infrastructure at the Village Panchayat level may be an asset for the formulation of the peoples participatory village development planning process and through sustained participation of the concerned village beneficiaries for the successful implementation of the integrated development programmes, with the view to improve the socio-economic conditions of the deprived poor multitudes living in the remote rural villages.

Archaeologically, historically and religiously Amethi has an importance for the tomb of Sufi Poet Malik Mohammad Jaisi and religious temple at Nand Mohar which is very famous for the worship of Yadav Community. Malik Mohammad Jaisi was born at Jais and composed many famous books in Hindi and Urdu literature. Jaisi memorial is also situated in the Jais town. There is no noteworthy archaeological importance in the Amethi. It has been observed that the chief land owning families of the past were the Rajputs of the various clans who possessed 76.16 per cent of the total land area of the Amethi. Among them Rajkumars alone held over one-fourth area of the Amethi while the Kinsmen Bachhgotis and Rajwaras owned 11.4 per cent and 3.4 per cent land respectively. The Rajkumars were the main proprietors of the Amethi and the chief of the Rajwaras were the Taluqdars of the revenue land tax collection. The next to the Bachhgotis and their kinsmen come the Bandhalgotis who owned almost the whole of Amethi Pargana. The other Rajputs with large properties in Amethi were the Bhale Sultans who owned 4.72 per cent and Kanhpurias with 4.7 per cent and the Bais with 2.8 per cent properties of the Bhale Sultan and of the Bhale Sultan's half were Hindus and half were Muslims. The Kanhpurias were chiefly confined to Pargana Gaura Jamo, almost the whole of which belonged to them. The Bais were scattered about in small groups. The backwardness of Amethi has been historical phenomenon due to kingship ruled estate, the land ownership was concentrated to the kings and their associated people.

An attempt has been made in this study to analyse the socio-economic-institutional infrastructural resources available at Village Panchayat level in Amethi Block.

The planning process for better and optimal utilization of available human resources has always been a great challenge to the policy makers and planners. It is necessary to evolve a planning strategy applicable at different levels, i.e. Village level-Block level-District level especially village as lowest unit of planning to strengthen Panchayat Raj system. In this study an attempt has been made to discuss vide range of issues which are very important for Local Area Development Planning. In the present context, efforts are being made to allocate resources at Village Panchayat level, it has become necessary to explain the human resources including socio-economic-institutional and man made infrastructural resources at Village Panchayat level in Amethi.

The man-made infrastructure especially the human resources plays an important role in the policy planning and need base planned programme implementation of the integrated rural land development. The human resources including the socio-economic-institutional infrastructural resources at the grassroots level plays a crucial role in the formulation of micro-level planning process.

The social infrastructure includes the population and population density, caste composition, workforce, educational profiles at the Village Panchayat level in Amethi.

The economic infrastructural resources include size of land holdings, land ownership pattern, source of irrigation and the irrigated area, agricultural production, use of agricultural implements, application of the fertilizer, economy from the animal husbandry and source of economy from primary, secondary and tertiary economy based on the workforce, etc. have been analysed at the Village Panchayat level in Amethi Block.

The Institutional infrastructure includes historical, religious and administrative infrastructure available at the Village Panchayat level in Amethi along with the communication network, telecommunication, drinking water facilities, energy, non-conventional sources of energy and electricity, animal hospitals, medical and health services, small scale industries and agro-industries, banking infrastructure, low cost housing, tourism infrastructure, Pancyati Raj Institutional infrastructure and the educational infrastructure available at the Village Panchayat level in Amethi Block.

The primary field survey at the grassroots level and the secondary sources of information has been the basic source of information for the collection and innovation of the human resources data including socio-economic-institutional infrastructural resources available at the Village Panchayat level in Amethi. The requisite indicator data have been collected through primary survey, grassroots level field observation and Village Patwari, Panchayat Secretary and village peoples representatives and other officials of the Amethi Block.

Various indicators related to the socio-economic-institutional infrastructural resources have been collected at the grassroots level especially covering 377 Purwas/Tolas/Hamlet villages and 82 revenue villages and 44 Village Panchayats of Amethi Block.

An attempt has been made to develop explanation mechanism for the uneven distribution of the various socio-economic-institutional infrastructural resources at the village panchayat level in Amethi.

Various cartographic techniques has been adopted to analyse the collected and collated data related to the socio-economic-institutional infrastructures available at Village Panchayat level in Amethi. Geographic Information System (GIS) techniques have been adopted for appropriate analysis of the socio-economic-institutional infrastructural resources distributed at the Village Panchayat level in Amethi.

The appropriate planning for the optimum utilization of the available socio-economic-institutional infrastructural resources has been analysed and to supervise the process of implementation of the planned programmes in order to find out eventual discrepancies and to set in motion adaptive achievements of the sustainable development at the grassroots level.

The village development means the evolution of the people in which the people acquires better perception and best control over the human resources, including especially socio-economic-institutional infrastructures available at the grassroots level. The village development means to fulfil the aspirations of the village people for the betterment and the welfare of the local level village people for their actions, aspirations and perceptions for better quality of life and also to feel good for an integrated development of the village.

It has been realized that there is a quest for evolving a model for village development planning. The village development planning and the implementation of the integrated rural development programmes can be made more accelerated and successful if it is planned through the peoples participation and the available human infrastructural resources are duly considered before the plan formulation, with the view to avoid the duplicacy of the already created socio-economic-institutions infrastructure at the village level.

In view of the above multi-disciplinary and multi-institutional Research and Development programme with a vision to provide appropriate scientific and technical inputs for operationalizing the concept of area specific decentralized planning at the grassroots level. The main objective of the programme has been to develop techno-scientific data base with an approach to support grassroots level planning.

The Human Resources Data Management System (HRDMS) includes socio-economic-institutional infrastructure available at the grassroots level, which may be an asset for the policy makers, planners of the rural development schemes. The innovation of the existing socio-economic-institutional infrastructural resources at the grassroots level will be helpful in the formulation of the need based village development planning and also the implementation of the peoples participatory integrated rural development.

The innovation of human resources along with socio-economic-institutional infrastructural resources data has been created and developed at the village panchayat level in Amethi which may be used as a base for the formulation of need base peoples participatory integrated village development planning. The innovation of the available socio-economic-institutional infrastructures at the grassroots level is most important exercise for the formulation of the policy planning, based on which the need base peoples participatory integrated rural development planning can be formulated for the sustainable development. The innovation of available man-made human infrastructure will be also helpful for the optimum utilization of the such resources already available at the grassroots level and it will also be helpful in the maintenance and management of ongoing implementation of various rural development programmes for the eco-friendly sustainable development and it will be an asset for meeting the ever increasing demand of the growing cattle and human population at village panchayat level through strengthening the grassroots level Panchayati Raj Institutions with the peoples participation to ensure integrated sustainable development of Amethi.

2
Social Infrastructure

1. INTRODUCTION

The man-made infrastructure plays an important role in the planning process and development of need based planning for an integrated development of any area. The policy planning for village development programmes are an information intensive task. The management of human resources data already available at the village level has not been properly geared up to meet the requisite information system for integrated village development planning. The conventional and traditional system of data collection, collation and its storage are not amenable for quick updation, retrieval and holistic approach of analysis and several problems has been realized because of the incompatible data base, in-efficient inter-sectoral data flow and lack of information system on the quality of data at the grassroots level.

It has been realized that the process of planning for an integrated approach requires a detailed knowledge of Human Resources Data Management System (HRDMS) and its interdependencies between various human infrastructural indicators, i.e. social sectoral indicators with the view to resolve often conflicting demands. It requires appropriate data management and the analysis of human resources sectoral data, especially the social infrastructural data base at village panchayat level.

The social infrastructure plays a key role in the planning process at the grassroots level and also in the implementation of the various planned rural development programmes. People's participation and their involvement in the formulation of the need base planning process and people's participation in the implementation of integrated rural development programmes. It will not only ensure successful implementation of the development programmes but it will be an asset and tool for maintenance and management of already completed and implemented village developmental programmes. Therefore, an attempt has been made in this study to analyse social infrastructural information system at Village Panchayat level in Amethi Block. The social infrastructure includes the population, caste composition, workers, educational profile and various associated indicators related to the social infrastructural resources, already available at the village panchayat level in Amethi Block. The collected information through primary field survey and based on the requisite secondary sources of information has been collated and analysed for area specific village development planning.

In view of the above an attempt has been made to analyse the available social infrastructural resources including the population distribution (Male and Female), population density per hectare and caste composition, workers distribution, educational profiles and its distribution at the village panchayat level in Amethi. The social system of Amethi has been historically backward. The social system of the Amethi has been interwoven with the professional occupation and working pattern with the kings. As per the occupational structure and services rendered to the kings working caste has been named, social security was looked by the kings, Brahmins were engaged in the worship programmes for the kings, kurmis were entrusted for the agricultural production activities, yadavs were supposed to provide milk and agricultural productivity and revenue taxes to the kings. Similarly, the other castes like carpenter, blacksmith, washerman, barbers and other service provider class has been professionally and occupationally associated with the caste. The composition of the caste plays an important role in the development of the society.

2. HUMAN INFRASTRUCTURE

The village information system has been developed at the village panchayat level in Amethi Block. The human infrastructure constitutes one of the major segment of the village information system. The human resources play an important role in the integrated development of an area. The human infrastructure at the grassroots level has been innovated through primary fieldwork, field observations and primary field survey at the village level in Amethi Block. The human infrastructural resources includes the social-economic-institutional infrastructure available at the village level.

The innovation of infrastructure and developing village information system consists of Natural and Human Resources which has been depicted in Table 2.5. The human resources includes *Social Economic-Institutional infrastructure* available at village level and it plays an important role in the policy planning for the integrated rural development and programme implementation through people's participation. Various indicators has been derived from the different implementing agencies engaged in the implementation of various rural development programmes at the grassroots level. Such rural developmental implementing agencies includes mainly Agriculture, Rural Development, Irrigation, Medical and Health, Welfare Programme, Labour, Water, Communication etc.

Human Resources Data Management System (HRDMS) or the Human Infrastructural indicators has been derived from the various sectoral indicators which include Socio-Economic-Institutional Infrastructure available at the village Panchayat level in Amethi. The sectoral indicators have been derived from the various implementing institutions working at the District Level. The human resources sectoral indicators have been explained in Table 2.6. The sectoral indicators of the human infrastructure includes Agriculture, Rural Developnent, Irrigation, Energy, Industry, Transport, Education, Economic Services, Science and Technology, Health, Information, Urban Development, Welfare Programmes, Labour and Social-Security implementing institutions working at the District level-Block level-Village Panchayat level.

The innovation of infrastructure and development of village information system has been divided into Natural Resources and Human Resources which have been sub-divided into social-economic-institutional infrastructure, has been mentioned in Table 2.7. The socio-economic-institutional infrastructure plays an important role in the formulation of need based village development planning and implementation of the various rural development programmes at Block level and Village Panchayat level including revenue villages along with Purwas/Tolas/Hamlet villages.

Table 2.5: Village Information System

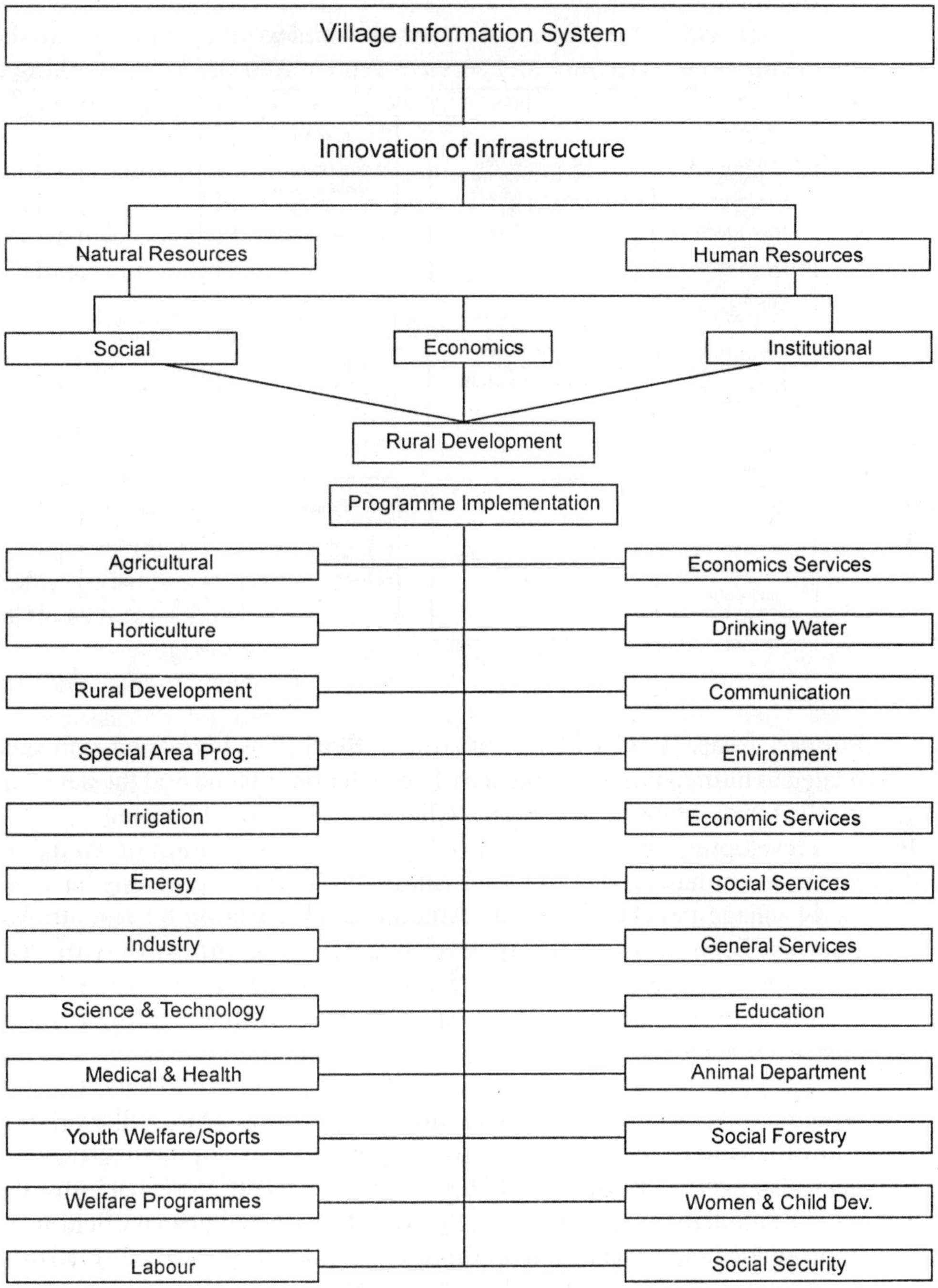

An effort has been made in this study to innovate the available human resources including socio-economic-institutional infrastructural resources at Village Panchayat level in Amethi Block through existing sources of data especially the revenue records, Block Economic Register, District-Statistical Hand Book and District Census Hand Book related to Amethi. The availability of the existing sources of Data has been shown in Table 2.8. The collection of the field level data has been ensured through involving People's Representatives, Revenue Lekhpal/Patwari, Village Panchayat Secretary and Primary Field Survey at Village Panchayat level including associated all revenue villages, and

Table 2.6: Sectoral Indicators

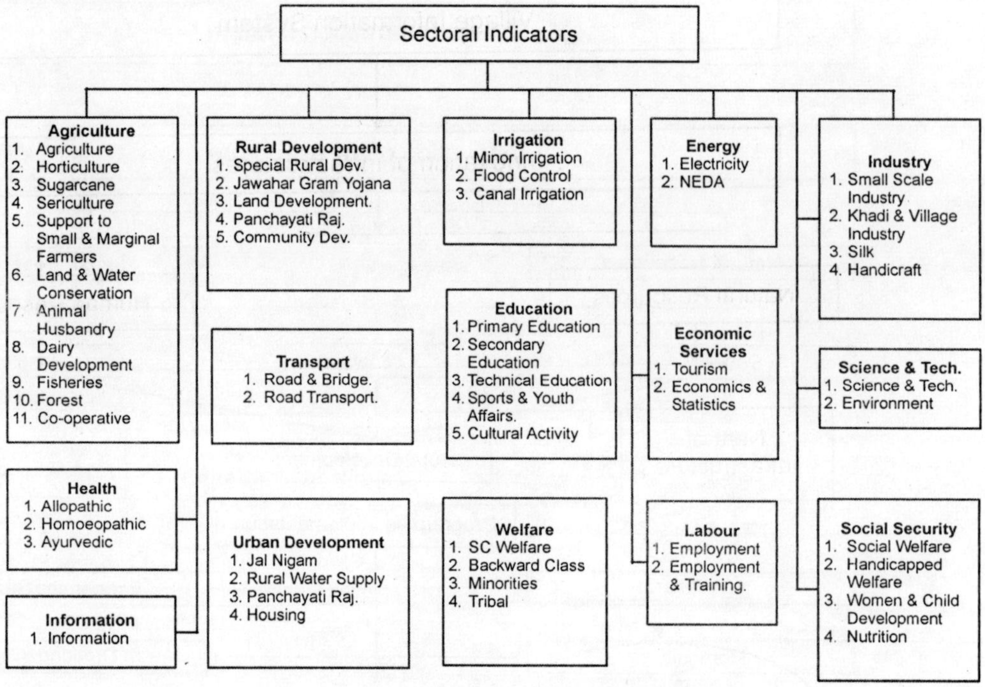

Purwas/Tolas/Hamlet villages of Amethi Block. The innovated, collected informations related to human infrastructure have been later on collated and the data has been analysed for the formulation of need based village development planning.

Developing Village Information System and innovation of available infrastructure for the formulation of need based village development planning have been ensured for all 44 village panchayats of the Amethi Block covering 82 revenue villages and 377 Purwas/Tolas/Hamlet villages of Amethi. The innovation of socio-economic-institutional infrastructural data has been collected through involving people's representatives, Block Development Officials and Implementing Institute Officials etc. have been depicted in Table 2.9.

The collection of the Village Information System has been done through people's representatives involving Village Pradhan in association with Village Panchayat Members and other interested village people. The Block Development officials of the Amethi have also been consulted involving village panchayat secretaries and Panchayat Mitra etc. The implementing institute officials have conducted primary field survey and ensured appropriate field observations at the grassroots level and the collected informations have been compared and collated through the already available secondary sources of information.

The financial flow for the integrated village development have been obtained at the National level - State level-District level-Block level-Village Panchayat level. The financial flow for the village development has been depicted in Table 2.10. It has been observed that the financial flow for village development has been achieved from the Central Government programmes, international agencies, state government programmes and other agencies. The District Rural Development Agency (DRDA), Zila Panchayat, Block Panchayat and Village Panchayat also provide financial support for the integrated village development. The Members of Parliament (Lok Sabha and Rajya Sabha) and Members

Table 2.7: Village Information System

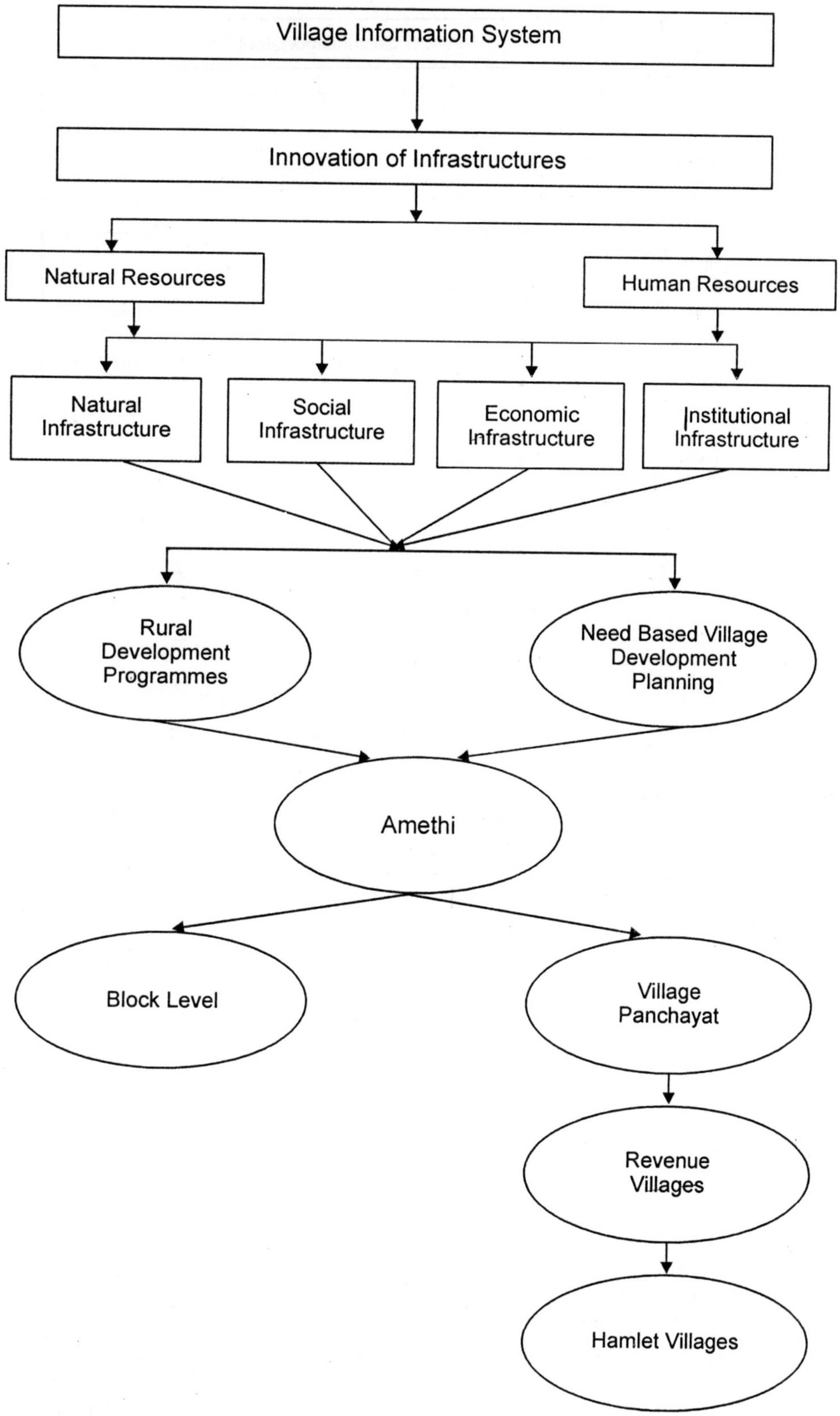

Table 2.8: Village Information System

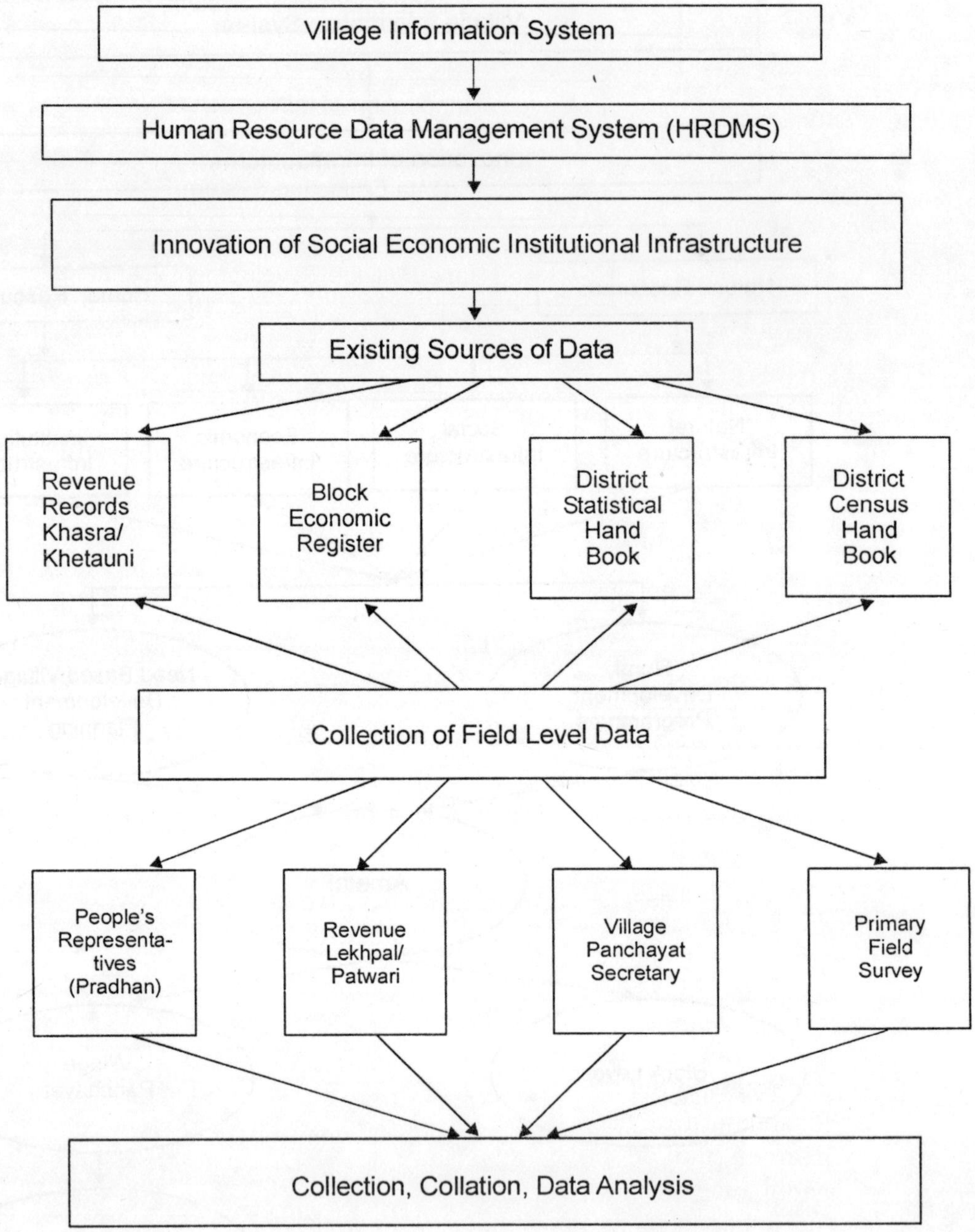

of Legislative Assembly and Members of Legislative Council of the State also provide financial assistance under the Local Area Development Scheme for integrated village development programmes. As per the constitutional and the Central and State Level provisions the financial support has also been made available under the District Development Planning (Zila Yojana), *Block Panchayat Development Planning and the Village Panchayat Development Planning* with the view to strengthen the three tier Panchayati Raj System. Thus the *Zila Yojana* is formulated by the *Zila Panchayat* and Block Yojana is formulated by the Block Panchayat and *Gram Yojana* is formulated by the Gram (Village) Panchayats, because the government has already given administrative and financial powers

Table 2.9: Village Information System

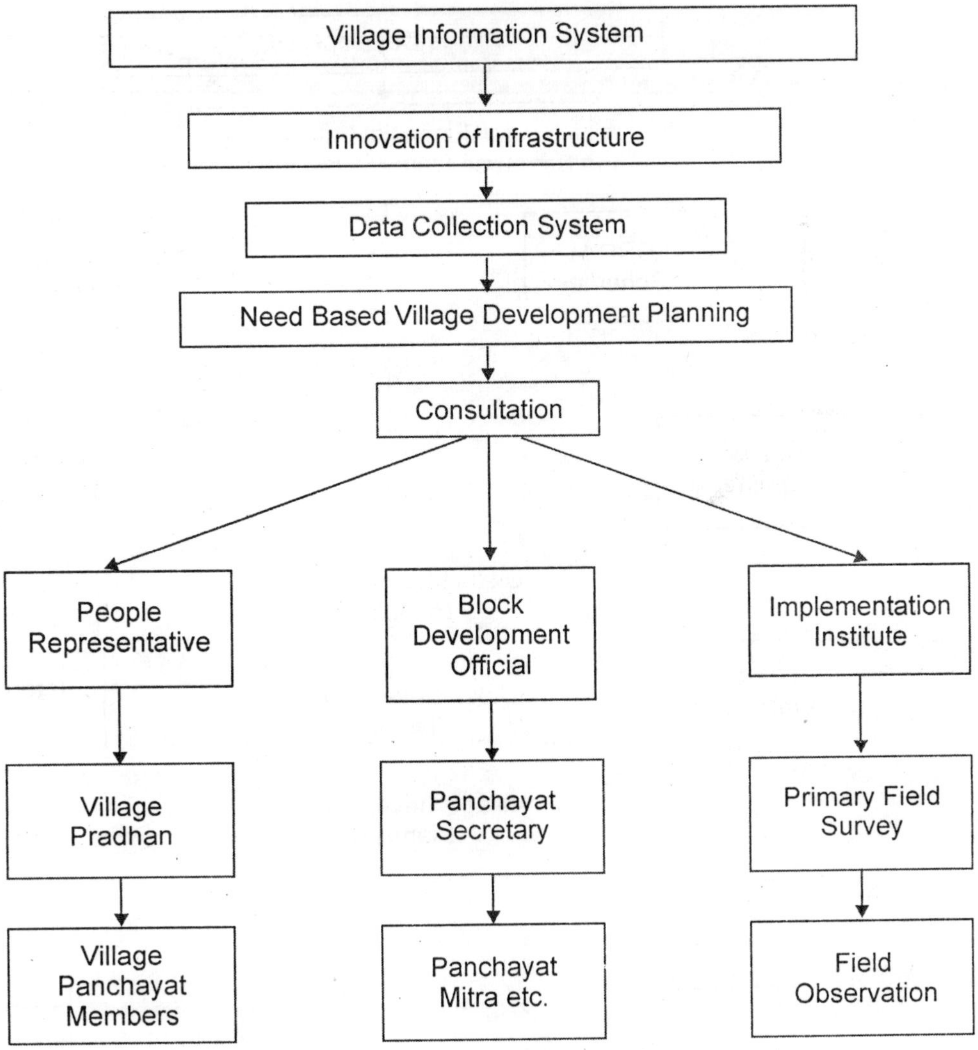

and rights to the District Panchayats = Block Panchayats = Village Panchayats for the formulation of need base village development planning and implementation of the planned rural development programmes under their control and also the maintenance and management of the created assets under the Panchayati Raj Institutions.

It has been realized that the innovation of already available human resources including socio-economic-institutional infrastructural resources and developing village information system at village panchayat level will be helpful in the formulation of the people's participatory need based integrated village development planning and successful implementation of the planned rural development programmes to fulfil the growing demand of ever increasing cattle and human population at the grassroots level.

3. SOCIAL INFRASTRUCTURE

The social infrastructure is one of the important part of the Human Resources. The social infrastructure plays an important role in the integrated development of an area. The social infrastructure include population pressure, caste composition, workforce and

Table 2.10: Village Development

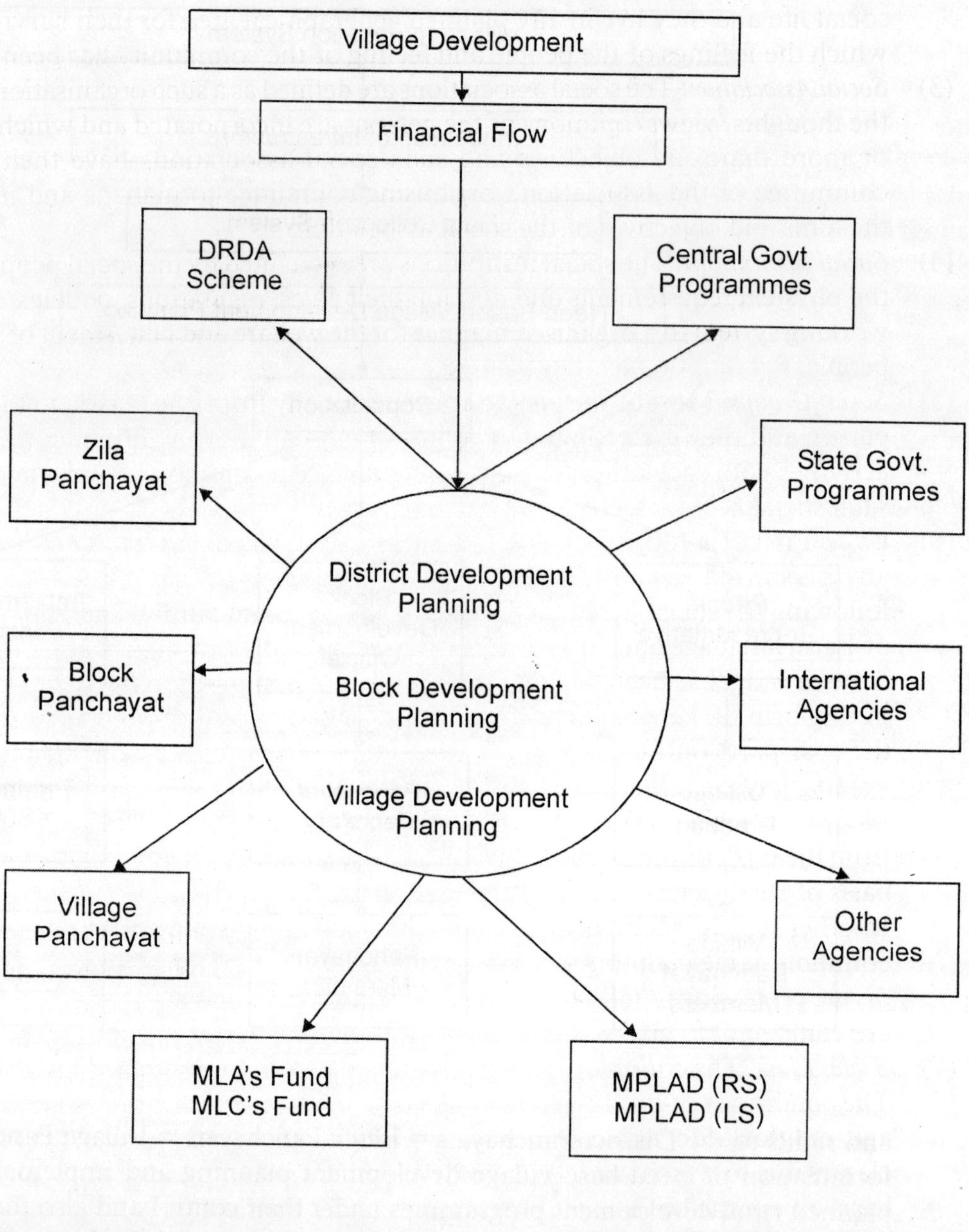

the educational profile along with various sub-indicators related to the social infrastructure.

The social system of an area covers the social class, society of the area, caste, community, social groups, association and social institutions. It is necessary to describe the social system of an area for better understanding to analyse the social infrastructure at the grassroots level.

(1) *Society*: "Society is the collection of individuals united by certain relations or modes of behaviour, which mark them off from others, who do not enter into these relations or who differ from them to behaviour."[1]
"Society is the system of usages and procedures of authority and mutual aid of many groups and divisions of control of human behaviours and of liberties."[2]

(2) *Community*: The community is a group of such people who participate in the general social life and they live in any planned geographical area for their survival and in which the feelings of the people and feeling of the community has been realized.

(3) *Social Association*: The social associations are defined as a such organisation in which the thoughts/views/opinions of the persons are incorporated and which have one or more than one objectives and such social associations have their working committee or the association's organising committee to manage and implement the aims and objectives of the social association.

(4) *Social Institutions*: The social institutions are accredited by the social people to fulfil the physical requirements and develop their rules, regulations, policies, plans and working system in a organised manner for the welfare and betterment of the social people.

(5) *Social Groups*: Most of the people affect personally from one person to the another person and they establish the relationship through meaningful inner feelings and activities with each other for the fulfilment of their common interests and through such social activities, social groups are formed in an area.

(6) *Caste*: First of all 'Garcia Deosta' used the word *'Caste'* and it has been said that if any person do not leave the hereditary profession of his father, and has been following the social hereditary rituals of the caste and family. The *'caste'* is a word of Latin language named as *'CAST US'* which means *caste* or *Jati*. The origin of the caste in India has been the joint system of caste composition from the *Vedic Period* in the form of *Varna* system. During the Vedic Period Society was distributed in the four parts on the basis of work and labour work. As per the labour and the *working profession Brahmin, Kshatriya, Vaisya and Shudra varna* emerged into *social varna system*. The caste is a such group whose membership is formed and decided from the birth of the person and their various social activities are performed on the basis of their caste or *varna* system and as per their hereditary and social rituals.
In other words, "caste is a collection of families or groups of families bearing a common name claiming a common descent from a mythical ancestor, human or divine professing to follow the same heredity calling, and recognised by those who are competent to give an opinion as forming a single homogenous community."

(7) *Social Class*: The conditions of the all persons are not common in the social system. The conditions of the differences from one person to the another varies due to sex, age, religion, education, profession etc. and the people are divided into different classes due to which various classes are formed. The division of the society on any basis except the birth has been termed as social class system.
"A social class in any portion of a community worked, off from the rest by social status"[3] may be defined as class.
'A social class is the aggregate of persons having essentially the some social status in a given society.'
The social class is an important phenomenon of the social infrastructure which affects directly or indirectly in the formulation of need based planning for the integrated development of an area including at the grassroots level through people's participation including the social class for whom such developmental plans are being formulated.

Thus the social infrastructure especially the *society,* social *community*, social *association*, social *institutions,* social *groups, castes,* social *class*, working class, and educational profile of any region play an important role in the integrated development of the area.

4. DEMOGRAPHY

The demography of the Amethi has been very diversely distributed from one village to another. The demographic diversities has been recorded from the historical period because the area was ruled by the kings and kings were only interested in the land revenue tax collection, due to which demographic variations continued, and it has adversely affected the social systems and economic growth of the people of Amethi.

The demography is a study of human population using information about births, deaths and movement of the population from one place to another.

The demography of the area has affected the socio-economic development of the Amethi. The demographic indicators include households, houses, population structure, male and female population and population density. The demographic pattern of the Amethi varies according to the land use pattern, soil structure, land capability and land quality cropping pattern of the area. The fertile land and the flat land has excessive population and settlement and populated area while undulated and unfertile land has poor settlement and very low population.

In view of the above, an attempt has been made in this study to innovate the proportionate distribution of houses, households, population and population density at the Village Panchayat Level in Amethi Block. The demographic distribution of Amethi has been mentioned in Table 2.11.

4.1 Houses

The distribution of houses in Amethi Block has been varying from one village to another due to establishment of the new settlements known as Purwas or Tolas or hamlet villages including revenue villages. There are 44 village panchayats in Amethi Block which have been considered as lowest unit of the development planning and lowest stage of the Three-Tier Panchayati Raj System. It has been recorded that there are 82 revenue villages along with 377 Tolas/Purwas/Hamlet Villages in Amethi Block.

It has been noticed that there are 18629 houses in the Block. The highest number of houses has been observed in the Jangal Ram Nagar having 48 revenue villages. The Jangal Ram Nagar is the highest village panchayat of the Amethi in terms of area, population, number of houses and also in the number of households. The total number of the houses of the Jangal Ram Nagar has been 1400 followed by the village panchayat Ramdaipur having 1340 number of houses. The distribution of houses has been depicted in Table 2.11 and the proportionate distribution of houses at the village panchayat level in Amethi Block has been shown in Map 2.3.

Medium number of houses ranging between 700 to 1000 houses has been noticed in the village Sarai Khema, Naraini, Kohara, Village Panchayat while low number of houses between 400 to 700 houses has been observed in Trilokpur, Mahmoodpur, Kherauna, Umapur Gana Patti, Nuwawan Mochawa, Korai Girdharshah, Gaderi, Ramgarh, Nainaha, Kakawa and Mahmoodpur village panchayats of the Amethi block. It has been noticed that less than 400 number of houses has been recorded in the Katara Maharani, Benipur, Parsawan, Kataraphul Kunwar, Hathaila, Dedhpaser, Rebha, Mahaso, Gangauli, Bhusahari, Himmatgarh, Dehara, Purabgaon, Dhanthudhar, Chaturbhujpur, Maharajpur, Agahar, Saidpur, Saraiya Duban Bhaganpur, Tala, Kushi Tali, Loharata and Darakha village panchayats of the Amethi Block. It has been observed that the number of the houses has been found more than the number of households

Table 2.11: Demography (Social Infrastructure)—Amethi Block

Sl. No.	Villages	No. of Houses	No. of Households	Total Population	Male	Female	Population density per hectare	%age of total Population	
								Male	Female
1	2	3	4	5	6	7	8	9	10
1.	Katra Maharani	335	324	1997	1014	983	15	51	49
2.	Sarai Khema	851	871	4868	2358	2510	9	49	51
3.	Trilokpur	525	492	2369	1206	1163	7	51	49
4.	Ramdaipur	1340	1327	3068	1533	1535	29	50	50
5.	Jangal Ram Nagar	1400	1363	8713	4458	4255	17	51	49
6.	Benipur	250	239	1335	705	630	10	53	47
7.	Parsawan	319	267	1537	800	737	5	52	48
8.	Mahmoodpur	500	430	2825	1468	1357	19	52	48
9.	Raipur Fulwari	319	283	1803	931	872	16	52	48
10.	Umapur Ganapatti	410	399	2376	1171	1205	17	49	51
11.	Bhaganpur	200	218	1296	647	649	19	50	50
12.	Tala	300	259	1472	772	700	8	52	48
13.	Kushi Tali	280	260	1429	708	721	14	50	50
14.	Loharta	190	222	1309	658	653	26	50	50
15.	Darkha	396	402	2347	1178	1169	18	50	50
16.	Mochwa	453	489	2749	1375	1374	16	50	50
17.	Nuwawan	501	419	2900	1480	1420	6	51	49
18.	Loniapur	300	251	1576	816	760	14	52	48
19.	Kherauna	480	461	3000	1596	1404	18	43	47
20.	Katra Phulkunwar	399	431	2548	1299	1249	14	51	49
21.	Hathkila	320	248	1571	785	786	17	50	50
22.	Rebha	235	217	1491	724	767	15	49	51
23.	Raidaipur	265	290	2205	1125	1080	18	51	49
24.	Korari Girdharshah	570	585	3317	1727	1590	7	52	48
25.	Dedhpasar	350	367	2701	1396	1305	19	52	48
26.	Mahaso	190	220	1912	1000	912	22	52	48
27.	Gangauli	258	284	1775	920	855	15	52	48
28.	Dhadhudhar	220	239	1733	888	845	13	51	49
29.	Gaderi	452	492	3049	1553	1496	11	51	49
30.	Bhusahari	250	277	1520	769	751	6	51	49
31.	Purabgaon	185	225	1403	723	680	16	52	48
32.	Chaturbhujpur	130	199	1202	608	594	10	51	49
33.	Mahrajpur	140	175	1184	561	623	17	47	53
34.	Aghar	225	211	1421	779	642	17	55	45
35.	Saidpur	270	265	1534	772	762	9	50	50
36.	Kakwa	635	651	3861	1948	1913	10	50	50
37.	Saraiya Duban	296	261	1574	831	743	5	50	50
38.	Kohra	710	651	3788	1911	1877	17	50	50
39.	Mahmpdpur	600	529	3107	1608	1499	17	52	48
40.	Naraini	780	723	4219	2052	2167	17	49	51
41.	Nainaha	480	504	2684	1421	1263	15	53	47
42.	Ramgarh	630	611	3810	1930	1880	16	51	49
43.	Himmatgarh	300	288	1672	821	851	14	49	51
44.	Dehara	390	431	3100	1586	1514	13	51	49
	Amethi Block	**18629**	**18530**	**107350**	**54609**	**52741**	**815**	**50.59**	**49.41**

because some of the families have also constructed another house in their field due to various personal reasons especially to look after their agricultural field and conjusted houses with much difficulties in the traditional houses in the hereditary old settlements.

4.2 Households

It has been observed that there is constant growth in the population and number of the houses at the village level in Amethi but there is significant growth in the number of households due to divisions of the families. The total number of households has been recorded 18530 in the Amethi Block. The proportionate distribution of households at the village panchayat level of Amethi Block has been depicted in Map 2.4. The highest number of households has been recorded in Jangal Ram Nagar (1363 Households) and 1327 houses in the village panchayat Ramdaipur of the Amethi Block. Proportionately medium number of households ranging between 700 and 1000 households has been observed in the Sarai Khema and Naraini village panchayats while low number of households between 400 and 700 households has been found in the Trilokpur, Mahmoodpur, Kherauna, Katra Phulkunwar, Korari Girdharshah, Nuwawan, Mochawa, Darkha, Gaderi, Ramgarh, Dehra, Nainaha, Kakawa, Kohara and Mahmoodpur village panchayats of Amethi Block. It has been recorded that very low number of households less than 400 households has been found in the Katara Maharani, Bhaganpur, Tala, Kushi Tali, Loharata, Umapurganapatti, Raipur Phulwari, Parsawana, Loniapur, Raidaipur, Rebha, Hathkila, Dedhpasar, Gangauli, Bhusahari, Himmatgarh, Dhandhudhar, Purabgaon, Chaturbhujpur, Maharajpur, Agahar, Saidpur and Saraiya Duban village panchayats of Amethi Block. Thus it has been noticed that the distribution of the households varies in accordance with the houses at the village panchayat level in Amethi which has also been significantly related to the distribution of population at the village panahcyat level including the associated revenue villages along with the Tolas/Purwas/Hamlet villages of Amethi Block.

4.3 Population

There is significant growth of the population in Amethi and 1,07,950 number of population including male and female has been recorded in the Amethi Block. The distribution of the population at the village panchayat level in the Amethi Block has been shown in Map. 2.5. It has been observed that more than 35,000 population has been found in the Sarai Khera, Jangal Ram Nagar, Kohara, Kakawa, Naraini and Ramgarh Village Panchayats of the Amethi Block. Medium population between 2500 and 3500 population has been found in the Ramdaipur, Mahmoodpur, Kherauna, Katara Phulkunwar, Dedhpasar, Korari Girdharshah, Mochawa, Nuwawan, Gaderi, Dehara, Nainaha, and Mahmoodpur village panchayats. Proportionately low distribution of population between 1500 and 2500 population has been observed in the Katara Maharani, Trilokpur, Parsawan, Hathkila, Raipur Phulwari, Umapur Ganapatti, Darakha, Dhandhudhar, Gangauli, Mahaso, Bhusahari, Himmatgarh and Saidpur village panchayats while very low distribution of population ranging between less than 1500 population has been recorded in the Bhaganpur, Tala, Kushi Tali, Loharata, Rebha, Agahar, Chaturbhujpur, Maharajpur, Purbgaon and Saraiya Duban village panchayats of Amethi Block. It has been noticed that the population has been distributed according to the land capability for agricultural productivity and approach to the town area including the commercial and industrial hubs which are closer to Purwas/Tolas/Hamlet villages or the revenue villages. Thus it can be stated that the population has been significantly distributed at village panchayat level in Amethi which has been an important component of the social infrastructure and the population plays an important significant positive role in the formulation of the need base planning and it implementation for the sustainable integrated village development.

4.4 MALE POPULATION

The distribution of the male population has been significantly distributed at the village panchayat level in Amethi which has been depicted in Map 2.6. The proportionate distribution of the Male population in numbers and also its percentage to the total population has been mentioned in Table 2.21. The female population percentage to the total population has been recorded 49.41 per cent in the Amethi Block. It has been observed that the highest number of the male population has been found 4458 males in Jangal Ram Nagar followed by 2358 in Sarai Khema and 1533 Male population in the Ramdaipur village panchayat and very low male population less than 1000 has been noticed in Benipur, Parsawan, Raipur Phulwari, Bhaganpur, Kushitali, Tala, Kushtali, Loharata, Loniapur, Hathkila, Rebha, Gangauli, Dhandhudhar, Bhusahari, Purabgaon, Chaturbhujpur, Maharajpur, Agahar Saidpur, Saraiya Duban and Himmatgarh village panchayats. Very high percentage distribution of the male population to total population having more than 53 per cent has been found in the Agahar Village Panchayat while medium percentage between 50 per cent and 53 per cent has been recorded in Katara Maharani, Trilokpur, Jangal Ram Nagar, Tala, Benipur, Parsawan, Mahmoodpur, Raipur Phulwari, Loniapur, Katara Phulkunwar, Raidaipur, Korarigirdharshah, Dhandhudhar, Nuwawan, Dedhpasar, Gangauli, Mahaso, Bhusahari, Dehara, Ramgarh, Nainaha, Purabgaon, Gaderi, Chaturbhujpur, Saraiya Duban, village panchayats of Amethi Block. Low percentage distribution of male population between 47 per cent and 50 per cent has been noticed in the Sarai Khema, Ramdaipur, Rebha, Hathkila, Himmatgarh, Darakha, Mochawa, Loharata, Kushi Tali, Umapur Gana Patti, Maharajpur, Naraini, Kohara, Kakawa and Saidpur village panchayats, while very low, less than 47 per cent male population to the total population has been found in the Kherauna village panchayat of Amethi Block.

4.5 FEMALE POPULATION

It has been recorded that there are 32741 total female population in Amethi Block (Map 2.7). The proportionate distribution of the female population at the village panchayat level has been illustrated in Table 2.11. It has been recorded that the highest female population has been found in the village panchayat Jangal Ram Nagar having 4255 female population followed by the 2358 female population in the village Sarai Khema and 1533 female population in the village panchayat Ramdaipur of the Amethi Block. Very low female population less than 1000 has been noticed in Katara Maharani, Benipur, Parsawan, Raipur Phulwari, Bhaganpur, Tala, Kushi Tali, Loharata, Loniapur, Hathkila, Rebha, Gangauli, Dhandhudhar, Bhusahari, Purabgaon, Chaturbhujpur, Maharajpur, Agahar, Saidpur and Saraiya Duban village panchayats of Amethi Block.

It has been recorded that more than 51 per cent female population to the total population has been found in the Maharajpur village panchayat and medium percentage between 49 and 51 per cent female population has been observed in the Saraikhema Ramdaipur, Bhaganpur, Kushitali, Loharata, Darakha, Mochawa, Umapur Gana Patti, Rebha, Hathkila, Saidpur, Kakawa, Kohara, Naraini and Himmatgarh village panchayats while low female population percentage to total population between 47 per cent to 49 per cent has been noticed in Katara Maharani, Trilokpur, Jangal Ram Nagar, Benipur,

Mahmoodpur, Parsawan, Raipur Phulwari, Kherauna, Katara Phulkunwar, Dedhpasar, Mahaso, Loniapur, Raidaipur, Korari Girdharshah, Dhandhudhar, Gangauli, Mahaso, Gaderi, Ramgarh, Dehara, Nainaha, Purabgaon, Chaturbhujpur, Saraiya Duban and Mohmadpur village panchayats of the Amethi Block. It has been recorded that there are 45 per cent female population in Agahar village panchayat of Amethi Block. It has been observed that proportionately female population has been reduced in some of the village panchayats due to ignorance and traditional sentimental feelings against the female child because the hereditary family will continue through the male child. The male child preferences has caused significant decrease in the famale child population, but the latest techno-scientific and educational programmes launched in the remote rural area has changed the minds of the rural poor and it has been felt that in near future female child ratio may increase in such village panchayats of Amethi Block.

4.6 POPULATION DENSITY

The population density per hectare has been computed at village panchayat level in Amethi. The population density of Amethi Block has been noticed 815 population per hectare (Map 2.8). The population density has been mentioned in Table 2.11. The distribution of the population density more than 18 population per hectare has been recorded in the Ramdaipur, Loharata and Mahaso village panchayats of the Amethi Block.

There is medium distribution of the population density between 12 and 18 per hectare has been recorded in Katra Maharani, Mochawa, Loniapur, Kherauna, Katara Phulkunwar, Rebha, Mochawa, Dhandhudhar, Nainaha and Dehara village panchayats of the Amethi Block, while low population density between 6 and 12 per hectare has been found in the Trilokpur, Saraikhema, Benipur, Mahmoodpur, Raipur Phulwari, Hathkila, Dedhpasar, Raidaipur, Korari Girdharshah, Jangal Ram Nagar, Umapur Ganapatti, Nuwawan, Darakha, Tala, Bhaganpur, Gaderi, Ramgarh, Bhusahari, Purabgaon, Chaturbhujpur, Maharajpur, Naraini, Agahar, Saidpur, Kakawa, Kohara and Mahmoodpur village panchayats of the Amethi Block. It has been observed that very low population density less than 6 per hectare has been found in Kushi Tali, Saraiya Duban, Parsawan, Gangauli and Himmatgarh village panchayats of Amethi Block.

It has been noticed that the population density has been significantly distributed in the Amethi Block because of Amethi Town Area and Hindustan Aeronautics Ltd. township area and marketing hubs at the Munshiganj and growth of the educational institutions in Amethi has led to a significant growth in the population and development of new settlements in the various revenue villages and Purwas/Tolas/Hamlet villages.

5. CASTE COMPOSITION

The caste means *Jati*. It has been said that if any person do not leave the hereditary profession of his father and has been following the social hereditary rituals of the caste and family. The caste composition had continued from Vedic period in the form of *Varna* system and the society was divided in the four parts on the basis of the work and labour work. As per the labour and the working profession Brahmin, Kshatriyas, Vaisya and Shudra varna emerged into the social *varna* system.

The caste is a such group whose membership is formed and decided from the birth of the person and their various social activities are performed on the basis of their caste or varna system and as per their hereditary and social rituals.

The Brahmins and Rajputs have been the main castes in the general category followed by the Vaisya which includes Gupta, Srivastava and other associated sub-castes in the general category which are insignificantly distributed at the village panchayat level in Amethi. In the varna system shudras have been significantly distributed in Amethi having various sub-castes categorised under the scheduled castes. Muslims have been categorised under the Minorities but significantly distributed in Amethi. The Muslims has also been categorised under the general caste, viz. Khan, Pathan and Shiya and Sunni Muslims but the Muslims are categorised as Backward castes which include Julaha or Ansari and there are several sub-castes and titles of the Muslims who are significantly distributed at the village panchayat level in Amethi Block.

It is a known fact from the historical period that the Amethi has been ruled by Kings and famous as Kingship ruled estate, due to which the kings required the service class people to fulfil their day-to-day requirements.

Kshatriya

Kshatriya were professionally involved for safety, security and protection of the estate and were known as *Yodha* of the Kings. The Kshatriya were given full liberty in the land ownership and were also involved in supporting the land revenue tax collection. The Kshatriyas enjoyed the benefits of the Kingship rulership at village panchayat level in Amethi.

Brahmins

The Brahmins played an important role not only during the Kingship rulership but also from the historical periods including the Vedic period. The Brahmins were engaged in the worships and in safeguarding the Kings through worshipping the God through adopting various religious ways and means. Thus the Brahmins were engaged in the worship programmes of the Kings and enjoyed the full liberty from the Kings including the land ownership. The Brahmins are significantly distributed at village panchayat level in Amethi.

Vaisya

The Vaisya included Srivastavas or Chitragupta and engaged for maintaining the land records. Accountancy work and land revenue records of the kings due to which very insignificant Vaisyas enjoyed the land rights and maximum facilities from the Kings.

Shudras

The Shudras as mentioned in the Varna system had been one of the most deprived section of the society and the shudras were the service providers including the various services to the kings but they were deprived of the land rights and land ownership from the kings. Thus the shudras were one of the most neglected, rejected and humiliated section of the society from the historical period, socially, religiously and institutionally.

Other Backward Castes

The other backward castes were also deprived of the land ownership and land rights but they were the service providers in the form of *agricultural activities* by Kurmi Caste, *Milking facility* by the *Ahirs* or *Yadavs*, *Vegetables supplied* by Maurya, *Cloth Stitching* by Tailor, *wood work* by *Badhai*/carpenter and Blacksmith workers, and various other service providers were professionally named as per their service to the kings as his caste, professionally.

Kurmis

Kurmis were engaged in the agricultural activities and they were providing the revenue tax in the form of cash or kind as per the instructions of the kings.

Yadavs

The Yadavs known as Ahir famous from historical period, especially the *Nand Vansh*, and also mentioned in *Mahabharata* has been famous for the *Milking* work and the Yadavs were providing milk to the kings but they were also deprived of land ownership and land rights from the kings.

Guptas

The Guptas were known as businessman and engaged in the commercial activities. The Guptas are insignificantly distributed in Amethi.

Carpenters

The carpenters had been providing services for the wood work activities to the kings including furnitures etc. The carpenter (*Badhai*) and Blacksmith (*Lohar*), etc. are insignificantly distributed in Amethi.

Other Backward Castes

The other backward castes include various other professional activities who were providing services to the kings. No doubt several other backward castes were the professionally service providers but these backward castes have been socially backward and economically very poor and these backward castes had been deprived of the land rights and land ownership from the kings and presently most of them are landless workers but they are surviving on their professional activities.

5.1 Scheduled Caste

The Scheduled Caste population historically known as Shudras has been socially-religiously-economically very deprived section of the society. The Scheduled Caste population has been significantly distributed at the Village Panchayat level in Amethi (Map 2.9). There are 23592 Scheduled Caste population in Amethi which contributed 21.9 per cent of the total population of Amethi Block.

The proportionate distribution of the Scheduled Caste population has been mentioned in Table 2.12.

Table 2.12: Caste Composition (Social-Infrastructure)—Amethi Block

Sl. No.	*Villages*	*Scheduled Caste Population*	*Kurmi*	*Yadav*	*Gupta*	*Carpentor*	*Other Backward Castes*	*Minorities*	*Brahmins*	*Rajput*
1	2	3	4	5	6	7	8	9	10	11
1.	Katra Maharani	396	190	500	73	5	90	145	378	220
2.	Sarai Khema	1132	610	800	250	50	100	500	776	650
3.	Trilokpur	874	100	500	400	20	25	100	250	100
4.	Ramdaipur	780	284	600	210	30	75	300	389	400
5.	Jangal Ram Nagar	1574	1000	1700	250	50	100	1000	1300	1739
6.	Benipur	582	178	270	50	5	5	70	35	140
7.	Parsawan	313	150	350	39	5	75	200	245	160
8.	Mahmoodpur	694	170	450	220	41	30	600	260	360
9.	Raipur Fulwari	451	170	300	120	10	15	210	302	225
10.	Umapur Ganapatti	580	228	450	100	58	90	300	390	180
11.	Bhaganpur	101	50	250	70	10	75	150	420	170
12.	Tala	388	150	240	80	20	15	105	292	182
13.	Kushi Tali	476	140	313	10	5	15	115	140	215
14.	Loharta	236	100	163	70	30	70	190	300	150
15.	Darkha	566	100	430	50	10	85	250	466	390
16.	Mochwa	664	200	580	144	30	75	300	576	180
17.	Nuwawan	680	220	546	200	20	67	308	559	300
18.	Loniapur	415	115	200	100	10	67	150	394	125
19.	Kherauna	700	250	800	240	10	25	265	330	380
20.	Katra Phulkunwar	487	200	521	60	20	70	290	520	380
21.	Hathkila	413	160	328	25	25	20	115	250	235
22.	Rebha	183	100	300	40	35	45	150	380	258
23.	Raidaipur	927	35	300	50	15	40	530	189	119
24.	Korari Girdharshah	711	200	536	100	70	100	700	500	400
25.	Dedhpasar	559	250	680	130	20	10	290	479	283
26.	Mahaso	400	180	530	120	20	7	100	225	330
27.	Gangauli	337	100	425	125	30	25	200	300	233
28.	Dhadhudhar	263	150	400	100	10	30	180	350	250
29.	Gaderi	629	200	650	140	10	100	398	542	380
30.	Bhusahari	370	50	350	40	10	60	190	250	200
31.	Purabgaon	207	100	390	30	5	75	125	286	185
32.	Chaturbhujpur	153	80	370	20	10	15	59	275	220
33.	Mahrajpur	255	70	300	35	5	44	90	205	180
34.	Aghar	245	50	350	15	5	50	180	300	226
35.	Saidpur	360	20	200	50	10	80	180	344	290
36.	Kakwa	840	200	800	200	100	100	520	601	500
37.	Saraiya Duban	214	100	358	40	10	86	180	386	200
38.	Kohra	867	300	622	280	50	150	443	623	453
39.	Mahmadpur	470	350	650	100	35	85	490	570	357
40.	Naraini	958	350	750	300	56	65	390	865	485
41.	Nainaha	433	245	500	66	50	70	320	510	490
42.	Ramgarh	850	300	800	200	20	150	280	710	500
43.	Himmatgarh	287	100	450	120	15	50	110	300	240
44.	Dehara	580	190	750	160	30	50	340	600	400
	Amethi Block	**23592**	**8485**	**21752**	**5230**	**1085**	**2676**	**12108**	**18362**	**14060**

The proportionate distribution of the caste composition to the total population has been illustrated in Table 2.13.

It has been observed that very high percentage of Scheduled Caste population, more than 40 per cent of the total population, has been found in Benipur, Raidaipur village panchayats of Amethi. Medium Scheduled Caste population between 30 per cent and 40 per cent and the total population has been noticed in the Trilokpur and Kushi Tali village panchayats, while low percentage between 20 per cent and 30 per cent Scheduled Caste population has been found in Ramdaipur, Sarai Khema, Mahmoodpur, Parsawan, Kherauna, Raipur Phulwari, Umapurganapatti, Tala, Darakha, Mochawa, Nuwawan, Korai Girdharshah, Loniapur, Mahaso, Dedhpasar, Hathkila, Bhusahari, Ramgarh, Gaderi, Maharajpur, Naraini, Saidpur, Kakawa and Kohara village panchayats of Amethi Block. Very low percentage distribution of Scheduled Caste less than 20 per cent and the total population has been noticed in the Katara Maharani, Jangal Ram Nagar, Bhaganpur, Loharata, Katara Phulkunwar, Rebha, Dhandhudhar, Gangauli, Himmatgarh, Dehara, Agahar, Chaturbhujpur, Purabgaon, Nainaha, Saraiya Duban and Mahmoodpur village panchayats of the Amethi Block and in these villages the upper caste population and the backward caste population has been significantly distributed and these villages have been well known as upper caste population dominant villages. These villages are socially and economically developed villages in comparison to the Scheduled Caste dominant villages of Amethi Block.

5.2 Kurmi

The Kurmi caste is one of the backward castes. The Kurmis are also the professional service providers to the Kings and the Kurmis main profession was been agricultural cultivation and the Kurmis were cultivating the land and in return they were providing land revenue taxes in cash or kind to the kings and these castes were also having land ownership and land rights. It has been observed that the Kurmis are significantly distributed in Amethi. The distribution of the Kurmi caste population has been mentioned in Table 2.13. It has been observed that the Kurmi caste has been highly distributed having more than 12 per cent and the total population in Saraikhema, Benipur village panchayats while medium Kurmi caste population between 9 per cent and 12 per cent has been distributed in Katara Maharani, Ramdaipur, Jangal Ram Nagar, Tala, Kushi Tali, Umapurganapatti, Raipur Phulwari, Parsawan, Hathkila, Dedhpasar, Mahaso, Nainaha village panchayats of the Amethi Block. It has been noticed that low percentage of Kurmi population between 6 per cent and 9 per cent and the total population has been found in Mahmoodpur, Katara Phulkunwar, Rebha, Loniapur, Korari Girdharshah, Dhandhudhar, Chaturbhujpur, Purabgaon, Gaderi, Ramgarh, Dehara, Naraini, Saraiya Duban and Kohara village panchayats of the Amethi Block. The proportionate distribution of the Kurmi caste population to the total population has been depicted in Map 2.10. Very low percentage less than 6 per cent Kurmi population of the total population has been found in Trilokpur, Bhaganpur, Kherauna, Raidaipur, Darakha, Gangauli, Bhusahari, Himmatgarh, Maharajpur, Saidpur, Agahar and Kakawa village panchayats of the Amethi Block.

5.3 Yadav

The Yadavs have been one of the dominant backward castes in Amethi. The main profession of the Yadavs is animal husbandry and dairy work. The milking has been the main activity of the Yadavs. The Yadavs contribute 20.3 per cent of the total population in the Amethi Block. Yadavs are significantly distributed in Amethi. The proportionate distribution of Yadav caste to the total population has been depicted in Map 2.11. It has been observed that more than 25 per cent Yadav population of the total population has been found in Kherauna, Dedhpasar, Mahaso, Purabgaon, Chaturbhujpur, Himmatgarh village panchayats of the Amethi Block. Medium percentage distribution of Yadavs between 20 per cent and 25 per cent has been noticed in Kushi Tali, Benipur, Parsawan, Katara Phulkunwar, Rebha, Hathkila, Dhandhudhar, Mochawa, Gaderi, Gangauli, Dehara, Bhusahari, Agahar, Kakawa, Saraiya Duban and Mahmoodpur village panchayats of the Amethi Block. Low percentage distribution of Yadavs between 15 per cent and 20 per cent of the total population has been recorded in Sarai Khema, Ramdaipur, Bhaganpur, Tala, Jangal Ram Nagar, Umapur Guna Patti, Mahmoodpur, Raipur Phulwari, Korari Girdharshah, Darakha, Nuwawan, Ramgarh, Nainaha, Naraini and Kohara village panchayats of Amethi. Very low percentage distribution of Yadav caste less than 15 per cent of the total population has been observed in Loniapur, Raidaipur, Loharata and Saidpur village panchayats of the Amethi Blcok. It has been observed that the Yadavs of Amethi have been socially and economically backward due to kingship ruled estate and the Yadavs were deprived of the land rights and land ownership. The main economic activity of the Yadavs is milking professional activity.

5.4 Gupta

The Guptas have been one of the important business communities. The Guptas are engaged in the commercial activities and trading business. The Guptas population has been insignificantly distributed in Amethi except the marketing places, town areas and other nodal places at the village panchayat level. The proportionate distribution of the Gupta population to the total population has been depicted in Map 2.12. Very high percentage of the Gupta population of the total population has been found in Trilokpur village panchayat having 16.8 per cent Gupta's population while medium Gupta's population between 6 per cent and 9 per cent has been found in the Ramdaipur, Mahmoodpur, Raipur Phulwari, Kherauna, Loniapur, Nuwawan, Mahaso, Gangauli, Himmatgarh, Naraini and Kohara village panchayats of the Amethi Block. It has been noticed that low percentage distribution of the Guptas, having 3 per cent to 6 per cent population, has been found in Katara Maharani, Saraikhema, Benipur, Bhaganpur, Tala, Loharata, Umapur Gana Patti, Mochawa, Dhandhudhar, Korai Girdharshah, Dedhpasar, Ramgarh, Gaderi, Dehara, Saidpur, Kakawa and Mahmoodpur village panchayats of the Amethi Block. It has been observed that very low percentage of Gupta population less than 3 per cent of the total population has been found in the Jangal Ram Nagar, Kushi Tali, Parsawan, Katara Phulkunwar, Raidaipur, Rebha, Hathkila, Darakha, Bhusahari, Agahar, Chaturbhujpur, Maharajpur, Purabgaon, Nainaha and Saraiya Duban village panchayats of Amethi Block.

5.5 Carpenter

The carpenters have been one of the service providers to the kings. The carpenters are locally known as '*Badhai*'. The carpenters are one of the backward castes who are socially and economically backward in Amethi. The carpenter has been the manufacturers of wood furniture and wood related agricultural implements. The carpenters are insignificantly distributed in Amethi. The proportionate distribution of the carpenters population to the total population has been depicted in **Map 2.13**. Very high percentage distribution of carpenters of the total population is more than 2 per cent in Loharata, Kakawa, Korari Girdharshah and Rebha village panchayats while medium percentage distribution of carpenter population of the total population between 1.5 per cent and

2.0 per cent has been found in Gangauli and Nainaha village panchayats of the Amethi Block. Low percentage between 1 per cent and 1.5 per cent carpenter population has been found in Sarai Khema, Jangal Ram Nagar, Mahmoodpur, Bhaganpur, Tala, Hathkila, Mahaso, Mochawa, Naraini, Kohara and Mahmoodpur village panchayats of Amethi. It has been observed that very low percentage distribution of the carpenter

Table 2.13: Proportionate Distribution of Castes (Social-Infrastructure)—Amethi Block

(%age of Total Population)

Sl. No.	*Villages*	*Scheduled Caste*	*Kurmi*	*Yadav*	*Gupta*	*Carpenter*	*Other backward Castes*	*Minorities*	*Brahmins*	*Rajput*
1	2	3	4	5	6	7	8	9	10	11
1.	Katra Maharani	19.8	10	25	4	0.2	4	7	19	11
2.	Sarai Khema	23.2	12.5	16.4	5.1	1	2	10.2	15.9	13.3
3.	Trilokpur	36.8	4.2	21.1	16.8	0.8	1	4.2	10.5	4.2
4.	Ramdaipur	25.4	9.2	20	6.8	0.9	2.4	9.7	12.6	13
5.	Jangal Ram Nagar	18.0	11.4	19.5	2.8	1	1.1	11.4	14.9	19.9
6.	Benipur	43.5	13.3	20.2	3.7	0.3	0.3	5.2	2.6	10.4
7.	Parsawan	20.3	9.7	22.7	2.5	0.3	4.8	13	15.9	10.4
8.	Mahmoodpur	24.5	6	15.9	7.7	1.4	1	21.2	9.2	12.7
9.	Raipur Fulwari	25	9.4	16.6	6.6	0.5	0.8	11.6	16.7	12.4
10.	Umapur Ganapatti	24.4	9.5	18.9	4.2	2.4	3.7	12.6	16.4	7.5
11.	Bhaganpur	8	3.8	19.2	5.4	0.7	5.7	11.5	32.4	13.1
12.	Tala	26.3	10.1	16.3	5.4	1.3	1	7.1	19.8	12.3
13.	Kushi Tali	33.3	9.7	21.9	0.6	0.3	1	8	9.7	15
14.	Loharta	18	7.6	12.4	5.3	2.2	5.3	14.5	22.9	11.4
15.	Darkha	24.1	4.2	18.3	2.1	0.4	3.6	10.6	19.8	16.6
16.	Mochwa	24.1	7.2	21	5.2	1.0	2.7	10.9	20.9	6.5
17.	Nuwawan	23.4	7.5	18.8	6.8	0.6	2.3	10.6	19.2	10.3
18.	Loniapur	26.3	7.2	12.6	6.3	0.6	4.2	9.5	25	7.9
19.	Kherauna	23.3	0.3	26.6	8	0.3	0.8	8.8	11	12.6
20.	Katra Phulkunwar	19.1	7.8	20.4	2.3	0.7	2.7	11.3	20.4	14.9
21.	Hathkila	26.2	10.1	20.8	1.5	1.5	1.2	7.3	15.9	14.9
22.	Rebha	12.2	6.7	20.1	2.6	2.3	3	10	25.4	17.3
23.	Raidaipur	42.4	1.5	13.6	2.2	0.6	1.8	24	8.5	5.3
24.	Korari Girdharshah	21.4	6	16.3	3	2.1	3	21.1	15	12
25.	Dedhpasar	20.6	9.2	25.1	4.8	0.7	0.8	10.7	17.7	10.4
26.	Mahaso	21	9.4	27.7	6.2	1	0.3	5.2	11.7	17.2
27.	Gangauli	19	5.6	23.9	7	1.6	1.4	11.2	17	13.1
28.	Dhadhudhar	15.1	8.6	23	5.7	0.5	1.7	10.3	20.1	14.4
29.	Gaderi	20.6	6.5	21.3	4.5	0.3	3.2	13	17.7	12.4
30.	Bhusahari	24.3	3.2	23	2.6	0.6	3.9	12.5	16.4	13.1
31.	Purabgaon	14.7	7.1	27.7	2.1	0.3	5.3	8.9	20.3	13.1
32.	Chaturbhujpur	12.7	6.6	30.7	1.6	0.8	3.6	4.9	22.8	14.9
33.	Mahrajpur	21.5	5.9	25.3	2.9	0.4	3.7	7.6	17.3	15.2
34.	Aghar	17.2	3.5	24.6	1	0.3	3.5	12.6	21.1	15.9
35.	Saidpur	23.4	1.3	13	3.2	0.6	5.2	11.7	22.4	18.9
36.	Kakwa	21.7	5.1	20.7	5.1	2.5	2.5	13.4	15.5	12.9
37.	Saraiya Duban	13.5	6.3	22.7	2.5	0.6	5.4	11.7	24.5	12.7
38.	Kohra	22.8	7.9	16.4	7.3	1.3	3.9	11.6	16.4	11.9
39.	Mahmadpur	15.1	11.2	20.9	3.2	1.1	2.7	15.7	18.3	11.4
40.	Naraini	22.7	8.2	17.7	7.1	1.3	1.9	9.2	20.5	11.4
41.	Nainaha	16.1	9.1	18.6	2.4	1.8	2.6	11.9	19	18.2
42.	Ramgarh	22.3	7.8	20	5.2	0.5	3.9	7.3	18.6	13.1
43.	Himmatgarh	17.1	5.9	26.9	7.1	0.8	2.9	6.5	17.9	14.3
44.	Dehara	18.7	6.1	24.1	5.1	0.9	1.6	10.9	19.3	12.9
	Amethi Block	**21.9**	**7.9**	**20.3**	**4.9**	**1.0**	**2.5**	**11.2**	**17.8**	**13.1**

population less than 1 per cent of the total population has been found in the Katara Maharani, Trilokpur, Ramdaipur, Parsawan, Raipur Phulwari, Kherauna, Katara Phulkunwar, Dedhpasar, Loniapur, Raidaipur, Darakha, Nuwawan, Dhandhudhar, Agahar, Maharajpur, Chaturbhujpur, Purabgaon, Ramgarh, Bhusahari, Himmatgarh, Dehara, Saidpur and Saraiya Duban village panchayats of Amethi Block.

5.6 Other Bakcward Castes

The other backward castes include Maurya, Blacksmith, Barber (*Nai*), Nishad/Kashyap, Kohar/Prajapati, Kanhar/Rajbhar, Gond, Bhuj, Muslim, Ansari and various other castes which have been included under the backward castes. The backward castes have been the service providers to the Kings. Presently, the various other sub-castes are professionally engaged for their survival based on their traditional/hereditary professional occupations. The proportionate distribution of the other backward caste population to the total population has been depicted in **Map 2.14**. It has been noticed that more than 5 per cent of other Backward Caste population of the total population have been found in Bhaganpur, Loharata, Purabgaon, Saidpur and Saraiya Duban village panchayats of Amethi. Medium percentage distribution of other backward castes between 3 per cent and 5 per cent of the total population has been recorded in Katara Maharani, Parsawan, Umapur Gana Patti, Darakha, Loniapur, Gaderi, Bhusahari, Ramgarh, Agahar, Chaturbhujpur, Maharajpur and Kohara village panchayats of the Amethi Block. It has been noticed that low percentage distribution of the other Backward castes ranging from 1 per cent to 3 per cent of the total population has been found in Trilokpur, Saraikhema, Ramdaipur, Jangal Ram Nagar, Mahmoodpur, Katara Phulkunwar, Hathkila, Rebha, Raidapur, Korari Girdharshah, Dhandhudhar, Mochawa, Nuwawan, Gangauli, Himmatgarh, Dehara, Naraini, Nainaha, Kakawa and Mahmoodpur village panchayats of the Amethi Block. Very low percentage distribution of the other backward caste population less than one per cent of the total population has been found in Benipur, Raipur Phulwari, Kherauna, Dedhpasar, Mahaso, Tala and Kushi Tali village panchayats of Amethi Block.

5.7 Minorities

The Muslims are the important religious population. The Muslims have been categorised under the Minorities religious population but in Amethi the Muslims contribute 11.2 per cent significant proportion to the total population. The proportionate distribution of the Minorities population including Muslims, Sikhs, Christians etc. to the total population has been depicted in **Map 2.15**. It has been observed that more than 20 per cent of Minorities population of the total population have been found in Mahmoodpur, Korari Girdharshah and Raidaipur village panchayats while medium percentage from 15 per cent to 20 per cent of minorities population have been found in Mahmoodpur village panchayat. Low percentage from 10 per cent to 15 per cent of minorities population have been seen in Saraikhema, Jangal Ram Nagar, Bhaganpur, Umapur Ganapatti, Loharata, Darakha, Mochawa, Nuwawan, Raipur Phulwari, Katara Phulkunwar, Rebha, Dedhpasar, Dhandhudhar, Gaderi, Gangauli, Bhusahari, Dehara, Nainaha, Agahar, Saidpur, Kakawa, Saraiya Duban and Kohara village panchayats of the Amethi Block. It has been observed that very low percentage of minorities population less than 10 per cent of the total population have been found in Katara Maharani, Trilokpur, Ramdaipur, Tala, Kushi Tali, Loniapur, Kherauna, Hathkila, Mahaso, Himmatgarh, Naraini,

Ramgarh, Purabgaon, and Himmatgarh village panchayats of the Amethi Block. Very low percentage distribution of the minorities population has been recorded because there are high percentage distribution of the upper caste and backward caste population in these village panchayats of the Amethi Block.

5.8 Brahmins

The Brahmins are significantly and proportionately distributed at the village panchayat level in Amethi. There are 17.8 per cent Brahmin caste population in the Amethi. The proportionate distribution of the Brahmin caste population has been depicted in the **Map 2.16.** It has been noticed that very high percentage more than 22 per cent Brahmin population to the total population has been seen in Bhaganpur, Loharata, Chaturbhujpur, Saraiya Duban, Saidpur, Loniapur and Rebha village panchayats of the Amethi. Medium percentage from 18 per cent to 22 per cent Brahmin population has been found in Katara Maharani, Tala, Darakha, Mochawa, Nuwawan, Dhandhudhar, Katara Phulkunwar, Dehara, Nainaha, Purabgaon, Ramgarh, Naraini, Agahar and Mahmoodpur village panchayats of the Amethi Block. Low percentage from 14 per cent to 18 per cent Brahmin population has been recorded in the Saraikhema, Jangal Ram Nagar, Umapur Ganapatti, Raipur Phulwari, Hathkila, Dedhpasar, Korai Girdharshah, Gaderi, Gangauli, Bhusahari, Himmatgarh, Maharajpur, Kakawa and Kohara village panchayats. Very low percentage less than 14 per cent Brahmin population has been noticed in Trilokpur, Ramdaipur, Kushitali, Raidaipur, Mahaso, Benipur, Mahmoodpur and Kherauna village panchayats of the Amethi Block.

5.9 Rajput

The Rajput castes constitute very important segment of the caste composition from the historical period. The Rajputs were basically kings or rulers of the estate or the land revenue tax collectors or the kins of the Kingship rulership. There are 13.1 per cent Rajput population of the total population in the Amethi Block. The proportionate distribution of the Rajput Caste to the total population has been depicted in **Map 2.17**. It has been observed that very high percentage more than 18 per cent Rajput population of the total population has been seen in Jangal Ram Nagar, Saidpur and Nainaha village panchayats while medium percentage between 15 per cent and 18 per cent Rajput population has been noticed in Darakha, Agahar, Rebha, Mahso village panchayats of Amethi Block. It has been observed that low percentage between 12 per cent and 15 per cent Rajput population has been seen in the Saraikhema, Ramdaipur, Mahmoodpur, Raipur Phulwari, Kherauna, Katara Phulkunwar, Hathkila, Koraigirdhar Shah, Dhandhudhar, Chaturbhujpur, Purabgaon, Gaderi, Dehara, Ramgarh, Himmatgarh, Bhusahari, Kakawa, Saraiya Duban village panchayats of the Amethi Block while very low less than 12 per cent Rajput population has been recorded in Katara Maharani, Trilokpur, Loharata, Umapur Ganapatti, Mochawa, Nuwawan, Loniapur, Raidaipur, Dedhpasar, Benipur, Parsawan and Naraini, Kohara and Mahmoodpur village panchayats of Amethi Block.

Thus, the caste composition of the Amethi plays an important role as the social infrastructure of the village panchayats. The structure of the caste which has been based on the professional/occupational services to the Kings from historical period has been still followed in the Amethi. The title name or the surname indicating the caste clearly indicates the occupational structure of the particular caste whether the person belongs to the backward caste or the upper caste. It has been noticed that there are 21.9 per cent Scheduled Caste population, followed by 7.9 per cent Kurmi, 20.3 per cent Yadavas, 4.9 per cent Gupta caste people and 1 per cent Carpenter caste and 2.5 per cent other backward caste people to the total population while the minorities share 11.2 per cent, and Brahmin 17.8 per cent and the Rajput caste population constitutes 13.1 per cent population of the total population in the Amethi Block. Thus the caste composition has been an important social infrastructure based on professional occupation from the historical period plays an important role in the socio-economic development of the Amethi.

6. WORKERS

Workforce of an area plays an important role in the socio-economic development of the region. As discussed earlier that Amethi has been the kingship ruled estate. The king has service class providers in the form of agricultural workers, farmers, service providers for the day-to-day requirements of the kings. As per the service class the caste of the person has been determined. The castewise professional and occupational structure has been existing not only in the Amethi but in most of the districts of the State. In this study an attempt has been made to analyse the distribution of the workers at the village panchayat level in Amethi Block.

The distribution of workers and its various categories at the village panchayat level has been depicted in Table 2.14. The proportionate distribution of the workers to the total population at the village panchayat level has been mentioned in Table 2.15. The proportionate distribution of workers to the total population has been depicted in **Map 2.18**. It has been observed that highest number of total workers more than 40 per cent of the total population has been found in the Katara Maharani, Mochawa and Gaderi village panchayats of the Amethi Block. Medium percentage distribution of workers between 30 per cent and 40 per cent has been seen in Trilokpur, Sarai Khema, Darakha, Dedhpasar, Korari Girdharshah, Gangauli, Bhusahari, Ramgarh, Himmatgarh, Purabgaon, Agahar, Saidpur and Kohara village panchayats of Amethi. Low percentage distribution of workers between 20 per cent and 30 per cent has been seen in Ramdaipur, Benipur, Tala, Loharata, Umapur Gana Patti, Raipur Phulwari, Kherauna, Katara Phulkunwar, Hathkila, Rebha, Raidaipur, Naraini, Nainaha, Kakawa, Saraiya Duban and Himmatgarh village panchayats of Amethi. Very low percentage less than 20 per cent workers to total population has been noticed in Kushi Tali, Bhaganpur, Jangal Ram Nagar, Mahmoodpur, Parsawan, Loniapur, Mahaso, Nuwawan and Chaturbhujpur village panchayats of Amethi Block.

6.1 Cultivators

The agriculture is main dominant source of income in Amethi. The farmers or cultivators are the important part of the occupational structure of Amethi. The proportionate distribution of cultivators at the village panchayat level has been depicted in Map 2.19. Proportionately very high percentage more than 20 per cent cultivators to the total population has been seen in Mochawa, Gangauli and Ramgarh village panchayats while medium percentage between 15 per cent and 20 per cent cultivators of the total population has been observed in Umapur Ganapatti, Darakha, Korari Girdharshah, Bhusahari, Himmatgarh, Purabgaon, Naraini, Agahar, Saidpur, Saraiya Duban and

Table 2.14: Workers (Social-Infrastructure)—Amethi Block

Sl. No.	*Villages*	*Total Workers*	*Cultivators*	*Agricultural Workers*	*Non-Skilled Workers*	*Skilled Workers*	*Plantation & Animal Husbandry*	*Construction Workers*	*Business Workers*	*Transportation Workers*	*Other & Office Workers*	*Small Scale & Agro Industries Workers*
1	2	3	4	5	6	7	8	9	10	11	12	13
1.	Katra Maharani	822	229	222	160	75	50	20	22	19	10	15
2.	Sarai Khema	1597	732	350	220	100	65	40	30	25	15	20
3.	Trilokpur	817	350	150	195	47	15	29	5	14	2	10
4.	Ramdaipur	848	392	193	139	74	11	10	10	9	3	14
5.	Jangal Ram Nagar	1713	880	420	200	105	25	15	20	25	10	13
6.	Benipur	285	160	40	45	25	5	3	2	3	1	1
7.	Parsawan	195	86	34	44	15	3	2	5	2	3	1
8.	Mahmoodpur	479	179	173	58	25	17	5	7	8	4	3
9.	Raipur Fulwari	362	70	144	90	25	11	8	7	4	1	2
10.	Umapur Ganapatti	712	397	138	100	50	5	3	8	7	1	3
11.	Bhaganpur	171	81	23	36	15	3	4	5	1	1	2
12.	Tala	299	150	31	52	20	14	8	5	8	4	7
13.	Kushi Tali	150	90	27	20	5	3	2	1	2	—	—
14.	Loharta	268	114	93	40	10	1	1	3	2	2	2
15.	Darkha	933	383	280	211	30	9	5	5	5	2	3
16.	Mochwa	899	511	264	75	25	5	6	7	3	1	2
17.	Nuwawan	267	132	47	37	20	10	5	5	3	—	8
18.	Loniapur	266	102	80	56	2	1	—	—	—	—	1
19.	Kherauna	657	305	125	90	50	20	15	17	12	18	5
20.	Katra Phulkunwar	643	260	235	70	35	4	3	18	5	—	5
21.	Hathkila	335	133	94	72	17	3	2	4	3	2	5
22.	Rebha	304	100	140	35	12	5	2	5	2	1	2
23.	Raidaipur	609	327	58	160	40	10	5	3	2	3	6
24.	Korari Girdharshah	1070	550	300	130	50	10	12	10	4	2	2
25.	Dedhpasar	927	400	292	150	50	10	8	5	3	4	5
26.	Mahaso	250	200	31	8	2	2	2	2	1	1	1
27.	Gangauli	626	379	124	70	20	5	3	10	2	3	10
28.	Dhadhudhar	498	200	150	70	25	15	10	7	8	3	10
29.	Gaderi	1285	610	459	144	30	10	10	7	5	—	10
30.	Bhusahari	518	271	86	73	25	10	10	15	10	3	15
31.	Purabgaon	472	248	110	80	10	5	8	5	3	—	3
32.	Chaturbhujpur	188	86	70	15	5	3	2	3	2	1	1
33.	Mahrajpur	347	159	75	60	20	10	8	6	3	1	5
34.	Aghar	445	215	109	50	30	16	5	5	8	6	1
35.	Saidpur	469	266	95	50	20	5	3	10	8	2	10
36.	Kakwa	869	468	230	100	40	5	10	10	4	—	2
37.	Saraiya Duban	468	250	121	55	20	8	3	2	5	1	3
38.	Kohra	1190	670	318	110	50	13	10	8	4	3	4
39.	Mahmadpur	866	340	290	117	66	15	10	8	7	3	10
40.	Naraini	917	688	105	77	20	8	5	4	3	2	5
41.	Nainaha	562	280	120	100	50	3	2	3	3	—	1
42.	Ramgarh	1300	798	280	122	34	10	10	10	20	12	4
43.	Himmatgarh	662	300	213	100	20	5	10	6	3	1	4
44.	Dehara	681	380	180	52	20	6	10	10	10	3	10
	Amethi Block	**28241**	**13921**	**7119**	**3938**	**1429**	**469**	**344**	**340**	**280**	**155**	**246**

Kohara village panchayats. It has been observed that low percentage distribution of cultivators between 10 per cent and 15 per cent of the total population has been found in Katara Maharani, Trilokpur, Saraikhema, Ramdaipur, Jangal Ram Nagar, Tala, Kherauna, Katara Phulkunwar, Dedhpasar, Raidaipur, Dhandhudhar, Maharajpur, Kakawa, Nainaha and Himmatgarh village Panchayats of Amethi Block. Very low percentage distribution of cultivators less than 10 per cent of the total population has been noticed in Bhaganpur, Kushi Tali, Loharata, Nuwawan, Chaturbhujpur, Mahaso, Rebha, Loniapur, Hathkila, Raipur Phulwari, Mahmoodpur and Parsawan village panchayats of Amethi Block.

6.2 Agricultural Labourers

The agricultural labourers are significantly distributed in Amethi. It has been observed that along with the cultivators some of the landless people are engaged as agricultural labourers in assisting the cultivators having large size of land holdings and needy cultivators. The proportionate distribution of agricultural labourers to the total population has been depicted in **Map 2.20**. It has been observed that more than 9 per cent agricultural labourers of total population has been found in Katara Maharani, Darakha, Mochawa, Katara Phulkunwar, Rebha, Dedhpasar, Korarigirdhar Shah, Gaderi, Himmatgarh, Darakha, Mochawa and Himmatgarh village panchayats while medium percentage between 7 per cent and 9 per cent agricultural workers has been found in Saraikhema, Raipur Phulwari, Loharata, Dhandhudhur, Agahar, Purabgaon, Ramgarh, Saraiya Duban and Kohara village panchayats of Amethi. Low percentage distribution of the agricultural labourers between 5 per cent and 7 per cent has been noticed in the Trilokpur, Ramdaipur, Umapur Ganapatti, Loniapur, Mahmoodpur, Hathkila, Bhusahari, Gangauli, Dehara, Chaturbhujpur, Maharajpur, Kakawa and Saidpur village panchayats while very low percentage of agricultural labourers less than 5 per cent of the total population has been seen in Bhaganpur, Tala, Kushi Tali, Jangal Ram Nagar, Benipur, Parsawana, Kherauna, Raidaipur, Mahaso, Nuwawan, Naraini, Nainaha village panchayats of the Amethi Block. It has been observed that the agricultural labourers are significantly distributed at the village panchayat level and they contribute a significant role in increasing the agricultural productivity of the village.

6.3 Non-Skilled Workers

The non-skilled workers are significantly distributed at the village panchayat level in Amethi. The proportionate distribution of non-skilled workers to the total population has been depicted in **Map 2.21**. It has been observed that more than 8 per cent non-skilled workers of the total population has been seen in Trilokpur and Darakha village panchayat while medium percentage between 5 per cent and 8 per cent non-skilled workers of total population has been recorded in Katara Maharani, Raidaipur, Dedhpasar, Himmatgarh, Purabgaon and Maharajpur village panchayat. It has been noticed that low percentage of non-skilled workers of total population has been seen in Saraikhema, Ramdaipur, Bhaganpur, Tala, Loharata, Umapur Ganapatti, Raipur Phulwari, Mahmoodpur, Benipur, Parsawan, Kherauna, Katara Phulkunwar, Hathkila, Rebha, Loniapur, Korari Girdharshah, Mochawa, Dhandhudhar, Gaderi, Gangauli, Bhusahari, Ramgarh, Nainaha, Agahar, Saidpur, Kakawa, Saraiya Duban, Kohara and Mahmoodpur village panchayats of Amethi Block. The very low percentage less than 2 per cent non-skilled workers has been found in Kushi Tali, Nuwawan, Mahaso, Naraini and Chaturbhujpur village panchayats of Amethi.

6.4 Skilled-Workers

The skilled workers includes trained workers including the Mason workers and educated technical workers like electrician etc. The skilled workers are significantly distributed at the village panchayat level in Amethi. The proportionate distribution of skilled workers to the total population has been depicted in **Map 2.22**. It has been observed that more than 3 per cent skilled workers of the total population has been found in the Katara Maharani village panchayat while medium percentage between 2 per cent and 3 per cent skilled workers of total population has been seen in Ramdaipur, Umapur Ganapatti, Agahar and Mahmoodpur village panchayats of the Amethi Block. Low percentage between one per cent and two per cent skilled workers of total population has been found in Trilokpur, Sarai Khema, Benipur, Jangal Ram Nagar, Bhaganpur, Tala, Raipur Phulwari, Kherauna, Katara Phulkunwar, Dedhpasar, Loniapur, Raidaipur, Korari Girdharshah, Dhandhudhar, Gangauli, Bhusahari, Himmatgarh, Maharajpur, Nainaha, Saidpur, Kakawa, Saraiya Duban and Kohara village panchayats of the Amethi Block. It has been observed that very low percentage less than one per cent skilled workers of total population has been found in Parsawan, Mahmoodpur, Hathkila, Rebha, Mahaso, Nuwawan, Loharata, Kushi Tali, Chaturbhujpur, Gaderi, Ramgarh, Dehara, Purabgaon and Naraini village panchayats of Amethi Block.

6.5 Plantation and Animal Husbandry Workers

The plantation and animal husbandry workers are those people who are engaged in the milking programme and engaged in the milking animals, sheep and goats keeping activities. The animal husbandry programmes are carried out by the Yadavs and Pals, i.e. Ahirs and Gadaria caste. The plantation and animal husbandry workers are proportionately insignificantly distributed at village panchayat level in Amethi. The proportionate distribution of animal husbandry workers has been mentioned in Table 2.15. It has been observed that 2.5 per cent plantation and animal husbandry workers has been found in the village panchayat Katara Maharani followed by 1.3 per cent in Sarai Khema and 1.1 per cent in Agahar village panchayats of Amethi Block and in these villages Yadavs are significantly distributed. The animal husbandry and plantation workers between 0.5 per cent and one per cent of the total population has been found in Trilokpur, Mahmoodpur, Raipur Phulwari, Tala, Kherauna, Dhandhudhar, Bhusahari, Maharajpur and Saraiya Duban village panchayats of the Amethi Block, while less than 0.5 per cent animal husbandry workers has been recorded in Korari Girdharshah, Dedhpasar, Raidaipur, Rebha, Gaderi, Purabgaon, Saidpur, Kohara, Mahmoodpur, Ramdaipur, Benipur, Darakha and Nuwawan village panchayats while less than 0.3 per cent animal husbandry workers has been found in the rest of the village panchayats of the Amethi Block.

6.6 Construction Workers

The construction workers are distributed in most of village panchayats of the Amethi Block. The proportionate distribution of the construction workers has been mentioned in the Table 2.15. It has been noticed that more than one per cent construction workers has been found in Katara Maharani and Trilokpur village panchayats while from 0.5 per cent and one per cent construction workers has been observed in Saraikhema, Tala, Kherauna, Dhandhudhar, Bhusehari, Purabgaon, Maharajpur and Himmatgarh village panchayats of the Amethi Block while low percentage between 0.3 per cent and 0.5 per cent construction workers has been observed in Ramdaipur, Raipur Phulwari, Bhoganpur, Tala, Korari Girdharshah, Dedhpasar, Gaderi, Agahar and Dehara village panchayats of the Amethi Block while low percentage less than 0.3 per cent construction workers has been found in the rest of the village panchayats of Amethi Block.

6.7 Business Workers

The business workers has been found in most of the village panchayats of Amethi Block. The business workers include trade workers, shopkeepers and other businessmen who are engaged in the business activities at the village panchayat level in Amethi. The proportionate distribution of the business workers in numbers has been mentioned in Table 2.14. It has been observed that more than 0.8 per cent business workers to total workers has been found in Katara Phulkunwar, Dhandhudhar and Bhusahari village panchayats while Katara Maharani village panchayat has 1.1 per cent business workers of the total population due to Munshiganj Marketing Centre and Hindustan Aeronautics Ltd. (HAL), Korwa, Munshiganj and in other villages there are local marketing centres or weekly markets located in the respective village panchayats. Medium percentage between 0.5 per cent and 0.8 per cent business workers has been seen in Saraikhema, Kherauna, Maharajpur, Saidpur Gangauli village panchayats of the Amethi Block. Low percentage between 0.2 per cent and 0.5 per cent business workers has been noticed in Trilokpur, Ramdaipur, Jangal Ramnagar, Parsawan, Mahmoodpur, Raipur Phulwari, Umapur Ganapatti, Bhaganpur, Tala, Loharata, Darakha, Mochawa, Nuwawan, Rebha, Korari Girdharshah, Gaderi, Purabgaon, Chaturbhujpur, Agahar, Kakawa, Kohara, Mahmoodpur, Ramgarh, Himmatgarh, Dehra village panchayats of Amethi Block. There is no business worker in the Loniapur village Panchayat while 0.1 per cent business workers has been noticed in rest of the village panchayats.

6.8 Transportation Workers

It has been noticed that very insignificant number of transportation workers are found in Amethi. Generally, exceptional number of people from the various villages are engaged in transportation works as Driver and cleaners in the total population has been mentioned in Table 2.15. It has been observed that more than 0.5 per cent transportation workers are found in Katara Maharani, Sarai Khema, Trilokpur Tala, Bhusahari, Agahar, Saidpur and Ramgarh village panchayats of Amethi Block. It has been noticed that there are 0.9 per cent transportation workers in the village panchayat Trilokpur followed by 0.8 per cent of the total population in the village panchayat Bhusahari due to marketing centres and nearness to the business and trade centres. It has been observed that medium percentage between 0.2 per cent and 0.5 per cent transportation workers has been seen in Rebha, Agahar, Ramgarh, Ramdaipur, Jangal Ram Nagar, Benipur, Mahmoodpur, Raipur Phulwari, Umapur Ganapatti, Tala, Darakha, Mochawa, Nuwawan and Kherauna village panchayats while village panchayat Loniapur has no transportation workers. It has been observed that 0.1 per cent transportation workers to total population has been recorded in the Parsawana, Bhaganpur, Kushi Tali, Loharata, Katara

Table 2.15: Proportionate Distribution of Workers (Social-Infrastructure)—Amethi Block

(%age of Total Population)

Sl. No.	*Villages*	*Total Workers*	*Cultivators*	*Agricultural Workers*	*Non-Skilled Workers*	*Skilled Workers*	*Plantation & Animal Husbandry*	*Construction Workers*	*Business Weorkers*	*Transportation Workers*	*Others & Office Workers*	*Small Scale & Agro Industries Workers*
1	2	3	4	5	6	7	8	9	10	11	12	13
1.	Katra Maharani	41.1	11.4	11.1	8	3.7	2.5	1	1.1	0.9	0.5	0.7
2.	Sarai Khema	32.8	15	7.9	4.5	2	1.3	0.8	0.6	0.5	0.3	0.4
3.	Trilokpur	34.4	14.7	6.3	8.2	1.9	0.6	1.2	0.2	0.5	0.4	0.4
4.	Ramdaipur	27.6	12.7	6.4	4.5	2.4	0.3	0.3	0.3	0.2	0.1	0.4
5.	Jangal Ram Nagar	19.6	10	4.8	2.2	1.2	0.2	0.1	0.3	0.2	0.2	0.1
6.	Benipur	21.3	11.9	2.9	3.8	1.8	0.3	0.2	0.1	0.2	0.1	0.1
7.	Parsawan	12.6	5.5	2.2	2.8	0.9	0.1	0.1	0.3	0.1	0.1	0.1
8.	Mahmoodpur	16.9	6.3	6.1	2.4	0.8	0.6	0.1	0.2	0.2	0.1	0.1
9.	Raipur Fulwari	20	3.8	7.9	4.9	1.3	0.6	0.4	0.3	0.2	0.1	0.2
10.	Umapur Ganapatti	29.8	16.6	5.7	4.1	2.3	0.2	0.1	0.3	0.3	0.1	0.1
11.	Bhaganpur	13.1	6.2	1.7	2.7	1.4	0.2	0.3	0.3	0.1	0.1	0.1
12.	Tala	20.3	10.1	2.4	3.5	1.3	0.9	0.5	0.3	0.5	0.2	0.4
13.	Kushi Tali	10.4	6.2	1.8	1.3	0.3	0.2	0.1	0.1	0.1	—	—
14.	Loharta	20.4	8.7	7.1	3.1	0.7	0.1	0.2	0.2	0.1	0.1	0.1
15.	Darkha	39.7	16.3	11.9	8.9	1.2	0.3	0.2	0.2	0.2	0.2	0.5
16.	Mochwa	51.4	29.2	15	4.2	1.4	0.2	0.2	0.3	0.2	0.2	0.2
17.	Nuwawan	9.2	4.5	1.6	1.2	0.6	0.3	0.2	0.2	0.2	—	0.2
18.	Loniapur	16.8	6.4	5.1	3.5	1.5	0.1	0.1	—	—	—	0.1
19.	Kherauna	21.9	10.1	4.1	3	1.6	0.6	0.8	0.5	0.4	0.6	0.2
20.	Katra Phulkunwar	25.2	10.2	9.2	2.7	1.8	0.1	0.1	0.9	0.1	—	0.1
21.	Hathkila	21.3	8.4	5.9	4.5	0.9	0.1	0.1	0.1	0.1	0.1	0.3
22.	Rebha	21.4	7.1	9.8	2.4	0.8	0.3	0.2	0.3	0.1	0.2	0.1
23.	Raidaipur	27.6	14.8	2.6	7.2	1.8	0.4	0.2	0.1	0.1	0.1	0.1
24.	Korari Girdharshah	32.2	16.5	9.1	3.9	1.5	0.3	0.3	0.3	0.1	0.1	0.1
25.	Dedhpasar	34.3	14.8	10.8	5.6	1.8	0.3	0.3	0.2	0.1	0.1	0.2
26.	Mahaso	13.1	10.4	1.6	0.4	0.1	0.1	0.1	0.1	0.1	0.1	0.1
27.	Gangauli	35.2	21.3	6.9	3.9	1.1	0.2	0.1	0.5	0.1	0.1	0.5
28.	Dhadhudhar	28.1	11.2	8.4	3.9	1.4	0.8	0.5	0.8	0.4	0.1	0.5
29.	Gaderi	42.1	20	15.1	4.7	0.9	0.3	0.3	0.2	0.3	—	0.3
30.	Bhusahari	34.1	17.8	5.6	4.8	1.6	0.8	0.8	0.9	0.8	0.1	0.9
31.	Purabgaon	33.6	17.6	7.8	5.7	0.7	0.3	0.5	0.3	0.2	—	0.2
32.	Chaturbhujpur	15.6	7.2	5.8	1.2	0.4	0.2	0.1	0.2	0.1	0.1	0.1
33.	Mahrajpur	29.3	13.4	6.3	5.1	1.6	0.8	0.6	0.5	0.2	0.1	0.4
34.	Aghar	31.3	15.1	7.6	3.5	2.3	1.1	0.3	0.3	0.5	0.4	0.1
35.	Saidpur	30.5	17.3	6.4	3.2	1.3	0.3	0.1	0.6	0.5	0.1	0.6
36.	Kakwa	22.5	12.1	5.9	2.5	1	0.1	0.2	0.2	0.1	—	0.1
37.	Saraiya Duban	29.7	15.8	7.8	3.4	1.3	0.5	0.1	0.1	0.3	0.1	0.1
38.	Kohra	31.4	17.6	8.3	2.9	1.3	0.3	0.2	0.2	0.1	0.1	0.1
39.	Mahmadpur	27.8	10.9	9.3	3.7	2.3	0.4	0.3	0.2	0.2	0.1	0.3
40.	Naraini	21.7	16.3	2.4	1.8	0.4	0.1	0.1	0.1	0.1	0.1	0.1
41.	Nainaha	20.9	10.4	4.4	3.7	1.8	0.1	0.1	0.1	0.1	0.1	0.1
42.	Ramgarh	34.1	20.9	7.4	3.2	0.8	0.2	0.2	0.2	0.5	0.3	0.2
43.	Himmatgarh	39.5	17.9	12.7	5.9	1.1	0.2	0.8	0.3	0.1	0.1	0.2
44.	Dehara	21.9	12.2	5.8	1.6	0.6	0.1	0.3	0.3	0.3	0.1	0.3
	Amethi Block	**26.3**	**12.9**	**6.6**	**3.6**	**1.3**	**0.4**	**0.3**	**0.3**	**0.2**	**0.1**	**0.2**

Phulkunwar, Hathkila, Rebha, Raidaipur, Korari Girdharshah, Dedhpasar, Mahaso, Gangauli, Chaturbhujpur, Kakawa, Kohara, Naraini, Nainaha and Himmatgarh village panchayats of Amethi Block.

6.9 Others and Office Workers

The other workers and the office workers are very insignificantly distributed at village panchayat level in Amethi. The distribution of other workers and office workers has been shown in Table 2.14. It has been observed that more than 0.5 per cent other workers and office workers has been found in the Kherauna and Katara Maharani village panchayat due to Hindustan Aeronautic Ltd., industrial area and also the marketing centres while medium percentage between 0.3 per cent and 0.5 per cent other workers and office workers has been found in Saraikhema, Trilokpur, Agahar and Ramgarh village panchayats. It has been observed that low percentage between 0.1 per cent and 0.2 per cent other workers and office workers has been found in the Jangal Ram Nagar, Tala, Darakha, Mochawa and Rebha village panchayats while 0.1 per cent other workers and office workers to the total population has been seen in Himmatgarh, Dehara, Nainaha, Naraini, Mahmoodpur, Kohara, Saraiya Duban, Kakawa, Saidpur, Maharajpur, Chaturbhujpur, Bhusahari, Dhandhudhar, Gangauli, Mahaso, Dedhpasar, Korari Girdharshah, Raidaipur, Hathkila, Loharata, Bhaganpur, Umapur gana patti, Raipur Phulwari, Mahmoodpur, Parsawana, Benipur and Ramdaipur village panchayats of the Amethi Block, while there is no other workers and office workers in Kushi Tali, Nuwawan, Loniapur, Katara Phulkunwar, Gaderi, Purabgaon and Kakawa village panchayats of Amethi Block.

6.10 Small Scale and Agro-Industries Workers

The small scale industries and Agro-Industries workers are nominally distributed at the village panchayat level in Amethi. The proportionate distribution of the small scale and Agro-Industries workers are mentioned in Table 2.15. It has been noticed that very high small scale and agro-industries workers to the total population has been found 0.9 per cent in Bhusahari, 0.7 per cent in Katara Maharani and 0.6 per cent in Saidpur and 0.5 per cent in Gangauli and Dhandhudhar village panchayats of the Amethi Block. It has been noticed that 0.4 per cent small scale and agro-industries workers of the total population has been observed in Sarai Khema, Trilokpur, Ramdaipur, Tala and Maharajpur village panchayats while 03 per cent small scale and agro-industries workers has been seen in Dehara, Mahmoodpur, Gaderi, Hathkila, village panchayats of the Amethi. It has been recorded that 0.2 per cent small scale and agro-industries workers has been found in Raipur Phulwari, Darakha, Mochawa, Nuwawan, Kherauna, Dedhpasar, Purabgaon, Ramgarh and Himmatgarh village panchayat while 0.1 per cent small scale and agro-industries workers of the total population has been found in Naraini, Nainaha, Kohara, Saraiya Duban, Kakawa, Agahar, Chaturbhujpur, Mahaso, Korari Girdharshah, Rebha, Raidaipur, Katara Phulkunwar, Loniapur, Loharata, Bhaganpur, Umapur Ganapatti, Mahmoodpur, Parsawan, Benipur and Jangal Ram Nagar village panchayats of the Amethi Block. It has been recorded that there is no small-scale and agro-industries workers in the Kushi Tali village panchayat of Amethi Block.

The workers has been an important part of the social infrastructure which plays an important role in the social and economic development of Amethi. There are 26.3 per cent total workers of the total population in Amethi Block while the cultivators contribute 12.9 per cent agricultural workers to the total population. The non-skilled workers share 3.6 per cent and skilled workers contribute 1.3 per cent workforce of the total population. The plantation and animal husbandry workers are found 0.4 per cent of the total population in the Amethi Block. The construction workers and the business workers contributed 0.3 per cent of the total population in the Amethi. The other workers and office workers are 0.1 per cent of the total population in Amethi. It has been noticed that the transportation workers and small scale and agro-industries workers are 0.2 per cent of the total population in Amethi Block. The workers are significantly distributed in Amethi because from historical period the service class people has been significantly found in Amethi to serve their kings. In view of the above concept of *Raja* and *Rank* is still continued because the rich people have become richest and the poor people have become poorest in the Amethi. The Techno-Scientific educational and professional training may upgrade the castewise skill development which may improve the quality and quantity productivity in their respective occupational castes, trades and profession.

7. LITERACY

Literacy has been an important tool for removal of ignorances, and traditional rituals during the twenty-first century. The literacy plays an important role in the overall socio-economic development of an area. The illiteracy creates several problems for the day-to- day routine life of the common people. It has been noticed that educationally, socially, institutionally and economically Amethi has been always backward from the historical period, due to kingship rulership; the common people's development was stagnent and they were supposed to only provide the services to the kings and they were deprived of the land ownership and land rights and also the common amenities required for their sustainance.

Due to the socio-economic backwardness the service providers has been unable to achieve their educational goals and they were forced to survive hand to mouth, that is why the 54.1 per cent people of Amethi are still illiterates which indicates social backwardness and non-availability of social and educational infrastructure at the grassroots level. It has been noticed that there are 45.9 per cent literate people of the total population of the Amethi Block. In spite of the various educational programmes including the adult education. The proportionate distribution of literacy has been half of the total population which has been a great challenge to the policy planners and educational institutional implementing agencies at the grassroots level in Amethi. The distribution of literates and literacy at various levels of educational system starting from primary education to higher education and professional education has been mentioned in the Table 2.16, at village panchayat level in the Amethi Block. The proportionate distribution of literacy to the total population at village panchayat level has been illustrated in the Table 2.17.

The distribution pattern of the total literates of the total population at village panchayat level in Amethi has been depicted in **Map 2.23**. It has been observed that very high percentage literates of the total population has been found in the Kherauna (55.6%), Katara Maharani (51.4%), Ramdaipur (55.6%), Katara Maharani (51.4%), Raipur Phulwari (51.3%), Hathkila (50.9%), Dedhpasar (51.4%), Raidaipur (50.8%), Dhandhudhar (52%), Chaturbhujpur (52.4%), Purabgaon (53.1%), and Kohara (52.7%) at village panchayat level in Amethi. Medium percentage of literates population between 45 per cent and 50 per cent has been recorded in Trilokpur, Sarai Khema, Jangal Ram

Table 2.16: Literacy (Social-Infrastructure)—Amethi Block

Sl. No.	*Villages*	*Total Literacy*	*Primary Education*	*Junior Education*	*High School Education*	*Intermediate Education*	*Graduate Education*	*Post-Graduate Education*	*Professional Education*
1	2	3	4	5	6	7	8	9	10
1.	Katra Maharani	1027	300	223	222	162	70	50	
2.	Sarai Khema	2232	730	545	415	320	111	80	31
3.	Trilokpur	1100	275	309	155	165	118	71	7
4.	Ramdaipur	1501	300	400	298	305	105	90	3
5.	Jangal Ram Nagar	4253	1000	700	800	500	700	550	3
6.	Benipur	600	215	122	100	85	48	30	
7.	Parsawan	750	195	240	75	125	60	55	
8.	Mahmoodpur	1397	400	270	290	250	119	63	3
9.	Raipur Fulwari	925	180	242	200	168	90	45	
10.	Umapur Ganapatti	1179	200	380	220	180	120	79	
11.	Bhaganpur	637	172	200	120	80	40	25	
12.	Tala	712	188	130	149	115	95	35	
13.	Kushi Tali	699	200	185	156	98	40	20	
14.	Loharta	653	193	170	100	75	90	25	
15.	Darkha	1162	300	250	250	100	162	95	5
16.	Mochwa	1211	231	300	280	325	50	20	5
17.	Nuwawan	1165	280	242	220	200	150	70	2
18.	Loniapur	770	250	150	115	100	90	65	
19.	Kherauna	1668	450	343	265	250	206	150	4
20.	Katra Phulkunwar	1147	412	300	150	120	95	70	
21.	Hathkila	800	340	196	90	95	50	25	4
22.	Rebha	710	180	170	150	100	60	50	
23.	Raidaipur	1122	528	265	185	95	35	14	
24.	Korari Girdharshah	1556	439	350	400	200	100	56	11
25.	Dedhpasar	1391	300	281	250	350	150	59	
26.	Mahaso	584	195	147	90	75	42	35	
27.	Gangauli	834	232	290	110	90	74	35	3
28.	Dhadhudhar	902	300	200	150	150	70	30	2
29.	Gaderi	1419	300	219	300	400	150	50	
30.	Bhusahari	368	120	70	130	20	18	10	
31.	Purabgaon	745	200	250	135	90	40	30	
32.	Chaturbhujpur	630	50	190	145	110	70	35	3
33.	Mahrajpur	493	190	95	50	53	75	30	
34.	Aghar	586	150	150	81	95	70	40	
35.	Saidpur	665	220	100	200	100	30	15	
36.	Kakwa	1875	420	380	370	330	200	170	5
37.	Saraiya Duban	722	200	216	150	75	50	30	1
38.	Kohra	2000	300	470	528	500	120	80	2
39.	Mahmadpur	1345	454	400	152	180	90	75	3
40.	Naraini	2040	500	627	380	250	190	90	3
41.	Nainaha	1150	300	320	310	100	70	50	
42.	Ramgarh	1866	600	424	380	263	120	75	4
43.	Himmatgarh	793	180	174	150	100	124	60	
44.	Dehara	1495	410	395	300	205	130	55	
	Amethi Block	**49357**	**13549**	**12085**	**9766**	**7749**	**3687**	**2597**	**104**

Nagar, Bhaganpur, Tala, Kushitali, Loharata, Darakha, Umapur Ganapatti, Loniapur, Korari Girdharshah, Gangauli, Himmatgarh, Dehara, Ramgarh, Gaderi, Naraini, Kakawa and Saraiya Duban village panchayats of the Amethi Block. Low percentage distribution of literates of the total population has been observed in the Saidpur, Agahar, Nuwawan, Mochawa, Mahmoodpur, Nainaha, Katara Phulkunwar and Benipur village panchayats of the Amethi Block. It has been noticed that very low percentage of literates less than 40 per cent of the total population has been found in Mahaso and Bhusahari village panchayats of Amethi.

7.1 Primary Education

The primary educated people in Amethi has been very insignificant. There are 12.6 per cent primary educated persons in the Amethi Block. The proportionate distribution of the primary education to the total population has been depicted in **Map 2.24**. It has been observed that more than 20 per cent primary literates of the total population has been found in Raidaipur (23.9%) and Hathkila (21.6%) village panchayats of Amethi. Medium percentage between 15 per cent and 20 per cent primary literates are found in Benipur, Katara Phulkunwar, Loniapur, Dhandhudhar, Maharajpur and Ramgarh village panchayats of the Amethi Block. Low percentage between 10 per cent and 15 per cent primary educated people of the total population has been seen in Katara Maharani, Trilokpur, Sarai Khema, Jangal Ram Nagar, Bhaganpur, Tala, Kushi Tali, Loharata, Darakha, Mahmoodpur, Parsawan, Kherauna, Rebha, Dedhpasar, Mahaso, Gangauli, Korari Girdharshah, Himmatgarh, Dehara, Purabgaon, Nainaha, Naraini, Agahar, Saidpur, Kakawa, Saraiya Duban and Mahmoodpur village Panchayats of Amethi. It has been recorded that less than 10 per cent primary educated people of the total population has been seen in Ramdaipur, Umapur Ganapatti, Raipur Phulwari, Nuwawan, Mochawa, Chaturbhujpur, Gaderi and Kohara village panchayats of Amethi Block.

7.2 Junior Education

The junior educated persons from 6th to 8th class have been comparatively very poor than the common education norms. The proportionate distribution of Junior educated persons to the total population has been shown in **Map 2.25**. It has been observed that high percentage more than 15 per cent of the total population of junior educated persons are found in Bhaganpur, Umapur Ganapatti, Parsawan, Gangauli, Purabgaon, Chaturbhujpur village panchayats of the Amethi. Medium percentage between 10 per cent to 15 per cent junior educated persons are seen in the Katara Maharani, Trilokpur, Ramdaipur, Saraikhema, Raipur Phulwari, Kherauna, Katara Phulkunwar, Raidaipur, Rebha, Hathkila, Dedhpasar, Korari Girdharshah, Dhandhudhar, Mochawa, Loharata, Darakha, Kushi Tali, Agahar, Naraini, Nainaha, Ramgarh, Himmatgarh, Dehara, Saraiya Duban, Kohara and Mahmoodpur village panchayats of Amethi. Low percentage between 5 per cent and 10 per cent Junior educated persons are recorded in Tala, Jangal Ram Nagar, Mahmoodpur, Benipur, Loniapur, Mahaso, Nuwawan, Gaderi, Maharajpur, Saidpur and Kakawa village panchayats of Amethi. Very low percentage less than 5.0 per cent Junior educated persons to the total population has been found in the Bhusahari village panchayat of the Amethi Block.

7.3 High School Education

The proportionate distribution of the high school educated persons in Amethi has been considerably low. The High School educated persons in Amethi has been recorded 9.0 per cent of the total population in Amethi. The proportionate distribution of High School educated persons of the total population has been depicted in **Map 2.26**. It has been observed that more than 11 per cent High School educated persons are recorded in Katara Maharani, Korari Girdharshah, Chaturbhujpur, Saidpur, Kohara and Nainaha village panchayats of Amethi. Medium percentage between 9 per cent and 11 per cent High School educated persons are found in the Ramdaipur, Jangal Ram Nagar, Bhaganpur, Tala, Kushi Tali, Umapur Ganapatti, Raipur Phulwari, Rebha, Dedhpasar, Darakha, Mochawa, Purabgaon, Gaderi, Ramgarh, Dehara, Kakawa and Saraiya Duban village panchayats. Low percentage distribution of High School educated persons ranging from 7 per cent to 9 per cent has been found in Sarai Khema, Benipur, Kherauna, Loniapur, Raidaipur, Loharata, Nuwawan, Dhandhudhar, Bhusahari, Himmatgarh and Naraini village panchayats of Amethi. It has been recorded that very low percentage less than 7 per cent High School educated persons of total population has been found in Trilokopur, Parsawan, Katara Phulkunwar, Hathkila, Gangauli, Mahaso, Agahar, Maharajpur and Mahmoodpur village panchayats of Amethi Block.

7.4 Intermediate Education

The Intermediate educated persons have been poorly distributed in Amethi. There are only 7.2 per cent Intermediate educated persons in Amethi. The proportionate distribution of the Intermediate educated persons to total population at village panchayat level has been depicted in **Map 2.27**. Very high percentage more than 10 per cent Intermediate educated persons of total population has been found in Dedhpasar, Mochawa, Gaderi, and Kohara village panchayats while medium percentage between 8 per cent and 10 per cent Intermediate educated persons are found in Katara Maharani, Ramdaipur, Mahmoodpur, Parsawan, Raipur Phulwari, Kherauna, Dhandhudhar, Chaturbhujpur and Kakawa village panchayats. Low percentage distribution, between 6 per cent and 8 per cent Intermediate educated persons of the total population has been recorded in Sarai Khema, Trilokpur, Benipur, Bhaganpur, Tala, Kushi Tali, Umapur Ganapatti, Loniapur, Rebha, Hathkila, Korari Girdharshah, Nuwawan, Ramgarh, Dehara, Purabgaon, Agahar and Saidpur village panchayats of the Amethi Block. It has been observed that very low percentage less than 6 per cent Intermediate educated persons of the total population has been seen in Jangal Ram Nagar, Loharata, Darakha, Katara Phulkunwar, Raidaipur, Gangauli, Mahaso, Bhusahari, Himmatgarh, Naraini, Nainaha, Saraiya Duban and Mahmoodpur village panchayats of the Amethi Block.

7.5 Graduate Education

The Graduate educated persons, having higher education are insignificantly distributed at village panchayat level in Amethi. The Graduate educated persons are 3.4 per cent of the total population in Amethi Block. The proportionate distribution of higher educated or graduate educated persons to the total population at village panchayat level in Amethi has been depicted in **Map 2.28**. It has been noticed that high percentage more than 8 per cent Graduate educated persons of the total population has been found in Jangal Ram Nagar village panchayat while medium percentage between 6 per cent and 8 per cent Graduate educated persons of the total population has been recorded in Tala, Loharata, Darakha, Kherauna, Himmatgarh and Maharajpur village panchayats of Amethi. Low percentage between 4 per cent and 6 per cent Graduate educated persons has been noticed in Trilokpur, Mahmoodpur, Raipur Phulwari, Umapur Ganapatti, Nuwawan, Loniapur, Rebha, Dedhpasar, Dhandhudhar, Gaderi, Gangauli, Dehara, Chaturbhujpur, Agahar,

Table 2.17: Proportionate Distribution of Literacy (Social-Infrastructure)—Amethi Block

(%age of Total Population)

Sl. No.	*Villages*	*Total Literacy*	*Primary Education*	*Junior Education*	*High School Education*	*Intermediate Education*	*Graduate Education*	*Post-Graduate Education*	*Professional Education*
1	2	3	4	5	6	7	8	9	10
1.	Katra Maharani	51.4	15	11.1	11.1	8.1	3.5	2.5	
2.	Sarai Khema	45.8	14	11.1	8.5	6.5	2.2	2	0.6
3.	Trilokpur	46.4	11.6	13	6.5	6.9	4.9	2.9	0.2
4.	Ramdaipur	48.9	9.7	13	9.7	9.9	3.4	2.9	0.09
5.	Jangal Ram Nagar	48.8	11.4	8	9.1	5.7	8	6.3	0.03
6.	Benipur	44.9	16.1	9.1	7.4	6.3	3.5	2.2	
7.	Parsawan	48.7	12.6	15.6	4.8	8.1	3.9	3.5	
8.	Mahmoodpur	49.4	14.1	9.5	10.2	8.8	4.2	2.3	0.1
9.	Raipur Fulwari	51.3	9.9	13.4	11	9.3	4.9	2.4	
10.	Umapur Ganapatti	49.8	8.4	15.9	9.2	7.5	5	3.3	
11.	Bhaganpur	49.1	13.2	15.4	9.2	6.1	3	1.9	
12.	Tala	48.3	12.7	8.8	10.1	7.8	6.4	2.3	
13.	Kushi Tali	48.9	13.9	12.9	10.9	6.8	2.7	1.3	
14.	Loharta	49.8	14.7	12.9	7.6	5.7	6.8	1.9	
15.	Darkha	49.5	12.7	10.6	10.6	4.2	6.9	4	0.2
16.	Mochwa	44	8.4	10.9	10.1	11.8	1.8	0.7	0.1
17.	Nuwawan	40.1	9.6	8.3	7.5	6.8	5.1	2.4	0.06
18.	Loniapur	48.8	15.8	9.5	7.2	6.3	5.7	4.1	
19.	Kherauna	55.6	15	11.4	8.8	8.3	6.8	5	0.1
20.	Katra Phulkunwar	45	16.1	11.7	5.8	4.7	3.7	2.7	
21.	Hathkila	50.9	21.6	12.4	5.1	6	3.1	1.5	0.2
22.	Rebha	47.6	12	11.4	10	6.7	4	3.3	
23.	Raidaipur	50.8	23.9	12	8.3	4.3	1.5	0.6	
24.	Korari Girdharshah	46.9	13.2	10.5	12	6	3	1.6	0.3
25.	Dedhpasar	51.4	11.1	10.4	9.2	12.9	5.5	2.1	
26.	Mahaso	30.5	10.1	7.6	4.7	3.9	2.1	1.8	
27.	Gangauli	46.9	13	16.3	6.1	5	4.1	1.9	0.1
28.	Dhadhudhar	52	17.3	11.5	8.6	8.6	4	1.7	0.1
29.	Gaderi	46.5	9.8	7.1	9.8	13.1	4.9	1.6	
30.	Bhusahari	24.2	7.8	4.6	8.5	1.3	1.1	0.6	
31.	Purabgaon	53.1	14.2	17.8	9.6	6.4	2.8	2.1	
32.	Chaturbhujpur	52.4	4.1	15.8	12	9.1	5.8	2.9	0.2
33.	Mahrajpur	41.6	16	8	4.2	4.4	6.3	2.5	
34.	Aghar	41.2	10.5	10.5	5.7	6.6	4.9	2.8	
35.	Saidpur	43.3	14.3	6.5	13	6.5	1.9	0.9	
36.	Kakwa	48.5	10.8	9.8	9.5	8.5	5.1	4.4	0.1
37.	Saraiya Duban	45.8	12.7	13.7	9.5	4.7	3.1	1.9	.06
38.	Kohra	52.7	7.9	12.4	13.9	13.1	3.1	2.1	0.05
39.	Mahmadpur	43.5	14.6	12.8	4.8	5.7	2.8	2.4	0.09
40.	Naraini	48.3	11.8	14.8	9	5.9	4.5	2.1	0.07
41.	Nainaha	42.8	11.1	11.9	11.5	3.7	2.6	1.8	
42.	Ramgarh	48.9	15.7	11.1	9.9	6.9	3.1	1.9	0.1
43.	Himmatgarh	47.4	10.7	10.7	8.9	5.9	7.4	3.5	
44.	Dehara	48.2	13.2	12.7	9.6	6.6	4.1	1.7	
	Amethi Block	**45.9**	**12.6**	**11.2**	**9**	**7.2**	**3.4**	**2.4**	**0.1**

Naraini and Kakawa village panchayats of the Amethi Block. Very low percentage less than 4 per cent Graduate educated persons of total population has been seen in Katara Maharani, Sarai Khema, Ramdaipur, Benipur, Parsawan, Katara Phulkunwar, Hathkila, Raidaipur, Mahaso, Korari Girdharshah, Bhusahari, Ramgarh, Nainaha, Purabgaon,

Saidpur, Saraiya Duban, Kohara and Mahmoodpur village panchayats of the Amethi Block.

7.6 Post Graduate Education

The Post Graduate educated persons at village panchayat level has been very insignificantly distributed in Amethi. There are 2.4 per cent Post Graduate educated persons of total population in Amethi. The proportionate distribution of Post Graduate educated persons to the total population has been depicted in **Map 2.29**. It has been observed that Jangal Ram Nagar has 6.3 per cent Post Graduate educated persons of the total population. Medium percentage between 4 per cent and 6 per cent Post Graduate educated person has been seen in Kherauna, Loniapur and Kakawa village panchayats. Low percentage between 2 per cent and 4 per cent Post Graduate educated persons has been seen in Katara Maharani, Trilokpur, Ramdaipur, Sarai Khema, Benipur, Mahmoodpur, Parsawan, Raipur Phulwari, Katara Phulkunwar, Rebha, Dedhpasar, Nuwawan, Derakha, Agahar, Chaturbhujpur, Maharajpur, Purabgaon, Agahar, Naraini, Kohara and Mahmoodpur village panchayats of the Amethi Block. It has been observed that very low, less than 2 per cent Post Graduate educated persons of total population has been found in Bhaganpur, Kushi Tali, Loharata, Mochawa, Korari Girdharshah, Dhandhudhar, Gaderi, Gangauli, Mahaso, Bhusahari, Ramgarh, Dehara, Nainaha, Saidpur and Saraiya Duban village panchayats of the Amethi Block.

7.7 Professional Education

The professionally educated persons in the Amethi are very insignificantly distributed. There are 0.1 per cent professionally educated persons in Amethi. Professionally educated persons proportionate distribution has been mentioned in Table 2.17. It has been noticed that there are 0.9 per cent professionally educated persons in village Jangal Ram Nagar and Mahmoodpur village panchayat while village panchayat Naraini is having 0.7 per cent professionally educated persons and 0.6 per cent professionally educated persons have been found in Sarai Khema, Nuwawan and Saraiya Duban village panchayats. It has been observed that village panchayat Kohara has 0.5 per cent professionally educated persons and 0.3 per cent professionally educated persons have been found in Jangal Ram Nagar, Korari Girdharshah village panchayats and 0.2 per cent professionally educated persons have been observed in Trilokpur, Darakha, Hathkila and Purabgaon village panchayats while, 0.1 per cent professionally educated persons of total population have been recorded in Mahmoodpur, Mochawa, Kherauna, Gangauli, Dhandhudhar, Kakawa and Ramgarh village panchayats of the Amethi Block. The professionally educated persons having Industrial Training, Polytechnic, Graduate, Engineering, Technocrats and Master of Business Administration (MBA) etc. has been mentioned in Table 2.18.

7.7.1 Industrial Training

There are 30 persons having Industrial training education in the village panchayat Trilokpur followed by 10 persons in Korari Girdharshah village panchayat because in these village panchayats there is Industrial Training Institute and the youths are aware of the importance of the Industrial Training for the employment generation. There are 5 persons having Industrial Training in the village panchayat Mochawa while 4 persons are industrially trained in Darakha village panchayat. It has been noticed that there are 3 persons having industrial training in Jangal Ram Nagar and Kherauna village panchayats and 2 persons having an Industrial Training are found in Nuwawan, Gangauli, Dhandhudhar, Chaturbhujpur, Kakawa, Kohara, Naraini and Ramgarh village panchayats of Amethi. It has been noticed that there is single Industrial Trained person in Ramdaipur, Saraiya Duban and Mahmoodpur village panchayats of Amethi while the rest of the village panchayats having not any Industrially Trained person in the Amethi Block.

7.7.2 Polytechnic

It has been observed that there are 3 polytechnic educated persons in Mahmoodpur and Kakawa village panchayats and 2 persons in Jangal Ram Nagar, Mahmoodpur and Ramgarh village panchayats and one polytechnic educated person has been recorded in Sarai Khema, Ramdaipur, Kherauna, Korari Girdharshah, Gangauli, Chaturbhujpur and Naraini village panchayats of Amethi.

7.7.3 Graduate Engineers

There are 5 graduate engineers in the village panchayat Trilokpur and 2 graduate technocrats in Jangal Ram Nagar and 1 graduate technocrat has been recorded in the village panchayat Sarai Khema, while in some of the village panchayats Graduate professionally educated persons including engineering and technology are continuing their education and in some of the village panchayats there are several emerging students who are engaged in obtaining the coaching classes to compete the entrance test for the admission in the graduate level engineering and technical education.

7.7.4 Business Administration

The Graduate level and Post Graduate level Business Administration programmes (B.B.A. and M.B.A.) educated two persons have been found in Trilokpur and Jangal Ram Nagar village panchayats and one person in Sarai Khema and Darakha village panchayats having Business Administration educational qualifications while many students are preparing for the test to qualify their admission examination for Business Administration, including Medical education and Pharmacy and other technical and managerial educational programmes in the various village panchayats of the Amethi Block.

The literacy ratio of Amethi has been very poor because there are only 45.9 per cent total literates in Amethi Block which have been very challenging task for the policy makers and the grassroots level implementing institutions. The primary educated persons are 12.6 per cent of the total population and Junior school educated persons are 11.2 per cent of the total population in the Amethi Block. There are 9.0 per cent High School educated persons and 7.2 per cent Intermediate educated persons in the Amethi Block, which has been very insignificant proportion and great concern for rural development planners and policy-makers. Graduate educated persons are 3.4 per cent and Post Graduate educated persons are 2.4 per cent of total population in Amethi Block. There are only 0.1 per cent professionally educated persons of the total population in the Amethi Block. Insignificant literacy ratio in Amethi indicates the poor literacy infrastructure of Amethi which has led to socio-economic backwardness of the people of Amethi.

Table 2.18: Professionally Educated Persons (Social-Infrastructure)—Amethi Block

Sl. No.	*Villages*	*I.T.I.*	*Polytechnic*	*Graduate*	*Engineering*
1	2	3	4	5	6
1.	Katra Maharani				
2.	Sarai Khema	30	1	1	1
3.	Trilokpur			5	2
4.	Ramdaipur	1	1		
5.	Jangal Ram Nagar	3	2	2	2
6.	Benipur				
7.	Parsawan				
8.	Mahmoodpur		3		
9.	Raipur Fulwari				
10.	Umapur Ganapatti				
11.	Bhaganpur				
12.	Tala				
13.	Kushi Tali				
14.	Loharta				
15.	Darkha	4			1
16.	Mochwa	5			
17.	Nuwawan	2			
18.	Loniapur				
19.	Kherauna	3	1		
20.	Katra Phulkunwar				
21.	Hathkila	4			
22.	Rebha				
23.	Raidaipur				
24.	Korari Girdharshah	10	1		
25.	Dedhpasar				
26.	Mahaso				
27.	Gangauli	2	1		
28.	Dhadhudhar	2			
29.	Gaderi				
30.	Bhusahari				
31.	Purabgaon				
32.	Chaturbhujpur	2	1		
33.	Mahrajpur				
34.	Aghar				
35.	Saidpur				
36.	Kakwa	2	3		
37.	Saraiya Duban	1			
38.	Kohra	2			
39.	Mahmadpur	1	2		
40.	Naraini	2	1		
41.	Nainaha				
42.	Ramgarh	2	2		
43.	Himmatgarh				
44.	Dehara				
	Amethi Block	**78**	**17**	**8**	**6**

8. CONCLUSION

The social infrastructure plays an important role in policy planning process and also in formulation of need base integrated development planning of an area. The innovation of the human resources and social-infrastructural information system at the grassroots level has always been information intensive task. The conventional and traditional systems of data collection, collation and its storage are not amenable for the quick updation, retrieval and holistic approach for analysis of several problems, has been realized due to incompatible data base, inefficient inter-sectoral data flow and lack of information on the quality of data at the village level.

It has been realized that the process of planning for an integrated approach requires a detailed knowledge of *Human Resources Data Management System (HRDMS)* and its interdependencies between various human infrastructural indicators with the view to resolve often conflicting demands. It require appropriate data management and the analysis of social sectoral data especially the social-infrastructural data base at village panchayat level.

The innovation of the social infrastructural data and developing Village Information System has been evolved through socio-economic-institutional infrastructure has been derived from the Sectoral Indicators and also from the various implementing institutions/agencies working at the District level. The collection of the socio-economic-institutional data have been ensured through the available sources at the Village/Block/District level and from the secondary sources of information and Primary Field Survey at the grassroots level.

The social infrastructure of an area includes the society, community, social association, social institution and groups, caste composition, social class, workforce and literacy. The various indicators related to population, caste composition, workers and literacy have been identified and their characteristics have been explained at Village Panchayat level in Amethi.

The demographic structure of the Amethi has been analysed. It has been recorded that there are 18629 houses and 18530 households in Amethi. Total number of population of Amethi has been 107350 which include 54609 males and 52741 females. The male population contributes 50.59 per cent and female population shares 49.41 per cent population of the total population.

It has been recorded that there are 21.9 per cent scheduled caste population in Amethi. There are 7.9 per cent Kurmi caste, 209.3 per cent Yadav population and Gupta caste contributes 4.9 per cent of the total population of the Amethi Block. There are 1.0 per cent share of the Carpenter caste and other backward castes including Maurya, Nishad, Nai, Lohar, Bhuj contribute 2.5 per cent of the total population of Amethi Block. Minorities community which include Muslims, Sikhs and Christians contribute 11.2 per cent of the total population of Amethi. There are 17.8 per cent Brahmin population and 13.1 per cent Rajput population in the Amethi Block. The social backwardness of the people of Amethi has been realized due to Kingship rulership from historical period. The local kings and land revenue tax collectors exploited the service class people and they were deprived of common minimum amenities including land ownership and land rights.

There are 26.3 per cent total workers of the total population in Amethi. There are highest 51.4 per cent workers in Mochawa village panchayat and lowest 9.2 per cent workers of the total population in Nuwawan village panchayat because this village is dominant by the Muslim population and they work outside in other Metropoliton cities. It has been noticed that there are 12.9 per cent cultivators and 6.6 per cent agricultural labourers and 3.6 per cent non-skilled workers and 1.3 per cent skilled workers of the total population in Amethi. The plantation and animal husbandry workers contribute 0.4 per cent, construction workers and business workers contributes 0.3 per cent of the total population of the Amethi Block. There are 0.2 per cent transportation workers and 0.1 per cent other workers including office workers while small scale and Agro-Industries workers share 0.2 per cent of the total population of Amethi.

The literacy profile of the Amethi has been recorded very poor. There are 45.9 per cent total literates in Amethi. The primary educated persons are 12.6 per cent, Junior school educated people are 11.2 per cent and High School educated persons are 9.0 per cent of the total population in Amethi. There are 7.2 per cent Intermediate educated persons, 3.4 per cent Graduate educated persons and 2.4 per cent Post Graduate educated persons in the Amethi Block. There are 0.1 per cent professionally educated persons of the total population in the Amethi Block. The insignificant literacy ratio in Amethi indicates the poor literacy infrastructure of Amethi at village panchayat level which has caused socio-educational backwardness of the people of Amethi.

In view of the above it has been realized that Amethi has Male dominated society and the Male population ratio has been found significantly higher than the female population, at the village panchayat level in Amethi. The flat land and agriculturally fertile land are highly populated and developed settlements with requisite amenities for the survival of the common people.

Amethi is an agrarian area. Agriculture is dominant occupation of the people of Amethi. More than 76 per cent population of the area depend on agricultural activities. The farming and cultivation are the significant occupational activities of the people of Amethi while landless agricultural workers also contributes significant proportion to the total population at the village panchayat level in Amethi. The skilled workers and non-skilled workers are also significantly distributed at village level in Amethi. The plantation and animal husbandry activities are carried out by the Yadav/Kurmis/Pals and few other interested persons who are engaged in the collection of milk and selling it in the marketing centres for various commercial purposes. The construction workers and business workers are very insignificantly distributed in Amethi while other workers and office workers are also nominally distributed at village panchayat level in Amethi. The small-scale and Agro-Industries workers are insignificantly and nominally distributed at the village panchayat level in Amethi.

Historically, is it known fact that Amethi was kingship ruled estate due to which the *Rajputs* were kins of the kings and land revenue tax collectors and working with the kings for safeguarding the estate of the kings, while *Brahmins* were engaged in the worship of the God for well-being of the kings and estate. *Vaisyas* were engaged in commercial and managerial activities of the estate and *Shudras* were engaged in providing the services to the kings. It has been noticed that the service class providers who have been providing various services to the kings, were given their surname of their caste as per their occupational activities like *Kurmi*—for agricultural activities, *Yadavs* for Milking and animal husbandry activities, *Guptas* for trading and business activities, *Pal/Gaderia* for animal husbandry activities, *Nishad* for fisheries etc., *Nai* for Hair cutting, *Dhobi* for washing the cloths, *Darji* for stitching the cloth, *Julaha* for cloth weaving, *Vaisya* for trading/management/accountancy, *Carpenters* for wood work and furnitures, *Lohar* for iron work/agricultural implement, Blacksmith, *Kohar* for (Mitti) Soil Bartan Work, *Brahmins* for worship of *the God* and *Rajputs* for safety and security of the estate etc. There are various other sub-castes in backward castes who are the service providing people as per their caste and occupational structure. *Scheduled Caste,* have also been the service providers to the Kings. It has been observed that the service class providing castes were exploited and deprived of their basic common amenities for livelihood including the land ownership and land rights, due to which these service class providers were socially backward and deprived of social upliftment. The scheduled caste people were landless and one of the most deprived multitudes of the society. The social backwardness of the people has also adversely affected the literacy ratio of Amethi due to which there are only 45.9 per cent literates in the Amethi Block and the primary educated people, Junior and High School educated people are only 32.8 per cent of the total population while Intermediate educated people are only 7.2 per cent of the total population of Amethi. There are 5.8 per cent Graduate and Post-Graduate educaterd persons of the total population in Amethi and very insignificant 0.1 per cent professionally educated people of the total population has been found in Amethi Block.

Thus it has been observed that Amethi has been socially backward since historical period. Occupational and caste composition has been based on the service class providers to the kings. The service class providers have not been properly developed and deprived of the common minimum infrastructure required for the integrated development of the caste oriented occupational people of the Amethi. The educational profile of the Amethi has been very poor which indicates the backwardness of the people of Amethi.

In view of the above it has become a challenging task for the policy makers, planners at the grassroots level implementing institutions to plan with the peoples involvement for the skill development of workers, occupation based caste composition and improve the educational standard quantitatively and qualitatively at each level of education including professional education. The integrated development of social infrastructure including caste composition, professionally and occupationally and provide skill development training programmes to all workers and sub-workers and increase literacy ratio *scientifically-educationally-institutionally-technically-professionally* for strengthening the available social infrastructure and its optimum utilization at village panchayat level in the Amethi Block, through ensuring people's participatory need based action oriented planning for their social upliftment and implementation of integrated village development programmes for self-sustenance of the people, for the people, with the people and by the people at the Village Panchayat level in Amethi.

NOTES

1. Ginsberg, M., *Sociology, Betterbirth*, London, 1934, p. 50.
2. MacIver, R.M., Page, C.H., *Society*, The Rine Hart & Company, London, 1953, p. 5.
3. MacIver, R.M. & Page, C.H., *Society*, MacMillan & Company, New York, 1950, p. 348.

3 Economic Infrastructure

1. INTRODUCTION

The soul of Amethi lives in villages excepting Amethi Town area, Munshiganj Industrial area and Munshiganj Marketing Centre. The agriculture is the main occupation of the people of Amethi. The economy of the Amethi has been agrarian. The traditional system of agricultural activities are still followed by the farmers/cultivators of Amethi, which has led to low agricultural productivity causing very poor economy, henceforth the economic backwardness of the people of Amethi. Poor land capability and low fertility status of the soil have caused poor agricultural productivity. Inappropriate sources of irrigation and improper application of organic and inorganic amendments has also led to poor agricultural productivity of Amethi. The traditional system of the application of low productive agricultural seeds and non-commercialization of agricultural activities has also caused the poor agricultural productivity of Amethi. Least application of High Yielding Variety (HYV) seeds and improper use of insecticides and pesticides have also been responsible for the low agricultural productivity. The low agricultural productivity and poor return from agricultural cropping pattern have caused economic backwardness of the people of Amethi.

The another factor which has been responsible for the economic backwardness of Amethi has been low agricultural productivity due to poor fertility status of the soil, large size of land holdings because the land has been concentrated among the 10 per cent people and the land owners could not manage the land properly for increasing agricultural production. The negligence of the agricultural cropping has caused poor fertility status of the soil and led to an increase in the Banjar land and Usarization of the soil due to which the fertility status of the soil has been reduced. After *Zamindari*/*Taluqdari* Abolition Act the excess land lying with the large size land holders has been given to the landless people and agricultural labourers, but such lands have been lying uncultivated land as wastelands for several years. Such lands has been unfertile for agricultural cropping. The *Patta* Banjar land allottees could not manage to reclaim the allotted *Patta* Banjar lands due to ignorance and poor financial status for maintaining the fertility status of the soil which has caused very poor agricultural productivity and very low income of such people and leading towards economic backwardness of the people of Amethi.

In view of the above an attempt has been made in this study to analyse the size of land holdings, sources of irrigation, use of agricultural implements, application of organic and inorganic amendments, use of insecticides and pesticides, use of High Yielding Variety of seeds, application of agricultural implements and average monthly income of the workers including cultivators/farmers, agricultural labourers and other workers at the Village Panchayat level in Amethi.

An effort has been made in this study to collect the various informations related to the size of land holdings and various agricultural inputs including irrigation, use of fertilizer and insecticides and pesticides, application of good quality seeds, use of agricultural implements and average monthly income of the workers at Village Panchayat level in the Amethi Block. The collection of the economic infrastructural data has been based on the secondary sources of information but the collected information has been finalized through Primary Field Survey and Investigations at field level including the farmers and other related people's representatives and officials engaged in the implementation of Agricultural, Horticultural, Agro-Forestry, Social-Forestry, Fisheries and Animal Husbandary Programmes at the Village Panchayat level or grassroots level in Amethi.

2. ECONOMIC INFRASTRUCTURE

Village Information System and Management of Economic Infrastructural Data related to economic sector have been the major programme of the Human Resources Data Management System (HRDMS). The various indicators related to economic sector need to be integrated for the remotely based village panchayats of the Amethi Block. The collection and collation of economic indicators data base in the framework of Spatial Information System for optimal management is required for sustainable economic integrated development of the village panchayats. Appropriate and proper linkage of economic data base within a framework of required suitable information system to enable customized retrieval and analysis of specific needs to be managed at grassroots level or village panchayat level in the Amethi Block. The Economic Resources Data Base Management System (ERDBMS) has to be visualised in a network based nodes covering Village Panchayat, Block Panchayat and District Panchayat. The innovation of economic infrastructure has to be popularised to promote existing abilities to initiate more activities in a better and faster system for the collection, collation of the available data at the Village Panchayat level to strengthen the Three-Tier Panchayati Raj Institutions. Nevertheless, not every innovation of infrastructure and development of Village Information System that looks like agricultural productivity, enhancing tools, agricultural implements, etc. eventually promote the role of the collection of information at the Village Panchayat level. There, if not carefully introduced, it may run counter to natural modes of expectations, thereby leading to rejection of the technology of the data collection. The economic sector based planning programmes at the Village Panchayat level requires routine basis updation of the data base at the Village, Block and District level, so that as per economic growth the process of planning can be formulated. The greatest constraints in the large scale economic process of planning has been non-availability of appropriate data base at the grassroots level. There are several limitations of collection of the existing available data base and available techniques regarding economic data collection and updation from grassroots level. It needs technology development and training initiatives for development of appropriate indices of economic sector data base. It also requires employment of hyper spectral economic data applications relating to agricultural cropping pattern, sources of irrigation, use of the agricultural implements, application of fertilizers and use of High Yield Variety Seeds, size of land holdings and average monthly income of the workforce at the grassroots level or village panchayat level.

It has been felt and realized that the economic development and commendable advances made by the nation in the diverse field of rural development, would in reality be incomplete, if they fail to translate into better and dignified life for the majority of people who are surviving in the remote rural villages. Economic development of an area should be participatory, tapping the local talent and available economic infrastructural resources at the grassroots level, in order to ensure sustainable planning for integrated development. Policy planning and people's participatory process of planning for economic development has been implemented aimed at sustainable development of the village people with a focus on enhancing the livelihood of weakers and vulnerable sections of the society. It has been the commitment of the Government to accord the foremost priority for integrated rural development for which a number of steps have been initiated to formulate planning programmes at the grassroots level or village panchayat level, to make the implementation of planned, rural development programmes, schemes more effective, accelerated through people's participation and their continued involvement in the implementation of various development programmes, henceforth, ensuring sustainable integrated development at the village panchayat level in Amethi.

In view of the above an effort has been made in this study to innovate the available economic infrastructure at village panchayat level and develop Village Information System through collecting economic infrastructural data including size of land holdings, sources of irrigation, use of high yielding variety of seeds, agricultural cropping pattern, application of organic and inorganic amendments, use of insecticides and pesticides, use of agricultural implements, average monthly income of the workers at the Village Panchayat level in Amethi. It has been realized and assumed that the economic indicators data may play an important role in the overall development of the village panchayats, therefore, the collected and collated data base related to economic indicators are analysed because these innovated economic infrastructural resources play an important role in the planning process, henceforth in the integrated village development planning and its successful implementation for the sustainable development. The various indicators of the economic infrastructural data have been collected, collated and analysed at village panchayat level in Amethi, because economic infrastructural data base has been one of the major important indicators of the Human Resources Data Management System (HRDMS).

3. LAND OWNERSHIP

The land ownership pattern has been diversely distributed at Village Panchayat level in Amethi. Approximately 10 per cent people of Amethi are holding 90 per cent land because Amethi had been the kingship ruled estate and the kings were not only rulers but also the land owners to a large extent. The farmers were cultivating the agricultural land and providing the land revenue taxes to the kings through their tax collectors but these cultivators were not having the land rights. The kings and their kinsmen, Taluqdars and their land revenue tax collectors possessed most of land due to which the large size of the land holdings been concentrated among those people while the farmers/cultivators were the landless workers in the agricultural fields, without land rights and land ownership as well. After Zamindari Abolition Act and Taluqdari Abolition Act, the excess land was distributed among the landless agricultural workers and later on they became the

Table 3.19: Land Ownership and Irrigation (Economic-Infrastructure)—Amethi Block

Sl. No.	*Villages*	*No. of Households (Land Ownership)*				*Source of Irrigation (Area in Hectares)*				
		Less than One Hectare	*1 - 2 hectares*	*2 - 4 hectares*	*More than 4 hectares*	*Net Irrigated Area*	*Canal Irrigated Area*	*Govt. Tube-well Irrigated Area*	*Private Tube-well Irrigated Area*	*Other sources of Irrigated Area*
1	2	3	4	5	6	7	8	9	10	11
1.	Katra Maharani	170	90	63	1	72	15	10	42	5
2.	Sarai Khema	380	325	166	—	240	—	20	210	10
3.	Trilokpur	220	180	90	2	162	5	5	152	—
4.	Ramdaipur	1000	205	120	2	50	5	5	40	—
5.	Jangal Ram Nagar	650	450	253	10	603	120	10	463	10
6.	Benipur	139	50	50	—	58	10	5	38	5
7.	Parsawan	160	70	37	—	1469	15	5	121	5
8.	Mahmoodpur	250	125	55	—	150	15	—	130	5
9.	Raipur Fulwari	165	79	38	1	130	20	—	110	—
10.	Umapur Ganapatti	190	125	75	9	145	10	10	125	—
11.	Bhaganpur	95	80	43	—	70	5	—	65	—
12.	Tala	135	82	39	3	85	5	—	80	—
13.	Kushi Tali	115	98	47	—	170	25	10	125	10
14.	Loharta	112	82	28	—	26	2	—	24	—
15.	Darkha	190	180	30	—	158	5	5	143	5
16.	Mochwa	254	130	100	5	80	5	5	70	—
17.	Nuwawan	210	179	30	—	244	10	5	229	—
18.	Loniapur	135	75	41	—	48	2	1	43	2
19.	Kherauna	219	170	65	7	75	3	1	70	1
20.	Katra Phulkunwar	200	171	54	6	78	3	2	68	5
21.	Hathkila	148	60	40	—	125	15	5	105	—
22.	Rebha	80	75	60	2	45	2	2	39	2
23.	Raidaipur	180	50	55	5	115	5	5	105	—
24.	Korari Girdharshah	280	200	100	5	170	5	3	160	2
25.	Dedhpasar	210	110	46	1	140	5	2	123	10
26.	Mahaso	120	74	26	—	40	1	—	36	3
27.	Gangauli	150	90	42	2	175	3	2	170	—
28.	Dhadhudhar	130	80	25	4	60	5	3	50	2
29.	Gaderi	222	180	85	5	120	2	—	118	—
30.	Bhusahari	170	100	7	—	125	20	—	100	5
31.	Purabgaon	115	80	30	—	105	10	5	90	—
32.	Chaturbhujpur	90	65	44	—	56	5	3	46	2
33.	Mahrajpur	105	80	30	—	93	4	—	88	1
34.	Aghar	108	70	45	—	112	15	10	82	5
35.	Saidpur	165	70	30	—	80	4	3	70	3
36.	Kakwa	280	220	140	11	160	3	4	153	—
37.	Saraiya Duban	120	80	60	1	130	5	7	123	1
38.	Kohra	320	280	43	8	275	15	7	250	—
39.	Mahmadpur	250	200	70	9	210	2	2	215	1
40.	Naraini	345	270	90	8	280	30	10	230	10
41.	Nainaha	210	180	100	14	90	2	5	82	1
42.	Ramgarh	311	200	90	10	295	10	10	265	10
43.	Himmatgarh	144	122	22	—	192	2	2	186	2
44.	Dehara	200	170	55	6	126	5	3	116	2
	Amethi Block	**9442**	**6052**	**2759**	**134**	**6109**	**455**	**192**	**5350**	**125**

land owners in revenue records. In view of the above it has been noticed that the large size land holding have been concentrated within the very nominal households belonging to Rajputs or the kins of the kingship rulers in Amethi. Due to large size land holdings the land owners could not pay much attention for the maintenance and management of the fertility status of the soil and due to over agricultural cropping most of the land has deteriorated fertility status of the soil leading towards an increase in the area under wastelands including Banjar land, Usar land and fallow land. The size of land holdings at Village Panchayat level has been mentioned in Table 3.19.

An attempt has been made in this study to explain the distribution of land ownership pattern and size of land holdings among the different level of households at the Village Panchayat level in the Amethi Block.

3.1 Size of Land Holdings Less than One Hectare

Very low size of land holdings less than one hectare has been among 9442 households in the Amethi Block. The highest number of households more than 800 households owning less than one hectare land has been recorded in the village panchayat Ramdaipur having 1000 households owning less than one hectare of land, while 650 households are the owners of less than one hectare land in the village panchayat Jangal Ram Nagar of Amethi. The distribution of less than one hectare size of land holdings of the number of households has been depicted in the **Map 3.30**. It has been observed that low size land holdings between 300 and 500 households have been noticed in Kohara, Naraini, Benipur, Ramgarh and Sarai Khema Village Panchayats of the Amethi Block. It has been recorded that very low less than 300 households are the owners of less than one hectare land in Katara Maharani, Trilokpur, Mahmoodpur, Parsawan, Raipur Phulwari, Kherauna, Katara Phulkunwar, Hathkila, Dedhpasar, Rebha, Loniapur, Ramdaipur, Korari Girdhar Shah, Dhandhudhar, Chaturbhujpur, Maharajpur, Nainaha, Gaderi, Gangauli, Mahaso, Bhusahari, Himmatgarh, Dehara, Bhaganpur, Tala, Kushitali, Loharata, Umapur Gana Patti, Darakha, Mochawa, Nuwawan, Agahar, Saidpur, Kakawa Saraiya Duban and Mahmoodpur Village Panchayats of the Amethi Block. Thus, it has been observed that most of the households of the Amethi are the owners of less than one hectare size of land holdings at Village Panchayat level in Amethi Block.

3.2 Size of Land Holdings Between One and Two Hectares

The size of land holdings between one hectare and two hectares land owning households has been recorded in Sarai Khema and Jangal Ram Nagar village panchayats. The size of land holdings between one hectare and two hectares ranging between 100 and 200 households at Village Panchayat level has been found in Mahmoodpur, Kherauna, Katara Phulkunwar, Dedhpasar, Umapur Ganapatti, Darakha, Mochawa, Nuwawan, Gaderi and Nainaha Village Panchayats of the Amethi Block, while 200 to 300 households owning one hectare to two hectares size of land holdings has been found in the Ramdaipur, Korari Girdharshah, Kakawa, Naraini, Ramgarh, Kohara and Mahmoodpur village panchayats of the Amethi Block. The proportionate distribution of size of land holdings between one hectare and two hectares among the households at village panchayat level in Amethi has been mentioned in Table 3.19. The distribution of land ownership between one hectare and two hectares at the household level among the village panchayats of Amethi has been depicted in **Map 3.31**. It has been recorded that very low size of land ownership less than 100 households owning one hectare to two hectares land has been noticed in the Katara Maharani, Trilokpur, Bhaganpur, Tala, Kushia Tali, Loharata, Benipur, Parsawan, Raipur Phulwari, Loniapur, Raidaipur, Rebha, Hathkila, Mahaso, Gangauli, Dhandhudhar, Purabgaon, Chaturbhujpur, Maharajpur, Agahar, Saidpur and Saraiya Duban Village Panchayats of the Amethi Block.

3.3 Size of Land Holdings Between 2 and 4 Hectares

The size of land holdings between two and four hectares of land among the households at village panchayat level has been depicted in Map 3.32. It has been recorded that land ownership between 2 and 4 hectares land among households more than 150 households have been found in Sarai Khema and Jangal Ram Nagar Village Panchayats of the Amethi Block. The medium number of households between 100 to 150 households owning 2 and 4 hectares size of land holdings has been noticed in Ramdaipur, Mochawa, Korari Girdharshah, Nainaha and Kakawa Village Panchayats of the Amethi Block. The size of land holdings among 50 to 100 households land owning 2-4 hectares land has been found in the Katara Maharani, Trilokpur, Benipur, Mahmoodpur, Kherauna, Katara Phulkunwar, Rebha, Raidaipur, Umapur Ganapatti, Gaderi, Ramgarh, Dehara, Naraini, Saraiya Duban and Mahmoodpur Village Panchayats of the Amethi Block. Very low number of households less than 50 households having 2-4 hectares size of land ownership has been recorded in Parsawan, Raipur Phulwari, Loniapur, Hathkila, Dedhpasar, Mahaso, Gangauli, Bhusahari, Himmatgarh, Purabgaon, Chaturbhujpur, Maharajpur, Agahar, Saidpur and Kohara Village Panchayats of the Amethi Block.

3.4 Size of Land Holdings More than 4 Hectares

The size of land holdings more than 4 hectares has been found among 10 households in Nainaha, Kakawa, Ramgarh and Jangal Ram Nagar village panchayats which has been the estates of the kings has been established during the historical period. The large size of land holding having more than 4 hectares of land among 9 household has been seen in Mahmoodpur and Umapur Ganapatti village panchayats while 8 householders owned land more than 4 hectares has been seen in Naraini, Kohara Village Panchayats and 7 households owning more than 4 hectares land has been found in Kherauna, and 6 households in Dehara and Katara Phulkunwar Village Panchayats of the Amethi Block. It has been recorded that 5 households owning more than 4 hectares of land has been seen in the Raidaipur, Korari Girdharshah, Gaderi and Mochawa village panchayats of the Amethi. The size of land holdings among the households owning more than 4 hectares of land has been mentioned in Table 3.19. It has been noticed that land ownership of more than 4 hectares among 4 households has been found in the Dhandhudhar and 3 households in Tala, village panchayat and among 2 households in Trilokpur, Ramdaipur, Rebha and Gangauli Village Panchayats of the Amethi Block. It has been recorded that one household owning more than 4 hectares of land has been seen in Katara Maharani, Raipur Phulwari, Dedhpasar and Saraiya Duban village panchayats of the Amethi Block.

It has been observed that very insignificant and nominal number of households are the owners of large size of land holdings at village panchayat level in Amethi having good quality fertile land while large number of households are owners of less than one hectare of land which has been agriculturally low productive and poor fertility status of the soil which has been the main reasons for the economic backwardness of the people of Amethi.

4. SOURCE OF IRRIGATION

The source of irrigation for irrigating agricultural land cropping to increase agricultural productivity has been an important input for maintaining agricultural productivity. The net irrigated area in Amethi has been recorded 6109 hectares. The distribution of irrigated area through different sources of irrigation has been mentioned in Table 3.19. The basic important source of irrigation has been the canal, Government Tube-wells, Private Tube-wells and other sources of irrigation has been noticed in Amethi from several years. The irrigation has been an important input of the agricultural cropping. An effort has been made in this study to analyse the distribution of irrigated area through different sources of irrigation at village panchayat level in the Amethi Block.

4.1 Net Irrigated Area

The net irrigated area in Amethi has been recorded 6109 hectares. The distribution of net irrigated area in hectares at village panchayat level has been depicted in Table 3.19. The proportionate distribution of Net Irrigated Area at Village Panchayat level in Amethi has been shown in Map 3.33. It has been noticed that more than 300 hectares of net irrigated area having 450 hectares net irrigated land has been seen in the village panchayat Jangal Ram Nagar. Net irrigated area between 200 and 300 hectares has been noticed in Sarai Khema, Nuwawan, Naraini, Ramgarh, Kohara and Mahmoodpur Village Panchayats of the Amethi Block while low net irrigated proportionate area between 100 and 300 hectares has been observed in Trilokpur, Mahmoodpur, Parsawan, Raipur Phulwari, Hathkila, Dedhpasar, Raidaipur, Korari Girdharshah, Umapur Ganapatti, Kushi Tali, Darakha, Purabgaon, Gaderi, Gangauli, Bhusahari, Himmatgarh, Dehara, Agahar, Kakawa and Saraiya Duban village panchayats of the Amethi Block. It has been noticed that less than 100 hectares net irrigated area has been found in Katara Maharani, Ramdaipur, Bhaganpur, Tala, Loharata, Mochawa, Kherauna, Katara Phulkunwar, Rebha, Mahaso, Loniapur, Dhandhudhar, Chaturbhujpur, Maharajpur, Nainaha and Saidpur village panchayats of the Amethi Block.

4.2 Canal Irrigated Area

The canal source of irrigation has been main source of irrigation in the Amethi Block except Sarai Khema Village Panchayat where there is no source of canal irrigation, while in the rest of the village panchayats of Amethi canal irrigation has been an important source of irrigation. The canal irrigated area in hectares has been depicted in Map 3.34. It has been recorded that more than 30 hectares of canal irrigated land has been found in Jangal Ram Nagar having 120 hectares canal irrigated area and 30 hectares of canal irrigated area in the Naraini village panchayat of the Amethi Block. It has been noticed that medium canal irrigated area between 20 hectares and 30 hectares has been found in Kushi Tali, Raipur Phulwari, and Bhusahari Village Panchayats while low canal irrigated area between 10 hectares and 20 hectares has been recorded in Katara Maharani, Benipur, Mahmoodpur, Parsawan, Hathkila, Umapur Ganapatti, Nuwawan, Ramgarh, Purabgaon, Agahar and Kohara village panchayats of the Amethi Block. Very low less than 10 hectares of canal irrigated area has been noticed in Trilokpur, Ramdaipur, Bhaganpur, Tala, Loharata, Darakha, Mochawa, Chaturbhujpur, Maharajpur, Nainaha, Himmatgarh, Dehara, Gaderi, Dhandhudhar, Korari Girdharshah, Gangauli, Mahaso, Raidaipur, Loniapur, Rebha, Dedhpasar, Katara

Phulkunwar, Kherauna, Saidpur, Kakawa, Saraiya Duban and Mahmoodpur village panchayats of the Amethi Block.

4.3 Government Tube-Well Irrigated Area

The government tube-well irrigation facilities have not been available in Bhaganpur, Tala, Loharata, Mahmoodpur, Maharajpur, Raipur Phulwari, Mahaso, Bhusari and Gaderi village panchayats of the Amethi Block. Proportionate distribution of the Government Tube-well Irrigated area in hectares at village panchayat level has been depicted in Map 3.35. It has been noticed that more than 9 hectares of the Government Tube-well Irrigated area has been found in Katara Maharani, Sarai Khema, Jangal Ram Nagar, Kushi Tali, Umapur Ganapatti, Agahar, Naraini and Ramgarh Village Panchayats of Amethi. The medium area under Government Tube-well Irrigation between 6 hectares and 9 hectares has been noticed in the Saraiya Duban and Kohara village panchayats while low area under Government Tube-well irrigation between 3 hectares and 6 hectares has been recorded in Benipur, Parsawan, Hathkila, Raidaipur, Korari Girdharshah, Dhandhudhar, Dehara, Purabgaon, Chaturbhujpur, Nainaha, Mochawa, Nuwawan, Darakha, Saidpur and Kakawa Village Panchayats of Amethi. Very low area under Government Tube-well irrigation less than 3 hectares has been recorded in Trilokpur, Ramdaipur, Kherauna, Katara Phulkunwar, Rebha, Dedhpasar, Loniapur, Gangauli, Himmatgarh and Mahamadpur village panchayats of the Amethi Block.

4.4 Private Tube-Well Irrigated Area

The proportionate private tube-well irrigated area has been recorded in most of the villages of Amethi. The private tube-well source of irrigation has been an important source of irrigation at the village panchayat level in the Amethi Block. The distribution of private tube-well irrigated area in hectares at the village panchayat level has been depicted in Map 3.36. It has been recorded that very high more than 300 hectares of private tubewell irrigated area has been found in Jangal Ram Nagar having 463 hectares area irrigated through private tube-wells. Medium area under private tube-well irrigation between 200 hectares and 300 hectares has been noticed in Saraikhema, Nuwawan, Ramgarh, Naraini, Kohara and Mahmoodpur Village Panchayats of the Amethi Block. Proportionately low area under private tube-well irrigation between 100 hectares and 200 hectares has been observed in Trilokpur, Mahmoodpur, Parsawan, Raipur Phulwari, Hathkila, Dedhpasar, Kushi Tali, Umapur Ganapatti, Darakha, Korari Girdharshah, Raidaipur, Gangauli, Bhusahari, Himmatgarh, Dehara, Gaderi, Kakawa and Saraiya Duban Village Panchayats of the Amethi Block. It has been recorded that very low area, less than 100 hectares, under private tube-well irrigation has been seen in Katara Maharani, Ramdaipur, Bhaganpur, Tala, Loharata, Mochawa, Purabgaon, Dhandhudhar, Loniapur, Benipur, Kherauna, Katara Phulkunwar, Rebha, Mahaso, Nainaha, Chaturbhujpur, Maharajpur, Agahar and Saidpur village panchayats of the Amethi Block.

4.5 Other Sources of Irrigated Area

The other sources of irrigation include pond irrigation, well-irrigation and rain water harvesting system. The traditional source of irrigation at village level has been rarely distributed in Amethi. The other sources of irrigated area having 10 hectares has been recorded in Sarai Khema, Jangal Ram Nagar, Kushi Tali, Dedhpasar, Naraini and

Ramgarh village panchayats of the Amethi Block. The other sources of irrigated area having 5 hectares land has been seen in Katara Maharani, Benipur, Parsawan, Mahmoodpur, Darakha, Katara Phulkunwar, Bhusahari, Agahar Village Panchayats of the Amethi Block. There are 3 hectares area under irrigation through other sources in Saidpur village panchayat and 2 hectares area under other sources of irrigation has been found in Loniapur, Rebha, Korari Girdharshah, Dhandhudhar, Chaturbhujpur, Himmatgarh and Dehara Village Panchayats of Amethi. It has been noticed that one hectare area under other sources of irrigation has been found in Kherauna, Maharajpur, Saraiya Duban, Mahmoodpur, Nainaha village panchayats of the Amethi Block. The traditional and other sources of irrigation has been insignificantly distributed at village panchayat level in Amethi.

It is known fact that the irrigation has been an important input in the agricultural cropping system. The irrigational input plays an important role in increasing the agricultural productivity and also maintaining the fertility status of the soil to produce the agricultural crops. It has been recorded that the available sources of irrigation and existing net irrigated area has been insufficient against the cultivable land and also for reclamation of the wastelands. The canal irrigation has adversely affected the fertility status of the soil, over irrigation has caused waterlogging and increasing salinity and alkalinity problem of the soil which has deteriorated the fertility status of the soil and decreased agricultural productivity of the area. The improvement and an increase in area under the irrigation has to be planned intensively through ensuring people's participation and effort must be ensured to bring more area under irrigation to increase the agricultural productivity of the various villages of Amethi. An effort must be initiated to develop rain water harvesting system to ensure good quality irrigation system for increasing agricultural productivity and also maintaining the deterioration of the fertility status of the soil. The people's participatory planning at the grassroots level for developing rain water harvesting and optimum utilization of natural water for appropriate conservation of available land and water natural infrastructural resources at the village panchayat level in Amethi.

5. AGRICULTURAL CROPPING

Agriculture has been the backbone of the economy of Amethi. More than 80 per cent people of the Amethi depend on agriculture. The agricultural farming is the main occupation of the Amethi. The agriculture has been the main source of economy of the people of Amethi. It has been noticed that traditional system of agricultural cropping pattern has been still adopted in most of the villages of Amethi. The techno-scientific and commercial agricultural system have not been adopted due to ignorance and socio-economic backwardness of the people of Amethi, which has led to poor agricultural productivity. The detailed agricultural cropping pattern at the village panchayat level has been mentioned in Table 3.20. An attempt has been made in this study to analyse the area under foodgrain and commercial crops at the village panchayat level especially the area under rice, wheat, barley, peas, mustard, sugarcane, potato and fodder agricultural cropping has been explained at village level in Amethi.

5.1 Rice Cropped Area

Rice has been an important food crop of Amethi. The area under rice crop at village panchayat level has been mentioned in Table 3.20. The proportionate distribution of the rice cropped area at the village panchayat level has been depicted in Map 3.37. It has been observed that more than 90 hectares area under rice cultivation has been recorded in Sarai Khema, Jangal Ram Nagar, Kohara, Naraini and Ramgarh Village Panchayats while medium area under rice cultivation between 60 hectares and 90 hectares has been noticed in Trilokpur, Mahmoodpur, Darakha, Mahmoodpur, Himmatgarh and Gangauli Village Panchayats of Amethi. Low rice cropped area between 30 hectares and 90 hectares has been recorded in Katara Maharani, Bhaganpur, Tala Kushi Tala, Mochawa, Nuwawan, Parsawan, Umapur Ganapatti, Raipur Phulwari, Kherauna, Katara Phulkunwar, Hathkila, Dedhpasar, Bhusahari, Dehara, Nainaha, Purabgaon, Gaderi, Maharajpur, Agahar, Saidpur and Saraiya Duban Village Panchayats of Amethi. Very low area under rice less than 30 hectares has been observed in Benipur, Ramdaipur, Loharata, Loniapur, Rebha, Mahaso, Dhandhudhar and Chaturbhujpur village panchayats of the Amethi Block. The rice has an important place in the agricultural cropping pattern of Amethi and the rice is main food crop at village level in Amethi.

5.2 Wheat Cropped Area

The wheat is another main food crop of Amethi. Total wheat cropped area of Amethi has been recorded 1701 hectares which has been comparatively lower than the rice cropped area because the cultivators used to crop various other Rabi crops along with the wheat crop and also irrigation has been another major factor for the reduction in the wheat cropped area. Most of the areas of Amethi have been low-lying and waterlogged land which has always been suitable for Rice cropping and such lands are locally known as *Jadhan* or *Dhan* or *Paddy* or *Rice* cropping specific land. The distribution of the wheat cropped area at village panchayat level has been mentioned in Table 3.20. The proportionate distribution of the wheat cropped area at the village panchayat level in Amethi has been depicted in Map 3.38. It has been noticed that more than 80 hectares of wheat cropped area has been recorded in Jangal Ram Nagar Village Panchayat having 190 hectares of the wheat cropped land. The village panchayat Jangal Ram Nagar has been the largest village panchayat of the Amethi Block due to which the area under the wheat crop has been comparatively higher than the other village panchayats. Medium area under the wheat cropped land between 50 hectares and 80 hectares has been observed in Sarai Khema, Ramgarh, Naraini, Kohara and Mahmoodpur Village Panchayats of Amethi. Proportionately low wheat cropped area between 20 hectares and 50 hectares has been noticed in Trilokpur, Bhaganpur, Tala, Kushi Tali, Darakha, Nuwawan, Umapur Ganapatti, Mahmoodpur, Parsawan, Kherauna, Katara Phulkunwar, Hathkila, Dedhpasar, Raipur Phulwari, Raidaipur, Dehara, Himmatgarh, Bhusahari, Gangauli, Purabgaon, Gaderi, Nainaha, Maharajpur, Agahar, Kakawa, Saidpur and Saraiya Duban Village Panchayats of the Amethi Block. Less than 20 hectares wheat cropped area has been recorded in Katara Maharani, Ramgarh, Loharata, Mochawa, Chaturbhujpur, Dhandhudhar, Loniapur, Benipur, Rebha and Mahaso village panchayats of the Amethi Block.

5.3 Barley Cropped Area

The Barley cropped area has been insignificantly distributed at village panchayat level in Amethi. The distribution of the Barley cropped area has been mentioned in Table 3.20. It has been recorded that very high proportionate area more than 15 hectares under barley crop has been found in Naraini and Ramgarh Village Panchayats while high

Table 3.20: Agricultural Cropping Pattern (Economic-Infrastructure)—Amethi Block

(Area in Hectares)

Sl. No.	*Villages*	*Agricultural Cropping Pattern*							
		Rice	*Wheat*	*Barley*	*Peas*	*Mustard*	*Sugarcane*	*Potato*	*Fodder*
1	2	3	4	5	6	7	8	9	10
1.	Katra Maharani	32	19	1	4	8	1	4	3
2.	Sarai Khema	90	50	8	20	40	2	15	15
3.	Trilokpur	60	35	9	10	20	1	17	10
4.	Ramdaipur	20	10	2	4	11	—	2	1
5.	Jangal Ram Nagar	203	190	10	50	73	2	50	25
6.	Benipur	28	18	2	1	6	—	2	1
7.	Parsawan	50	30	5	18	28	—	10	5
8.	Mahmoodpur	60	30	1	12	24	1	12	10
9.	Raipur Fulwari	45	33	1	8	22	—	13	8
10.	Umapur Ganapatti	52	34	2	15	22	—	15	5
11.	Bhaganpur	30	20	1	3	10	—	4	2
12.	Tala	35	20	—	3	13	—	8	6
13.	Kushi Tali	58	37	5	12	28	—	20	10
14.	Loharta	12	8	—	1	3	—	1	1
15.	Darkha	63	38	3	9	23	—	18	4
16.	Mochwa	31	19	—	5	15	—	8	2
17.	Nuwawan	35	25	1	8	16	2	10	8
18.	Loniapur	20	10	—	2	8	—	5	3
19.	Kherauna	33	20	1	2	10	2	5	2
20.	Katra Phulkunwar	30	22	1	4	11	3	5	2
21.	Hathkila	50	35	1	8	20	1	10	1
22.	Rebha	22	15	1	1	4	—	1	1
23.	Raidaipur	49	34	1	2	15	1	8	5
24.	Korari Girdharshah	54	40	5	18	24	1	18	10
25.	Dedhpasar	40	20	1	8	18	—	10	3
26.	Mahaso	20	10	2	1	3	—	2	2
27.	Gangauli	70	40	9	12	20	—	14	10
28.	Dhadhudhar	25	17	1	4	5	—	5	3
29.	Gaderi	50	35	2	10	8	1	8	6
30.	Bhusahari	48	36	1	11	14	—	8	7
31.	Purabgaon	41	30	1	7	12	—	8	6
32.	Chaturbhujpur	22	18	—	2	6	—	5	3
33.	Mahrajpur	32	20	2	5	17	1	12	4
34.	Aghar	38	27	1	13	18	—	8	7
35.	Saidpur	32	24	—	5	9	—	6	4
36.	Kakwa	52	38	7	16	24	5	18	6
37.	Saraiya Duban	55	34	4	4	19	1	10	3
38.	Kohra	90	75	12	18	40	2	18	10
39.	Mahmadpur	76	50	12	18	25	—	20	9
40.	Naraini	90	75	18	22	35	3	25	12
41.	Nainaha	32	22	3	8	12	—	8	5
42.	Ramgarh	90	75	15	30	40	2	30	12
43.	Himmatgarh	60	45	10	20	27	—	20	10
44.	Dehara	45	33	1	11	18	2	13	3
	Amethi Block	**2170**	**1701**	**163**	**445**	**824**	**33**	**509**	**264**

proportionate area between 10 hectares and 15 hectares has been seen in Jangal Ram Nagar, Himmatgarh Kohara and Mahmoodpur Village Panchayats of the Amethi Block. Medium area under barley crop between 5 hectares and 10 hectares has been recorded in Sarai Khema, Trilokpur, Kakawa, Parsawan, Kushi Tali, Korari Girdhar Shah and

Gangauli village panchayats of the Amethi. Proportionately low area under barley crop has been noticed in Dehara, Nainaha, Saraiya Duban, Agahar, Maharajpur, Purabgaon, Bhusahari, Gaderi, Dhandhudhar, Mahaso, Dedhpasar, Raidaipur, Rebha, Hathkila, Katara Phulkunwar, Nuwawan, Darkha, Bhaganpur, Umapur Ganapatti, Raipur Phulwari, Mahmoodpur, Benipur, Ramdaipur and Katara Maharani village panchayats of the Amethi Block. While Tala, Loharata, Mochawa, Loniapur, Chaturbhujpur and Saidpur Village Panchayats of the Amethi Block are without barley cropped area. Barley is less preferred crop in Amethi due to which the area under barley crop has been found insignificant.

5.4 Peas Cropped Area

The pea is an important food crop of Amethi. The plea is important pulse crop which has been significantly cultivated by the farmers for their personal family use in a nominal area to meet their day to demands but not for commercial purpose. The proportionate peas cropped area at village panchayat level in Amethi has been depicted in Map 3.39. It has been noticed that high pea cropped area more than 15 hectares has been found in Sarai Khema, Jangal Ram Nagar, Parsawan, Umapur Ganapatti, Agahar, Gaderi, Dehara, Bhusahari, Gangauli, Kushi Tali, and Mahmoodpur Village Panchayats of the Amethi Block. Proportionately medium peas cropped area between 10 hectares and 15 hectares has been observed in Trilokpur, Kushi Tali, Mahmoodpur, Agahar, Gaderi, Gangauli, Bhusahari and Dehara village panchayats. Proportionately low peas cropped area between 5 hectares and 10 hectares has been noticed in Hathkila, Dedhpasar, Darakha, Mochawa, Nuwawan, Saidpur, Maharajpur, Purabgaon, Nainaha and Raipur Phulwari village panchayats, while very low proportionate area under peas crop less than 5 hectares has been noticed in Katara Maharani, Ramdaipur, Bhaganpur, Tala, Loharata, Saraiya Duban, Chaturbhujpur, Dhandhudhar, Loniapur, Raidaipur, Mahaso, Rebha, Kherauna, Katara Phulkunwar and Benipur Village Panchayats of the Amethi Block.

5.5 Mustard Cropped Area

Mustard has been an important commercial crop of Amethi. The mustard cultivation is being used by the farmers for their household use. The distribution of the Mustard cropped area at village panchayat level has been depicted in Map 3.40. Proportionately very high mustard cropped area more than 30 hectares has been noticed in Sarai Khema, Jangal Ram Nagar, Ramgarh, Naraini and Kohara Village Panchayats of the Amethi Block. Medium area under mustard crop between 20 hectares and 30 hectares has been recorded in Trilokpur, Kushi Tali, Darakha, Umapur Ganapatti, Mahmoodpur, Parsawan, Raipur Phulwari, Hathkila, Korari Girdharshah, Gangauli, Himmatgarh, Kakawa and Mahmoodpur Village Panchayats of the Amethi Block. Low area under the mustard crop between 10 hectares and 20 hectares has been noted in Ramdaipur, Bhaganpur, Tala, Kherauna, Katara Phulkunwar, Dedhpasar, Raidaipur, Bhusahari, Dehara, Nainaha, Purabgaon, Maharajpur, Nuwawan, Mochawa, Agahar, Nainaha and Saraiya Duban Village Panchayats of Amethi. Proportionately very low mustard cropped area less than 10 hectares has been recorded in Katara Maharani, Loharata, Benipur, Rebha, Mahaso, Loniapur, Dhandhudhar, Gaderi, Chaturbhujpur and Saidpur Village Panchayats of the Amethi Block.

5.6 Sugarcane Cropped Area

The sugarcane is an important commercial crop of Amethi. The sugarcane cropping has been noticed mostly for the household purposes. The proportionate distribution of the sugarcane cropped area at village panchayat level has been mentioned in Table 3.20. It has been noticed that sugarcane cropping in Amethi has been insignificantly distributed at village panchayat level in Amethi. The total area under sugarcane crop has been found 33 hectares. It has been recorded that 5 hectares area under sugarcane crop has been founded in Kakawa Village Panchayat and 3 hectares area under sugarcane crop has been recorded in Katara Phulkunwar and Naraini Village Panchayats of the Amethi Block. It has been recorded that 2 hectares area under the sugarcane crop has been found in Saraikhema, Jangal Ram Nagar, Nuwawan, Kherauna, Kohara, Ramgarh and Dehara Village Panchayats of the Amethi Block, while one hectare area under sugarcane crop has been noticed in the Saraiya Duban, Maharajpur, Gaderi, Korari Girdharshah, Raidaipur, Mahmoodpur, Trilokpur and Katara Maharani Village Panchayats of Amethi. It has been observed that out of 44 village panchayats of the Amethi Block 26 village panchayats has very insignificant or without sugarcane cropped area at village panchayat level in Amethi.

5.7 Potato Cropped Area

The potato has been an important crop in Amethi but potato cultivation has been done for household consumption while commercial potato agricultural cropping has been done very insignificantly and nominally at village level. The excess potatos are sold locally but not at larger commercial scale. The proportionate distribution of the potato cropped area at the village panchayat level in Amethi has been depicted in Map 3.41. It has been recorded that more than 30 hectares area under potato crop has been found in Jangal Ram Nagar and Ramgarh Village Panchayats of Amethi. Medium potato cropped area between 20 hectares and 30 hectares has been recorded in Kashi Tali, Mahmoodpur, Naraini and Himmatgarh Village Panchayats while low potato cropped area between 10 hectares and 20 hectares has been noticed in the Trilokpur, Sarai Khema, Mahmoodpur, Parsawan, Raipur Phulwari, Hathkila, Dedhpasar, Umapur Ganapatti, Darakha, Nuwawan, Korari Girdharshah, Gangauli, Makarajpur, Kohara, Saraiya Duban and Kohara Village Panchayats. Proportionately very low potato cropped area less than 10 hectares has been recorded in the Katara Maharani, Ramdaipur, Bhaganpur, Tala, Loharata, Mochawa, Dhandhudhar, Bhusahari, Mahaso, Rebha, Raidaipur, Loniapur, Katra Phulkunwar, Kherauna, Benipur, Gaderi, Purabgaon, Chaturbhujpur, Agahar, Nainaha and Saidpur Village Panchayats of Amethi.

5.8 Fodder Cropped Area

The fodder cropped area has been nominally distributed in Amethi. It has been noticed that there is 264 hectares area under the fodder crop in Amethi. The proportionate distribution of fodder cropped area at village panchayat level has been shown in Map 3.42. It has been noticed that more than 15 hectares area under fodder crop has been found in Sarai Khema and Jangal Ram Nagar Village Panchayat. Medium fodder cropped area between 10 hectares and 15 hectares has been noticed in Trilokpur, Kushi Tali, Mahmoodpur, Korari Girdharshah, Gangauli, Himmatgarh, Ramgarh Naraini and Kohara Village Panchayats of the Amethi Block. It has been observed that low fodder cropped area between 5 hectares to 10 hectares has been recorded in the Tala, Umapur Ganapatti, Nuwawan, Raidaipur, Phulwari, Parsawan, Bhusahari, Gaderi, Nainaha, Purabgaon, Agahar, Kakawa and Mahmoodpur village panchayats. Proportionately very low fodder cropped area less than 5 hectares has been noticed in the Katara Maharani, Ramdaipur, Bhaganpur, Loharata, Darakha, Mochawa, Chaturbhujpur, Maharajpur, Saidpur, Saraiya Duban, Mahaso, Dedhpasar, Rebha, Hathkila, Katara Phulkunwar, Kherauna and Benipur Village Panchayats of the Amethi Block.

In view of the above, it has been observed that the rice agricultural food crop has maximum 2170 hectares land, because Amethi has mostly Dhan/Dhankhar/Jadhan Khet is paddy land due to low-lying and waterlogged land and the soil is also appropriate for rice cropping due to which rice has been one of the major food grain crop of the Amethi. The rice foodgrain agricultural cropping is carried out during Kharif cropping season. The agro-climatic conditions of the Amethi has been favourable and suitable for the rice/paddy agricultural cropping at village level in the Amethi. Wheat has been another important foodgrain crop in Amethi. There is 1701 hectares area under wheat crop in Amethi. Wheat foodgrain crop has been an important crop of the Rabi agricultural cropping season. The excess wheat and rice foodgrains are sold by the farmers in the local markets including Krishi Utpadan Mandi Samiti at Amethi. The area under the barley crop has been very insignificantly distributed in Amethi. There is 163 hectares area under barley crop in Amethi. The peas has also been an important food crop and the peas foodgrains are used as pulses in the Amethi. The area under peas foodgrain crop has been 445 hectares in Amethi Block. The Mustard is an important oil seed crop of the area. There is 824 hectares area under the mustard oil seed crop in Amethi. The mustard oil crop is cropped in Amethi for the household purpose by the people. The sugarcane agricultural cropping has been very insignificantly cropping has been very insignificantly cropped in Amethi. There is only 33 hectares sugarcane agricultural cropped area in Amethi. The potato agricultural cropping has been significantly cropped at village panchayat level in Amethi. It has been observed that potato agricultural cropping has been done for cultivators household purposes and potato is being used as an important vegetable crop in Amethi. It has been recorded that there is 509 hectares area under potato crop in Amethi. The fodder cultivation has been significantly cropped in Amethi. It has been noticed that there is 264 hectares area under fodder cropping for cattle feed at village panchayat level in Amethi. The policy planners and agricultural scientists including soil scientists must initiate an effort for maintaining the fertility status of the soil and also ensuring the techno-scientific methods of the reclamation of available wastelands including waterlogged land, Usar land, Banjar land, old fallow land, fallow land, other types of waste lands and Kankarili land lying waste at village panchayat level in Amethi, with the view to increase the area under cultivation and also to increase the agricultural productivity and to strengthen the economic infrastructural resources at the village panchayat level in Amethi, because the economic backwardness of the people at village panchayats level in Amethi and also improving, maintaining the eco-friendly agricultural cropping system at the field level in Amethi.

6. SEEDS

The application of good quality seed for agricultural cropping plays an important role in determining the agricultural productivity of the area. It has been noticed that the cultivators of the Amethi are still using traditional system of seeds. The appropriate

High Yielding Variety seeds are not used effectively in the various villages of Amethi. The application of High Yielding Variety (HYV) seeds may increase the agricultural productivity. It has been noticed that the general variety of seeds are used in 2137 hectares area while the High Yield Variety (HYV) seeds are used in 1235 hectares of the cultivable land in Amethi. It has been observed that the high yielding variety seeds are applied in the less area while tradition and general seeds are applied which are responsible for low agricultural productivity. The traditional seeds are sown in most of the net cultivated areas at the village panchayat level in Amethi. The use of seeds in hectares at village panchayat level has been mentioned in Table 3.21. An effort has been made in this study to analyse the application of traditional seeds and High Yielding variety seeds at village panchayat level in the Amethi Block.

6.1 Seeds

The traditional system of seeds, which has low agricultural productivity are generally sown in the maximum net cultivated areas at the village panchayat level in Amethi. The proportionate distribution of area under traditional system of seeds at village panchayat level in Amethi has been depicted in Map 3.43. It has been observed that more than 60 hectares area are being sown through general quality seeds processed by the farmers in Jangal Ram Nagar, Mahmoodpur, Katara Phulkunwar, Hathkila, Umapurganapatti, Korari Girdharshah, Darakha, Ramgarh, Mahmoodpur, Agahar, Naraini, Kakawa, Himmatgarh Village Panchayats of the Amethi Block. Medium area between 40 hectares and 60 hectares has been sown through general seeds has been noticed in Trilokpur, Sarai Khema Parsawan, Raipur Phulwari, Kherauna, Loniapur, Raidaipur, Bhusahari, Gaderi, Purabgaon, Maharajpur, Mochawa, Kushi Tali, Tala, Bhaganpur, Saidpur and Kohara Village Panchayats of Amethi. It has been observed that the general seeds are used between 20 hectares and 40 hectares area has been found in Katara Maharani, Raidaipur, Loharata, Nuwawan, Ramdaipur, Katara Maharani, Rebha, Dedhpasar, Mahaso, Gangauli, Dhandhudhar, Chaturbhujpur, Nainaha, Dehara and Saraiya Duban village panchayats of Amethi. It has been observed that the cultivators of village panchayat Benipur has used general seeds only in 15 hectares area. It has been observed that the general seeds are applied in most of the cultivated areas under the Kharif, Rabi and Jaid cropping seasons in Amethi.

6.2 High Yielding Variety Seeds

The High Yielding Variety (HYV) seeds are applied by the few farmers due to which the area under the HYV seeds has been found nominal and less than the general seeds at village panchayat level in Amethi. The proportionate area under the high yielding variety seeds at village panchayat level has been depicted in Map 3.44. It has been observed that the high yielding variety seeds are used in more than 30 hectares cultivated land has been found in Jangal Ram Nagar, Mahmoodpur, Umapur Ganapatti, Darakha, Katara Phulkunwar, Hathkila, Dedhpasar, Korari Girdharshah, Gaderi, Gangauli, Bhusahari, Ramgarh, Himmatgarh, Nainaha, Dehara, Maharajpur, Agahar, Saidpur, Kakawa and Mahmoodpur Village Panchayats of the Amethi Block. The application of High Yielding Variety seeds between 20 hectares and 30 hectares cultivated land has been observed in Trilokpur, Ramdaipur, Bhaganpur, Tala, Kushi Tali, Parsawan, Kherauna, Loniapur,

Table 3.21: Use of Seeds and Fertilizers (Economic-Infrastructure)—Amethi Block

Sl. No.	*Villages*	*Use of Seeds (Area in Hectares)*		*Use of Insecticides & Pesticides*	*Use of Fertilizers (Area in Hectares)*				*No. of Bio-Gas*
		Seeds	*HYV Seeds*		*Nitrogen*	*Phosphate*	*Potash*	*Compost*	
1	2	3	4	5	6	7	8	9	10
1.	Katra Maharani	30	10	15	30	10	1	25	15
2.	Sarai Khema	47	19	15	72	13	2	35	10
3.	Trilokpur	41	22	20	55	7	2	30	10
4.	Ramdaipur	30	20	15	25	5	2	35	18
5.	Jangal Ram Nagar	70	30	35	190	25	5	60	8
6.	Benipur	15	5	10	20	7	1	20	8
7.	Parsawan	40	20	10	50	8	2	25	11
8.	Mahmoodpur	100	35	15	50	7	2	20	8
9.	Raipur Fulwari	40	15	10	45	9	2	35	4
10.	Umapur Ganapatti	60	30	10	50	10	1	25	9
11.	Bhaganpur	50	23	10	30	9	1	20	9
12.	Tala	40	20	12	35	8	1	15	6
13.	Kushi Tali	43	29	8	60	8	2	25	8
14.	Loharta	35	10	7	15	8	1	10	11
15.	Darkha	60	30	10	55	6	2	30	7
16.	Mochwa	50	20	8	30	9	1	15	14
17.	Nuwawan	38	29	12	80	9	4	40	7
18.	Loniapur	40	21	9	20	10	1	10	8
19.	Kherauna	55	20	15	30	9	2	15	11
20.	Katra Phulkunwar	70	30	17	30	9	1	15	10
21.	Hathkila	70	30	15	45	10	2	20	6
22.	Rebha	30	20	10	40	10	1	20	10
23.	Raidaipur	53	28	12	55	8	2	25	8
24.	Korari Girdharshah	60	50	25	47	10	1	26	10
25.	Dedhpasar	20	40	10	17	9	2	10	6
26.	Mahaso	30	10	10	56	7	1	269	9
27.	Gangauli	35	40	20	20	8	1	10	5
28.	Dhadhudhar	30	22	15	36	8	1	18	9
29.	Gaderi	50	30	20	37	9	2	15	6
30.	Bhusahari	50	46	12	31	6	1	13	6
31.	Purabgaon	40	25	15	26	8	1	10	5
32.	Chaturbhujpur	35	15	10	27	5	1	12	5
33.	Mahrajpur	50	40	10	33	9	1	14	7
34.	Aghar	70	30	15	24	9	1	10	5
35.	Saidpur	50	32	18	48	7	3	22	9
36.	Kakwa	60	50	22	24	10	2	16	9
37.	Saraiya Duban	30	19	15	82	8	1	18	4
38.	Kohra	50	25	17	63	9	2	23	7
39.	Mahmadpur	70	30	25	84	6	1	38	6
40.	Naraini	90	15	15	27	10	4	13	7
41.	Nainaha	30	50	20	88	7	3	14	8
42.	Ramgarh	80	50	25	57	10	2	22	8
43.	Himmatgarh	70	30	20	45	9	2	25	4
44.	Dehara	30	70	15	40	7	2	20	8
	Amethi Block	**2137**	**1235**	**659**	**2024**	**385**	**76**	**945**	**359**

Raidaipur, Rebha, Dedhpasar, Purabgaon, Dhandhudhar and Kohara Village Panchayats of Amethi. It has been noticed that the area between 10 hectares and 20 hectares using high yielding variety seeds has been found in Katara Maharani, Sarai Khema, Raipur Phulwari, Mahaso, Loharata, Chaturbhujpur, Naraini and Saraiya Duban village panchayats of the Amethi Block.

It has been observed that the cultivators/farmers are still using the traditional system of agricultural practices including the application of the general seeds. The ignorance and social backwardness and low size of land holdings have been the major reasons but some of the scientifically-technically aware farmers are applying High Yielding Variety seeds due to which the area under general seeds has been comparatively higher than the area under the High Yielding Variety seeds. An effort must be made to popularize and demonstrate the application of the good quality High Yielding Variety of seeds and also the application of latest developed techno-scientific techniques for increasing the agricultural productivity of the area.

7. USE OF INSECTICIDES AND PESTICIDES

The control of the insects and various other problems of the agricultural crops, the use of insecticides and pesticides is necessary to increase the quality production of the agricultural crops. The use of insecticides and pesticides at village panchayat level has been mentioned in Table 3.21. It has been observed that more than 30 hectares of cultivated area in Jangal Ram Nagar village panchayat has been used for the insecticides and pesticides. The use of insecticides and pesticides in the net cultivated area at village panchayat level in Amethi has been depicted in Map 3.45. The medium cultivated area between 20 hectares and 30 hectares using insecticides and pesticides has been noticed in Trilokpur, Korari Girdharshah, Gangauli, Gaderi, Himmatgarh, Ramgarh, Nainaha, Kakawa and Mahmoodpur Village Panchayats of the Amethi Block. It has been recorded that proportionately low cultivated area between 10 hectares and 20 hectares using insecticides and pesticides has been found in the Katara Maharani, Sarai Khema, Ramdaipur, Bhaganpur, Tala, Darakha, Umapur Ganapatti, Nuwawan, Dhandhudhar, Purabgaon, Bhusahari, Dehara, Mahaso, Dedhpasar, Hathkila, Katara Phulkunwar, Rebha, Raidaipur, Kherauna, Raipur Phulwari, Mahmoodpur, Parsawan, Benipur, Chaturbhujpur, Maharajpur, Naraini, Agahar, Saidpur, Saraiya Duban and Kohara Village Panchayats of the Amethi. Very low area less than 10 hectares using insecticides and pesticides has been noticed in the Kushi Tali, Loharta, Mochawa village panchayats of the Amethi Block.

The ignorance and adoption of the traditional techniques in the agricultural cropping pattern has led towards low agricultural productivity in Amethi. An effort should be initiated to propogate and demonstrate technically-scientifically an appropriate use of insecticides and pesticides for the control of insects and pests. It has also been observed that the various schemes and programmes launched by the government has not been successfully implemented and demonstrated among the deprived resourceless cultivators of Amethi. The government facilities especially the plant protection and protection of the agricultural crops for the control of the insects and pests has not been properly provided among the resourceless farmers at the grassroots level. Even if some of the interested cultivators desire and require to obtain the requisite insecticides and pesticides the appropriate proven items are not made available to the farmers due to which the cultivators have lost their faith in the Government schemes for increasing the agricultural productivity and the slogan of the *"Produce More Foodgrain"* (*Adhik Ann Upjao*) has been failed at grassroots level.

8. USE OF FERTILIZERS

The use of chemical fertilizer has been insignificantly used in Amethi. It has been observed that the traditional system of fertilizer application has been used through cow dung and compost fertilizer and organic amendment has also been used especially the green manuring, viz. Sanai/Dhaincha, etc. The chemical fertilizers are not appropriately used as per the fertility requirement of the soil. The application of Nitrogen, Phosphate and Potash (NPK) has not been properly used. It has been observed that the application of fertilizer as per the fertility status of the soil has not been used, scientifically. The improper use of NPK fertilizer has caused low agricultural productivity and deteriorated the fertility status of the soil. The area specific use of fertilizer at the village panchayat level has been mentioned in Table 3.21. An attempt has been made in this study to explain the Nitrogen, Phosphate and Potash (NPK) use of the fertilizer at the village panchayat level in Amethi.

8.1 Use of Nitrogen Fertilizer

The application of the Nitrogen fertilizer has been significantly used in Amethi. The proportionate distribution of the cultivated area using Nitrogen fertilizer at village panchayat level in Amethi has been depicted in Map 3.46. It has been noticed that more than 60 hectares cultivated land using Nitrogen fertilizer has been seen in Sarai Khema, Jangal Ram Nagar, Kushi Tali, Nuwawan, Nainaha, Saraiya Duban, Kohara and Mahmoodpur Village Panchayats of the Amethi. The cultivated area between 40 hectares and 60 hectares, using nitrogen fertilizer has been recorded in Parsawan, Mahmoodpur, Trilokpur, Darakha, Umapur Ganapatti, Raipur Phulwari, Hathkila, Rebha, Mahaso, Raidaipur, Korari Girdharshah, Himmatgarh, Ramgarh, Dehara and Saidpur village panchayats of the Amethi Block. The area between 20 hectares and 40 hectares using Nitrogen fertilizer has been noticed in Katara Maharani, Ramdaipur, Bhaganpur, Tala, Benipur, Kherauna, Loniapur, Mochawa, Dhandhudhar, Purabgaon, Gaderi, Gangauli, Bhusahari, Chaturbhujpur, Maharajpur, Agahar, Naraini and Kakawa Village Panchayats of Amethi. The cultivated area less than 20 hectares using Nitrogen fertilizer has been recorded in Loharata, and Dedhpasar village panchayats of the Amethi Block.

8.2 Use of Phosphate Fertilizer

The Phosphate fertilizer has been nominally used at the village panchayat level in the Amethi Block. The proportionate distribution of cultivated area using Phosphate fertilizer at the village panchayat level has been depicted in Map 3.47. It has been recorded that more than 11 hectares area using Phosphate fertilizer has been seen in Sarai Khema, Jangal Ram Nagar village panchayats and Darakha, Chaturbhujpur, Mahmoodpur and Bhusahari village panchayats of the Amethi Block. The agricultural land ranging from 9 hectares to 11 hectares using Phosphate fertilizers has been seen in Katara Maharani, Bhaganpur, Mochawa, Nuwawan, Umapur Ganapatti, Raipur Phulwari, Kherauna, Katara Phulkunwar, Hathkila, Dedhpasar, Rebha, Loniapur, Korari Girdharshah, Gaderi, Ramgarh, Himmatgarh, Naraini, Maharajpur, Agahar, Kakawa and Kohara Village Panchayats. The proportionate area between 7 hectares and 9 hectares land using Phosphate fertilizer has been noticed in Trilokpur, Tala, Kushi Tali, Loharata, Benipur, Mahmoodpur, Parsawan, Raidaipur, Dhandhudhar, Purabgaon, Nainaha, Dehara, Gangauli, Mahaso, Saidpur, Saraiya Duban Village Panchayats of the Amethi Block. The net cultivated area less than 7 hectares using Phosphate fertilizer has been recorded in Ramdaipur, Darakha, Chaturbhujpur, Mahmoodpur and Bhusahari Village Panchayats of the Amethi Block.

8.4. Use of Compost Fertilizers

The Compost fertilizers has been significantly used in the all villages of the Amethi. The *Gobar khad*/cow dung/green manuring or compost fertilizers has been used by the cultivators of Amethi from the historical period. The use of the Compost fertilizers in the cultivated area has been depicted in Map 3.48. It has been observed that the application of the Compost fertilizer in the cultivated area more than 35 hectares land has been seen in Ramdaipur, Jangal Ram Nagar, Sarai Khema, Raipur Phulwari, Nuwawan and Mahamadpur Village Panchayats of the Amethi Block. The use of Compost fertilizers applied between 25 hectares and 35 hectares has been found in Katara Maharani, Trilokpur, Parsawan, Mahmoodpur, Kushi Tali, Umapur Ganapatti, Darakha, Himmatgarh, Dehara, Korari Girdharshah, Mahaso and Raidaipur Village Panchayats of the Amethi Block. The use of Compost fertilizer within 15 hectares of the agricultural land has been recorded in Loharata, Loniapur, Dedhpasar, Gangauli, Bhusahari, Purabgaon, Nainaha, Naraini, Maharajpur, Chaturbhujpur and Agahar Village Panchayats of the Amethi Block.

It has been observed that the application of Nitrogen fertilizer has ben ensured in 2024 hectares of agricultural land in Amethi. The agricultural land covering 385 hectares area has been facilitated by the Phosphate fertilizer. The agricultural land covering 76 hectares land has been facilitated through the Potash fertilizer in the Amethi Block. The use of inorganic fertilizers has been insignificantly used in the Amethi due to ignorance and economic backwardness. There is inefficient and improper use of chemical fertilizers in Amethi. The scientific testing of the soils have not been carried out to know the requirement of the fertilizers to produce the agricultural crop. The Compost fertilizer has been applied in 945 hectares of agricultural land. The scientific demonstration of the soil testing and application of the organic and inorganic amendments as per the needs of the soil to produce agricultural crops must be ensured to increase the agricultural productivity and also to improve the economic conditions of the cultivators/farmers of the Amethi.

9. USE OF BIO-GAS

The bio-gas is one of the best scientific system to utilize the cowdung for producing the household cooking gas and compost fertilizer for its application in the cultivated land to increase the agricultural productivity of the field. The Bio-Gas installation is an appropriate scientific technique for optimum and multi-utilization of cowdung for obtaining cooking gas and compost fertilizer for maintaining the fertility status of the soil. The distribution of number of Bio-gas plants at village panchayat level has been depicted in Map. 3.49. It has been recorded that more than 15 numbers of bio-gas plants have been found in Katara Maharani and Ramdaipur Village Panchayats while 10 to 15 numbers of bio-gas plants have been noticed in Trilokpur, Sarai Khema, Loharata, Mochawa, Korari Girdharshah, Rebha, Katara Phulkunwar, Kherauna and Parsawana Village Panchayats of the Amethi Block. It has been recorded that 5 to 10 numbers of bio-gas plants have been found in Bhaganpur, Tala, Darakha, Nuwawan, Kushi Tali, Umapur Ganapatti, Jangal Ram Nagar, Benipur, Mahmoodpur, Loniapur, Raidaipur, Hathkila, Dedhpasar, Mahaso, Gangauli, Bhusahari, Dehara, Ramgarh, Nainaha, Naraini, Purabgaon, Gaderi, Dhandhudhar, Maharajpur, Chaturbhujpur, Naraini, Agahar, Saidpur, Kakawa, Kohara and Mahmoodpur Village Panchayats of the Amethi Block. It has been recorded that less than 5 numbers of bio-gas plants has been installed in Saraiya Duban, Himmatgarh and Raipur Phulwari Village Panchayats of the Amethi Block. It has been noticed that there has been 359 bio-gas plants installed and functional in the various village panchayats of the Amethi Block. The appropriate scientific demonstration of the Bio-gas installation will facilitate the farmers for availing the cooking gas and compost fertilizers and it can be used for improving the fertility status of the soil and also conserve the environmental conditions of the area.

10. AGRICULTURAL IMPLEMENTS

The agricultural implements plays an important role in the agricultural farming. The old, traditional agricultural implements are time taking and inefficient and low agricultural productive while high-tech, latest developed techno-scientific agricultural implement are quick and efficient and increases the agricultural productivity but the high-tech-scientific agricultural implements are expensive and effectively used in the large size of land holdings and it is beyond the economic limits of the low size land holders and poor resourceless cultivators. The high-tech and scientific agricultural implements must be facilitated to the cultivators at the field level by the government agricultural implementing agencies to increase the quality and quantity agricultural productions at the grassroots level. The distribution of agricultural implement at village panchayat level has been mentioned in Table 3.22. An attempt has been made in this study to analyze the distribution of agricultural implement including wood-cultivator, iron-cultivator, High-Tech-Cultivator, agricultural implements/tools, tractors and other agricultural implements/machinery used at village panchayat level in the Amethi Block.

10.1. Use of Wood Cultivator

The wood cultivator has been used by the cultivators of Amethi from the historical period. The use of wood cultivators has been traditional with the help of local carpenter and blacksmith (*Badhai* and *Lohar*) the wood cultivator is being prepared at the village level. The wood cultivator can cultivate the agricultural land normally not deeply. The deep ploughing is not possible by the wood cultivator. The distribution of the wood cultivator at village panchayat level has been depicted in Map 3.50. It has been recorded that more than 60 wood cultivators have been found in Saraiya Duban, Mahmoodpur, Dehara and Jangal Ram Nagar village panchayats. The use of 40 and 60 wood cultivators have been used in Bhaganpur, Tala, Loharata, Nuwawan, Ramgarh, Bhusahari village panchayats while 20 to 40 wood cultivators are being used in the Katara Maharani, Trilokpur, Mahmoodpur, Parsawan, Raipur Phulwari, Kherauna, Umapur Ganapatti, Darakha, Mochawa, Korari Girdharshah, Gaderi, Purabgaon, Naraini, Kakawa and Kohara Village Panchayats of the Amethi Block. Proportionately less than 20 wood cultivators have been used in the Ramdaipur, Sarai Khema, Kushi Tali, Benipur, Katara Phulkunwar, Hathkila, Dedhpasar, Rebha, Loniapur, Raidaipur, Mahaso, Gangauli, Dhandhudhar, Himmatgarh, Chaturbhujpur, Maharajpur, Agahar and Saidpur Village Panchayats of the Amethi Block. It has been observed that most of the cultivators of Amethi are still using traditional wood cultivators for cultivating their agricultural land in Amethi.

10.2 Use of Iron Cultivators

The iron cultivators are insignificantly used in Amethi. It has been recorded that only

Table 3.22: Agricultural Implements (Economic-Infrastructure)—Amethi Block

Sl. No.	*Villages*	*Agricultural Implements*					
		Wood Cultivator	*Iron Cultivator*	*High Tech Cultivator*	*Agricultural Implements/ Tools*	*Tractors*	*Other Agricultural Implements/ Machinery*
1	2	3	4	5	6	7	8
1.	Katra Maharani	30	10	2	5	5	2
2.	Sarai Khema	12	8	3	4	8	2
3.	Trilokpur	25	10	2	3	7	1
4.	Ramdaipur	14	7	2	1	7	—
5.	Jangal Ram Nagar	80	20	3	5	10	12
6.	Benipur	158	3	5	5	3	—
7.	Parsawan	20	10	1	3	3	2
8.	Mahmoodpur	30	10	2	4	6	2
9.	Raipur Fulwari	25	10	1	3	3	1
10.	Umapur Ganapatti	22	12	—	3	4	2
11.	Bhaganpur	47	7	1	2	3	—
12.	Tala	40	4	1	1	3	—
13.	Kushi Tali	14	8	2	3	6	1
14.	Loharta	42	13	2	1	3	—
15.	Darkha	24	18	2	3	17	2
16.	Mochwa	25	15	5	3	8	3
17.	Nuwawan	42	18	2	2	15	3
18.	Loniapur	12	5	4	2	8	3
19.	Kherauna	35	10	3	4	7	2
20.	Katra Phulkunwar	18	9	2	3	16	3
21.	Hathkila	12	8	2	4	4	2
22.	Rebha	14	9	2	1	4	2
23.	Raidaipur	10	8	3	2	15	1
24.	Korari Girdharshah	20	14	5	4	10	3
25.	Dedhpasar	10	5	2	3	15	1
26.	Mahaso	10	8	1	5	5	1
27.	Gangauli	14	8	4	2	18	2
28.	Dhadhudhar	14	7	3	2	5	2
29.	Gaderi	34	15	3	2	5	2
30.	Bhusahari	48	7	2	2	13	1
31.	Purabgaon	25	10	2	1	13	4
32.	Chaturbhujpur	15	8	1	3	3	2
33.	Mahrajpur	15	7	1	2	4	2
34.	Aghar	18	4	1	3	5	3
35.	Saidpur	14	12	2	2	14	2
36.	Kakwa	20	9	4	3	9	2
37.	Saraiya Duban	63	15	1	2	5	1
38.	Kohra	23	13	2	1	5	1
39.	Mahmadpur	69	12	3	4	15	10
40.	Naraini	25	15	3	3	15	4
41.	Nainaha	74	10	3	2	7	1
42.	Ramgarh	44	8	4	5	9	4
43.	Himmatgarh	14	7	3	2	15	3
44.	Dehara	72	12	4	2	7	2
	Amethi Block	**1249**	**438**	**109**	**119**	**372**	**99**

438 iron cultivators are used in Amethi. The proportionae distribution of iron cultivators at village panchayat level has been depicted in Map. 3.51. It has been noticed that more than 15 iron cultivators are used in Jangal Ram Nagar, Darakha, Mochawa, Nuwawan, Gaderi, Naraini and Saraiya Duban Village Panchayats of Amethi Block. The iron

cultivators between 10 and 15 numbers have been used in Katara Maharani, Trilokpur, Loharata, Umapur Ganapatti, Raipur Phulwari, Mahmoodpur, Parsawan, Kherauna, Korari Girdharshah, Purab Gaon, Nainaha, Saidpur, Kohara and Mahmoodpur Village Panchayats of the Amethi Block. It has been noticed that 5 to 10 iron cultivators are used in Sarai Khema, Ramdaipur, Bhaganpur, Kushi Tali, Katara Phulkunwar, Hathkila, Dedhpasar, Rebha, Raidaipur, Mahaso, Gangauli, Bhusahari, Himmatgarh, Ramgarh, Dhandhudhar, Chaturbhujpur, Maharajpur and Kakawa village panchayats of the Amethi Block. Less than 5 iron cultivators have been used in Tala, Benipur and Agahar Village Panchayats of the Amethi Block. It has been noticed that due to ignorance and economic backwardness and low size land holding has led to very less and insignificant use of the iron cultivators at the village panchayat level in Amethi Block.

10.3 Use of High-Tech Cultivators

The high-tech cultivators are very insignificanly used in the Amethi Block. It has been noticed that there are 109 high-tech cultivators in the Amethi Block. The use of 5 high-tech cultivators has been observed in the Benipur, Mochawa, Korari Girdharshah Village Panchayats while 4 high-tech cultivators are used in the Dehara, Ramgarh, Kakawa, Gangauli, Loniapur Village Panchayats and 3 high-tech cultivators have been recorded in Sarai Khema, Jangal Ram Nagar, Kherauna, Raidaipur, Dhandhudhar, Gaderi Mahmoodpur, Naraini, Nainaha and Himmatgarh Village Panchayats of the Amethi Block. It has been observed that 2 high-tech cultivators are used in Kakawa, Saidpur, Purabgaon, Bhusahari, Dedhpasar, Rebha, Hathkila, Katara Phulkunwar, Nuwawan, Darakha, Loharata, Kushti Tali, Mahmoodpur, Ramdaipur, Trilokpur and Katara Maharani village panchayats of Amethi Block. The use of one high-tech cultivator has been recorded in Parsawan, Raipur, Phulwari, Bhaganpur, Tala, Mahaso, Chaturbhujpur, Maharajpur, Agahar and Saraiya Duban Village Panchayats of the Amethi Block. It has been observed that there is no high-tech cultivator in the Village Panchayats Umapur Ganapatti. The least and insignificant use of high-tech cultivator in the Amethi indicates low agricultural productivity and economic backwardness of the people of Amethi.

10.4 Use of Agricultural Implements/Tools

The use of agricultural implements/tools has been insignificant due to low size of the land holdings, ignorance and economic backwardness and poverty of the people of Amethi. The application of agricultural implements/tools at village panchayat level has been mentioned in the Table 3.22. It has been recorded that 5 number of high-tech tools and agricultural implements are used in Ramgarh, Mahaso, Benipur, Jangal Ram Nagar and Katara Mahari Village Panchayats of Amethi. The use of 4 agricultural implements/tools are used in Sarai Khema, Mahmoodpur, Kherauna, Hathkila, Korari Girdharshah and Mahmoodpur Village Panchayats while 3 numbers of agricultural implements/tools are used in the Naraini, Kakawa, Agahar, Chaturbhujpur, Dedhpasar, Katara Phulkunwar, Mochawa, Darakha, Kushi Tali, Umapur Gangapatti, Raipur Phulwari, Parsawan and Trilikpur Village Panchayats of Amethi. The application of the 2 numbers of the agricultural implements/tools has ben recorded in the Bhaganpur, Nuwawan, Loniapur, Raidaipur, Gangauli, Dedhpasar, Bhusahari, Gaderi, Dehara, Maharajpur, Saidput, Saraiya Duban Nainaha and Himmatgarh Village Panchayats of the Amethi Block. It has been recorded that the use of one number of agricultural implements/tools has been found in the Ramdaipur, Tala, Loharata, Rebha, Purabgaon, and Kohara village panchayats of the Amethi Block.

10.5 Tractors

It has been observed that the tractors are significantly used in Amethi at Village Panchayat level. The economically well of and agriculturally-commercially oriented cultivator have been the owners of the tractors for cultivating the agricultural land and transportation of agricultural goods and transporting the Bricks, etc. The large size of land holders are possessing the tractors for various purposes. The proportionate distribution of the tractors are village panchayat level has been mentioned in Table 3.22. It has been observed that more than 15 tractors have been found in the Darakha, Nuwawan, Katara Phulkunwar, Raidaipur, Dedhpasar, Gangauli, Mahmoodpur, Naraini and Himmatgarh village panchayats of Amethi. It has been noticed that the use of 10 to 15 tractors have been found in Jangal Ram Nagar, Korari Girdharshah, Bhusarai, Purabgaon, and Saidpur Village panchayats while the application and ownership of 5 to 10 tractors have been recorded in Dehara, Ramgarh, Nainaha, Sarai Duban, Kakawa, Agahar, Gaderi, Dhandhudhar, Mahaso, Loniapur, Kherauna, Mochawa, Kushi Tali, Mahmoodpur, Ramdaipur, Trilokpur, Sarai Khema and Katara Maharani Village Panchayats of the Amethi Block. The use of less than 5 tractors has been recorded in the Benipur, Parsawan, Raipur Phulwari, Bhaganpur, Tala, Loharata, Hathkila, Rebha, Chaturbhujpur, Maharajpur Village Panchayats of Amethi Block.

10.6 Use of Other High-Tech Agricultural Implement and Machinery

The use of other high-tech agricultural implement and machinery has been very insignificantly used in Amethi. The Village Panchayats Ramdaipur, Benipur, Bhaganpur, Tala, Loharata are without use fo other other high-tech agricultural implement and machinery. It has been noticed that village panchayat Jangal Ram Nagar has 12 other high-tech agricultural implement and machinery and 10 high-tech agricultural implement and machinery in Mahmoodpur village panchayat of Amehti. The use of 4 other high-tech agricultural implements has been found in the Purabgaon, Varaini and Ramgarh Village Panchayats while 3 other high-tech agricultural implement and machinery has been found in Himmatgarh, Agahar, Korari Girdharshah, Katara Phulkunwar, Loniapur, Nuwawan, Mochawa, village panchayats. The use of one other high-tech agricultural implements and machinery has been found in Trilokpur, Raipur Phulwari, Kushi Tali, Raidaipur, Dedhpasar, Mahaso, Bhusahari, Saraiya Duban, Kohara and Nainaha village panchayats of the Amethi Block.

It has been observed that the traditional system of wood cultivator are being used in Amethi. The excess use of 1249 wood cultivator indicates the tradition system of the agricultural land cultivation. The low size land holding farmers and economically poor cultivators are using traditional cultivation system. The use of iron-cultivators has been comparatively less than the wood cultivator. The large size land holders scientifically awarded cultivators are the users of iron-cultivators. There are 438 iron cultivators are being used in Amethi which has very less than the wood cultivators. Simultaneously, 109 high-tech cultivators are used in Amethi. The high-tech agricultural implements are insignificantly used in Amethi and only 124 high-tech agricultgural implements/tool has been used in the Amethi Block. There are 363 tractors owned and used by the large size land holding cultivators for agricultural land cultivation and other commercial use for generating income. It has been noticed that use of 99 high-tech other agricultural implements/machinery and agricultural equipments has been owned by the cultivators of Amethi. It has been noticed the economically weaker/poor and low size land holding cultivator/farmers are forced to use/own tradition system of agricultural implements/machinery/equipment. The large size land holding farmers and economically developed cultivators are the users and owners of the high-tech expensive cultivators/agricultural implements/machinery and agricultural equipments at village panchayat level in the Amethi Block.

11. ANIMAL HUSBANDRY

Animal husbandry has been an important source of economy for the downtrodden deprived multitudes. The backward castes, viz. Yadav/Pal has been animal husbandry workers. The Yadavs were engaged in the milking work while Pals were engaged in the sheep and goat rearing activities from the historical period. It has been noticed that the cows, buffalowes, goats, horses, pigs and hens/cocks have been significantly distributed in Amethi. The pigs animal husbandry work has been done by the Scheduled Caste people and hens/cocks have been kept the Muslim population not only in Amethi but in the other areas of Uttar Pradesh as well. The distribution of different animals at the village panchayat level has been mentioned in Table 3.23. An attempt has been made in this study to analyse the distribution of cows, buffalowes, cows, horses, pigs and hens etc. at village panchayat level in Amethi.

11.1 Cows

Religious and historically the cows has been an important animal in the Hindu religion. The cow milk has important religious use from the historical period including Vedas. The importance of the cows has been clearly mentioned in the *Vedas* and *Puranas*. The cows has been worshipped as '*Go Mata*' while the cowdung has an important role in the worship programmes. The calf of the cow or male cow or bulls has been used for cultivating the agricultural land through cultivators. The distribution of the cows at village panchayat level has been mentioned in Table 3.23. The cows has been significantly distributed at village panchayat level in Amethi. The distribution of cows at village panchayat level in Amethi has been depicted in **Map 3.52**. It has been recorded that more than 200 cows have been seen in Jangal Ram Nagar, Mahmoodpur and Kherauna Village Panchayats of the Amethi Block. The number of cows between 150 and 200 has been found in Hathkila, Korari Girdharshah, Nuwawan and Naraini Village Panchayats. It has been noticed that 100 to 150 cows have been recorded in Trilokpur, Ramdaipur, Benipur, Katara Phulkunwar, Dedhpasar, Rebha, Raidaipur, Loniapur, Raipur Phulwari, Umapur Ganapatti, Kushi Tali, Tala, Darakha, Mochawa, Nainaha, Ramgarh, Dehara, Bhusahari, Gangauli, Gaderi, Maharajpur, Agahar, Kakawa, Saraiya Duban and Kohara Village Panchayats of Amethi. It has been observed that less than 100 cows has been found in the Katara Maharani, Sarai Khema, Parsawan, Mahaso, Himmatgarh, Purabgaon, Bhaganpur, Loharata, Chaturbhujpur and Saidpur village panchayats of the Amethi Block.

11.2 Buffalowes

The buffalow has been an important milking animal and a basic source of the economy

Table 3.23: Animal Husbandry (Economic-Infrastructure)—Amethi Block

Sl. No.	*Villages*	*Cow*	*Buffallowes*	*Goats*	*Horses*	*Pigs*	*Hen/Cocks*
1	2	3	4	5	6	7	8
1.	Katra Maharani	95	40	25	4	—	15
2.	Sarai Khema	70	40	30	7	4	10
3.	Trilokpur	100	70	30	7	12	25
4.	Ramdaipur	120	70	40	10	20	15
5.	Jangal Ram Nagar	320	150	90	25	20	20
6.	Benipur	105	75	40	1	—	25
7.	Parsawan	90	40	30	—	—	25
8.	Mahmoodpur	205	105	90	4	25	35
9.	Raipur Fulwari	115	70	25	3	10	20
10.	Umapur Ganapatti	125	90	47	3	28	15
11.	Bhaganpur	95	70	20	5	12	15
12.	Tala	105	85	40	4	19	23
13.	Kushi Tali	104	56	38	3	16	20
14.	Loharta	95	65	40	10	—	25
15.	Darkha	135	90	38	8	—	45
16.	Mochwa	120	70	40	—	20	30
17.	Nuwawan	159	75	35	4	10	20
18.	Loniapur	115	75	40	—	—	35
19.	Kherauna	213	110	53	5	20	21
20.	Katra Phulkunwar	120	80	35	4	20	30
21.	Hathkila	153	94	15	—	—	10
22.	Rebha	101	72	40	—	25	30
23.	Raidaipur	120	70	45	7	20	15
24.	Korari Girdharshah	150	90	40	7	10	35
25.	Dedhpasar	110	75	35	3	20	25
26.	Mahaso	73	36	20	1	7	4
27.	Gangauli	110	70	40	10	25	30
28.	Dhadhudhar	75	40	25	3	15	20
29.	Gaderi	125	90	40	10	—	25
30.	Bhusahari	125	70	45	10	35	20
31.	Purabgaon	90	65	15	8	—	—
32.	Chaturbhujpur	90	65	35	4	—	21
33.	Mahrajpur	105	70	25	—	—	40
34.	Aghar	110	85	40	—	—	—
35.	Saidpur	90	60	30	7	15	20
36.	Kakwa	120	80	40	12	20	40
37.	Saraiya Duban	120	75	40	5	10	20
38.	Kohra	125	60	25	—	158	20
39.	Mahmadpur	150	95	50	—	2	40
40.	Naraini	165	75	40	5	18	48
41.	Nainaha	110	70	25	3	20	30
42.	Ramgarh	145	70	60	10	35	40
43.	Himmatgarh	90	60	35	2	11	20
44.	Dehara	115	70	35	8	18	20
	Amethi Block	**5373**	**3233**	**1716**	**222**	**575**	**1032**

for the backward class and milk providers of Amethi. The buffalowes has been significantly distributed at village level in Amethi. The proportionate distribution of the buffalowes at the village panchayat level has been depicted in **Map 3.53**. It has been recorded that more than 90 buffalowes has been found in Hathkila, Kherauna, Mahmoodpur, Jangal Ram Nagar, Umapur Ganapatti, Darakha, Korari Girdharshah, Gaderi and Mahmoodpur Village Panchayats while medium distribution of cows between 70 and 90 cows has been noticed in Trilokpur, Ramdaipur, Benipur, Bhaganpur, Tala,

Raipur Phulwari, Katara Phulkunwar, Loniapur, Raidaipur, Rebha, Dedhpasar, Gangauli, Bhusahari, Dehara, Ramgarh, Nainaha, Mochawa, Nuwawan, Naraini, Agahar, Maharajpur, Kakawa and Saraiya Duban village panchayat of Amehti. It has been observed that the distribution of 70 and 90 buffalowes has been found in the Trilokpur, Ramdaipur, Bhaganpur, Tala, Benipur, Raipur, Raidaipur, Loniapur, Nuwawan, Mochawa, Gangauli, Bhusahari, Dehara, Ramgarh, Nainaha, Naraini, Maharajpur, Agahar, Kakawa and Saraiya Duban Village Panchayats of the Amethi Block. The distribution of buffalowes between 50 and 70 buffalowes has been recorded in Himmatgarh, Chaturbhujpur, Purabgaon, Kohara and Saidpur Village Panchayats of Amthi. It has been observed that less than 50 buffalows have been found in Mahaso, Dhandhudhar, Parsawan, Sarai Khema and Katara Maharani Village Panchayats of the Amethi Block.

11.3 Goats

The goats have been kept by the Minorities and Pals. The minorities are keeping the goats for milking and meat needs while the Pals/Gaderia caste people are keeping the goats and sheep as their professional heriditary occupation. The goats are significantly distributed at the village panchayat level in Amethi. The distribution of goats at village panchayat level has been depicted in **Map 3.54**. It has been noticed that more than 50 goats have been found in Jangal Ram Nagar, Mahmoodpur, Kherauna, Ramgarh and Mahmoodpur Village Panchayats, while medium distribution between 40 and 50 goats have been recorded in Ramdaipur, Benipur, Tala, Loharata, Umapur Ganapatti, Mochawa, Korari Girdhar Shah, Loniapur, Raidaipur, Rebha, Gangauli, Bhusahari, Gaderi, Naraini, Agahar, Kakawa and Saraiya Duban Village Panchayats of the Amethi Block. Low distribution of goats between 30 and 40 has been noticed in Trilokpur, Sarai Khema, Parsawan, Katara Phulkunwar, Dedhpasar, Kushi Tali, Darakha, Nuwawan, Chaturbhujpur, Himmatgarh, Dehara, Dhandhudhar, Saidpur Village Panchayats of Amethi. Very low distribution of goats less than 30 goats in Katara Maharani, Bhaganpur, Raipur Phulwari, Hathkila, Mahaso, Dhandhudhar, Purabgaon, Nainaha, Maharajpur, Kohara village panchayats of Amethi.

11.4. Horses

The horses have been significantly distributed at village panchayat level in Amethi. The horses have been used for transportation work through *Tanga/Ekka* and other social purposes. The distribution of horses has been mentioned in Table. 3.23. Maximum 25 horses have been found in the village panchayat Jangal Ram Nagar and more than 10 horses have been recorded in Ramdaipur, Loharata, Gangauli, Gaderi, Bhusahari, Kakawa and Ramgarh Village Panchayats while 5 to 10 horses have been found in Naraini, Sarai Khema, Trilokpur, Darakha, Raidaipur, Korari Girdharshah, Purabgaon, Saidpur, Saraiya Duban and Dehara Village Panchayats of Amethi. It has been observed that less than 5 horses have been seen in Himmatgarh, Nainaha, Mahaso, Chaturbhujpur, Dedhpasar, Katara Maharani, Benipur, Mahmoodpur, Raipur Phulwari, Umapur Ganapatti, Tala Kushi Tali, Nuwawan and Katara Phulkunwar Village Panchayats of Amethi. It has been observed that there is availability of horses in Parsawan, Loniapur, Mochawa, Hathkila, Rebha, Maharajpur, Agahar, Rebha, Kohara and Mamadpur village panchayats of the Amethi Block.

11.5 Pigs

The pigs husbandry activities are carried out by the Scheduled Caste people in Amethi. The distribution of pigs at village panchayat level in Amethi has been mentioned in Table 3.23. It has been recorded that more than 30 pigs have been found in Bhusahari and Ramgarh village panchayats while 20 to 30 pigs have been noticed in Nainaha, Mahmoodpur, Kakawa, Gangauli, Dedhpasar, Raidaipur, Rebha, Kherauna, Katara Phulkunwar, Mochawa, Umapur Ganapatti, Mahmoodpur, Jangal Ram Nagar and Ramdaipur Village Panchayats of the Amethi Block, while the distribution of 10 to 20 pigs has been recorded in Trilokpur, Raipur Phulwari, Bhaganpur, Tala, Kushi Tali, Nuwawan, Korari Girdharshah, Dhandhudhar, Saidpur, Saraiya Duban, Kohara, Naraini, Himmatgarh and Dehara Village Panchayats of the Amethi Block. It has been noticed that less than 10 pigs have been recorded in the Sarai Khema and Mahaso village panchayats while nil husbandry of pigs have been observed in Agahar, Maharajpur, Chaturbhujpur, Purabgaon, Gaderi, Hathkila, Loniapur, Darakha, Loharata, Parsawan, Benipur and Katara Maharani Village Panchayats of the Amethi Block.

11.6 Hens/Cocks

The hens/cocks have been significantly distributed at village panchayat level in Amethi. The distribution of the hens/cocks at village panchayat level has been depicted in **Map 3.55**. It has been recorded that more than 30 hens/cocks are found in Mahmoodpur, Katara Phulkunwar, Rebha, Loniapur, Korari Girdharshah, Loniapur, Gangauli, Ramgarh, Nainaha, Naraini, Kohara, Mahmoodpur, Mochawa and Darakha village panchayats of the Amethi Block. Medium distribution of hens/cocks between 25 to 30 hens/cocks has been recorded in Trilokpur, Parsawan, Benipur, Dedhpasar, Gaderi and Loharta village panchayats. Low distribution of hens/cocks between 20 and 25 hens/cocks has been observed in Tala, Kushi Tali, Jangal Ram Nagar, Raipur Phulwari, Kherauna, Dhandhudhar, Chaturbhujpur, Maharajpur, Bhusahari, Himmatgarh, Dehara, Saidpur, Saraiya Duban and Kohara Village Panchayats while less than 20 hens/cocks has been noticed in the Katara Maharani, Ramdaipur, Sarai Khema, Baganpur, Umapur Ganapatti, Raidaipur, Hathkila, and Mahaso Village Panchayats. The Village Panchayats of Agahar and Purabgaon have been found without hens/cocks. The hens/cocks husbandry has been done by the downtrodden section of the society for the personal use of the obtaining eggs and chicken, etc. and excess of it has been mentioned and sold for generating income of the minorities and downtrodden section of the society.

It has been noticed that the animal husbandry activities through traditional animals are carried out by the resourceless, deprived rural poor section of the society while hybrid/inseminated cows/buffalow/pigs/hens, etc. are kept by the socially, scientifically and economically better status beneficiaries at village panchayat level in Amethi. It has been recorded that 5273 cows and 3233 buffalows and 1716 goats are kept by the cultivators/farmers/village people of the Amethi Block. The horses are nominally distributed and 222 horses has been noted in the various villages of the Amethi Block. It has been noticed that there are 575 pigs and 1032 hens/cocks are found in Amethi while the pigs are kept by the Scheduled Caste people and the hens/cocks are kept by the minorities and downtrodden Scheduled Caste beneficiaries in the different villages of the Amethi Block.

12. INCOME

An average monthly income of the agricultural workers, cultivators and various trade workers has been computed based on their day-to-day generated income and average per month income has been calculated which has been computed for the related total workers of the respective village panchayats. The average monthly income of the workers at the village level has been calculated which has been mentioned in Table 3.24. An attempt has been made in this study to analyse the average monthly income of the cultivators agricultural labourers, non-skilled workers, skilled workers, animal husbandry workers, business workers, transportation workers and agro-industries workers at the village panchayat level in Amethi.

12.1 Average Monthly Income of Cultivators

Average monthly income of the cultivators at village panchayat level in Amethi has been depicted in **Map 3.56**. It has been noticed that average monthly income of the cultivators of Amethi has been found very nominal and indicates the economic backwardness of Amethi. It has been noticed that an average monthly income lakh rupees of the cultivators more than 30.0 lakhs has been found in Kohara and Jangal Ram Nagar Village Panchayats. The average monthly income of the cultivators between 20.0 and 30.0 lakh rupees has been recorded in Sarai Khema, Kakawa, Naraini, Ramgarh Village Panchayats and average monthly income, between 10 and 20 lakh rupees, of the cultivators has been observed in Trilokpur, Ramdaipur, Dedhpasar, Korari Girdharshah, Gangauli, Gaderi, Mochawa, Darakha and Mahmoodpur Village Panchayats. It has been recorded that average monthly income of the cultivators less than rupees 10.0 lakh has been found in Katara Maharani, Bhaganpur, Tala, Kushi Tali, Loharta, Umapur Ganapatti, Nuwawan, Benipur, Mahmoodpur, Parsawan, Raipur Phulwari, Kherauna, Katara Phulkunwar, Hathkila, Rebha, Raidaipur, Loniapur, Dhandhudhar, Purabgaon, Dehara, Bhusahari, Himmatgarh, Nainaha, Chaturbhujpur, Maharajpur, Agahar, Saraiya Duban and Kakawa Village Panchayats of the Amethi Block.

12.2 Average Monthly Income of Agricultural Workers

An average monthly income of the agricultural workers in lakh rupees at the village panchayat level in Amethi has been depicted in **Map 3.57**. The average monthly income of the agricultural workers has been computed based on the per day wages earned by the agricultural workers at village level. It has been recorded that an average monthly income of the agricultural workers more than 8.0 lakh rupees has been found in Jangal Ram Nagar and Korari Girdharshah Village Panchayats while average monthly income of the agricultural labourers between 6.0 and 8.0 lakh rupees has been found in Sarai Khema, Mochawa, Gaderi, Ramgarh and Kohara Village Panchayats of the Amethi Block. Average monthly income between 4.0 and 6.0 lakh rupees of the agricultural workers has been recorded in Trilokpur, Darakha, Gangauli and Kakawa Village Panchayats of the Amethi Block. It has been recorded that an average monthly income, less than rupees 4.0 lakh rupees of the agricultural labourers has been found in the Katara Maharani, Ramdaipur, Bhaganpur, Tala, Loharta, Kushi Tali, Umapur Ganapatti, Nuwawan, Benipur, Mahmoodpur, Parsawan, Raipur Phulwari, Loniapur, Raidaipur, Rebha, Dedhpasar, Hathkila, Katara Phulkunwar, Kherauna, Bhusahari, Himmatgarh,

Dehara, Nainaha, Purabgaon, Chaturbhujpur, Maharajpur, Naraini, Agahar, Saidpur, Saraiya Duban and Mahmoodpur village panchayats of the Amethi Block.

12.3. Average Monthly Income of Non-Skilled Workers

The average monthly income of the non-skilled workers of Amethi has been computed based on their per day wages earned by them Map 3.58. Average monthly income of non-skilled workers more than 6.0 lakh rupees has been recorded in the Darakha Village Panchayats and average monthly income between 4.0 and 6.0 lakh rupees of the non-skilled workers has been observed in Sarai Khema, Jangal Ram Nagar and Gaderi Village Panchayats of the Amethi Block, while average monthly income between 2.0 and 4.0 lakh rupees of the non-skilled workers has been noticed in Trilokpur, Katara Maharani, Ramdaipur, Umapur Ganapatti, Raipur Phulwari, Kherauna, Dedhpasar, Raidaipur, Korari Girdhar Shah, Himmatgarh, Ramgarh, Kakawa, Kohara and Mahamadpur Village Panchayats of the Amethi Block. An average monthly income less than 2.0 lakh rupees of the non-skilled workers has been observed in Bhaganpur, Tala Kushi Tali, Loharta, Nuwawan, Mochawa, Dhandhudhar, Benipur, Mahmoodpur, Parsawan, Katara Phulkunwar, Hathkila, Rebha, Loniapur, Gangauli, Mahaso, Bhusahari, Dehara, Nainaha, Purabgaon, Chaturbhujpur, Maharajpur, Naraini, Agahar, Saraiya Duban and Saidpur village panchayats of Amethi Block.

12.4. Average Monthly Income of Skilled Workers

An average monthly income of the skilled workers has been computed based on the daily wages earned by the skilled workers at the village level. The average monthly income of the skilled workers in lakh rupees has been depicted in Map 3.59. The average monthly income more than 5.0 lakh rupees of the skilled workers has been recorded in Katara Maharani, Sarai Khema, Ramdaipur, and Jangal Ram Nagar Village Panchayats of Amethi. Average monthly income of the skilled workers between 3.0 and 5.0 lakhs rupees has been observed in Trilokpur, Umapur Ganapatti, Kherauna, Dedhpasar, Korari Girdharshah, Nainaha and Kohara village panchayats of the Amethi Block. Average monthly income between 1.0 and 3.0 lakh rupees of the skilled workers has been noticed in Tala, Bhaganpur, Darakha, Mochawa, Nuwawan, Benipur, Mahmoodpur, Parasawan, Raipur Phulwari, Katara Maharani, Hathkila, Raidaipur, Dhandhudhar, Gaderi, Gangauli, Bhusahari, Himmatgarh, Ramgarh, Dehara, Naraini, Maharajpur, Agahar, Saidpur, Kakawa, Saraiya Duban and Mahmoodpur village panchayats of Amethi. The average monthly income less than rupees one lakh of the skilled workers has been observed in Loniapur, Rebha, Mahaso, Chaturbhujpur, Purabgaon, Loharata and Kushi Tali village panchayats of the Amethi Block.

12.5. Average Monthly Income of Animal Husbandry Workers

The average monthly income of the animal husbandry workers has been calculated based on the per day income of the animal husbandry workers. The average monthly income of the animal husbandry workers in thousand rupees has been depicted in **Map 3.60**. The average monthly income more than hundred thousand rupees has been found in Katara Maharani and Sarai Khema Village Panchayats of the Amethi Block. The average monthly income, between 70 and 100 thousand rupees of the animal husbandary workers has been recorded in Jangal Ram Nagar and Parsawan village panchayats while

Table 3.24: Average Monthly Income (Economic-Infrastructure)—Amethi Block

Sl. No.	*Villages*	*In Lakh Rupees*				*In Thousand Rupees*			
		Cultivators	*Agricultural Workers*	*Non-Skilled Workers*	*Skilled Workers*	*Animal Husbandry Workers*	*Business Workers*	*Transportation Workers*	*Agro-Industries Workers*
1	2	3	4	5	6	7	8	9	10
1.	Katra Maharani	9.1	3.99	2.8	5.4	150	88	95	22
2.	Sarai Khema	21.9	7	4.4	7.2	160	120	150	32
3.	Trilokpur	10.5	4	3.9	3.38	45	15	56	15
4.	Ramdaipur	11.7	2.9	3.47	5.3	33	30	36	21
5.	Jangal Ram Nagar	35.2	10.5	5	7.5	75	60	125	20
6.	Benipur	3.2	1.4	1.12	1.8	10	6	12	2
7.	Parsawan	1.7	1	1.1	1	9	15	10	2
8.	Mahmoodpur	5.3	3	1.45	1.8	42	24	32	6
9.	Raipur Fulwari	1.4	1	2.25	1.8	27	24	35	3
10.	Umapur Ganapatti	9.9	3	2.5	3.6	15	28	3	6
11.	Bhaganpur	1.6	1	0.9	1	9	12	32	4
12.	Tala	3	1	1.3	1.4	42	12	28	14
13.	Kushi Tali	1.8	1	0.9	0.36	27	3	6	—
14.	Loharta	2.2	1.10	1	0.76	3	12	6	3
15.	Darkha	11.4	4.2	6.33	2.16	27	20	17	6
16.	Mochwa	15.3	6.1	1.87	1.8	15	21	10	3
17.	Nuwawan	3.3	1.1	0.9	1.4	30	15	10	20
18.	Loniapur	12	1	1.12	0.14	3	—	—	—
19.	Kherauna	9.15	3.35	2.7	3.6	60	68	72	15
20.	Katra Phulkunwar	6.5	2	1.75	2.5	12	54	17	15
21.	Hathkila	2.6	1	1.50	1.22	9	12	9	15
22.	Rebha	2	1	0.7	0.86	15	15	6	5
23.	Raidaipur	6.5	2.13	3.2	2.88	30	9	6	16
24.	Korari Girdharshah	19.2	8.8	3.25	3.6	30	30	16	5
25.	Dedhpasar	10	3	3	3.6	30	15	12	15
26.	Mahaso	3	1.1	0.2	1.4	6	6	4	3
27.	Gangauli	11.3	5.2	1.8	1.44	15	30	8	25
28.	Dhadhudhar	4	1.1	1.75	1.8	45	24	36	25
29.	Gaderi	18.3	6.3	4.32	2.16	30	24	20	20
30.	Bhusahari	6.7	2.4	1.82	1.8	30	45	45	25
31.	Purabgaon	4.9	1.25	1.6	0.7	15	15	12	7
32.	Chaturbhujpur	1.2	1	0.3	0.36	9	10	7	2
33.	Mahrajpur	2.3	1	1.5	1.44	30	18	12	15
34.	Aghar	4.3	2.18	1	2.16	48	15	36	2
35.	Saidpur	4	1.42	1	1.44	15	35	36	25
36.	Kakwa	23.4	5.75	3	2.88	15	35	18	5
37.	Saraiya Duban	7.5	2.8	1.37	1.44	24	6	20	7
38.	Kohra	30.1	7.1	3.3	3.6	39	28	18	10
39.	Mahmadpur	11.9	3.2	2.34	4.75	45	28	24	25
40.	Naraini	27.5	3.15	1.54	1.44	24	12	12	10
41.	Nainaha	7	2.1	1.5	3.6	9	9	12	2
42.	Ramgarh	23.9	7	3	2.44	30	35	70	10
43.	Himmatgarh	8.7	3	2	1.44	15	18	10	10
44.	Dehara	9.5	3.19	1	1.44	18	35	40	20
	Amethi Block	**415.95**	**135.78**	**92.75**	**102.43**	**1370**	**1136**	**1241**	**513**

average monthly income between 40 and 70 thousand rupees of the animal husbandry workers has been observed in Trilokpur, Mahmoodpur, Kherauna, Dhandhudhar, Tala, Agahar and Mahmoodpur Village Panchayats of the Amethi Block. It has been observed that average monthly income less than 40 thousand rupees of the animal husbandry workers has been found in Ramdaipur, Benipur, Bhaganpur, Kushi Tali, Loharata,

Darakha, Mochawa, Nuwawan, Umapur Ganapatti, Raipur Phulwari, Loniapur, Katara Phulkunwar, Raidaipur, Korari Girdharshah, Hathkila, Dedhpasar, Mahaso, Gangauli, Bhusahari, Himmatgarh, Dahara, Ramgarh, Gaderi, Nainaha, Purabgaon, Naraini, Chaturbhujpur, Maharajpur, Saidpur, Saraiya Duban, Kakawa and Kohara Village Panchayats of the Amethi Block.

12.6 Average Monthly Income of the Business Workers

The average monthly income of the business workers has been calculated based on the daily business income of the business workers. The average monthly income of the business workers in thousand rupees at village panchayat level has been depicted in **Map 3.61**. The average monthly income of the business workers more than seventy thousand rupees has been recorded in Katara Maharani, Sarai Khema village panchayats. It has been recorded that average monthly income between 40 and 70 thousand of the business workers has been observed in Jangal Ram Nagar, Kherauna, Katara Phul Kunwar and Bhusahari Village Panchayats while average monthly income, between 10 and 40 thousand of the business workers has been recorded in Trilokpur, Ramdaipur, Bhaganpur, Tala Loharata, Darakha, Mochawa, Nuwawan, Umapur Ganapatti, Raipur Phulwari, Mahmoodpur, Parsawan, Hathkila, Dedhpasar, Rebha, Korari Girdharshah, Dhandhudhar, Gangauli, Purabgaon, Gaderi, Ramgarh, Dehara, Chaturbhujpur, Maharajpur, Naraini, Agahar, Mahmoodpur, Saidpur, Kakawa, Kohara Village Panchayats of the Amethi Block. The village panchayat Loniapur is not having the business workers due to which the monthly income of the business workers has not been depicted in the map and mentioned as the income of the business workers is not applicable in the village panchayat Loniapur of the Amethi Block.

12.7 Average Monthly Income of the Transportation Workers

The average monthly income of the transportation workers has been computed based on the daily wage income generated or earned by the transportation workers. It has been noticed that village panchayat Loniapur has not transportation workers due to which the average monthly income of the transportation workers has not been shown in the Map 3.62. The average monthly income of the transportation workers in thousand rupees at the village panchayat level has been depicted in **Map 3.62**. It has been observed that average monthly income more than 70 thousand rupees has been recorded in Katara Maharani, Sarai Khema, Jangal Ram Nagar, Kherauna, and Ramgarh Village Panchayats of the Amethi Block. It has been noticed that average monthly income, between 40 and 70 thousands of the transportation workers has been found in Trilokpur, Bhusahari and Dehara Village Panchayats while average monthly income between 10 and 40 thousand rupees of the transportation workers has been found in Ramdaipur, Bhaganpur, Tala, Darakha, Mochawa, Nuwawan, Benipur, Mahmoodpur, Parsawan, Raipur Phulwari, Katara Phulkunwar, Dedhpasar, Korari Girdharshah, Dhandhudhar, Gaderi, Purabgaon, Nainaha, Dedhpasar, Maharajpur, Agahar, Naraini, Saidpur, Kakawa, Saraiya Duban, Kohara and Mahamadpur Village Panchayats of Amethi. It has been recorded that less than 10 thousand rupees average monthly income of the transportation workers has been found in Chaturbhujpur, Loharta, Kushi Tali, Umapur Ganapatti, Gangauli, Raidaipur, Rebha, Mahaso and Hathkila village panchayats of the Amethi Block.

12.8 Average Monthly Income of the Agro-Industries Workers

The average monthly income of the small scale and agro-industries workers has been computed based on their daily wage remuneration. It has been noticed that village panchayats Kushi Tali and Loniapur do not have small scale and agro-industries workers due to which the average monthly income has not been shown in the Map. The average monthly income of the small scale and agro-industries workers at village panchayat level has been depicted in **Map 3.63**. It has been recorded that more than 20 thousand rupees average monthly income of the small scale and agro-industries workers has been found in Katara Maharani, Sarai Khema, Ramdaipur, Jangal Ram Nagar, Nuwawan, Saidpur, Mahmoodpur, Nuwawan, Dhandhudhar, Gaderi, Gangauli, Bhusahari, Dehara, Saidpur and Mahmadput Village Panchayats of the Amethi Block. It has been noticed that average monthly income of the small scale and agro-industries workers between 15 and 20 thousand rupees has been found in Trilokpur, Kherauna, Katara Phulkunwar, Hathkila, Dedhpasar, Raidaipur and Maharajpur Village Panchayats of the Amethi Block. Average monthly income between 10 and 15 thousand of the small scale and agro-industries workers has been noticed in Tala, Himmatgarh, Ramgarh, Naraini and Kohara village panchayats of the Amethi Block. The average monthly income, less than 10 thousand rupees of the small scale and agro-industries workers has been found in the Bhaganpur, Umapur Ganapatti, Benipur, Mahmoodpur, Parsawan, Raipur Phulwari, Rebha, Mahaso, Korari Girdharshah, Loharta, Darakha, Mochawa, Purabgaon, Nainaha, Chaturbhujpur, Agahar, Kakawa and Saraiya Duban Village Panchayats of the Amethi Block.

The average monthly income of the various workers of Amethi has been insignificantly and very nominal than the per day wages fixed the labour norms of Government. The very poor income of the workers has forced the people of Amethi to survive hand to mouth. The low income of the people of Amethi has forced them to pass their life in economic hardship. The economic hardship of the poor people of Amethi has led to economic backwardness. The average monthly income of the cultivators of Amethi has been noticed 415.95 lakh rupees and agricultural workers average monthly income has been recorded 135.78 lakh rupees for the Amethi Block. It has been recorded that average monthly income of the non-skilled workers has been 92-75 lakh rupees upgradation of the skill to ensure quantity production which should less labour oriented but increasing the productivity with the view to increase the workers per day income and improving the economic conditions of the resourceless, ignorant, deprived, rural poor workers of Amethi.

13. CONCLUSION

The agriculture is the backbone of the economy of Amethi. The agriculture is the main occupation of the peoples of Amethi. The deteriorated fertility status of the soil and inappropriate agricultural inputs has caused very poor agricultural productivity which has led to very poor economy of the peoples of Amethi. The ignorance, and socio-economic backwardness and small size of land holdings of the farmers has also been responsible for the poor agricultural productivity of the area. It is known fact that after the Zamindari Abolition the excess land lying waste has been allotted to the landless workers due to which the most of the population of Amethi has less than one hectare of the land, i.e. very small size of land holdings while large size of land has been concentrated among very nominal cultivators. The average monthly income of the skilled workers of

Amethi has been 102.43 lakh rupees, which has been very nominal and poor income of the deprived resourceless poor workers of Amethi. The average monthly income of the animal husbandry workers has been recorded 1370 thousand rupees and the average monthly income of the business workers has been found 1136 thousand rupees of the Amethi Block. Thus, it has been observed that very low average monthly income of the transportation workers has been observed 1241 thousand rupees and the average monthly income of the small scale and agro-industries workers has been noticed 513 thousand rupees for the whole Amethi which has been very low wages as per the wage rates fixed by the Government.

In view of the above, it has become an important task of the policy-makers and planners to propagate and demonstrate the latest developed scientific-techniques and tools, equipments, machinery and new system for ensuring the quality production by the workers and also imparting training for the skill development and among the limited land holders of Amethi.

Village Information System and the management of economic infrastructural data collection, collation and analysis have been ensured at the village panchayat level in Amethi. The collection of the Economic Resources Data Management System has been visualized in a network based notes covering Village-Block-District Panchayat. The innovation of economic infrastructural data base has been popularized to promote existing abilities to initiate more activities in a better and faster system for the collection, collation of the available resources of the data base. The major constraints in the large scale economic process of planning has been non-availability of appropriate data base at the grassroots level. The economic development of an area should be through tapping the local talent, and available economic infrastructural resources at the village level in order to ensure sustainable planning for the integrated development. In view of the above an attempt has been made in this study to innovate and analyse the available economic infrastructural data and develop information system for the policy makers and the village development planners engaged in the implementation of the integrated rural development programmes at the village level.

The land ownership pattern of Amethi has been diversified the large size land has been concentrated among very few land holders. The land concentration in Amethi has adversely affected the agricultural productivity of Amethi. It has been observed that very insignificant and nominal number of thouseholds has been the owners of large size land holdings at village panchayat level in Amethi. The good quality, fertile land are owned by the large size landholders and the small size landholders owning very nominal lands has been the wastelands, which has the deteriorated fertility status of soil and very poor agricultural productivity and providing very low income to the resourceless poor cultivators of Amethi. The small size of land holdings and deteriorated fertility status of the soil has caused poor agricultural productivity, hence forth it has caused economic backwardness for the peoples surviving in the remote rural areas of Amethi.

The irrigation has been an important agricultural input for producing agricultural crops. The irrigational facilities in Amethi has been in appropriate. The irrigational facilities as an agricultural input plays an important role in maintaining the fertility status of the soil for increasing agricultural productivity and also improves the moistures retaining capacity of the soil. It has been noticed that the existing sources of irrigation and available net irrigated area in Amethi has been improper and insufficient in Amethi. The over irrigation and excess canal water has adversely affected the net cultivated area leading to usarization, waterlogging and deterioration of the fertility status of the soil and caused for poor agricultural productivity. The planned scientific irrigational system as per the need of the soil and agricultural crops may be implemented through peoples participation. The canal irrigation and over irrigation of the agricultural crops and proper construction of the drainage system for the removal of excess irrigated water and rainy water has to be ensured to check the growth of wastelands. The Government Tube-well and Tube-well irrigation system may be promoted and propogated to check the water logging and also control the usarization of the soil. An effort must be initiated to develop rain water harvesting systems to provide good quality irrigation for increasing the agricultural productivity and maintaining the deteriorated fertility status of the soil. The techno-scientific and appropriate irrigational system as per the soil and agricultural crops requirements must be propogated, popularized and the cultivators/farmers should be motivated and trained for optimum utilization of available irrigational and natural rain water resources.

Amethi is a rice bowl of the area and rice has been the main agricultural food grain crop having 2170 hectares agricultural land. The matiyar soil and low-lying, waterlogged land has facilitated appropriate agro-climatic favourable conditions for the Paddy/ Jadhan/Dhan/Rice foodgrain cropping in Amethi. Wheat has been an important foodgrain crop in Amethi has 1701 hectares wheat cropped area in Amethi. The area under 446 hectares agricultural land under the peas as pulse crop while the mustard oil seed crop has 824 hectares cropping in Amethi. The sugarcane area has been only 33 hectares in Amethi, while the potato a vegetabe crop has been cultivated in the 509 hectares land in Amethi. The fodder has been an important cattle feed which has been cultivated by the animal owners, the total area under fodder crop has been recorded 264 hectares agricultural land in Amethi. The policy planners and the agricultural scientist, soil scientists and agricultural extension workers to promote, propogate, motivate and practically demonstrate for the optimum utilization of the available agricultural land, water, wasteland resources and also to conserve the available wastelands for agricultural productivity to meet the ever increasing demand of growing population for meeting fuel wood, fodder, fibre, fruits, foodgrains, fisheries (F^6) and vegetable.

The ignorance and adopted traditional techno-scientific agricultural practices has reduced poor agricultural productivities. The proper application of insecticides and pesticides and organic and inorgtanic amendments may be helpful in increasing the agricultural productivity. The Government facilities especially the plant protection and the control of insects and pests have not been properly applied in the agricultural crops which have not only affected the crops but also adversely affected the fertility status of the soil. The appropriate proven use of insecticides and pesticides, as per the need of the agricultural crops, in a scientific system may be an asset not only in increasing the agricultural productivity but also maintaining the fertility status of the soil.

The use of chemical fertilizers has been improperly and insignificantly used in Amethi. The green manuring and compost fertilizers and organic and inorganic amendments are not properly applied as per the need of the soil to produce the crop and also to maintain the fertility status of the soil. It has been recorded that the application of the Nitrogen fertilizer has been found in the 2024 hectares agricultural cropped land. The Phosphate fertilizer has been used in the 385 hectares agricultural cropped land. The potash fertilizer has been used in the 76 hectares of the Amethi Block. The organic and inorganic inappropriate and insignificant use of the chemical fertilizers have caused poor agricultural productivity and also deteriorated the fertility status of the soil. The soil testing has not been carried out to know the requirement of the soil to produce the agricultural crops. The green manuring of the agricultural land must be ensured for the proper conservation of the cropping land. It has been recorded that the compost fertilizer has been applied in the 945 hectares in Amethi. The scientific and appropriate need based demonstration of the use of organic and inorganic amendments, green manuring of the land and compost fertilizer including *Gobar khad* must be ensured through people's participation to increase the agricultural productivity and to fulfil the slogan of the Government for the *"Adhik Ann Upjao"* or *"Produce more Foodgrains"*.

The use of bio-gas has been very insignificantly used in Amethi. It has been recorded that there are 359 bio-gas plants installed and functional in Amethi. The proper use of available cow dung and animal's *gobar* should be utilized through the bio-gas plants for availing cooking gas and the compost fertilizer with the view to improve the fertility status of the soil and also to conserve the environmental conditions of Amethi.

The agricultural implements plays an important role in increasing the agricultural productivity of the land. The old, traditional agricultural implements are time taking, inefficient for ensuring quality agricultural activities. The latest developed scientific and technically proven agricultural implements are efficient, sufficient, effective in performing the quick agricultural practices but the high-tech, scientific agricultural implements are costly and beyond the reach of the deprived, resourceless, rural poor agricultural cultivators of the Amethi Block. The proper scientific and technical demonstration of the high-tech agricultural implements may increase the agricultural productivity of the Amethi Block. It has been noticed that 1249 wood cultivators and 348 iron cultivators are used in the Amethi Block. There are 109 high-tech cultivators used in Amethi and 124 high-tech agricultural implements/machinery, etc. are used by the large size land holders in the Amethi Block. It has been recorded that there are 362 tractors used for the land cultivation and other agricultural activities including transportation of the agricultural and commercial commodities. It has been noticed that other high-tech 99 agricultural implements/equipments are used in the Amethi Block. It has been recorded that small size land holders and weaker cultivators has been using traditional agricultural implements and large size land holders and rich cultivators are applying the high-tech scientific and latest developed agricultural implements for ensuring quantity and quality of agricultural production at the grassroots level in Amethi.

Animal husbandry has been an important source of income generation for the down-trodden deprived animal husbandry workers in Amethi. It has been recorded that there are 5273 cows, 3233 buffalowes, 1716 goats and 222 horses in the Amethi Block. It has been noticed that there are 575 pigs, 1032 hens/cocks in the Amethi Block.

It has been observed that the traditional cows/buffalowes are kept by the deprived poor people like Yadavs and others while rich and large size land holding persons are keeping hybrid and inseminized cows and buffalowes which produce more milk and are economically viable. The pigs are kept by the Scheduled Caste people and hens/cocks are kept by Muslims and others for availing eggs and chickens for their household use. The economy through animal husbandry activities has been very nominal and insufficient income generation. The inseminization of the existing milking animals like cows, buffalowes and goats should be promoted and scientific promotion of pigs and hens/cocks should be promoted with the view to increase quality and quantity production to increase the income and generate employment of the deprived animal husbandry workers.

The average income of the workers of Amethi has been found insufficient, for ensuring the livelihood of the common people of Amethi. The average monthly income of the cultivators has been estimated 415.95 lakh rupees and agricultural workers monthly income has been recorded rupees 135.78 lakhs and non-skilled workers monthly income 92.75 lakhs rupees and skilled workers monthly income rupees 102.43 lakh has been recorded for Amethi.

It has been observed that the average monthly income of the animal husbandry workers has been found 1370 thousand rupees, business workers' monthly average income has been found 1136 thousand rupees and the transportation workers average monthly income has been noticed 1241 thousand ruppes and the average monthly income of the small scale and agro-industries workers has been found 513 thousand rupees for the Amethi Block.

In view of the above, it has become an important task of the policy-makers and planners to propogate, promote and demonstrate the latest developed technologies, tools, equipments, machinery and scientific system for ensuring the quantity and quality production through participation of the workers. The special skill development training programmes for the skill upgradation of the workers to ensure quality and quantity production should be ensured which should be less labour oriented but it can increase the productivity with the view to increase the daily wages income of the workers and generate employment and increase the income of the resourceless, deprived rural poor workers living in hardship, hand to mouth, surviving in the remote rural areas.

4

Institutional Infrastructure

1. INTRODUCTION

Institutional Infrastructure available in an area plays an important role in the integrated village development. The available institutional infrastructure plays a key role in planning process. The integrated approach of planning process, requires detail knowledge of the inter-relations and inter-dependencies between various sectoral indicators, to resolve often conflicting requirements and available institutional infrastructure at the grassroots level. Therefore, it becomes necessary to analyse the available institutional infrastructure at the village level. The available institutional infrastructural resources may provide a base for the plan formulation of common minimum need based requirements of the downtrodden deprived rural poor multitudes and ensuring the peoples participation for sustainable development, because the formulated plans without people's participation and without incorporating the needs of the local people, the planning process cannot be made successful. Therefore, the available institutional infrastructural resources must be considered before initiation of the planning process at the grassroots level or at village panchayat level in the Amethi Block. In view of the above, an attempt has been made in this study to analyse the available institutional infrastructural resources at the village Panchayat level because the developed and established institutional infrastructural resources plays a vital role and supports as a back bone for the initiation and formulation of the planning process at the village panchayat level.

2. INSTITUTIONAL INFRASTRUCTURAL RESOURCES DATA MANAGEMENT SYSTEM (IIRDMS)

It has been realized that there is largest known tradition of systematically collection of spatial institutional infrastructural data through various institutions at macro level. Several line departments has been engaged in the collection of Non-Spatial Data in a strong traditional system. The Government has emphasized on the management of the spatial data base for efficient and effective local level area specific development planning. The management of institutional infrastructural data base is a multi-disciplinary and multi-institutional, Research and Development programme with a vision to provide an appropriate scientific and technological inputs for operationalizing the concept of decentralized integrated village development planning. The main objectives of the development of institutional infrastructural resources are to develop scientific data base approach to support the local level area specific village development planning. Various efforts have been made to evolve and develop institutional infrastructural resources spatial data management technologies for integrated village development planning and its demonstration in the local level decision-making process. In the context of institutional infrastructural resources data management system, any institutional resource which is important for local area development is relevant for this study.

Institutional Infrastructural Resources Data Management System has been focusing on the technological and institutional capacity building in a multi-level framework, so that the people utilizing the local resources, can utilize for the area specific development planning, institutional infrastructure available at the grassroots level has been helpful for its potential utilization and generating alternative scenarios for integrated village development planning at village level.

In spite of the macro level efforts, a large segment of end users are yet to explore the full potential of the system and its optimum utilization in the planning activities because the policy planning and implementing institutions lack the technical organizational and institutional capacity. To reduce the impediments in the widespread use of the technologies and make it an effective tool in the process of local level integrated development planning. Institutional infrastructural resources Data management focuses in the research and development for simplifying the methods and techniques for collection of the data, collation and analysis of the collected information and to device suitable strategies to transfer the techniques for its adoption by the end users in the planning system.

In view of the recent trends in the development of spatial data technologies, the emerging changes in the system of the formulation of the need based planning process and institutionalization of the available informations at grassroots level, to meet the aspirations of the grassroots level users and in the support of the overall transformation in the concept of information sharing the felt needs for refocusing the research and development thrusts of developing Village Information System and collection, collation and the analysis of the available institutional infrastructural resources at the Village Panchayat level.

An attempt has been made in this study to analyse the available institutional infrastructural resources existing at the Village Panchayat level in Amethi. An effort has been made to develop spatial data management system and analyzing techniques for incorporation of existing institutional infrastructural resources available at grassroots level. It has been attempted to develop advanced technology applications in the large scale spatial data collection, collation of the data at the Village Panchayat level. Effort has been made to explain the transfer of technology and capacity building programmes for the micro-level policy planners and the implementing institutions at the Village Panchayat level in Amethi.

It has been visioned to enable the people, societies, communities and institutions of self-governance with spatial data technologies through sustained people's participation in the decision making for the integrated village development planning. The main objectives of this study are to strengthen the science and technology inputs for integrated institutional resource management through development of appropriate tools and techniques in the data collection, collation and its analysis for policy planning for the integrated village development. Necessary initiatives has been ensured for the technical capacity building at various levels of administrative, i.e. Village Panchayat-Block Panchayat-District Panchayat for enabling the adoption of the technologies developed in the integrated village development planning.

In view of the above an attempt has been made in this study to analyse the spatial data technologies Institution Infrastructural Resources for micro-level planning.

In order to implement at least some of the institutional infrastructure related activities with the vision of Village Information System and collection, collation of the grassroots level data support from a large segment of the scientists and entrepreneurs are required. It is expected to stimulate the imagination of the research community to relate specific problems in their areas of interests and evolve suitable research proposals to persue line of investigation and imagination of the research community to relate specific problems in the related fields, and to arrive at meaningful solutions of the problems as well as in advancing the existing knowledge in certain spheres of the micro-level planning activities, thereby adding to the overall integrated village development planning.

In view of the above the Government has constituted such local level institutions with definite mandate to collect revenues, draw up and implement integrated development programmes. It requires capacity building at the institutions of local self-governance to prepare and implement local specific integrated village development programmes by assessing and utilizing the available institutional infrastructural resources at the grassroots level. The formulation of the need base policy planning and implementation of the rural development programmes has been an information intensive task. In this study an effort has been made to analyse the institutional infrastructural resources developed by the Village Panchayat-Block Panchayat-District Panchayat to analyse the responsibilities and activities carried out by the Village Pradhan-Block Pramukh-Chairman (District Development Committee) District Panchayat.

3. PANCHAYATI RAJ

It has been realized that commendable advances have been made in the diverse field of rural development programmes, would in reality may be incomplete because such rural development programmes failed to translate into better and dignified life for the majority of the people surviving in the remote rural areas. The appropriate and faster development of the rural areas are required to fulfil the ever increasing demand of growing population.

It has been felt that the development should be participatory and it should be planned according to the local needs of the resourceless deprived rural poor multitudes. The development should be planned through tapping local level available institutional infrastructural resources in order to make the implemented rural development programme self-sustainable. It has been noticed that various rural development programmes are being implemented aiming at sustainable development of the rural areas, with a focus on enhancing the livelihoods of weakers and vulnerable sections of the society. In confirmity with the commitment to accord foremost priority to rural development, a number of steps have been initiated to make the implementation of on going programmes more effective, efficient and accelerated.

The implementation of various rural development programmes can be made more effective through sustained people's participation. Thus the rural development should be for the people, and it should be implemented, maintained and sustained through the village people. The participatory planning of the need based programmes and integrated development should be initiated at the grassroots level.

It has been mentioned in the Constitution of India that, "*Government should evolve methods to unite the Village Panchayat and provide such powers and rights, which can be helpful to work out as an unit of the Self-Government.*"

Institutional changes has been brought to implement this strategy through the *73rd* and *74th Constitutional Amendments Act* (1992 and 1993). The State Governments were empowered from the instituitions of Local Self Governance right from the Village level-Block level-District level and within the Municipal jurisdiction in Village Panchayats and Nagar Palikas in the context of rural and urban development respectively. The Eleventh and Twelfth Schedules of the Constitution while specifying the sectors for the Panchayats have also defined the role for the multi-level institutions of Governance in the Planning and Implementation of the Integrated Rural Development Programmes. The State Governments have accordingly constituted the local level bodies with definite mandates to collect revenues, to formulate need based action plan and implement the integrated village development programmes. It requires capacity building at instutions of local level self-governance to prepare and implement area specific integrated village development programmes by assessing and utilizing the local level available institutional infrastructural resources.

It has been stated by Mahatma Gandhi ji that, *"In the Panchayati Raj System each village should be self-sustained and independent, the implementation of welfare programmes of rural masses, can be implemented in a better manner in the villages of vast rural India."*

In view of the above, as per the policy of the Government of India, the State Government of Uttar Pradesh established Self-Government in the rural areas. Historical and revolutionary decisions have been taken to allot the work, to allocate the financial resources to implement the planned programmes and allocated the financial and administrative rights to provide the Self-Governance to the Village Panchayat-Block Panchayat-District Panchayat.

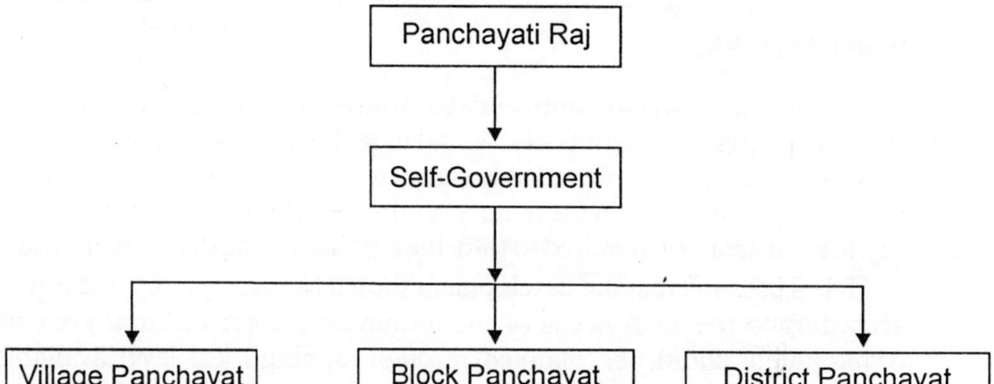

The grassroots level or micro level development unit shall be the Village Panchayat including the revenue villages and Tolas/Purawas/Hamlet villages. In this system of decentralization village shall be the central focal point for the development. In reality, it will be meaningful exercise to transfer this in the integrated planning and development schemes, its control and management should be ensured through people's participation. The formulation of plan and the planning process should be initiated from the bottom to top, i.e. Village Panchayat level-Block Panchayat level-District Panchayat level. After Independence first of all revolutionary steps of decentralization has been started with the view to bring total changes in the life of rural poor villagers and also to provide a new era for integrated development of the rural areas.

The real meaning of democracy is the importance of the people and people's participation in the planning process and implementaion of the planned programmes. The self-government is the main sole of village development. The governmance, management, finanacial and administrative control of village Panchayat and continued participation and co-operation for establishing Village Panchayat—for Self-Government, for the formulation of people participatory planning and implementation of various village development programmes for self-sustenance and socio-economic development of the village people.

The Government has allocated the rights, administrative and financial powers to the Village Panchayat, Block Panchayat and District Panchayat for the implementation and maintenance of assets created at the grassroots level through people's participation.

Village Panchayat has been allocated education, tube-wells, hand pumps, youth welfare, medical, health, women and child development, animal, agriculture, food supply, Panchayati Raj, rural development and all types of pensions and scholarships.

Block Panchayats has been allocated rural development, primay health centres, animal hospitals, seed and marketing centres, to look the additional village's activities and maintenance of the created assets.

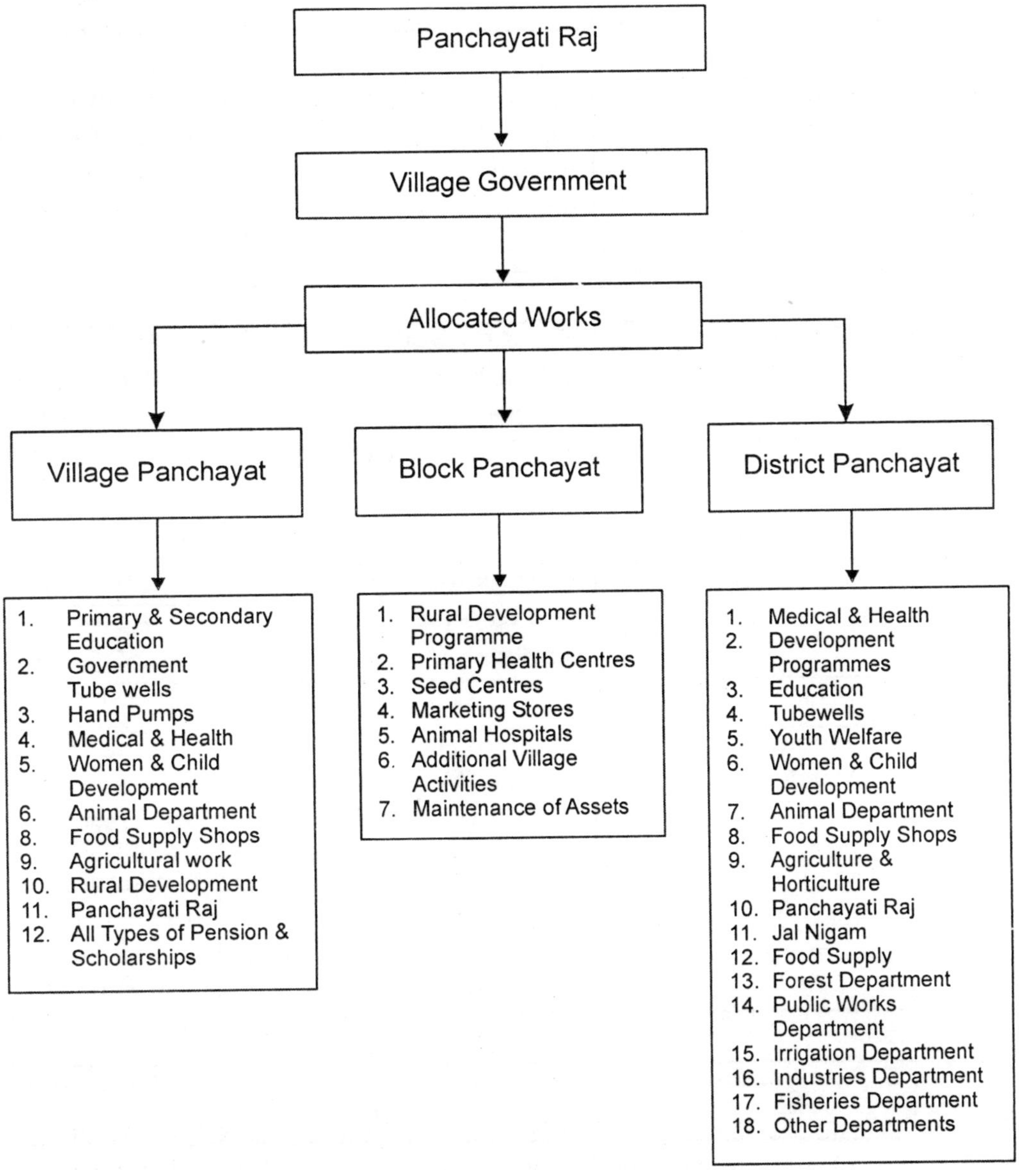

District Panchayat has been allocated Medical and Health, Development programmes, Tube-wells, Youth Welfare, Women and Child development, Animal, Agriculture and Horticulture Department, Food Supply shops, Panchayati Raj, Jal

Nigam, Food Supply, Forest and Public Works Departments, Irrigation Department, Fisheries Department and other departments.

The Government has also formed various committees to work and the Village Panchayat-Block Panchayat-District Panchayat. The Chairmen of these committees are elected by the respective Panchayats. The main important committees, their works and the constitution of these committees are illustrated below—

Committees of Panchayats

Committees	Allocated Works	Composition of Committee
1. Planning and Development	Plan Formulation & Agriculture, and poverty Alleviation programmes	1. Chairman 2. 6 other Members (one member each from S.G., DBG & Women)
2. Education	Primary, Secondary Education, Information, Educational Literacy etc.	1. Chairman 2. 4 other Members 3. Head Master 4. 3 Guardians
3. Construction	All construction works and to ensure quality works	1. Chairman 2. 4 other Members (SC, OBC & Women)
4. Health, Welfare	Medical Health, Family Welfare, Women & Child Development, Social Welfare, S.C., B.C., Minorities Classes Development Programmes	1. Chairman 2. 4 other Members (SC, OBC & Women)
5. Administrative	Personnel Staff related all works	1. Chairman 2. 4 other Members

The District Rural Development Agency (DRDA) has been reconstituted, i.e. Chairman, DRDA at present is the Chairman District Panchayat. In the Governing Body of DRDA 5 Additional Members are included, viz. Chairman of the 5 Standing Committees of the District Panchayat. The District Fisheries Development Agency is chaired by the Chairman. District Panchayat and 5 Chairmen of the Standing Committees of the District Panchayat.

The Chairman of the Sinchai Bandhu is the Member of the District Panchayat. Various rural development schemes are being implemented through Financial support from the Government by the Chief Development Officer (CDO) through the District Rural Development Agency (DRDA) in which various District Level implementing line departments are transferred under the control and supervision of the District Panchayats.

District Planning Committee has been formulated which is chaired by the nominated Minister by the State Government and the Chairman, District Panchayat as its Vice-Chairman and the District Magistrate. Local Body Chairman is the Vice-Chairman of Zila Yojana Samiti and Members of Parliament, Members of Legislative Assembly are the permanent Members of Zila Yojana Samiti. Chief Executive Officer is the Member Secretary and District Economics and Statistical offices, is the Joint Secretary of the District Planning Committee and other members are nominated by the Government. Village-Block-District Plan is formulated every year. Thus the decentralization system of the Government, i.e. Self-Government, i.e. from Village-Block, District Panchayat has been ensured and the Panchayats have been provided administrative and financial rights for the formulation of various village development programmes through people's participation and implementation of the need based planned programmes and ensuring the implemented village development programmes self-sustained under the Panchayati Raj System.

4. INSTITUTIONAL INFRASTRUCTURE

The institutional infrastructure plays an important role in policy planning for the integrated village development. The area specific integrated village development policy plan formulation requires assessment and the utilization of the already available institutional infrastructure at the grassroots level or village panchayat level.

The people's participatory need based integrated village development formulation of the policy planning should be initiated through tapping local level available institutional infrastructural resources, in order to make the already implemented rural development programmes more sustainable. An attempt has been made in this study to analyse the drinking water facilities available at the Village Panchayat level in Amethi. The established small scale industries and Agro-Industries distributed at the Village Panchayat level in Amethi has been explained. The sources of energy including the non-conventional sources of energy and the household-wise connections of the electricity consumption including the commercial use of the electricity has been analyzed at the grassroots level in Amethi. The constructed road including the National High Ways, Pucca Road, Kharanza Road, Kuchcha Road, etc. has been analysed at the Village Panchayat level in Amethi. The religious and historical infrastructures available at Village Panchayat level including religious Temples, historical buildings etc. have been analysed. It has been recorded that the Panchayat Bhawan an important institutional infrastructure has been constructed at every Village Panchayat in Amethi Block. The established Anganwadi Kendra, Assistant Nursing Midwife Centres and Post Offices facilities available at Village Panchayat level in Amethi has been explained. The transportation facilities including the Bus, Jeep, Tempo etc. has been analysed at the Village Panchayat level in Amethi. The established functional educational infrastructures, Animal Hospitals, Medical Health Centres, Banking infrastructures, the Hindus Temples, Muslim's Masjid, Idgah and Telecommunication facilities available at the Village Panchayat level in Amethi has been explained. The

Table 4.25: Institutional Infrastructure—Amethi Block

Sl. No.	Villages	Water Supply (No. of Houses)	India Mark-II Hand Pumps	Hand Pumps	Other Sources of Drinking Water	Small Scale and Agro-Industries	Low Cost Houses	Non-Conventional Source of Energy	House Hold Electricity	Commercial Electricity
1	2	3	4	5	6	7	8	9	10	11
1.	Katra Maharani	–	25	190	10	4	6	10	205	4
2.	Sarai Khema	10	145	300	8	11	8	10	435	15
3.	Trilokpur	–	55	105	5	3	6	10	315	5
4.	Ramdaipur	23	60	145	7	11	10	20	800	12
5.	Jangal Ram Nagar	25	125	385	20	15	16	20	900	20
6.	Benipur	–	15	45	5	2	6	10	110	4
7.	Parsawan	–	45	115	8	7	10	10	200	10
8.	Mahmoodpur	–	50	115	14	6	10	8	220	10
9.	Raipur Fulwari	16	65	115	7	8	10	8	120	8
10.	Umapur Ganapatti	16	55	125	4	6	8	7	225	6
11.	Bhaganpur	–	45	120	3	6	10	6	120	6
12.	Tala	–	80	130	4	2	10	10	159	5
13.	Kushi Tali	8	55	105	7	6	5	15	130	15
14.	Loharta	–	25	120	3	4	10	5	120	10
15.	Darkha	15	55	120	4	6	15	20	220	12
16.	Mochwa	20	65	170	8	10	10	15	250	16
17.	Nuwawan	10	35	145	8	6	8	10	235	10
18.	Loniapur	10	40	110	8	6	8	12	170	8
19.	Kherauna	25	65	225	8	5	10	15	330	10
20.	Katra Phulkunwar	–	55	140	7	9	9	10	190	15
21.	Hathkila	15	40	80	5	3	4	9	210	7
22.	Rebha	15	45	125	4	5	8	15	175	8
23.	Raidaipur	8	105	230	17	—	4	9	180	6
24.	Korari Girdharshah	50	70	350	10	15	20	20	390	20
25.	Dedhpasar	10	35	280	3	8	9	20	290	13
26.	Mahaso	–								
27.	Gangauli	25	45	125	7	7	8	21	175	12
28.	Dhadhudhar	–	60	135	4	9	10	10	180	8
29.	Gaderi	20	55	165	5	11	20	15	380	7
30.	Bhusahari	15	40	130	3	7	20	15	180	10
31.	Purabgaon	—	40	135	5	6	8	10	160	5
32.	Chaturbhujpur	15	40	115	3	4	5	10	80	5
33.	Mahrajpur	5	35	125	4	3	10	10	80	10
34.	Aghar	20	45	148	36	5	10	16	150	12
35.	Saidpur	25	40	170	3	6	9	17	180	10
36.	Kakwa	40	60	125	10	16	15	18	420	20
37.	Saraiya Duban	—	35	180	3	10	10	22	180	15
38.	Kohra	—	65	143	3	10	10	10	525	20
39.	Mahmadpur	20	60	200	7	14	15	15	490	16
40.	Naraini	20	80	345	10	9	15	10	580	13
41.	Nainaha	—	45	390	10	15	10	25	381	18
42.	Ramgarh	30	65	190	10	9	10	22	510	14
43.	Himmatgarh	—	35	190	4	8	9	20	280	12
44.	Dehara	—	65	290	8	5	6	15	280	10
	Amethi Block	**499**	**2380**	**7326**	**262**	**319**	**430**	**595**	**12190**	**478**

constructed, established and maintained institutional infrastructures at the Village Panchayat level plays a vital key role before initiation of the policy plan formulation at the grassroots level, through peoples participation to ensure quality work and sustenance of the implemented works. Thus the importance of the institutional infrastructures already available at the Village Panchayat level must be protected an maintained successfully for the purpose for which it has been constructed.

The available infrastructures related to institutional resources provide a base for the formulation of the common minimum needs of the resourceless, downtrodden deprived rural poor multitudes and ensuring the people's participation and the incorporation of the existing institutional infrastructural resources in the policy planning for integrated village development may be an asset and helpful in the successful implementation of the planned village development programmes through ensuring proper maintenance and management of the completed rural development programmes, to ensure its self-sustenance.

An effort has been made in this study to analyze the available institutional infrastructures constructed and established at the grassroots level, i.e. Village Panchayat level in the Amethi Block. The major and important institutional infrastructures available at the Village Panchayat level data have been collected, collated and analyzed in this study but there are several other institutional infrastructures and other resources which are not visible directly or indirectly have not been incorporated, in this study due to some reason or the other, also plays an important role, in deciding the further scope for the integrated village development.

The important common minimum social amenities required for the day-to-day life of the downtrodden resourceless poor deprived multitudes have been incorporated in this study like water, communication, health, education and various other institutional infrastructural resources have been selected for analysing the impact of institutional infrastructures available at the Village Panchayat level in Amethi.

5. DRINKING WATER

The drinking water is one of the most important requirements for the survival of the human being. The availability of the good quality drinking water protects the health hazard problems of the common people. It has been observed that traditionally and historically the drinking water facilities have been availed through dugwells, later on the Kuchcha dugwells was made Puccawells. The drinking waters fetched from the wells has been found of good quality drinking water but later on the excessive use of the chemical fertilizers, use of insecticides and pesticides and over irrigation through canal irrigation has contaminated and polluted the underground water. It has led to the health hazards and created various water borne diseases among the resourceless deprived rural poor people surviving in the remote rural areas. In view of the contaminated drinking water available through wells, Government has launched various programmes to provide good quality drinking water facilities to the resourceless rural poors. The tap water supply has been made available in most of the villages which are highly populated and conjusted settlements. The India Mark-II Hand Pumps have been installed at all the Village Panchayats covering associated revenue villages along with the Tolas/Purwas/Hamlet villages. The special financial supports have been made available through Members of Parliament's Local Area Development Fund (MP-LAD) and Members of Legislative Assembly Local Area Development fund (MLA-LAD) and District Rural Development Agency (DRDA) and District Panchayat-Block Panchayat-Village Panchayats. Various other sources provided financial support to promote the Drinking Water Mission programmes with the view to provide good quality drinking water facilities at the grassroots level or village Panchayat level in Amethi. The village people who has not been covered under the good quality drinking water mission have attempted and installed their own Private Hand Pumps to obtain the facilities of the drinking water for their household members. Exceptionally very nominal households are still obtaining the drinking water through wells. In view of the above an attempt has been made in this study to analyse the distribution of water supply through various sources of the drinking water supply at the Village Panchayat level in Amethi.

5.1 Water Supply

The tap water supply for the drinking water for the village people has been made available in most of the villages of the Amethi Block except few villages. The drinking water supply through tap water has not been made available in Katara Maharani, Trilokpur, Benipur, Parsawan, Mahmoodpur, Bhaganpur, Tala, Loharata, Katara Phulkunwar, Mahaso, Dhadhudhar, Purabgaon, Saraiya Duban, Kohara, Nainaha, Himmatgarh and Dehara Village Panchayats of the Amethi Block. It has been recorded that more than 30 households have been facilitated through tap drinking water supply has been found in Kakawa, Ramgarh and Korari Girdharshah Village Panchayats of the Amethi Block.

The tap water supply among the households at Village Panchayat level in Amethi has been depicted in **Map 4.64.** The distribution of drinking water at Village Panchayats level in the Amethi Block has been mentioned in Table 4.25. It has been noticed that there are 20 and 30 households, facilitated tap drinking water supply has been found in Ramdaipur, Jangal Ram Nagar, Kherauna, Mochawa, Gaderi, Gangauli, Naraini, Agahar and Saidpur Village Panchayats of the Amethi Block. It has been observed that 10 to 20 households who have been provided tap drinking water facility has been found in Sarai Khema, Umapur, Ganapatti, Raipur Phulwari, Darakha, Chaturbhujpur, Hathkila, Nuwawan, Loniapur, Dedhpasar, Rebha, Bhusahari, Chaturbhujpur Village Panchayats of the Amethi Block. It has been observed than less than 10 households being facilitated tap drinking water supply has been found in Kushi Tali, Raidaipur, and Mahrajpur Village Panchayats of the Amethi Block. Thus it has been recorded that only 499 households have been facilitated tap drinking water supply in the various Village Panchayats of the Amethi Block. Thus it is very unfortunate to learn that most of the families or households are still deprived of the tap drinking water facility in the various Village Panchayats of the Amethi Block. Therefore, an attempt must be ensured to provide tap drinking water facilities in the all Village Panchayats of the Amethi Block.

5.2 India Mark-II Hand Pumps

India Mark-II hand pumps have been installed by the various Government agencies including District Rural Development Agency (DRDA) and Members of Parliament Local Area Development Fund and Members of Legislative Assembly Local Area Development Fund and various other organisations to fulfil the increasing demand of the good quality drinking water facility at the village level. The distribution of the India Mark-II Hand Pumps at village panchayat level has been mentioned in Table 4.25. The distribution of the India Mark-II Hand Pumps varies from the village panchayat to another based on the population and number of households and need of the people and also support from the Village Pradhan, Block Pramukh, Chairman and Members of the Zila Panchayat and also the Members of Parliament and Members of the local Village Panchayats for sanction and installation of the India Mark-II hand pumps in their interested places. The distribution of the India Mark-II hand pumps at village panchayat level have been depicted in **Map. 4.65**. It has been recorded that more than 80 India Mark-II hand pumps have been installed in Sarai Khema, Jangal Ram Nagar, Tala, Raidaipur, and Naraini Village Panchayats of the Amethi Block. It has been noticed that the installation of India Mark-II hand pumps between 60 and 80 hand pumps has been found in the Ramdaipur, Raipur Phulwari, Kherauna, Korari Girdharshah, Mochawa, Kohara and Mahmoodpur Village Panchayats of the Amethi Block. It has been noticed that the installation of India Mark-II hand pumps between 40 and 60 pumps has been found in Trilokpur, Bhaganpur, Kushi Tali, Umapur Ganapatti, Darakha, Loniapur, Rebha, Mahmoodpur, Parsawan, Katara Phulkunwar, Hathkila, Rebha, Gangauli, Bhusahari, Gaderi, Purabgaon, Nainaha, Chaturbhujpur, Agahar and Saidpur Village Panchayats of the Amethi Block. It has been noticed that less than 40 India Mark-II hand pumps has been recorded in Saraiya Duban, Maharajpur, Himmatgarh, Loharta, Nuwawan, Mahaso, Dedhpasar, Benipur and Katara Maharani Village Panchayats of Amethi Block. It has been observed that still there are several Purwas/Tolas/Hamlet villages, revenue villages and settlement colonies are deprived of India Mark-II hand pump drinking water facilities. In view of the above, attempts should be made by the policy planners to facilitate the installation of the India Mark-II hand pumps in the most problem oriented and contaminated drinking water settlement colonies on priority basis.

5.3 Hand Pumps

The private hand pumps has been installed by the individual household to fulfil the increasing demand of the drinking water to protect themselves from the health hazards, because these households/families could not avail the India Mark-II hand pumps from the Government agencies. The private hand pumps are technically and scientifically of the poor quality in comparison to the India Mark-II hand pumps. The distribution of private hand pumps at the village panchayat level in Amethi Block has been mentioned in Table 4.25. It has been noticed that the installation of the private hand pumps has been recorded more than the government facilitated installation of the India Mark-II hand pumps. The detailed distribution of the installed private hand pumps at village panchayat level in the Amethi Block have been depicted in **Map 4.66**. It has been recorded that more than 300 private hund pumps have been installed in Sarai Khema, Jangal Ram Nagar, Korari Girdharshah, Naraini and Nainaha village panchayats of the Amethi Block. It has been observed that the distribution of private hand pumps between 200 and 300 hand pumps has been found in Kherauna, Raidaipur, Dedhpasar, Dehara and Mahmoodpur village panchayats of the Amethi Block. It has been noticed that the distribution and installation of the private hand pumps between 100 and 200 hand pumps has been found in Katara Maharani, Trilokpur, Ramdaipur, Bhaganpur, Tala, Kushi Tali, Loharta, Darakha, Mochawa, Nuwawan, Rebha Katara Phulkunwar, Raipur Phulwari, Mahmoodpur, Parsawan, Dhandhudhar, Gangauli, Bhusahari, Himmatgarh, Ramgarh, Gaderi, Purabgaon, Chaturbhujpur, Saraiya Duban, Kohara, Kakawa and Saidpur village panchayats of the Amethi Block. It has been recorded that the distribution of the Private hand pumps less than 100 has been found in Hathkila, Benipur, and Mahaso Village Panchayats of the Amethi Block. It has been observed that the deprived of and left out families from the installation of India Mark-II hand pumps has been forced to install their personal hand pumps to obtain proper drinking water facilities. The installation of private hand pumps has been found comparatively very high which indicates that the policy planners and the government agencies should initiate installation of the India Mark-II hand pumps, at war footing level, in each settlement Colonies/ Purwas/Tolas/Hamlet villages or revenue villages to fulfil the increasing demand of the good quality drinking water facilities with the view to control the health hazard problems of the deprived rural poor multitudes surviving in the remote rural areas.

5.4 Other Sources of Drinking Water

The resourceless, deprived, helpless, hopeless families/households who could not avail the tap water facilities, installed India Mark-II hand pumps and private hand pumps are still forced and bound to avail the drinking water from the dug wells and other sources of the drinking water. The distribution of the drinking water from other sources at village panchayat level has been mentioned in Table 4.25. The distribution of the other sources of drinking water facilities at the village panchayat level in Amethi Block has been depicted in **Map 4.67**. It has been recorded that more than 15 drinking water facilities from other sources have been found in Jangal Ram Nagar and Raidaipur village panchayats of the Amethi Block. It has been noticed that the distribution of the drinking water facilities from other sources between 10 and 15 has been found in Katara Maharani, Mahmoodpur, Korari Girdharshah, Ramgarh, Nainaha, Naraini and Kokawa village panchayats of the Amethi Block. It has been observed that the distribution of the other sources of drinking water between 10 and 15 has been found in Trilokpur, Ramdaipur, Sarai Khema, Benipur, Parsawan, Raipur Phulwari, Kherauna, Katara Phul Kunwar, Hathkila, Loniapur, Mochawa, Nuwawan, Kushi Tali, Gangauli, Gaderi, Purabgaon, Dehara, and Mahmoodpur Village Panchayats of the Amethi Block. It has been observed that the other sources of drinking water facilities less than 5 have been found in Bhaganpur, Tala, Loharata, Darakha, Umapur Ganapatti, Rebha, Dedhpasar, Mochawa, Bhusahari, Himmatgarh, Dhandhudhar, Chaturbhujpur, Maharajpur, Agahar, Saidpur, Saraiya Duban and Kohara Village Panchayats of the Amethi Block. The other sources of the drinking water including wells have been recorded in Purwas/Tolas/Hamlet villages or settlement colonies belonging to the downtrodden, deprived, resourceless, landless, poor families. The government agencies should initiate on priority basis to install the India Mark II hand pumps in such settlements which are deprived of the common minimum amenities like good quality drinking water facility because the good quality drinking water support is the right of the people and the government has also been giving due attention to facilitate good quality drinking water at every level.

It has been noticed that the Tap water supply has been provided at the village panchayat level in the Amethi Block, while 2380 India Mark II hand pumps have been installed through various funding agencies which is very insufficient to fulfil the ever increasing demand of the growing population and increasing settlement colonies in the form of extension of houses as Purwas/Tolas/Hamlet villages. It has been recorded that most of the families/households have been deprived of the good quality drinking water facilities supported by the Government. The individual families/households have installed their own personal hand pumps to fetch the drinking water with the view to avail good quality drinking water facilities. It has been observed that the private hand pumps installed by the individual households are not successful because the depth of the boring of the hand pumps are not deep and the accessories installed in the hand pumps are of the poor quality due to which the contaminated water is being availed for the drinking purposes. In view of the such circumstances there are 7326 households/ families have been installed their personal/private hand pumps to avail the drinking water facilities. It is surprising to learn that there are 292 households/families in the Amethi Block who are forced to fetch the drinking water from the wells and other sources or availing the drinking water from other's hand pumps.

In view of the above, it is very unfortunate to learn that there are only 499 tap water supply to the households and 2380 installed India Mark II hand pump facilities to the families/households which is very insignificant and insufficient against the total households/families at the village panchayat level in the Amethi Block. Therefore, it has become an important task of the policy planners and the local people's representatives to provide special package for the installation of India Mark II hand pumps among the deprived, resourceless, rural poor surviving in the remote Purwas/Tolas/Hamlet villages and revenue villages of the Amethi Block.

6. SMALL SCALE AND AGRO-INDUSTRIES

The small scale and agro-industries are very insignificantly distributed in Amethi. It has been noticed that there are 319 small scale and agro-industries established in the Amethi Block. There is lack of agro-industries in the Amethi Block. The produced agricultural foodgrains, pulses and oilseeds processing is necessary for the value addition of the agricultural products and generating employment to the resourceless rural poor villagers and also increasing the income of the cultivators and unemployed rural youth at larger extent. The upgradation and establishment of the institutional infrastructure through installation of small scale industries and agro based industries must be promoted and propagated for appropriate utilization of agricultural produces and optimum utilization of available human resources at the village panchayat level in the Amethi Block. The distribution of small scale and agro-industries at village panchayat level in the Amethi Block has been mentioned in Table 4.25. The insufficient distribution and establishment of the agro-industries and small scale industries has led to economic backwardness of the people of Amethi. The small scale and agro-industries distribution at the village panchayat level has been depicted in **Map 4.68**. It has been recorded that more than 15 small scale and agro-industries have been found in Jangal Ram Nagar, Korari Girdharshah, Kakawa and Nainaha village panchayats at the Amethi Block. The distribution of the small scale and agro-industries between 10 and 15 agro-industries have been established and functional in Ramdaipur, Sarai Khema, Mochawa, Gaderi, Saraiya Duban, Kakawa and Mahmoodpur village panchayats of the Amethi Block. It has been observed that the distribution of small scale and agro-industries between 5 and 10 agro-industries has been found functional in Bhaganpur, Kushi Tali, Darakha, Nuwawan, Dhandhudhar, Umapur Ganapatti, Mahmoodpur, Parsawan, Raipur Phulwari, Kherauna, Katara Phulkunwar, Rebha, Dedhpasar, Loniapur, Gangauli, Bhusahari, Himmatgarh, Ramgarh, Dehara, Purabgaon, Naraini, Agahar and Saidpur village panchayats of the Amethi Block. It has been observed that less than 5 small scale and agro-industries have been seen in Katara Maharani, Trilokpur, Tala, Loharata, Benipur, Hathkila, Mahaso, Chaturbhujpur, and Maharajpur village panchayats of the Amethi Block. In view of the above, the installation of the small scale and agro-industries should be promoted and special package should be sanctioned for the establishment of small scale industries and agro-industries for the optimum utilization of agricultural products for its value addition and to provide appropriate value for their agricultural products on the one hand and to generate employment and increase the income of the deprived rural poor at village level in the Amethi Block.

7. LOW COST HOUSING

Low cost housing has been very insignificantly facilitated to the landless, houseless, below poverty line deprived rural poor multitudes surviving in the remote Purwas/Tolas/Hamlet villages of the Amethi Block. It has been recorded that there are only 430 low cost houses provided by the government agencies at village panchayat level in Amethi Block. The available low cost houses at village level are very insignificant against the total requirement of the houseless households or families who are surviving the mud wall and thatched roof houses which are badly ruined by the fire during the summer season and very unsuitable during rainy season. The distribution of the low cost houses at village panchayat level in Amethi has been mentioned in Table 4.25. The proportionate distribution of the low cost houses at village panchayat level has been depicted in **Map 4.69**. It has been recorded that more than 20 low cost houses have been distributed in Korari Girdharshah, Gaderi, Bhusahari village panchayats of the Amethi Block. The distribution of low cost houses between 15 and 20 houses has been found in the Jangal Ram Nagar, Darakha, Kakawa, Mahmoodpur and Naraini village panchayats of the Amethi Block. It has been observed that medium distribution of low cost houses between 10 and 15 houses have been found in Ramdaipur, Tala, Loharata, Bhaganpur, Mochawa, Dhandhudhar, Mahmoodpur, Parsawan, Raipur Phulwari, Kherauna, Ramgarh, Nainaha, Maharajpur, Agahar, Saraiya Duban and Kohara village panchayats of the Amethi Block. Very minimum less than 10 low cost houses have been found in Katara Maharani, Trilokpur, Sarai Khema, Benipur, Katara Phulkunwar, Hathkila, Dedhpasar, Rebha, Mahaso, Gangauli, Raidaipur, Loniapur, Umapur Ganapatti, Kushi Tali, Nuwawan, Himmatgarh, Dehara, Purabgaon, Chaturbhujpur and Saidpur village panchayats of the Amethi Block. In view of the above, an effort must be initiated by the policy-makers, planners and the local level people's representatives to provide special package for construction of low cost houses for the landless, houseless, below poverty line people surviving in the mud wall and thatched roof houses in the remote rural Purwas/Tolas/Hamlet villages of the Amethi Block.

8. ENERGY

The energy play an important role in the economic development and an area and also indicated and aspirations for the better quality of life of the rural poor people. The use of energy including non-conventional sources of energy, household electricity and commercial electricity consumptions at the grassroots level may play an import key role in the integrated economic development of the various villages of the Amethi Block. The proportion at distribution of the various sources of energy at the village panchayat level in Amethi Block has been mentioned in Table 4.25. An attempt has been made in this study to analyze the distribution of non-conventional sources of Energy, Household electricity consumptions and commercial electricity consumptions at the village panchayat level in Amethi Block. It has been observed that there are only 595 non-conventional sources of energy which includes mainly solar light which has been facilitated in the various village panchayats. The household electricity connections have been recorded among 12190 household electricity connection under Rajiv Gandhi Vidyutikarana Yojana and other personal level in Amethi. It has been observed that 478 commercial electricity connections for the various commercial and industrial use at village panchayat level in the Amethi Block which has been very nominal commercial electricity consumption and indicates slow rate economic development of Amethi.

8.1 Non-Conventional Sources of Energy

The non-conventional sources of energy have been very insignificantly used at the village level in Amethi. The distribution of non-conventional sources of energy including solar light and solar pumps etc. has been mentioned in Table 4.25. The proportionate distribution of non-conventional sources of energy at village panchayat level in Amethi has been depicted in **Map 4.70**. It has been observed that more than 20 non-conventional sources of energy especially solar lights etc. has ben provided in the Ramdaipur, Jangal Ram Nagar, Darakha, Dedhpasar, Korari Girdharshah, Gangauli, Himmatgarh, Ramgarh, Nainaha and Saraiya Duban village panchayats of the Amethi Block. It has been recorded that non-conventional sources of energy between 15 and 20 numbers have been found in the Kherauna, Rebha, Bhusahari, Dehara, Gaderi, Mochawa, Kushi Tali, Agahar, Mahmoodpur, Kakawa and Saidpur village panchayats of the Amethi Block. It has been noticed that non-conventional sources of energy between 10 and 15 numbers have been found in Katara Maharani, Trilokpur, Sarai Khema, Benipur, Parsawan, Katara Phulkunwar, Mahaso, Loniapur, Dhandhudhar, Nuwawan, Purabgaon, Tala, Chaturbhujpur, Maharajpur, Naraini and Kohara village panchayats. It has been recorded that less than 10 numbers of solar lights etc. and non-conventional sources of energy have been found in Bhaganpur, Loharta, Umapur Ganapatti, Mahmoodpur, Raipur, Phulwari, Hathkila, Raidaipur village panchayats of Amethi Block. In view of the electricity crisis in Amethi, it has become an important task of the policy planners and the government agencies and administrative authorities to promote and propagate for the installation of the solar lights etc. as an alternate source of energy to fulfil the increasing demand of the electricity and also to save the energy.

8.2. Household Electricity

The household/residential electricity connection has been very insignificantly distributed at village panchayat level. The distribution of the household level electricity connection at village panchayat level has been mentioned in Table 4.25. The Rajiv Gandhi Vidyutikaran Yojana has been launched but most of the Revenue Villages, Purwas, Tolas, Hamlet villages, settlement colonies are still not facilitated by the electricity while the electricity supply in Amethi has been very poor. It has been observed that more than 12 hours, there is no electricity supply at village panchayat level in Amethi Block. The distribution of household level electricity connection and consumers in number at village panchayat level in Amethi has been depicted in **Map 4.71**. It has been recorded that more than 800 number of residential/household level connections of the electricity have been found in the Ramdaipur and Jangal Ram Nagar village panchayats of the Amethi Block. The residential electricity connections between 500 and 800 household level electricity consumers have been found in Kohara, Naraini and Ramgarh village panchayats of the Amethi Block. It has been recorded that household electricity connections between 200 and 500 residential consumers of the electricity have been noticed in Katara Maharani, Trilokpur, Sarai Khema, Mahmoodpur, Parsawan, Kherauna, Katara Phul Kunwar, Hathkila, Dedhpasar, Umapur Ganapatti, Darakha, Mochawa, Nuwawan, Korari Girdharshah, Dhandhudhar, Gaderi, Gangauli, Himmatgarh, Kohara, Nainaha, Kakawa and Mahmoodpur Village Panchayats of the Amethi Block. It has been recorded that less than 200 numbers of household/residential electricity connections have been found in Bhaganpur, Tala, Kushi Tali, Loharta, Benipur, Raipur Phulwari, Loniapur, Raidaipur, Rebha, Mahaso, Bhusahari, Purabgaon, Chaturbhujpur, Maharajpur, Agahar, Saidpur and Saraiya Duban Village Panchayats of the Amethi Block.

It has been observed that there are total 12190 numbers of household/residential electricity connections at village panchayat level in Amethi which have been found comparatively insignificant against ever increasing population, number of households and growing new settlement colonies/Tolas/Purwas/Hamlet villages in Amethi Block. In view of the above, an effort must be made to facilitate all the households/families or residential houses by the residential electricity connections under the Rajiv Gandhi Grameen Vidyutikaran Yojana with the view to facilitate all the left out and deprived resourceless rural poor multitudes belonging to below poverty line families surviving in the remote rural settlement areas. An effort must be made to provide continued electricity supply not only for the agricultural activities including irrigational activities but the sustained and continued electricity should be provided as per the needs of the resourceless villagers of the Amethi Block.

8.3. Commercial Electricity

The consumption of the commercial electricity has been very insignificantly distributed at the village panchayat level in Amethi. It has been noticed that there are 478 commercial connection availed for commercial activities at village panchayat level in Amethi which has been very nominal consumption and indicates very poor economic development of the area. The detailed distribution of the commercial electricity connection at the village panchayat level has been mentioned in Table 4.25. The commercial electricity connection includes electricity supply to the shops, small scale industries, agro-industries and other agricultural activities including irrigational activities and other activities than household or residential connections. The proportionate distribution of the commercial electricity connection at village panchayat level has been depicted in **Map 4.72**. It has been recorded that more than 15 numbers of commercial electricity connections have been availed in Sarai Khema, Jangal Ram Nagar, Kushi Tali, Katara Phulkunwar, Korari Girdharshah, Mochawa, Nainaha, Kakawa, Saraiya Duban, Kohara and Mahmoodpur Village Panchayats of the Amethi Block. It has been observed that the commercial electricity having 10 to 15 numbers of connections have been found in Ramdaipur, Loharta, Darakha, Nuwawan, Mahmoodpur, Parsawan, Kherauna, Dedhpasar, Gangauli, Bhusahari, Himmatgarh, Dehara, Ramgarh, Naraini, Maharajpur, Agahar and Saidpur village panchayats of the Amethi Block. It has been noticed that 5 to 10 numbers of the commercial electricity connections has been found in Trilokpur, Bhaganpur, Tala, Umapur Ganapatti, Raipur Phulwari, Hathkila, Loniapur, Raidaipur, Rebha, Mahaso, Dhandhudhar, Gaderi, Purabgaon, Chaturbhujpur Village Panchayats of Amethi Block. It has been observed that less than 5 numbers of commercial electricity connections have been found in Katara Maharani and Benipur Village Panchayats of the Amethi Block. In view of the above, it has been observed that the commercial electricity connections have been very nominally and insignificantly distributed at the village panchayat level in Amethi.

The energy has become lifeline not only for the survival of the common man but also for the growth of an area. The ever increasing population and growing settlement colonies/Purwas/Tolas/Hamlet villages have doubled the problem of energy. The developed infrastructures in the energy sector have not been multiplied but the already available energy infrastructural system has been deteriorated due to overloading and excessive pressure, which has resulted in the deterioration and disturbances in the energy supply even in the urban areas what to say about the remote rural villages. Therefore, it has become a necessary task to promote the non-conventional sources of energy in the remote rural areas through people's participation. Need based availability of Solar light, Solar lamps, wind mills and solar water pumps etc. should be promoted and provided to the interested village people on the subsidized rates as the Petrol, Diesel, Cooking Gas and other fuel or energy sources are made available at the national level. The household or residential electricity connection as per the need of the village people should be provided and the electricity as per requirements of the agricultural activities and cropping needs and post harvest technology. The scheduled time frame electricity should be made available to avoid the wastage and misuse of the electricity in the remote rural areas. The electricity infrastructural facilities should be strengthened and maintained to avoid the mishappenings, misuse and to ensure sustained supply of the electricity in the remote rural areas because the energy has become a basic necessity for the survival of the common people. In fact, there is least commercial activity in Amethi except shops and oil, rice and *Aata Chakki* functional in most of the village panchayats for which commercial electricity connections have been obtained but the agro-industries and small scale industries in Amethi are very insignificant. The commercial electricity connections have also been provided for agricultural machinery, equipments repair and maintenance shops but it has been observed that not only the residential electricity but also the commercial electricity facilities are not provided appropriately and as per the agricultural cropping requirements due to which the agricultural work and cropping system has been oftenly disturbed and it has adversely affected the agricultural activities leading towards poor agricultural productivity. Therefore, it has become an important task of the policy-makers, planners at the grassroots level to formulate the need based planning for strengthening the energy resources especially the non-conventional sources of energy and the households electricity supply and also the commercial electricity supply the consumers located in the remote rural villages to strengthen agricultural activities at village panchayat level in Amethi.

9. ROAD

The communication plays an important role in the economic growth and an integrated development of an area. The road network including National Highways, State Highways, District level roads, including pucca roads, kuchha roads, Kharanza roads and chuk roads i.e. roads network from the National Road → State Road → District Road → Block Level Road → Village Panchayat level road → Revenue village's road and chuk road network play a key role for people's movement and also transportation facilities from the grassroots level to the urban marketing centres. Recently, it has been noticed that the State level pucca roads have been incorporated under the National Highway Authority of India and the important roads from the Block and Tehsil Headquarters of the Amethi have been connected with the National Highway road which has facilitated proper maintenance and upgradation of the roads. It has facilitated the proper movement and transportation of the roads for marketing purposes of the agricultural products from the Krishi Utpadan Mandi Samiti. The state level supported roads and District Panchayat → Block Panchayat → Village Panchayat level roads have been well connected from one village to another village but the maintenance and management of such constructed roads have been very poor which has created much difficulties for the movement on the deteriorated constructed roads. In this study an attempt has been made to analyse the distribution of National Highway, Pucca road, Kharanza and Kuchha roads at village panchayat level in Amethi. The distribution of various road's distance in kilometres at village panchayat level has been depicted in Table 4.26. Effort has been made to analyse the approximate distance of the constructed road related to National → State → District → Block → village panchayat level roads having network at the grassroots level and field level including chuk roads and kharanza roads.

9.1 National Highways

It has been observed that most of the State Highways have been upgrated as National Highways (Map 4.73). The road network from Amethi to Sultanpur, Amethi to Munshiganj and Musafirkhana, Amethi to Gauriganj, Amethi to Kakawa and Amethi to Durgapur and Amethi to Sangrampur roads have been upgraded to National Highways and the road has been developed as per the standards and norms of the National Highway Authority of India. It has been noticed that the village panchayats of Raidaipur, Rebha, Mahaso, Purabgaon and Ramgarh are not connected by the National Highway road. It has been observed that more than four kilometres distance has not been connected with National Highway road has been found in Sarai Khema Village Panchayat of the Amethi Block. It has been observed that 3 to 4 kilometre distance of the National Highway road connecting the village panchayat Katara Maharani, Jangal Ram Nagar, Bhaganpur, Tala, Umapur Ganapatti, Kherauna village panchayats. It has been observed that some of the roads constructed under the Pradhan Mantri Gram Sadak Yojana (PMGSY) has also been included under the National Highway Authority of India for appropriate maintenance and management and sustenance of the constructed pucca road. It has been observed that National Highway road connecting 2 to 3 kilometre distance has been found in Trilokpur, Ramdaipur, Mahmoodpur, Parsawan, Raipur Phulwari, Loniapur, Katara Phulkunwar, Hathkila, Dedhpasar, Gangauli, Bhusahari, Nuwawan, Chaturbhujpur, Maharajpur, Naraini, Agahar, Saidpur, Saraiya Duban and Kakawa Village Panchayats of the Amethi Block. It has been observed that less than 2 kilometres distance of the National Highway roads connecting the village panchayats Benipur, Loharata, Mochawa, Dhandhudhar, Dehara, Gaderi, Nainaha and Mahmoodpur village panchayats has been noticed in the Amethi Block.

9.2. Pucca Road

It has been observed that most of the village panchayats → revenue villages → Purwas → Tolas → Hamlet villages and settlement colonies have been well connected by the pucca road in Amethi Block. The pucca road has been constructed by the District Rural Development Agency, District Panchayat, Block Panchayat, Member of Parliament, Local Area Development Fund, Members of Legislative Assembly Local Area Development Fund and State Government financial support and also through the Prime Minister Gram Sadak Yojana (PMGSY) in the various village panchayats of the Amethi Block. The detailed distribution of pucca road has been mentioned in Table 4.26. It has been noticed that most of the village panchayats has been well connected by the pucca road. The proportionate distribution of the pucca road at village panchayat level in Amethi has been depicted in **Map 4.74**. It has been noticed that more than 12 kilometres pucca road connecting village panchayats Ramdaipur has been found because this village has been well connected from all corners of the village connecting the other pucca road and other villages of the Amethi Block. Pucca road between 8 and 12 kilometres distance has been found in Trilokpur, Jangal Ram Nagar, Umapur Ganapatti, Darakha, Kherauna, Katara Phulkunwar and Kakawa Village Panchayats of Amethi Block. It has been observed that pucca road covering 4 - 8 kilometres distance has been found in Sarai Khema, Bhaganpur, Tala, Kushi Tali, Loharata, Mahmoodpur, Parsawan, Raipur Phulwari, Korari Girdhar Shah, Raidaipur, Gangauli and Himmatgarh Village Panchayats of the Amethi Block. It has been recorded that less than 4 kilometres distance pucca road has been found in the Katara Maharani, Benipur, Loniapur, Rebha, Hathkila,

Dedhpasar, Mahaso, Bhusahari, Dehara, Ramgarh, Nainaha, Gaderi, Purabgaon, Chaturbhujpur, Maharajpur, Naraini, Agahar, Saidpur, Saraiya Duban, Kohara and Mahmoodpur village panchayats of the Amethi Block.

9.3. Kharanza Road

The Kharanza road has been mostly constructed in the village panchayats of the Amethi Block. The construction of kharanza road with the village panchayats and connecting the Revenue villages/Purwas/Tolas/Hamlet villages and settlement colonies have been constructed by the Village Panchayat and Block Panchayat. The distribution of the Kharanza road has been mentioned in Table 4.26. The proportionate distribution of kharanza road in kilometres at village panchayat level in Amethi has been depicted in **Map 4.75**. It has been observed that more than 15 kilometres kharanza road has been found in Loniapur and Saraiya Duban Village Panchayats of the Amethi Block. Constructed kharanza road between 10 and 15 kilometres distance has been noticed in Ramdaipur, Raipur Phulwari, Kherauna, Raidaipur, Gangauli, Mochawa, Chaturbhujpur, Agahar and Kakawa village panchayats. The kharanza road constructed between 5 and 10 kilometres distance has been seen in Katara Maharani, Trilokpur, Sarai Khema, Jangal Ram Nagar, Mahmoodpur, Parsawan, Hathkila, Rebha, Korari Girdharshah, Dhandhudhar, Nuwawan, Darakha, Kushi Tali, Tala, Himmatgarh, Dehara, Ramgarh, Maharajpur, Naraini, Saraiya Duban, Mahmoodpur and Kohara Village Panchayats of the Amethi Block. It has been noticed that less than 10 kilometres kharanza road has been constructed in Benipur, Bhaganpur, Loharta, Umapur Ganapatti, Dedhpasar, Mahaso, Bhusahari, Gaderi, Nainaha, Purabgaon Village Panchayats of the Amethi Block. It has been noted that most of the kharanza road are constructed through village panchayats and also maintained by the respective village panchayats.

9.4. Kuchcha Road

The kuchcha roads are constructed by village panchayats and through *Shramdaan* and also under the MNREGA programme, being implement under the supervision of the village panchayats. The village panchayats are constructing the kuchcha road or the earth work road under the MNREGA with the view to generate 100 days Guarantee Employment Generation with the village panchayat itself. The village panchayats has been given administrative, financial and formulation of the need base plan for the integrated village development including the issue of Job Card to the land less, agricultural workers, labourers, living under the Below Poverty Line or B.P.L. Card Holders families or households and to ensure 100 days guaranteed Employment Generation through earth work or labour oriented kuchcha work including the road etc. The distribution of the kuchcha road at village panchayat level in Amethi has been mentioned distribution of the kuchcha road constructed at the village panchayat level has been depicted in **Map 4.76**. It has been noticed that more than 12 kilometres constructed kuchcha road has been found in Korari Girdharshah, Agahar and Kakawa village panchayats of the Amethi Block. It has been observed that constructed kuchha road between 8-12 kilometres distance has been found in Katara Maharani, Trilokpur, Sarai Khema, Jangal Ram Nagar, Raipur Phulwari, Kherauna, Katara Phulkunwar, Hathkila, Dedhpasar, Raidaipur, Mahaso, Gangauli, Bhusahari, Himmatgarh, Ramgarh, Nainaha, Naraini, Purabgaon, Maharajpur, Mochawa, Nuwawan, Saidpur, Saraiya Duban, Kohara and Mahmoodpur village panchayats of the Amethi Block. It has been observed that the constructed kuchcha

Table 4.26: Institutional Infrastructure—Amethi Block

Sl. No.	*Villages*	*Road Distance in km.*				*Educational Infrastructure*
		National Highway	*Pucca*	*Kharanja*	*Kuchcha*	
1	2	3	4	5	6	7
1.	Katra Maharani	3	3	8	8	4
2.	Sarai Khema	4	5	6	10	6
3.	Trilokpur	2	9	8	9	3
4.	Ramdaipur	2	12	12	7	5
5.	Jangal Ram Nagar	3	10	5	10	5
6.	Benipur	1	3	2	3	1
7.	Parsawan	2	5	8	5	4
8.	Mahmoodpur	2	7	6	3	4
9.	Raipur Fulwari	2	7	10	8	4
10.	Umapur Ganapatti	3	8	2	4	4
11.	Bhaganpur	3	7	3	5	2
12.	Tala	3	6	8	4	1
13.	Kushi Tali	2	5	8	6	1
14.	Loharta	1	4	3	7	3
15.	Darkha	3	10	6	5	3
16.	Mochwa	1	3	10	8	4
17.	Nuwawan	2	2	7	9	2
18.	Loniapur	2	3	15	6	2
19.	Kherauna	3	8	12	10	3
20.	Katra Phulkunwar	2	11	8	10	4
21.	Hathkila	2	3	6	10	2
22.	Rebha	—	3	7	5	3
23.	Raidaipur	—	5	10	10	2
24.	Korari Girdharshah	3	4	8	12	7
25.	Dedhpasar	2	1	4	10	3
26.	Mahaso	—	2	3	9	2
27.	Gangauli	2	5	10	10	2
28.	Dhadhudhar	1	2	5	8	4
29.	Gaderi	1	2	4	9	3
30.	Bhusahari	2	2	3	9	2
31.	Purabgaon	—	3	4	10	3
32.	Chaturbhujpur	2	2	10	6	2
33.	Mahrajpur	2	2	5	10	3
34.	Aghar	2	3	10	12	4
35.	Saidpur	2	2	15	11	3
36.	Kakwa	3	4	12	13	3
37.	Saraiya Duban	2	3	9	10	2
38.	Kohra	2	2	7	8	5
39.	Mahmadpur	1	3	6	9	3
40.	Naraini	2	3	5	8	4
41.	Nainaha	1	2	3	10	3
42.	Ramgarh	—	3	7	10	4
43.	Himmatgarh	2	4	7	11	1
44.	Dehara	1	2	8	7	5
	Amethi Block	**80**	**180**	**315**	**380**	**140**

road between 4 and 8 kilometres distance has been found in the Ramdaipur, Parsawan, Bhaganpur, Tala, Kushi Tali, Loharta, Darakha, Umapur Ganapatti, Rebha, Loniapur, Chaturbhujpur and Dehara village panchayats of the Amethi Block. It has been noticed that less than 4 kilometres distance constructed kharanza road has been found in the Benipur and Mahmoodpur village panchayats of the Amethi Block.

It has been observed that there are 80 kilometres National Highway road being connected to the most of village panchayats and revenue village of the Amethi Block. The State Highways and the road constructed under the Pradhan Mantri Gram Sadak Yojana (PMGSY) has been included under the Natioanl Highway Authority of India (NHAI) as National Highway Road due to which the roads under the National Highway has been found significantly distributed at village panchayat level in Amethi. It has been noticed that there are 195 kilimetres pucca road constructed, through various financial supports, at the village panchayat level in Amethi Block. The Kharanza road constructed through Village Panchayats and Block Panchayats and also through the Funds sanctioned by the local people representatives has been found 315 kilometres total distance at the village panchayat level in the Amethi Block. It has been recorded that kuchcha road, earth work has been constructed under the supervision of the Village Panchayats and Village Pradhan. It has been noticed that there are 380 kilometres kuchcha road constructed at the village panchayat level in the Amethi Block. The construction of the kuchha road, earth work has been done at the grassroots level under the Mahatma Gandhi National Rojgar Guarantee Act of the Government of India to generate 100 days guarantee employment for the MNREGA Job Card Holders belonging to the Below Poverty Line (BPL) families and landless, agricultural workers, labourers, belong to the respective village panchayats of the Amethi Block. It has been noted that all the village panchayats of the Amethi Block have been well connected through National Highway, pucca road and the village panchayats have well road network with the revenue villages and Purwas/Tolas/Hamlet villages and settlement colonies through kuchcha road and kharanza road constructed by the village panchayats of Amethi. The well connected road network as an institutional infrastructure has been as asset for the economic growth of the Amethi through strengthening the transportation network for the agricultural products to the marketing centre and it has also been helpful in the integrated village development of the peoples of Amethi through generating employment and increasing the income of deprived rural poor multitudes living in the remote villages of the Amethi Block.

10. EDUCATIONAL INFRASTRUCTURE

The educational infrastructure plays an important role in the economic development of an area. The elementary education/primary education and junior high school educational infrastructure has been distributed at the village panchayat level in the Amethi Block but the high school and intermediate educational infrastructure facilities or schools are very insignificantly distributed at village panchayat level in Amethi Block. The higher education and the professional education institutional infrastructure are very insignificant in Amethi except one Post Graduate, Graduate, Pharmacy, Management and Business Administration and Graduate level Engineering and Technology, Graduate level Computer Science and Information Technology institutional infrastructures have been established in the Amethi Block.

The distribution of the educational infrastructure at village panchayat level in Amethi has been mentioned in Table 4.26. The distribution of the number of educational institutions at village panchayat level has been depicted in **Map 4.77**. It has been observed that more than 6 numbers of educational institutions has been found in Sarai Khema and Korari Girdharshah village panchayats of the Amethi Block. The educational institutions between 4 and 6 institutions have been found in Katara Maharani, Ramdaipur, Jangal Ram Nagar, Mahmoodpur, Parsawan, Raipur Phulwari, Katara Phulkunwar, Mochawa, Dhandhudhar, Ramgarh, Dehara, Agahar, and Kohara village panchayats of the Amethi Block. It has been noticed that educational institutions between 2 and 4 schools have been found in Trilokpur, Nuwawan, Loniapur, Raidaipur, Rebha, Hathkila, Mahaso, Dedhpasar, Gangauli, Bhusahari, Gaderi, Purabgaon, Nainaha, Chaturbhujpur, Maharajpur, Saidpur, Kakawa, Saraiya Duban and Mahmoodpur village panchayats of Amethi. It has been noted that less than 2 numbers of educational institutional infrastructures have been found in Benipur, Tala, Kushi Tali and Himmatgarh village panchayats of Amethi.

It has been recorded that there are 140 numbers of educational institutional infrastructures distributed at village panchayat level in the Amethi Block, which has been very insignificant institutional infrastructure against ever increasing population and to generate employment and increase the income of the deprived rural poor multitudes of Amethi.

It has been noticed that there are three primary schools in Sarai Khema, Ramdaipur, Katara Phulkunwar, Mochawa and Korari Girdharshah village panchayats and the primary school has been found in Benipur, Parsawan, Tala, Kushi Tali, Nuwawan, Loniapur, Himmatgarh and Dehara village panchayats while two primary schools have been established and functional in the rest of 31 village panchayats of the Amethi Block. Thus, there are total 85 primary schools established and functional at village panchayat level in Amethi.

Highly populated larger village panchayats having more child strength are having three primary schools and medium populated village panchayats are having two primary schools and low populated small size village panchayats as per norms of the government are having only one primary school in the respective village panchayats of the Amethi Block.

It has been observed that there are 34 Junior High Schools up to the 8th standard of education while Benipur, Parsawan, Tala, Kushi Tali, Hathkila, Mahaso, Gaderi, Bhusahari, Chaturbhujpur and Himmatgarh village panchayats are without Junior High School in Amethi, and rest of the villages of the Amethi Block are having one Junior High School each in the respective village panchayats.

There are 9 High Schools in the Amethi Block. It has been noted that Umapur Ganapatti, Korari Girdharshah, Dhandhudhar, Gaderi, Maharajpur, Agahar, Kohara and Dehara village panchayats are having one High School each in the respective villages while rest of the village panchayats are without High School institutional facility.

It has been recorded that there are 4 Intermediate Colleges in the Amethi Block. Village Panchayat Jangal Ram Nagar, Korari Girdharshah, Saraiya Duban and Dehara are having one Intermediate College each in the respective villages of the Amethi Block. There is one Government Boys Intermediate College and Government Girls Intermediate College in Amethi Town area of the Amethi Block. There is no graduate and post-graduate college at the village panchayat level in Amethi excepting the Post Graduate College and the Women Degree College have been established and functional in the Amethi town area of the Amethi Block but the remote rural village are deprived of higher educational infrastructural facilities and the students are forced to visit the Amethi town area, Block and Tehsil Headquarter for higher educational studies in Amethi.

The professional educational infrastructural institutions are very insignificant in the Amethi Block. There is one Industrial Training Institute in Mahmoodpur and Korari Girdharshah village panchayat and one Government Girls and Boys Polytechnic Institute in Amethi. There is one Pharmacy College, one Management College and one Engineering and Technology College under the self-financing scheme at the village panchayat Sarai Khema and Jangal Ram Nagar in Amethi Block. It has been noticed that there are 7 other educational institutional infrastructures in Sarai Khema village panchayat having two educational institutions with primary education and one primary/junior level private schools are functional in Katara Maharani, Ramdaipur, Jangal Ram Nagar, Raipur Phulwari and Nainaha village panchayats of the Amethi Block.

11. RELIGIOUS AND HISTORICAL INFRASTRUCTURE

The religious and historical institutional infrastructures are significantly distributed at village panchayat level in Amethi. It has been noted that there are old historical temples in Saraiya Duban, Saidpur, Chaturbhujpur, Purabgaon, Dhandhudhar, Gangauli, Mahaso, Katara Phulkunwar, Kherauna, Darakha village panchayats of the Amethi Block. There is Kali Temple in Katara Maharani, Umapur Ganapatti and Nainaha village panchayats while Shiv Mandir (Shiva Temples) has been found in Himmatgarh, Dedhpasar, Rebha, Hathkila, Mochawa, Mahmoodpur, Benipur and Sarai Khema village panchayats of Amethi. The distribution of the religious and historical institutional infrastructures has been mentioned in Table 4.27. The religiously famous Kali Mandir has been found in Katara Maharani, Umapur Ganapatti, and Nainaha village panchayats while Durga Mata religious temple has been found in the Loharata and Devi Patan Mandir in Raipur Phulwari in the Amethi Block. Old Muslim religious Masjid has been noticed in Kohara, Korari Girdharshah, and historically and religiously famous Mazar at Loniapur village panchayat and famous *vatica* in the village panchayats Jangal Ram Nagar and Saheed Smarak in the village panchayat Trilokpur, Old Bargad (*Vat*) tree in Ramdaipur and Kushi Tali, Nuwawan, Agahar, Naraini village panchayats of Amethi. Muslim religious Idgaah and Masjid has been found in Sarai Khema, Loniapur, Korari Girdharshah, Gaderi, Agahar, Kakawa, Mahmoodpur village panchayats. There is 75 years old Pond (*Talab*) in Kakawa, and historically famous *Talab* in Mahmoodpur, Maharajpur, Raidaipur, Bhaganpur and Tala village panchayats of the Amethi Block. Thus various villages of the Amethi Block are having religious and historical institutional infrastructures and monuments which have to be maintained, managed, sustained and protected through the government support. There are 14 masjids and Idgaahs in Amehti Block and 42 Hindu Temples at village level in the Amethi Block.

12. PANCHAYAT INSTITUTIONAL INFRASTRUCTURE

It has been noticed that each village panchayat of the Amethi Block has Panchayat Bhawan which has one office room and meeting room and varandah. The Panchayat Bhawan is the office secretariat of the village panchayats where the official activities and meeting of the village panchayats are conducted. The Panchayat Secretary an official representative of the Block Development officer used to act as Secretary of the village panchayat on behalf of the government. The village level all developmental activities and formulation of the policy planning as per the needs of the village people is being implemented through the village panchayat under the supervision of the village pradhan. The Panchayat Bhawan is an important institutional infrastructural assets of the village panchayat.

13. ANGAN BADI KENDRA

The Angan Badi Kendra has been established in the 16 village panchayats of the Amethi Block. Integrated Child Development Centres are functional in the different village panchayats for supporting downtrodden, resourceless, below poverty line households' children. The mid-day meal, elementary education, health care facilities, etc. are provided to the selected children. The elementary education has been provided through Angan Badi Karya Kartri at village level. The Angan Badi Kendras and the facilities for the children are one of the most important institutional infrastructure of the Integrated Child Development Scheme (ICDS) of the Department of the Women and Child Development of the Government of Uttar Pradesh. The Angan Badi Karya Kartris are supervised and guided through ICDS supervisor and the Block level and District level programme officer. The Angan Badi Kendras are functional in Katara Maharani, Sarai Khema, Mahmoodpur, Raipur Phulwari, Bhaganpur, Darakha, Mochawa, Nuwawan, Kherauna, Katara Phulkunwar, Raidaipur, Bhusahari, Purabgaon, Saraiya Duban, Kohara and Himmatgarh Village Panchayats of the Amethi Block. The main function of the Angan Badi Kendras are to provide nutritious food and mid-day meal to the mal-nutritious children surviving in the remote villages of the Amethi Block.

14. ASSISTANT NURSING MIDWIFE CENTRES

Assistant Nursing Midwife Centres are functional in the selected village panchayats of Trilokpur, Jangal Ram Nagar, Loharta, Hathkila, Korari Girdharshah, Dedhpasar, Gangauli, Dhandhudhar, Maharajpur, Kakawa, Saraiya Duban, Mahmoodpur, Naraini, Ramgarh and Himmatgarh village panchayats of the Amethi Block. There are 15 Assistant Nursing Midwife Centres in the Amethi Block. The ANMs are working under the Medical Officer of the Primary Health Centres. The ANMs are responsible for providing health services, nursing assistance to the mother and child including immunization, and health facilities at the village panchayat level in Amethi. The rest of the villages are not facilitated through ANM centres but the women and child health care and immunization facilities are provided through Primary Health Centre and Health Workers at the village level in Amethi. The mother and child health care support is being provided free of cost of the needy and interested deprived, resourceless poor village beneficiaries at the village level, because the rural health services and better health for all has been one of the most important vision, mission and priorities of the government.

15. SUB-POST OFFICE

The sub-post office has been one of the most important postal communication institutional infrastructural facilities of the Government of India. There are 10 sub-post offices functional in the various village panchayats of the Amethi Block. It has been noticed that village panchayats Trilokpur, Jangal Ram Nagar, Umapur Ganapatti, Darakha, Naraini, Ramgarh of the Amethi Block are having sub-post office institutional infrastructure to facilitate the postal services to the villagers of the Amethi.

16. TRANSPORT COMMUNICATION

The communication network through Road Transport has been well connected with all the village panchayats of the Amethi Block. The distribution of the transport communication at village panchayat level in Amethi has been mentioned in Table 4.27. It has been noticed that Bus, Jeep, Tempo transportant facilities are available in Katara Maharani, Trilokpur, Sarai Khema, Jangal Ram Nagar, Benipur, Parsawan, Maharajpur, Mahmoodpur, Raipur Phulwari, Tala, Kushi Tali, Katara Maharani, Hathkila, Gaderi,

Table 4.27: Institutional Infrastructure (Religious, Transportation & Others)—Amethi Block

Sl. No.	Villages	Religious hand Historical Infras-tructure	Panchayat Bhawan	Anganbiari Kendra	ANM Centre	Sub-Post Office	Transportation Communication		
1	2	3	4	5	6	7	8	9	10
1.	Katra Maharani	Kali Temple	1	1	—	—	Bus	Jeep	Tempo
2.	Sarai Khema	Shiv Temple	1	—	—	—	Tempo	Jeep	Bus
3.	Trilokpur	Shaheed Smarak	1	—	1	1	Bus	Jeep	Tempo
4.	Ramdaipur	Bargad Vriksh	1	—	—	—	Bus	Tanga	Tempo
5.	Jangal Ram Nagar	Vatika	1	—	1	1	Bus	Jeep	Tempo
6.	Benipur	Shiv Temple	1	—	—	—	Bus	Jeep	Tempo
7.	Parsawan	Durga Temple	1	—	—	—	Bus	Jeep	Tempo
8.	Mahmoodpur	Shiv Temple	1	1	—	—	Bus	Jeep	Tempo
9.	Raipur Fulwari	Devipatan Temple	1	1	—	—	Bus	Jeep	Tempo
10.	Umapur Ganapatti	Kali Temple	1	—	—	1	Tanga	Jeep	Tempo
11.	Bhaganpur	Pond	1	1	—	—	Tanga	Jeep	Tempo
12.	Tala	Pond	1	—	—	—	Bus	Jeep	Tempo
13.	Kushi Tali	Bargad Vriksh	1	—	—	—	Bus	Jeep	Tempo
14.	Loharta	Durga Temple	1	—	1	—	Tanga	Jeep	Tempo
15.	Darkha	Temple	1	1	—	1	Tanga	Jeep	Tempo
16.	Mochwa	Shiv Temple	1	1	—	—	Tanga	Jeep	Tempo
17.	Nuwawan	Virksh	1	1	—	—	Tanga	Jeep	Tempo
18.	Loniapur	Majar	1	—	—	—	Tanga	Jeep	Tempo
19.	Kherauna	Temple	1	1	—	—	Tanga	Jeep	Tempo
20.	Katra Phulkunwar	Temple	1	1	—	—	Tanga	Jeep	Tempo
21.	Hathkila	Shiv Temple	1	—	—	—	Bus	Jeep	Tempo
22.	Rebha	Shiv Temple	1	—	—	1	Tempo	Jeep	Tanga
23.	Raidaipur	Pond	1	1	—	—	Tempo	Jeep	Tanga
24.	Korari Girdharshah	Masjid	1	—	1	1	Tempo	Jeep	Bus
25.	Dedhpasar	Shiv Temple	1	—	1	—	—	Tempo	Jeep
26.	Mahaso	Temple	1	—	—	—	—	Tempo	Tanga
27.	Gangauli	Temple	1	—	1	—	—	Tempo	Jeep
28.	Dhadhudhar	Temple	1	—	1	—	Rickshaw	Tempo	Jeep
29.	Gaderi	Well	1	—	—	1	Bus	Tempo	Jeep
30.	Bhusahari	Smarak	1	1	—	—	Tempo	Bus	Jeep
31.	Purabgaon	Temple	1	1	—	—	—	Jeep	Jeep
32.	Chaturbhujpur	Temple	1	—	—	—	Tempo	Jeep	Tanga
33.	Mahrajpur	Pond	1	—	1	—	Tempo	Jeep	Bus
34.	Aghar	Bargad Virksh	1	—	—	—	—	Jeep	Tempo
35.	Saidpur	Temple	1	—	—	—	—	Jeep	Tempo
36.	Kakwa	Pond (75 years old)	1	—	1	1	Tempo	Tempo	Bus
37.	Saraiya Duban	Temple	1	1	1	—	—	Jeep	Tempo
38.	Kohra	Masjid	1	1	—	—	—	Jeep	Jeep
39.	Mahmadpur	Pond	1	—	1	—	—	Jeep	Jeep
40.	Naraini	Virksh	1	—	1	1	Tempo	Tanga	Jeep
41.	Nainaha	Kali Temple	1	—	—	—	—	Jeep	Tempo
42.	Ramgarh	Durga Temple	1	—	1	1	Jeep	Tempo	Tanga
43.	Himmatgarh	Shiv Temple	1	1	1	—	Jeep	Tempo	
44.	Dehara	Shiv Temple	1	—	—	—	Jeep	Tempo	Tanga
	Amethi Block		**44**	**16**	**15**	**10**	—	—	—

Korari Girdharshah, Bhusahari, Kakawa village panchayats of the Amethi Block. Bus, Tanga, Tempo transportation facilities are available in Ramdaipur, village panchayat and Tanga, Jeep, Bus transport facilities have been found in Bhaganpur. Tanga, Jeep, Tempo Transports are found in Rebha, Raidaipur, Purabgaon, Chaturbhujpur, Loharta,

Mochawa, Nuwawan, Kherauna, Naraini, Ramgarh, Dehara village panchayats of the Amethi Block. Jeep, Tempo transport facilities are noticed in the Dedhpasar, Gangauli, Agahar, Saidpur, Saraiya Duban, Darakha, Kohara, Nainaha and Himmatgarh village panchayats of the Amethi Block. It has been noticed that Bus and Jeep transport facilities are available in Mahmoodpur and Riksha, Tempo, Jeep transport communication are found in Dhandhudhar village panchayat of the Amethi Block. Tanga, Jeep transport facilities are found in Loniapur village panchayat of Amethi. It has been observed that most of the village panchayats of the Amethi Block has been well communicated through Transport network. The private transportation network system plays an important role in the communication of the village people. The transport network has been one of the most important communication institutional infrastructures at the village panchayat level in the Amethi Block.

17. TELECOMMUNICATION

It has been noticed that the telecommunication institutional infrastructures are significantly distributed in the Amethi Block at village panchayat level. The distribution of telecommunication facilities at village panchayat level has been mentioned in Table 4.28. It has been observed that the Bharat Sanchar Nigam Ltd. (BSNL) public call telephone, mobile booths are available in Katara Maharani, Mahmoodpur, Loharta, Trilokpur, Darakha, Loniapur, Kherauna, Hathkila, Rebha, Raidaipur, Dedhpasar, Gangauli, Bhusahari, Ramdaipur, Purabgaon, Maharajpur, Agahar, Saidpur, Kakawa, Kohara, Mahmoodpur, Naraini, Ramgarh and Dehara village panchayats of the Amethi Block. Public Call BSNL land line telephone booth and mobile booths etc. have been found in Sarai Khema, Jangal Ram Nagar, Parsawan, Raipur Phulwari, Umapur Ganapatti, Tala, Bhaganpur, Kushi Tali, Mochawa, Nuwawan, Katara Phulkunwar, Korari Girdharshah, Mahaso, Dhandhudhar, Gaderi, Chaturbhujpur and Nainaha village panchayats of the Amethi Block. It has been recorded that the Bharat Sanchar Nigam Ltd. Telephone Booth or Public Call Centres are functional in a private system mostly in the market centres while at the village level mostly mobile booth and telephone network institutional infrastructural facilities are recorded at the Purwas/Tolas/Hamlet villages/revenue villages and village panchayat level in Amethi.

18. ANIMAL HOSPITAL

Animal Hospitals are established at Umapur Ganapatti, Kherauna, Korari Girdharshah, Bhusahari, Agahar, Kakawa, Saraiya Duban, Kohara, Naraini and Himmatgarh village panchayats of the Amethi Block. It has been recorded that there are 10 Animal Hospitals at village panchayat level in Amethi, while the rest of the Animal Husbandry worker visits to the block level Animal Hospitals located at Amethi. The Animal Hospitals infrastructural facilities are very insignificant against the ever increasing growth of cattle at village panchayat level in Amethi.

19. MEDICAL HEALTH

The Medical Health institutional infrastructural facilities are available in the Sarai Khema, Benipur, Umapur Ganapatti, Tala, Darakha, Nuwawan, Kherauna, Korari Girdhar Shah, Kakawa, Kohara, Mahmoodpur village panchayats of the Amethi Block while there is a medical health centre at Hindustan Aeronautics Ltd. Korwa, Munshiganj and one Eye

Hospital and Medical Health Hospital at Munshiganj Amethi while the rest of the village are not facilitated by the Medical Health Centre and the needy patients visits the Primary Health Centre at Amethi or approach the private medical practitioner at village panchayat level in Amethi. The Medical Health institutional infrastructure are very insignificantly distributed against the ever increasing population and occurrence of the water borne diseases and other medical health problems among the village people surviving in the remote villages of the Amethi Block.

20. BANKING INFRASTRUCTURE

It has been noticed that there are 20 Banks functional at village panchayat level in Amethi Block. It has been noticed that there are 3 nationalized banks in the village panchayat Sarai Khema due to Munshiganj Marketing Centre, while Banks including Baroda Kshetriya Grameen Banks and other Banks are frunctional in Trilokpur, Ramdaipur, Darakha, Mochawa, Korari Girdharshah, Gangauli, Dhandhudhar, Gaderi, Bhusahari, Kakawa, Saraiya Duban, Kohara, Mahmoodpur, Naraini, Ramgarh, Himmatgarh and Dehara village panchayats of Amethi. It has been noticed that the Banking institutional infrastructures are significantly distributed at village panchayat level in Amethi while rest of the villages are not having banking facilities and the needy villagers are using the banking facilities available at Amethi Town area and nearest banks available in other village panchayats. It has been observed that banking institutional infrastructures are appropriately disturbed at village panchayat level to fulfil the increasing demand of the banking support to the village people living in the remote villages of the Amethi Block.

In spite of the above there are various other institutional infrastructural resources available in Amethi, viz. Hindustan Aeronautics Ltd. (HAL) Korawa, Munshiganj, HAL Public School and Marketing Centre and Army Recruitment Centre at Amethi, Ministry of Defence, Government of India, New Delhi. Historical Place of the Kings of Amethi known at Bhupati Bhawan at Amethi is also an important institutional infrastructural available at village panchayats Jangal Ram Nagar in the Amethi Block.

There is developed Railway station at Amethi, under the Northern Railway and Sanjay Gandhi Hospital and Indira Gandhi Eye Hospital at Munshiganj, Amethi. There is Tourist Rest House at Munshiganj, Amethi. The Post Graduate College and Women Degree College are also an important institutional infrastructural available in the Amethi town area. There are various other institutional infrastructural and resources available at village panchayat level like local level marketing shops to fulfil the day-to-day requirements of the local village people while weekly markets in the various village panchayats also play an important role in the village development as an marketing institutional infrastructural resources which has not been documented the records of the government. It view of the above there are various other institutional infrastructural resources which plays an important key role directly or indirectly in the integrated village development of Amethi.

21. CONCLUSION

The institutional infrastructural available at the grassroots level plays a vital key role in the planning process of the integrated village development. The integrated approach of the Planning process requires detail knowledge of the inter-relations and interdependencies between various sectoral indicators to resolve often-conflicting requirements and available institutional infrastructural at the grassroots level. The existing

Table 4.28: Institutional Infrastructure (Telecommunication)—Amethi Block

Sl.No.	*Villages*	*Tele Communication*
1	2	3
1.	Katra Maharani	BSNL Mobile Booths
2.	Sarai Khema	Mobile Telephone Booth
3.	Trilokpur	BSNL Mobile Booths
4.	Ramdaipur	BSNL Mobile Booths
5.	Jangal Ram Nagar	Telephone Booth
6.	Benipur	BSNL P&T
7.	Parsawan	BSNL Mobile
8.	Mahmoodpur	BSNL Land Line, Mobile
9.	Raipur Fulwari	Public Telephone Booth
10.	Umapur Ganapatti	Telephone Booth, P.C.O.
11.	Bhaganpur	Public Telephone Booth Mobile
12.	Tala	P.C.O., Land Line, Mobile
13.	Kushi Tali	BSNL Mobile
14.	Loharta	BSNL Mobile
15.	Darkha	BSNL Mobile
16.	Mochwa	Telephone Booth Mobile
17.	Nuwawan	Public Booth, Mobile
18.	Loniapur	Mobile
19.	Kherauna	BSNL
20.	Katra Phulkunwar	Public Telephone Booth
21.	Hathkila	BSNL Mobile
22.	Rebha	BSNL Mobile
23.	Raidaipur	BSNL Mobile
24.	Korari Girdharshah	Public Telephone Booth
25.	Dedhpasar	BSNL Mobile
26.	Mahaso	Public Telephone Booth, Mobile
27.	Gangauli	BSNL, Mobile
28.	Dhadhudhar	Public Telephone Booth, Mobile
29.	Gaderi	Telephone Booth, Mobile
30.	Bhusahari	BSNL, Mobile
31.	Purabgaon	BSNL, Mobile
32.	Chaturbhujpur	Public Telephone Booth, Mobile
33.	Mahrajpur	BSNL, Mobile
34.	Aghar	BSNL, Mobile
35.	Saidpur	BSNL, Mobile
36.	Kakwa	BSNL, Mobile
37.	Saraiya Duban	Public Telephone Booth, Mobile
38.	Kohra	BSNL, Mobile
39.	Mahmadpur	BSNL, Mobile
40.	Naraini	BSNL, Mobile
41.	Nainaha	Telephone Booth, Mobile
42.	Ramgarh	BSNL, Mobile
43.	Himmatgarh	Public Telephone Booth, Mobile
44.	Dehara	BSNL, Mobile
	Amethi Block	

institutional infrastructural resources may provide a base for the formulation of need base, peoples participatory, sustainable integrated village development planning. Therefore, the available institutional infrastructural resources must be considered before initiation of the planning process.

The Institutional Infrastructural Resources Data Management System (IIRDMS) is multi-disciplinary and multi-institutional research and development programme with vision to provide appropriate scientific and technological inputs for operationalizing the concept of decentralized integrated village development planning.

The main objectives of the institutional infrastructural resources has been to develop the scientific data base approach to support the local level area specific village development planning, various efforts has been made to evolve and develop institutional infrastructural resources spatial data management system for integrated village development planning and its demonstration in the local level decision making process.

In view of the above, an attempt has been made in this study to analyse the available institutional infrastructural resources existing at village panchayat level in the Amethi Block. An effort has been made to develop spatial data management system and analysing techniques for the incorporation of the existing institutional infrastructural resources available at the grassroots level in the Amethi Block. In order to implement at least some of the institutional infrastructural related activities with the vision of Village Information System and collection, collation of the grassroots level data support from a large segment of the scientists and entrepreneurs are required. It has been expected to stimulate the imagination of the research community to relate specific problems in their areas of interests and to evolve suitable research proposals to pursue line of investigation and imagination of the research community and to arrive at meaningful solutions for the integrated village development planning.

It has been realized that the development should be participatory and it should be planned according to the local needs of the resource less deprived rural poor multitudes. The development should be planned through tapping local level existing institutional infrastructural resources in order to make the implemented rural development programmes self-sustainable.

It has also been mentioned in the Constitution of India that *"Government should evolve methods to unite the village panchayats and provide such powers and rights which can be helpful to workout as an unit of self-government."*

In the Panchayati Raj system each village should be self-sustained and independent, and the implementation of the welfare programmes can be implemented in a better manner in the various village panchayats of Amethi. The self-government is the main sole of the village development. To strengthen the Panchayati Raj Institutions, government has allocated the rights, administrative and financial powers to *Village Panchayat → Block Panchayat → District Panchayat* for implementation and maintenance of assets created at the grassroots level through peoples participation.

The institutional infrastructure plays an important role in the policy planning for the integrated village development. The people's participatory need based integrated village development formulation of the policy planning should be initiated through tapping local level available institutional infrastructural resources in order to make the already implemented rural development programmes.

The drinking water is one of the most important requirement for the survival of human being. It has been recorded that the tap water supply has been provided to 499 households in Amethi and there are 2380 India Mark II hand pumps installed at village panchayat level in Amethi, which has been very insufficient to fulfil the ever increasing demand of the growing population and increasing settlement colonies. The individual households have constructed and installed their own private hand pumps to fetch the drinking water facilities. It has been recorded that there are 7326 private hand pumps installed by the individual households at village panchayat level in Amethi. It has been noticed that there are 292 households in Amethi Block who are forced to fetch drinking water facilities from the wells and other sources of drinking water including borrowing from other individuals drinking water sources at village panchayat level in Amethi. In view of the above, it has become an important task for the policy planners and local level people's representatives to provide special package for the installation of the India Mark II hand pumps among the deprived resourceless, rural poor surviving in the remote rural areas of the Amethi Block.

It has been recorded that there are only 319 small scale industries and agro-industries functional at Amethi. Therefore, it has become necessary to promote the establishment of small scale industries and agro-industries to ensure the value addition of the agricultural produce and to generate the employment and also increase the income of the deprived rural poor people.

It has been noted that there are 430 low cost houses in the various villages of the Amethi Block which is very insignificant and an effort must be made to provide special package for the construction of low cost houses for the roofless, mud house and thatched roof house owners, landless labourers and to provide shelter for everyone as per the policy of the government to provide shelters for the houseless people living in the remote rural areas of Amethi.

The energy an important institutional infrastructure plays an important role in the economic development of an area. It has been noticed that there are 595 non-conventional sources of energy including solar lights, solar water pumps, solar lantern and other sources of the non-conventional energy being used in Amethi. There are 12190 household electricity consumers at village panchayat level in Amethi and very insignificant 478 commercial electricity consumptions have been found at village panchayat level in Amethi. The electricity consumers are very insignificantly distributed at village level in Amethi due to very poor and irregular, nominal 6-8 hours electricity supply which has adversely affected the commercial consumption of the electricity. The proper supply of the electricity, appropriate electricity and energy infrastructural resources may be helpful in the economic development of the Amethi Block.

The road communication plays a key role in the economic growth and an integrated development of an area. The National Highway, *pucca*, *kuchcha*, *kharanza* roads especially for linking the villages from one village to another village plays a key role in the economic growth and transportation of the agricultural produce to the Krishi Utpadan Mandir Samiti. It has been noted that there are 80 kilometres National Highway and 195 kilometres pucca road including State Highway and 315 kilometres kharanza road and 380 kilometres kuchcha road for connecting District, Tehsil, Block to the various village panchayats. The road network not only facilitates the communication support from one village to another but it has become the lifeline for the resourceless village poors in Amethi. Thus, the road network plays a key role in the economic development of not only the village panchayats but it supports for the integrated village development of the Amethi Block.

The educational infrastructure also plays a vital role in the integrated village development of an area. The educational infrastructure has been very insignificantly distributed at village panchayat level in Amethi. There are 140 educational institutional infrastructures available at village panchayat level in Amethi. It has been noticed that, there are 3 primary schools in the Sarai Khema, Mochawa, Ramdaipur, Korari Girdhar-shah and Katara Phulkunwar village panchayats of the Amethi Block. One primary school has been noticed in Benipur, Parsawan, Tala, Kushi Tali, Nuwawan, Loniapur, Himmatgarh and Dehara Village Panchayats while two primary schools has been recorded in the rest of the Village Panchayats of the Amethi Block. Thus, there are 85 primary schools established and functional at village panchayat level in Amethi Block. It has been noted that there are 34 Junior High Schools and 9 High Schools in various village panchayats of the Amethi Block. It has been observed that there are 4 Intermediate

Colleges in Amethi Block including government girls and government boys intermediate colleges in Amethi Town Area in Amethi Block. The graduate level girls college and post graduate level college is functional in Amethi Town area which has been an important higher educational infrastructure available in Amethi Block. There is one government boys and girls polytechnic in Amethi and one Industrial Training Institute has been noted in the Mahmoodpur and Korari Girdharshah village panchayats of Amethi Block. There is one Pharmacy, one Management and onc Engineering and Technology colleges functional in Jangal Ram Nagar and Sarai Khema village panchayats respectively. There are 7 other educational institutional infrastructures available at village panchayat level in Amethi. Thus, the educational institutions and professional educational institutional infrastructures are very insignificantly distributed in Amethi which has to be strengthened and promoted at village panchayat level in the Amethi Block.

It has been noted that there are old historical Temples in Sarai Khema, Saidpur, Chaturbhujpur, Purabgaon, Dhandhudhar, Gangauli, Mahaso, Katara Phulkunwar, Kherauna and Darakha village panchayats. There is Kali temple in Katara Maharani, Umapur Ganapatti and Nainaha village panchayat while Shiv Mandir has been found in Himmatgarh, Dedhpasar, Rebha, Hathkila, Mochawa, Mahmoodpur, Benipur and Sarai Khema village panchayats of the Amethi Block. Various historically and religiously Kali Mandir has been found in Katara Maharani, Umapur Ganapatti, Nainaha and Durga Mata Mandir in Loharta and Devi Patan Mandir in Raipur Phulwari has been found in the Amethi Block. Muslim religious Masjid and Idgah have been found in Sarai Khema, Loniapur, Korari Girdharshah, Gaderi, Agahar, Kakawa and Mahmoodpur village panchayats of the Amethi Block. There is 75 years old historical pond in the Kakawa village panchayat and famous old pond has been found in the Mahmoodpur, Maharajpur, Raidaipur, Bhaganpur and Tala village panchayats of the Amethi Block.

There are Panchayat Bhawan or Village Panchayat Office Secretariat functional at all village panchayats in Amethi Block. The ANM centres are functional in Trilokpur, Jangal Ram Nagar, Loharata, Hathkila, Korari Girdharshah, Dedhpasar, Gangauli, Dhandhudhar, Maharajpur, Kakawa, Saraiya Duban, Mahmoodpur, Naraini, Ramgarh and Himmatgarh village panchayats of the Amethi Block. There are 10 sub-psot office functioinal in Trilokpur, Jangal Ram Nagar, Umapur Gangapatti, Darakha, Rebha, Korari Girdharshah, Dhandhudhar, Kakawa, Naraini, Ramgarh village panchayats of the Amethi Block. Most of the village panchayats of the Amethi Block have been connected through bus, jeep, tempo, tanga etc. transportation facilities for commuting from one village to another and also Tehsil and Block Headquarters of Amethi. It has been noted that Public Call Office, Bharat Sanchar Nigam Limited (BSNL) Telephone Booth, Land Line Telephones and Mobile Telephones or Telecommunications facilities are significantly distributed at village panchayat level in the Amethi Block.

The Animal Hospital Institutional Infrastructure are functional in Umapur Ganapatti, Kherauna, Korari Girdharshah, Bhusahari, Agahar, Kakawa, Sarai Duban, Kohara, Naraini and Himmatgarh village panchayat of Amethi. The medical health institutional infrastructures facilities are available in the Sarai Khema, Benipur, Umapur Ganapatti, Tala, Darakha, Nuwawan, Kherauna, Korari Girdharshah, Kakawa, Kohara, Mahmoodpur village panchayats of the Amethi Block.

The Banking institutional infrastructures are significantly distributed in Amethi. There are 20 Banks functional at village panchayat level in Amethi. There are 3 nationalized Banks functional in the village panchayats Sarai Khema, Munshiganj and at Hindustan Aeronautics Ltd. (HAL) Korwa, Munshiganj, Baroda Kshetriya Grameen Banks are functional in the various village panchayats to facilitate the village beneficiaries for the financial transaction in the banks.

In view of the above, it has been noted that the drinking water, small scale and agro-industries, low cost housing and energy sources are very insignificantly distributed at village panchayat level in Amethi. The existing institutional infrastructure users have to be properly maintained and managed for its appropriate utilization for the purpose for which it has been established and made available to the village peoples of Amethi. The road network has been significantly and appropriately available at village panchayat level in Amethi and it requires appropriate maintenance and management for its sustenance. The educational infrastructures are very insignificantly distributed except the Primary Schools but the quality of the Schools and standard of the Primary education has been found very poor in comparison to the Public school due to which most of the children and their guardians prefer to obtain public school education in every village panchayats of the Amethi Block. The intermediate, high school educational institutional infrastructures are very insignificant and the higher education and the professional educational infrastructures are very poor and it requires to be strengthen at village panchayat level in view of the ever increasing demand of the growing population. The available religious and historical infrastructures must be protected, maintained and managed for its sustenance at village panchayat level. The number of Angan Badi Kendras and ANM Centres, Animal Hospitals and Medical Health Centres have to be promoted to facilitate the increasing population and growing diseases and medical health problems at village panchayat level. The transportation network has to be supported through Uttar Pradesh State Road Transport Corporation (UPSRTC) Buses facilitating to the village people to travel from one village to another place. Therefore, it has become an important task of the policy planners to protect and maintain the available institutional infrastructures at village panchayat level and also to establish more institutional infrastructural resources as per needs of the growing cattles and human population to meet their growing demand of *Roti, Kapada and Makan* (Food, Cloth and Shelter) for the resourceless deprived rural poor multitudes surviving in the remote villages of Amethi.

5

Conclusion

The sustained, integrated economic development has been realized and commendable advances have been made in the diverse field of rural development. The development programmes have been in reality incomplete because such rural development programmes have been failed to translate into better and dignified life for the majority of the people who live in the remote rural areas because the benefit of the development must reach to the dow ntrodden deprived resourceless ruralpoor *equally*, *effectively* and *efficiently*.

The poverty and backwardness has been recorded comparatively more in the rural areas than the urban areas. The government has formulated various policies and development planning programmes to bridge the gap between rural and urban.

It has been realized that the development should be participatory and it should be planned according to the local needs of the deprived rural multitudes. The development should be planned through tapping the available human resources including socio-economic-institutional infrastructure at Village Panchayat level, in order to ensure the proper implementation of the need based rural development programmes self-sustainable.

Various rural development schemes are being implemented aiming at the sustainable, integrated development of the remote rural areas with the focus on enhancing the livelihood of weakers and vulnerable sections of the society inconformity with the commitments to accord foremost priority to the integrated village development. In this regard a number of steps have been initiated to make the implementation of the ongoing rural development programmes more effective and accelerated. The formulation and implementation of various rural development programmes at the grassroots level is an intensive, innovative, informative and infrastructure oriented activity.

The human resources play an important role in the policy planning and in the formulation of need based action plans for an integrated development of the remote villages. The human resources include the socio-economic-institutional infrastructure available at the grassroots level. The social infrastructure plays crucial role in the formulation of the development planning process. The available economic and institutional infrastructure at the grassroots level, must be considered before the formulation of need based people's participatory planning process. The developed institutional infrastructure at the grassroots level should be considered as an asset for the formulation of the policy planning.

In the Panchayati Raj System each village should be self-sustained and independent, the implementation of the Welfare programmes of rural masses, can be implemented in a better manner when socio-economic-institutional infrastructures already available at the village level are innovated, requisite data are collected and collated for analysing the need based policy planning for the remote rural areas.

The real meaning of democracy is important to the people and Self-Government is the main soul of rural development, management of financial and administrative control of the Village Panchayats and continued participation, co-operation of the local people to establish village panchayats for Self-Government through people's participatory planning process.

The optimum utilization of the available socio-economic-institutional infrastructural resources to meet the increasing demand of the growing population and to generate employment and increase the income of the deprived resourceless poor multitudes surviving in the remote rural areas.

In view of the above an attempt has been made to analyse the available socio-economic-institutional infrastructural resources available at the Village Panchayat level in the Amethi Block. The innovation of the existing socio-economic-institutional infrastructure at the Village Panchayat level may be an asset for the formulation of the peoples participatory village development planning process and through sustained participation of the concerned village beneficiaries for the successful implementation of the integrated development programmes, with the view to improve the socio-economic conditions of the deprived poor multitudes living in the remote rural villages.

Archaeologically, historically and religiously Amethi has an importance for the tomb of Sufi Poet Malik Mohammad Jaisi and religious temple at Nand Mahar which is very famous for the worship of Yadav community. Malik Mohammad Jaisi was born at Jais and composed many famous books in Hindi and Urdu literature. Jaisi memorial is also situated in the Jais town. There is no noteworthy archaeological importance in Amethi. It has been observed that the chief land owning families of the past were the Rajputs of the various clans who possessed 76.16 per cent of the total land area of Amethi. Among them Rajkumars alone held over one-fourth area of Amethi while the Kinsmen Bachhgotis and Rajwars owned 11.4 per cent and 3.4 per cent land respectively. The Rajkumars were the main proprietors of Amethi and the chief of the Rajwars were the Taluqdars of the revenue land tax collection. The next to the Bachhgotis and their kinsmen come the Bandhalgotis who owned almost the whole of Amethi Pargana. The other Rajputs with large properties in Amethi were the Bhale Sultans who owned 4.72 per cent and Kanhpurias with 4.7 per cent and the Bais with 2.8 per cent properties of the Bhale Sultan and of the Bhale Sultan's half were Hindus and half were Muslims. The Kanhpurias were chiefly confined to Pargana Gaura Jamo, almost the whole of which belonged to them. The Bais were scattered about in small groups. The backwardness of Amethi has been historical phenomenon due to kingship ruled estate, the land ownership was concentrated in the kings and their associated people.

An attempt has been made in this study to analyse the socio-economic-institutional infrastructural resources available at Village Panchayat level in the Amethi Block.

The planning process for better and optimal utilization of available human resources has always been a great challenge to the policy-makers and planners. It is necessary to evolve a planning strategy applicable at different levels, i.e. Village level-Block level-District level especially village as lowest unit of planning to strengthen Panchayati Raj system. In this study an attempt has been made to discuss vide range of issues which are very important for Local Area Development Planning. In the present context, efforts are being made to allocate resources at Village Panchayat level, it has become necessary to explain the human resources including socio-economic-institutional and man made infrastructural resources at Village Panchayat level in Amethi.

The man-made infrastructure especially the human resources play an important role in the policy planning and need based planned programme implementation of the integrated rural land development. The human resources including the socio-economic-institutional infrastructural resources at the grassroots level plays a crucial role in the formulation of micro-level planning process.

The social infrastructure includes the population and population density, caste composition, workforce, educational profiles at the Village Panchayat level in Amethi.

The economic infrastructural resources include size of land holdings, land ownership pattern, source of irrigation and the irrigated area, agricultural production, use of agricultural implements, application of the fertilizers, economy from the animal husbandry and source of economy from primary, secondary and tertiary economy based on the workforce etc. has been analysed at the Village Panchayat level in the Amethi Block.

The Institutional infrastructure includes historical, religious and administrative infrastructure available at the Village Panchayat level in Amethi along with the communication network, telecommunication, drinking water facilities, energy, non-conventional sources of energy and electricity, animal hospitals, medical and health services, small scale industries and agro-industries, banking infrastructure, low cost housing, tourism infrastructure, Pancyati Raj Institutional infrastructure and the educational infrastructure available at the Village Panchayat level in the Amethi Block.

The primary field survey at the grassroots level and the secondary sources of information have been the basic source of information for the collection and innovation of the human resources data including socio-economic-institutional infrastructural resources available at the Village Panchayat level in Amethi. The requisite indicators data has been collected through primary survey, grassroots level field observation and Village Patwari, Panchayat Secretary and village people's representatives and other officials of the Amethi Block.

Various indicators related to the socio-economic-institutional infrastructural resources have been collected at the grassroots level especially covering 377 Purwas/Tolas/Hamlet villages and 82 revenue villages and 44 Village Panchayats of the Amethi Block.

An attempt has been made to develop explanation mechanism for the uneven distribution of the various socio-economic-institutional infrastructural resources at the village panchayat level in Amethi.

Various cartographic techniques have been adopted to analyse the collected and collated data related to the socio-economic-institutional infrastructures available at Village Panchayat level in Amethi. Geographic Information System (GIS) techniques have been adopted for appropriate analysis of the socio-economic-institutional infrastructural resources distributed at the Village Panchayat level in Amethi.

The appropriate planning for the optimum utilization of the available socio-economic-institutional infrastructural resources has been analysed and to supervise the process of implementation of the planned programmes in order to find out eventual discrepancies and to set in motion adaptive achievements of the sustainable development at the grassroots level.

The village development means the evolution of the people in which the people acquires better perception and best control over the human resources, including especially socio-economic-institutional infrastructures available at the grassroots level. The village development means to fulfil the aspirations of the village people for the betterment and the welfare of the local level village people for their actions, aspirations and perceptions for better quality of life and also to feel good for an integrated development of the village

It has been realized that there is a quest for evolving a model for village development planning. The village development planning and the implementation of the integrated rural development programmes can be made more accelerated and successful if it is planned through the people's participation and the available human infrastructural resources are duly considered before the plan formulation, with the view to avoid the duplicacy of the already created socio-economic-institutions infrastructure at the village level.

In view of the above multi-disciplinary and multi-institutional Research and Development programme with a vision to provide appropriate scientific and technical inputs for operationalizing the concept of area specific decentralized planning at the grassroots level. The main objective of the programme has been to develop techno-scientific data base with an approach to support grassroots level planning.

The Human Resources Data Management System (HRDMS) include socio-economic-institutional infrastructure available at the grassroots level, which may be an asset for the policy makers, planners of the rural development schemes. The innovation of the existing socio-economic-institutional infrastructural resources at the grassroots level will be helpful in the formulation of the need based village development planning and also the implementation of the people's participatory integrated rural development.

The innovation of human resources along with socio-economic-institutional infrastructural resources data have been created and developed at the village panchayat level in Amethi which may be used as a base for the formulation of need base peoples participatory integrated village development planning. The innovation of the available socio-economic-institutional infrastructures at the grassroots level is most important exercise for the formulation of the policy planning, based on which the need based people's participatory integrated rural development planning can be formulated for the sustainable development. The innovation of available man-made human infrastructure will also be helpful for the optimum utilization of the such resources already available at the grassroots level and it will also be helpful in the maintenance and management of ongoing implementation of various rural development programmes for the eco-friendly sustainable development and it will be an asset for meeting the ever increasing demand of the growing cattle and human population at village panchayat level through strengthening the grassroots level Panchayati Raj Institutions with the people's participation to ensure integrated sustainable development of Amethi.

SOCIAL INFRASTRUCTURE

The social infrastructure plays an important role in policy planning process and also in the formulation of need based integrated development planning of an area. The innovation of the human resources and social-infrastructural information system at the grassroots level has always been information intensive task. The conventional and traditional system of data collection, collation and its storage are not amenable for the quick updation, retrieval and holistic approach for analysis of several problems, has been realized due to incompatible data base, inefficient inter-sectoral data flow and lack of information on the quality of data at the village level.

It has been realized that the process of planning for an integrated approach requires a detailed knowledge of Human Resources Data Management System (HRDMS) and its interdependencies between various human infrastructural indicators with the view to resolve often conflicting demands. It require appropriate data management and the analysis of social sectoral data especially the social-infrastructural data base at village panchayat level.

The innovation of the social infrastructural data and developing Village Information System has been evolved through socio-economic-institutional infrastructure has been derived from the Sectoral Indicators and also from the various implementing institutions/agencies working at the District level. The collection of the social-economic-institutional data has been ensured through the available sources at the Village/Block/District level and from the secondary sources of information and Primary Field Survey at the grassroots level.

The social infrastructure of an area includes the society, community, social association, social institution and groups, caste composition, social class, workforce and literacy. The various indicators related to population, caste composition, workers and literacy has been identified and their characteristics have been explained at Village Panchayat level in Amethi.

The demographic structure of Amethi has been analysed. It has been recorded that there are 18629 houses and 18530 households in Amethi. Total number of population of Amethi has been 107350 which include 54609 males and 52741 females. The male population contributes 50.59 per cent and female population shares 49.41 per cent population to the total population.

It has been recorded that there are 21.9 per cent Scheduled Caste population in Amethi. There are 7.9 per cent Kurmi caste, 209.3 per cent Yadav population and Gupta caste contributes 4.9 per cent of the total population of the Amethi Block. There are 1.0 per cent share of the Carpenter's caste and other backward castes including Maurya, Nishad, Nai, Lohar, Bhuj and other backward castes which contribute 2.5 per cent of the total population of the Amethi Block. Minorities community which includes Muslims, Sikhs and Christians contribute 11.2 per cent and the total population of Amethi. There are 17.8 per cent Brahmin population and 13.1 per cent Rajput population in Amethi Block. The social backwardness of the people of Amethi has been realized due to Kingship rulership from historical period. The local kings and land revenue tax collectors exploited the service class people and they were deprived of common minimum amenities including land ownership and land rights.

There are 26.3 per cent total workers to the total population in Amethi. There are highest 51.4 per cent workers in Mochawa Village Panchayat and lowest 9.2 per cent workers to the total population in Nuwawan Village Panchayat because this village is dominant by the Muslim population and they work outside in other Metropoliton cities. It has been noticed that there are 12.9 per cent cultivators and 6.6 per cent agricultural labourers and 3.6 per cent non-skilled workers and 1.3 per cent skilled workers to the total population in Amethi. The plantation and animal husbandry worker contributes 0.4 per cent, construction workers and business worker contributes 0.3 per cent of the total population of the Amethi Block. There are 0.2 per cent transportation workers and 0.1 per cent other workers including office workers while small scale and Agro-Industries workers share 0.2 per cent of the total population of Amethi.

The literacy profile of Amethi has been recorded very poor. There are 45.9 per cent total literates in Amethi. The primary educated persons are 12.6 per cent, Junior school educated people are 11.2 per cent and high school educated persons are 9.0 per cent of the total population in Amethi. There are 7.2 per cent Intermediate educated persons in Amethi and 3.4 per cent Graduate educated persons and 2.4 per cent Post Graduate educated persons in the Amethi Block. There are 0.1 per cent professionally educated persons to the total population in Amethi Block. The insignificant literacy ratio in Amethi indicates the poor literacy infrastructure of the Amethi at village panchayat level which has caused social-educational backwardness of the people of Amethi.

In view of the above it has been realized that Amethi has Male dominated society and the Male population ratio has been found significantly higher than the female population, at the village panchayat level in Amethi. The flat land and agriculturally fertile land are highly populated and developed settlements with requisite amenities for the survival of the common people.

Amethi is an agrarian area. Agriculture is dominant occupation of the peoples of Amethi. More than 76 per cent population of the area depends on agricultural activities. The farmers and cultivators are the significant occupational activities of the peoples of Amethi while land less agricultural workers also contributes significant proportion to the total population at the Village Panchayat level in Amethi. The skilled workers and non-skilled workers are also significantly distributed at village level in Amethi. The plantation and Animal husbandry activities are carried out by the Yadav/Kurmi's/Pals and few other interested persons who are engaged in the collection of Milk and selling it in the marketing centres for various commercial purposes. The construction workers and business workers are very insignificantly distributed in Amethi while other workers and office workers are also nominally distributed at village panchayat level in Amethi. The small-scale and Agro-Industries workers are insignificantally and nominally distributed at the village panchayat level in Amethi.

Historically, it has been known fact that Amethi had been kingship ruled estate due to which the *Rajputs* were kins of the kings and land revenue tax collectors and working with the kings for safeguarding the estate of the kings while *Brahmins* were engaged in the worship of the God for well-being of the kings and estate while *Vaisya* were engaged in commercial and managerial activities of the estate and *Shudras* were engaged in providing the services to the kings. It has been noticed that the service class providers who have been providing various services to the kings were given their occupational activities and their surname as their caste, like *Kurmi*—for agricultural activities, *Yadavs*—for milking and animal husbandry activities, *Guptas* — for trading and business activities, *Pal/Gaderia* — for animal husbandry activities, *Nishad* — for fisheries etc., *Nai* — for Hair cutting, *Dhobi* — for washing the cloths, *Darji* — for stitching the cloth, *Julaha* — for cloth weaving, *Vaisya* — for trading/management/accountancy, *Carpenters* — for wood work and furnitures, *Lohar* — for iron work/agricultural implement, Blacksmith, *Kahar* — for (Mitti) Soil Bartan Work, *Brahmins* — for worship of *the God* and *Rajputs* — for safety and security of the estate, etc. There are various other sub-castes in backward caste who are the service providing people as per their caste and occupational structure. *Scheduled Caste* has also been the service providers to the Kings. It has been observed that the service class providing caste were exploited and deprived of their basic common amenities for livelihood including the land ownership and land rights, due to which these service class providers were the socially backward and deprived of social upliftment. The Scheduled Caste people were landless and one of the most deprived multitudes of the society. The social backwardness of the people has also adversely affected the literacy ratio of the Amethi due to which there are only 45.9 per cent literates in the Amethi Block and the primary educated people, junior and high school educated people are only 32.8 per cent of the total population while intermediate educated people are only 7.2 per cent to the total population of Amethi. There are 5.8 per cent Graduate and Post-Graduate educaterd persons to the total population in Amethi and very insignificant 0.1 per cent professionally educated people to the total population has been found in the Amethi Block.

Thus it has been observed that Amethi has been socially backward since historical period. Occupational and caste composition have been based on the service class providers to the kings. The service class providers have not been properly developed and deprived of the common minimum infrastructure required for the integrated development of the caste oriented occupational people of Amethi. The educational profile of Amethi has been very poor which indicates the backwardness of the people of Amethi.

In view of the above it has become a challenging task for the policy-makers, planners at the grassroots level implementing institutions to plan with the peoples involvement for the skill development of workers, occupation based caste composition and improve the educational standard quantitatively and qualitatively at each level of education including professional education. The integrated development of social infrastructure including caste composition, professionally and occupationally and provide skill development training programmes to all workers and sub-workers and increase literacy ratio *scientifically-educationally — institutionally — technically — professionally* for strengthening the available social infrastructure and its optimum utilization at village panchayat level in the Amethi Block, through ensuring peoples participatory need base action oriented planning for their social upliftment and implementation of integrated village development programmes for self-sustenance of the people, for the people, with the people and by the people at the Village Panchayat level in Amethi.

ECONOMIC INFRASTRUCTURE

The agriculture is the backbone of the economy of Amethi. The agriculture is the main occupation of the people of Amethi. The deteriorated fertility status of the soil and inappropriate agricultural inputs have caused very poor agricultural productivity which has led to very poor economy of the people of Amethi. The ignorance, and socioi-economic backwardness and small size of land holdings of the farmers have also been responsible for the poor agricultural productivity of the area. It is known fact that after the Zamindari Abolition the excess land lying waste has been allotted to the landless workers due to which the most of the population of Amethi less than one hectare of the land, i.e. very small size of land holdings while large size of land has been concentrated among very nominal cultivators. The average monthly income of the silled workers of Amethi has been 102.43 lakh rupees, which has been very nominal and poor income of the deprived resourceless poor workers of Amethi. The average monthly income of the animal husbandry workers has been recorded 1370 thousand rupees and the average monthly income of the business workers has been found 1136 thousand rupees of the Amethi Block. Thus, it has been observed that very low average monthly income of the transportation workers has been observed 1241 thousand rupees and the average monthly income of the ssmall scale and agro-industries workers has been noticed 513 thousand rupees for the whole Amethi which has been very low wages as per the wage rates fixed by the government.

In view of the above, it has become an important task of the policy-makers and planners to propagate and demonstrate the latest developed scientific-techniques and tools, equipments, machinery and new system for ensuring the quality production by the workers and also imparting training for the skill development and among the limited land holders of Amethi.

Village Information System and the management of economic infrastructural data collection, collation and analysis have been ensured at the village panchayat level in Amethi. The collection of the Economic Resources Data Management System has been visualized in a network based notes covering Village-Block-District Panchayat. The innovation of economic infrastructural data base has been popularized to promote existing abilities to initiate more activities in a better and faster system for the collection, collation of the available resources of the data base. The major constraints in the large scale economic process of planning has been non-availability of appropriate data base at the grassroots level. The economic development of an area should be through tapping the local talent, and available economic infrastructural resources at the village level in order to ensure sustainable planning for the integrated development. In view of the above an attempt has been made in this study to innovate and analyse the available economic infrastructural data and develop information system for the policy-makers and the village development planners engaged in the implementation of the integrated rural development programmes at the village level.

The land ownership pattern of Amethi has been diversified the large size land has been concentrated among very few land holders. The land concentration in Amethi has adversely affected the agricultural productivity of Amethi. It has been observed that very insignificant and nominal number of households has been the owners of large size land holdings at village panchayat level in Amethi. The good quality fertile lands are owned by the large size land holders and the small size land holders owning very nominal lands have been the wastelands, which has the deteriorated fertility status of soil and very poor agricultural productivity and providing very low income to the resourceless poor cultivators of Amethi. The small size of land holdings and deteriorated fertility status of the soil has caused poor agricultural productivity, henceforth it has caused economic backwardness for the people surviving in the remote rural areas of Amethi.

The irrigation has been an important agricultural input for producing agricultural crops. The irrigational facilities in Amethi has been inappropriate. The irrigational facilities as an agricultural input plays an important role in maintaining the fertility status of the soil for increasing agricultural productivity and also improves the moistures retaining capacity of the soil. It has been noticed that the existing sources of irrigation and available net irrigated area in Amethi has been improper and insufficient. The over irrigation and excess canal water has adversely affected the net cultivated area leading to usarization, waterlogging and deterioration of the fertility status of the soil and caused for poor agricultural productivity. The planned scientific irrigational system as per the need of the soil and agricultural crops may be implemented through people's participation. The canal irrigation and over irrigation of the agricultural crops and proper construction of the drainage system for the removal of excess irrigated water and rainy water has to be ensured to check the growth of wastelands. The Government Tube-well and Tube-well irrigation system may be promoted and propogated to check the water logging and also control the usarization of the soil. An effort must be initiated to develop rain water harvesting systems to provide good quality irrigation for increasing the agricultural productivity and maintaining the deteriorated fertility status of the soil. The techno-scientific and appropriate irrigational system as per the soil and agricultural crops requirements must be propogated, popularized and the cultivators/farmers should be motivated and trained for optimum utilization of available irrigational and natural rain water resources.

Amethi is a rice bowl of the area and rice has been the main agricultural foodgrain crops having 2170 hectares agricultural land. The matiyar soil and low lying, water logged land has facilitated appropriate agro-climatic favourable conditions for the Paddy/Jadhan/Dhan/Rice foodgrain cropping in the Amethi. Wheat has been an important foodgrain crop in Amethi 1701 hectares wheat cropped area in Amethi. The area under 446 hectares agricultural land under the peas as pulse crop while the mustard oil seed crop has 824 hectares cropping in Amethi. The sugarcane area has been only 33 hectares in Amethi, while the potato a vegetabe crop has been cultivated in 509 hectares land in Amethi. The fodder has been an important cattle feed which has been cultivated by the animal owners, the total area under fodder crop has been recorded 264 hectares agricultural land in Amethi. The policy planners and the agricultural scientist, soil scientists and agricultural extension workers to promote, propogate, motivate and practically demonstrate for the optimum utilization of the available agricultural land, water, wasteland resources and also to conserve the available wastelands for agricultural productivity to meet the ever increasing demand of growing population for meeting fuel wood, fodder, fibre, fruits, food grains, fisheries (F^6) and vegetable.

The ignorance and adopted traditional techno-scientific agricultural practices has reduced poor agricultural productivities. The proper application of insecticides and pesticides and organic and inorganic amendments may be helpful in increasing the agricultural productivity. The governent facilities especially the plant protection and the control of insects and pests has not been properly applied in the agricultural crops which has not only affected the crops but also adversely affected the fertility status of the soil. The appropriate proven use of insecticides and pesticides, as per the need of the agricultural crops, in a scientific system may be an asset not only in increasing the agricultural productivity but also maintaining the fertility status of the soil.

The use of chemical fertilizers has been improperly and insignificantly used in Amethi. The green manuring and compost fertilizers and organic and inorganic amendments are not properly applied as per the need of the soil to produce the crop and also to maintain the fertility status of the soil. It has been recorded that the application of the Nitrogen fertilizer has been found in 2024 hectares agricultural cropped land. The Phosphate fertilizer has been used in 385 hectares agricultural cropped land. The Potash fertilizer has been used in 76 hectares of the Amethi Block. The organic and inorganic, Inappropriate and insignificant use of the chemical fertilizers has caused poor agricultural productivity and also deteriorated the fertility status of the soil. The soil testing has not been carried out to know the requirement of the soil to produce the agricultural crops. The green manuring of the agricultural land must be ensured for the proper conservation of the cropping land. It has been recorded that the compost fertilizer has been applied in 945 hectares in Amethi. The scientific and appropriate need base demonstration of the use of organic and inorganic amendments, green manuring of the land and compost fertilizer including. Gobar khad must be ensured through people's participation to increase the agricultural productivity and to fulfil the slogan of the government for the *"Adhik Ann Upjao"* or "*Produce more Food Grain*s".

The use of bio-gas has been very insignificantly used in Amethi. It has been recorded that there are 359 bio-gas plants installed and functional in the Amethi. The proper use of available cow dung and animals gobar should be utilized through the bio-gas for availing cooking gas and the compost fertilizer with the view to improve the fertility status of the soil and also to conserve the environmental conditions of Amethi.

The agricultural implements plays an important role in increasing the agricultural productivity of the land. The old, traditional agricultural implements are time taking, inefficient for ensuring quality agricultural activities. The latest developed scientific and technically proven agricultural implements are efficient, sufficient, effective in performing the quick agricultural practices but the high-tech, scientific agricultural implements are costly and beyond the reach of the deprived, resourceless, rural poor agricultural cultivators of the Amethi Block. The proper scientific and technical demonstration of the high-tech agricultural implements may increase the agricultural productivity of the Amethi Block. It has been noticed that 1249 wood cultivators and 348 iron cultivators are used in the Amethi Block. There are 109 high-tech cultivators used in Amethi and 124 high-tech agricultural implements/machinery etc. are used by the large size land holders in the Amethi Block. It has been recorded that there are 362 tractors used for the land cultivation and other agricultural activities including transportation of the agricultural and commercial commodities. It has been noticed that other high-tech 99 agricultural implements/equipments are used in the Amethi Block. It has been recorded that small size land holders and weaker cultivators has been using traditional agricultural implements and large size land holders and rich cultivators are applying the high-tech scientific and latest developed agricultural implements for ensuring quantity and quality agricultural production at the grassroots level in Amethi.

Animal husbandry has been an important source of income generation for the down-trodden deprived animal husbandry workers in Amethi. It has been recorded that there are 5273 cows, 3233 buffalowes, 1716 goats and 222 horses in the Amethi Block. It has been noticed that there are 575 pigs, 1032 hens/cocks in the Amethi Block.

It has been observed that the traditional cows/buffalows are kept by the deprived poor people like Yadav and others while rich and large size land holding persons are keeping hybrid and inseminized cows and buffalow which produces more milk which are economically viable. The pigs are kept by the Scheduled Caste people and hens/cocks are kept by Muslims and others for availing eggs and chickens for their household use. The economy through animal husbandry activities has been very nominal and insufficient income generation. The inseminization of the existing milking animal like cows, buffalows and goats should be promoted and scientific promotion of pigs and hens/cocks should be promoted with the view to increase quality and quantity production to increase the income and generate employment of the deprived animal husbandry workers.

The average income of the workers of the Amethi has been found insufficient, for ensuring the livelihood of the common people of Amethi. The average monthly income of the cultivators has been estimated 415.95 lakh rupees and agricultural workers monthly income has been recorded rupees 135.78 lakhs and non-skilled workers monthly income of 92.75 lakhs rupees and skilled workers monthly income rupees 102.43 lakh has been recorded for Amethi.

It has been observed that the average monthly income of the animal husbandry workers has been found 1370 thousand rupees, business workers' monthly average income has been found 1136 thousand rupees and the transportation workers' average monthly income has been noticed 1241 thousand rupees and the average monthly income of the small scale and agro-industries workers has been found 513 thousand rupees for the Amethi Block.

In view of the above, it has become an important task of the policy makers and planners to propagate, promote and demonstrate the latest developed technologies, tools, equipments, machinery and scientific system for ensuring the quantity and quality production through participation of the workers. The special skill development training programmes for the skill upgradation of the workers to ensure quality and quantity production should be ensured which should be less labour oriented but it can increase the productivity with the view to increase the daily wages income of the workers and generate employment and increase the income of the resourceless, deprived rural poor workers living in hardship, hand to mouth, surviving in the remote rural areas.

INSTITUTIONAL INFRASTRUCTURE

The institutional infrastructural available at the grassroots level plays a vital key role in the planning process of the integrated village development. The integrated approach of the planning process requires detail knowledge of the inter-relations and interdependencies between various sectoral indicators to resolve often-conflicting requirements and available institutional infrastructural at the grassroots level. The existing institutional infrastructural resources may provide a base for the formulation of need base, people's participatory, sustainable integrated village development planning. Therefore, the available institutional infrastructural resources must be considered before initiation of the planning process.

The Institutional Infrastructural Resources Data Management (IIRDMS) is multi-disciplinary and multi-institutional research and development programme with vision to provide appropriate scientific and technological inputs for operationalizing the concept of decentralized integrated village development planning.

The main objectives of the institutional infrastructural resources have been to develop the scientific data base approach to support the local level area specific village development planning, various efforts has been made to evolve and develop institutional infrastructural resources spatial data management system for integrated village development planning and its demonstration in the local level decision-making process.

In view of the above, an attempt has been made in this study to analyse the available institutional infrastructural resources existing at village panchayat level in the Amethi Block. An effort has been made to develop spatial data management system and analysing techniques for the incorporation of the existing institutional infrastructural resources available at the grassroots level in the Amethi Block. In order to implement at least some of the institutional infrastructural related activities with the vision of Village Information System and collection, collation of the grassroots level data support from a large segment of the scientists and entrepreneurs are required. It has been expected to stimulate the imagination of the research community to relate specific problems in their areas of interests and to evolve suitable research proposals to pursue line of investigation and imagination of the research community and to arrive at meaningful solutions for the integrated village development planning.

It has been realized that the development should be participatory and it should be planned according to the local needs of the resourceless deprived rural poor multitudes. The development should be planned through tapping local level existing institutional infrastructural resources in order to make the implemented rural development programmes self-sustainable.

It has also been mentioned in the Constitution of India that *"Government should evolve methods to unite the village panchayats and provide such powers and rights which can be helpful to workout as an unit of self-government."*

In the Panchayati Raj system each village should be self-sustained and independent, and the implementation of the welfare programmes can be implemented in a better manner in the various village panchayats of Amethi. The self-government is the main sole of the village development. To strengthen the Panchayati Raj Institutions, government has allocated the rights, administrative and financial powers to *Village Panchayat → Block Panchayat → District Panchayat* for implementation and maintenance of assets created at the grassroots level through peoples participation.

The institutional infrastructure plays an important role in the policy planning for the integrated village development. The peoples participatory need base integrated village development formulation of the policy planning should be initiated through tapping local level available institutional infrastructural resources in order to make the already implemented rural development programmes.

The drinking water is one of the most important requirement for the survival of human being. It has been recorded that the tap water supply has been provided to the 499 households in Amethi and there are 2380 India Mark II hand pumps installed at village panchayat level in Amethi, which has been very insufficient to fulfil the ever increasing demand of the growing population and increasing settlement colonies. The individual households have constructed and installed their own private hand pumps to fetch the drinking water facilities. It has been recorded that there are 7326 private hand pumps installed by the individual households at village panchayat level in Amethi. It has been noticed that there are 292 households in Amethi Block who are forced to fetch the drinking water facilities from the wells and other sources of drinking water including borrowing from other individuals drinking water sources at village panchayat level in Amethi. In view of the above, it has become an important task for the policy planners and local level peoples representatives to provide special package for the installation of the India Mark II hand pumps among the deprived resourceless, rural poor surviving in the remote rural areas of the Amethi Block.

It has been recorded that there are only 319 small scale industries and agro-industries functional at Amethi. Therefore, it has become necessary to promote the establishment of small scale industries and agro-industries to ensure the value addition of the agricultural produce and to generate the employment and also increase the income of the deprived rural poor people.

It has been noted that there are 430 low cost houses in the various villages of the Amethi Block which is very insignificant and an effort must be made to provide special package for the construction of low cost houses for the roofless, mud house and thatched roof house owners, landless labourers and to provide shelter for everyone as per the policy of the government to provide shelters for the houseless people living in the remote rural areas of Amethi.

The energy an important institutional infrastructure plays an important role in the economic development of an area. It has been noticed that there are 595 non-conventional sources of energy including solar lights, solar water pumps, Solar Lanterns and other sources of the non-conventional energy being used in Amethi. There are 12190 household electricity consumers at village panchayat level in Amethi and very insignificant 478 commercial electricity consumptions have been found at village panchayat level in Amethi. The electricity consumers are very insignificantly distributed at village level in Amethi due to very poor and irregular, nominal 6-8 hours electricity supply which has adversely affected the commercial consumption of the electricity. The proper supply of the electricity, appropriate electricity and energy infrastructural resources may be helpful in the economic development of the Amethi Block.

The road communication plays a key role in the economic growth and an integrated development of an area. The National Highway, *pucca*, *kuchcha*, *kharanza* roads especially for linking the villages from one village to another village plays a key role in the economic growth and transportation of the agricultural produce to the Krishi Utpadan Mandir Samiti. It has been noted that there are 80 kilometres National Highway and 195 kilometres pucca road including State Highway and 315 kilometres kharanza road and 380 kilometres kuchcha road for connecting District, Tehsil, Block to the various village panchayats. The road network not only facilitates the communication support from one village to another but it has become the life line for the resource less village poors in Amethi. Thus, the road network plays a key role in the economic development of not only the village panchayats but it supports for the integrated village development of the Amethi Block.

The educational infrastructure also plays a vital role in the integrated village development of an area. The educational infrastructure has been very insignificantly distributed at village panchayat level in Amethi. There are 140 educational institutional infrastructures available at village panchayat level in Amethi. It has been noticed that there are 3 primary schools in Sarai Khema, Mochawa, Ramdaipur, Korari Girdharshah and Katara Phulkunwar village panchayats of the Amethi Block. One primary school has been noticed in Benipur, Parsawan, Tala, Kushi Tali, Nuwawan, Loniapur, Himmatgarh and Dehara village panchayats while two primary schools have been recorded in the rest of the village panchayats of the Amethi Block. Thus, there are 85 primary schools established and functional at village panchayat level in Amethi Block. It has been noted that there are 34 Junior High Schools and 9 High Schools in the various village panchayats of the Amethi Block. It has been observed that there are 4 Intermediate Colleges in the Amethi Block including Government Girls and Government Boys Intermediate College in the Amethi Town Area in the Amethi Block. The graduate level girls college and post graduate level college is functional in Amethi Town area which has been an important higher educational infrastructure available in Amethi Block. There is one government boys and girls polytechnic in Amethi and one Industrial Training Institute has been noted in Mahmoodpur and Korari Girdharshah village panchayats of the Amethi Block. There are one Pharmacy, one Management and one Engineering and Technology college functional in the village panchayat Jangal Ram Nagar and Sarai Khema village panchayats respectively. There are 7 other educational institutional infrastructures available at village panchayat level in Amethi. Thus, the educations institutions and professional educational institutional infrastructures are very insignificantly distributed in Amethi which have to be strengthened and promoted at village panchayat level in the Amethi Block.

It has been noted that there are old historical Temples in Sarai Khema, Saidpur, Chaturbhujpur, Purabgaon, Dhandhudhar, Gangauli, Mahaso, Katara Phulkunwar, Kherauna and Darakha village panchayats. There is Kali temple in the Katara Maharani, Umapur Ganapatti and Nainaha village panchayat while Shiv Mandir has been found in Himmatgarh, Dedhpasar, Rebha, Hathkila, Mochawa, Mahmoodpur, Benipur and Sarai Khema village panchayats of the Amethi Block. Various historical and religious temples are found in various Village Panchayats in Amethi, like Kali Mandir has been found in Katara Maharani, Umapur Ganapatti, Nainaha; Durga Mata Mandir in Loharata; and Devi Patan Mandir in Raipur Phulwari has been found. Muslim religious Masjid and Idgah has been found in Sarai Khema, Loniapur, Korari Girdharshah, Gaderi, Agahar, Kakawa and Mahmoodpur village panchayats of the Amethi Block. There is one 75 years old historical pond in Kakawa village panchayat and famous old pond has been found in Mahmoodpur, Maharajpur, Raidaipur, Bhaganpur and Tala village panchayats of the Amethi Block.

There are Panchayat Bhawan or Village Panchayats Office Secretariat functional at all village panchayats in Amethi Block. The ANM centres are functional in Trilokpur, Jangal Ram Nagar, Loharata, Hathkila, Korari Girdharshah, Dedhpasar, Gangauli, Dhandhudhar, Maharajpur, Kakawa, Saraiya Duban, Mahmoodpur, Naraini, Ramgarh and Himmatgarh village panchayats of the Amethi Block. There are 10 sub-post office functioinal in Trilokpur, Jangal Ram Nagar, Umapur Gangapatti, Darakha, Rebha, Korari Girdharshah, Dhandhudhar, Kakawa, Naraini, Ramgarh village panchayats of the Amethi Block. Most of the village panchayats of the Amethi Block have been connected through bus, jeep, tempo, tanga etc. transportation facilities for commuting from one village to another and also Tehsil and Block Headquarters of Amethi. It has been noted that Public Call Office, Bharat Sanchar Nigam Limited (BSNL) Telephone Booths, Land Line Telephones and Mobile Telephones or Telecommunications facilities are significantly distributed at village panchayat level in Amethi Block.

The Animal Hospital Institutional Infrastructures are functional in Umapur Ganapatti, Kherauna, Korari Girdharshah, Bhusahari, Agahar, Kakawa, Saraay Duban, Kohara, Naraini and Himmatgarh village panchayats of Amethi. The medical health institutional infrastructure facilites are available in Sarai Khema, Benipur, Umapur Ganapatti, Tala, Darakha, Nuwawan, Kherauna, Korari Girdharshah, Kakawa, Kohara, Mahmoodpur village panchayats of the Amethi Block.

The Banking institutional infrastructures are significantly distributed in Amethi. There are 20 Banks functional at village panchayat level in Amethi. There are 3 nationalized Banks functional in village panchayats Sarai Khema, Munshiganj and at Hindustan Aeronautics Ltd. (HAL) Korwa, Munshiganj, Baroda Kshetriya Grameen Banks are functional in the various village panchayats to facilitate the village beneficiaries for the financial transaction in the banks.

In view of the above, it has been noted that the drinking water, small scale and agro-industries, low cost housing and energy sources are very insignificantly distributed at village panchayat level in Amethi. The existing institutional infrastructure users have to be properly maintained and managed for its appropriate utilization for the purpose for which it has been established and made available to the village people of Amethi. The road network has been significantly and appropriately available at village panchayat level in Amethi and it requires appropriate maintenance and management for its sustenance. The educational infrastructures are very insignificantly distributed except the Primary Schools but the quality of the Schools and standard of the Primary education has been found very poor in comparison to the Public school due to which most of the children and their guardians prefer to obtain public school education in every village panchayats of the Amethi Block. The intermediate, high school educational institutional infrastructures are very insignificant and the higher education and the professional educational infrastructures are very poor and it requires to be strengthen at village panchayat level in view of the ever increasing demand of the growing population. The available religious and historical infrastructures must be protected, maintained and managed for its sustenance at village panchayat level. The number of Anganwadi Kendras and ANM Centres, Animal Hospitals and Medical Health Centres have to be promoted to facilitate the increasing population and growing diseases and medical health problems at village panchayat level. The transportation network has to be supported through Uttar Pradesh State Road Transport Corporation (UPSRTC) Buses facilitating to the village people to travel from one village to another place. Therefore, it has become an important task of the policy planners to protect and maintain the available institutional infrastructures at village panchayat level and also to establish more institutional infrastructural resources as per needs of the growing cattles and human population to meet their growing demand of *Roti, Kapada and Makan (Food, Cloth & Shelter)* for the resource less deprived rural poor multitudes surviving in the remote villages of Amethi.

Thus the Human Infrastructural resources contribute an important segment of the Village Information System. The collection, collation, storage and analysis of the available Human Resources Data Management System at Village Panchayat Level → Block Panchayat Level → District Block Panchayat Level may be an important asset for the policy-makers, planners for formulating the need based peoples participatory planning at the micro-level. It has been realized that already available Human Resources, i.e. Social–Economic–Institutional Infrastructural Resources play an important key role in plan formulation. It has been noticed that already existing Human Infrastructural Resources are not properly considered and due to lack of the information the duplicacy of the programmes and non-people's participation and non-willingness of the people has adversely affected the successful implementation and sustenance of the completed programmes. Therefore, it has become an important task for the grassroots level policy makers and planners to innovate the available Human-Social-Economic-Institutional Infrastructural resources and to develop the Village Information System at village panchayat level.

In view of the above, the innovated and developed Village Information System at village panchayat level in Amethi on Human Infrastructure including Social Infrastructure-Economic Infrastructure-Institutional Infrastructural Resources has been analysed at the grassroots levels i.e. Village Panchayat level in Amethi.

It has been noted that the available Human Infrastructural Resources including Social-Economic-Institutional Infrastructures has been appropriately available and distributed at Village Panchayat Level which has proved a mile-stone in the formulation of the integrated village development planning. It has been realized that the available the Social-Economic-Institutional Infrastructural Resources has not been properly tapped and innovated which led to Socio-Economic-Institutional backwardness of Amethi. The appropriate and optimum utilization of Social-Economic-Institutional Infrastructural Resources will be helpful for the integrated village development and it will be helpful in fulfilling the ever increasing demand of growing cattle and Human Population for Fuel wood, Fodder, Fibre, Fruits, Fisheries and Foodgrains (F^6) and vegetables and generate the employment and increase the average income of the deprived resourceless rural poor multitudes surviving in the remote villages of Amethi.

The creation of Human Infrastructural Resources Data Management System will be an asset for developing need based action plan to strengthen the Social Infrastructural Resources for optimum utilization of population, service providing caste with occupational structures especially to develop techno-scientific skills of professional castes for the quality and quantity production with the view to generate employment and increase their income. It will be helpful for optimum utilization of the workforce/workers, promoting and developing the educational system and various other social/society/community based programmes for their integrated development.

The Economic Infrastructural Resources creation of data will be helpful for appropriate utilization of the size of land holdings, land ownership, developing source of the irrigation and increasing the area under foodgrains and commercial crops, upgradation of the agricultural implements and also increasing the agricultural productivity of the area.

The creation of the Institutional Infrastructural Resources Data will be an asset for maintaining the created assets and optimum utilization of the developed assets and also in the formulation of the need base rural development programmes for Road, Education, Medical and Health. Small Scale Industries, Agricultural Inputs, Animal Husbandry, Sanitation, Drinking Water, Land Development and various other programmes as per the increasing demand of the ever growing population and rural settlements. Thus, it can be concluded that the creation of Human Infrastructural Resources Data Management System (HIRDMS) along with Social-Economic-Institutional Resources data will be an asset for fulfilling the common minimum requirements of the *Roti-Kapada-Makan* or *Food-Cloth-Shelter* for the downtrodden deprived rural poor multitudes living in the remote villages so that the Amethiwala may also survive and move *equally, effectively, efficiently* along with the other *Rurban* and *Urban elites.*

References

I. BOOKS

Babarata, K.C., *Planning for Forest Resources and Bio-Diversity Management*, published by Concept Publishing Co. Pvt. Ltd., New Delhi.

Bhattacharya, J.P., *Study of Soil Conservation for Agricultural Land*, New Delhi, 1964.

Bland Fort, H.F., *The Climates and Weather of India*, Cylon and Burma (London), 1889.

Browrigg, F.W., *Settlement Report*, District Sultanpur, 1898.

Chauhan, D.S., *Studies in Utilization of Agricultural Land*, Aggarwal Publication, Agra, 1966.

Ganguli, H.N., *Restoration of Soil Structures with Gypsum*, Bikaner Gypsum Ltd., Bikaner, 1954.

Ginsbarg, M., *Sociology,* Better Birth, London, 1934, p. 50.

Govinda Rajan, S.V. and Gopal Rao, H.G., *Studies on Soils of India*, New Dehli, 1978.

Krishnan, M.S., *Geology of India and Burman*, Madras, 1960.

Kuldeep, K.P., *The Climates of Continents*, Oxford University Press, Oxford 1927.

Leather, J.W., *Investigation of Usar Land in United Provinces*, Government Press, Allahabad, 1914.

McIver, R.M.S. & Page, C.H. *Society*, MacMillans & Company, New York, 1950, p. 348.

Mishra, R.P., *Regional Planning*, 1992, Concept Publishing Co. Ltd., New Delhi.

Mishra, R.P. (Ed.) *Changing Deceptions of Development Problems*, Singapore, Maruze in Asia, 1983.

Mohammad Ali, *Dynamics of Agricultural Development in India*, Concept Publishing Co. Pvt. Ltd., New Delhi, 1978.

Nevill, H.R., *District Gazetteer of the District Sultanpur*, Allahabad, 1903.

Rae Chaudhury, S.P., *Land and Soil*, National Book Trust, New Delhi, 1966.

Rao, K.L., *India's Water Wealth: Its assessment, Uses and Projections*, Orient Longman, New Delhi, 1979.

Risley, H. *The People of India*, London, 1951, p. 1.

Shafi, M., *Land Utilization in Eastern Uttar Pradesh*, Aligarh Muslim University, Aligarh, 1960.

Shame, K.B. & Rae Chaudhary, S.P., *Rating of Soils of India*, IARI, New Delhi, 1960.

Singh, A.K. *et al.*, *Forest Resource Economy and Environment*, Concept Publishing Co., New Delhi, 1987.

Srivastava, K.G., *Agro-Forestry*, Central Book House, Rajpur, M.P., 1995.

Tejwani, K.G., *Agro-Forestry in India*, Concept Publishing Co., New Delhi, 2001.

Wadia, D.N., *Geology of India*, London, 1960.

Yadav, H.R., *Agro-Afforestation Management on Wastelands*, Concept Publishing Co., New Delhi, 2011.

Yadav, H.R., *Dimension of Wastelands Development*, Concept Publishing Co., New Delhi, 1988.

Yadav, H.R., *Genesis and Utilization of Wastelands*, Concept Publishing Co., New Delhi, 1986.

Yadav, H.R., *Reclaiming Wastelands*, Concept Publishing Co., New Delhi, 1990.

Yadav, H.R., *Village Development Planning*, Concept Publishing Co., New Delhi, 2009.

Yadav, H.R., *Village Information System (Innovation of Natural Infrastructure)*, Concept Publishing Co. Pvt. Ltd., New Delhi, 2012.

Yadav, H.R., *Wastelands Diagnosis and Treatment*, Concept Publishing Co., New Delhi, 1987.

II. ARTICLES

Abrol, I.P., *Reclamation of Wastelands and World Food Prospects*, Trans, Int. Cong. Soil Science, New Delhi, 1982.

Aggarwal, L.I. & Mehrotra, C.L., *Soil Survey and Soil Work in U.P.*, Vol. I, Allahabad, 1952.

Aggarwal, R.R. & Mehrotra, C.L., "Quality of Water Irrigation Waters in U.P.", India J. Science, 31, (1966).

Aggarwwal, L.I., *Soil Survey and Soil Work in U.P.*, Vol. II, Allahabad, 1952.

Aggarwwal, L.I., *Soil Survey and Soil Work in U.P.*, Vol. III, Allahabad, 1954.

Aggarwwal, L.I., *Soil Survey and Soil Work in U.P.*, Vol. IV, Allahabad, 1954.

Bland Food, *H.F., "The Rainfall of India*, Mem., Indian Met. Deptt. Vol. 3, 1986-88.

Bland Ford, H.F., *Hotwinds of Northern India*, Mem., Indian Met, Deptt., Vol. 6, 1986.

Choudhary, Kamala, "Greening of India", *Indian Express*, 21 December, 1982.

Clark, K.G.T., "The Vicissitudes of Summer Rainfall of the Indo-Gangetic Plain and the Valley", *Geography*, 18 (Pt. IV), 1932.

Dhawan C.L., *Land Reclamation*, Central Board of Irrigation and Power, Publication No. 43, Vol. III, 1.

Eliot, J., "The Hot Winds of Northern India" Indian Met., Mem. 6 (Pt.) (III), 1980.

Hart, D.R.D. & Stands, M.W., "Sustainable Land Use System Research and Development" in International Workshop on Sustainable Land Use System Research February, 12-16, p. 13.

Hill, S.P., "Variations of Rainfall in Northern India", Indian Met., Mem. 1 (Pt. III) 1897.

Kanwar, J.S., "Reclaiming Retriorated Soils" *Fertilizer News*, 6 (21) 1961.

Leather, J.W., "Agriculture Soils" in *Agriculture Ledger* (3) 1898.

Mathur, R.K., "Economics of Agro-Forestry for wastelands Reclamation", *Agriculture Ledger*, 1983, (175-87).

Rae Chaudhary, S.P., "Extension of Cultivated Areas for Increased Agricultural Production," Producing of Symposium of Science and India's Food Problem, ICAR, New Delhi, 1971.

Rae Chaudhary, S.P., "Final Report of the All India Soil Survey Scheme": *Bulletina*, India Council of Agricultural Research, 1952, 13.

St. Duster, S.A. "Intervening Opportunities: A theory relating Mobilizing and Distance", *American Sociological Review*-Vol.-II, Dec. 840, pp. 845-67.

Stamp, L.D., "The Land Utilization Survey of Britain, *Geographic Journal*, London, (78), 1931.

Taylor, C.C., "Weed Control" *Indian Farming*, 9 (4) 1948.

Tewari, D.N., "Technology for Sustainable Development", National Seminar on *Technology for Sustainable Developments*, March, 12-18, Guru Ghasi Das University, 1980, p. 17.

III. GOVERNMENT AND U.N. PUBLICATIONS

Agricultural Census of Uttar Pradesh, 1990-71, Agricultural Statistics of Uttar Pradesh, 1971.

District Census Hand Book, Sultanpur District 2001.

Economic Register, Block Development Office, Amethi.

F.A.O. Frame Work for Land Evaluation *Soil Bulletin No. 1*, 1976

I.A.R.I., Resources Analysis of the District Rae Bareli, 1989.

I.A.R.I., Resources Analysis of the District Sultanpur, 1989.

I.C.A.R. *Hand Book of Agriculture*, 1969.

I.C.A.R., *Final Report of All India Soil Survey Scheme*, 1958.

Land Revenue Records (Khasara Register and Khasara Maps) Amethi Tehsil, Distt. Amethi.

National Thematic Maps Organisation (NATMO), Govt. of India.

State Soil Conservation Research, Annual Reprot, U.P. p. 61.

Statistical Book, District Raebareli, 2001.

Statistical Book, District Sultanpur, 2001.

Survey of India, Topographical Sheets NO. 63F/11, 63F/10, 63F/12, 63F/14, 63F/15, 63F/16, 63J/3, 63J/4, 63J/5, 63J/8, 63J/11, 63J/12, 63K/3, 63K/9.

The Imperial Gazetteer of India, Vol. XXIII, Singhbhumi to Transhialchod-Zong, Reprint Edition, (Today and Tomorrow Printers and Publishers) New Delhi, 1974, 130-37.

U.S.D.A., *A Manual on Conservation of Soil and Water, Hand Book of Professional Agriculture Workers*, Oxford Publishing Co., 1984.

Coloured Maps

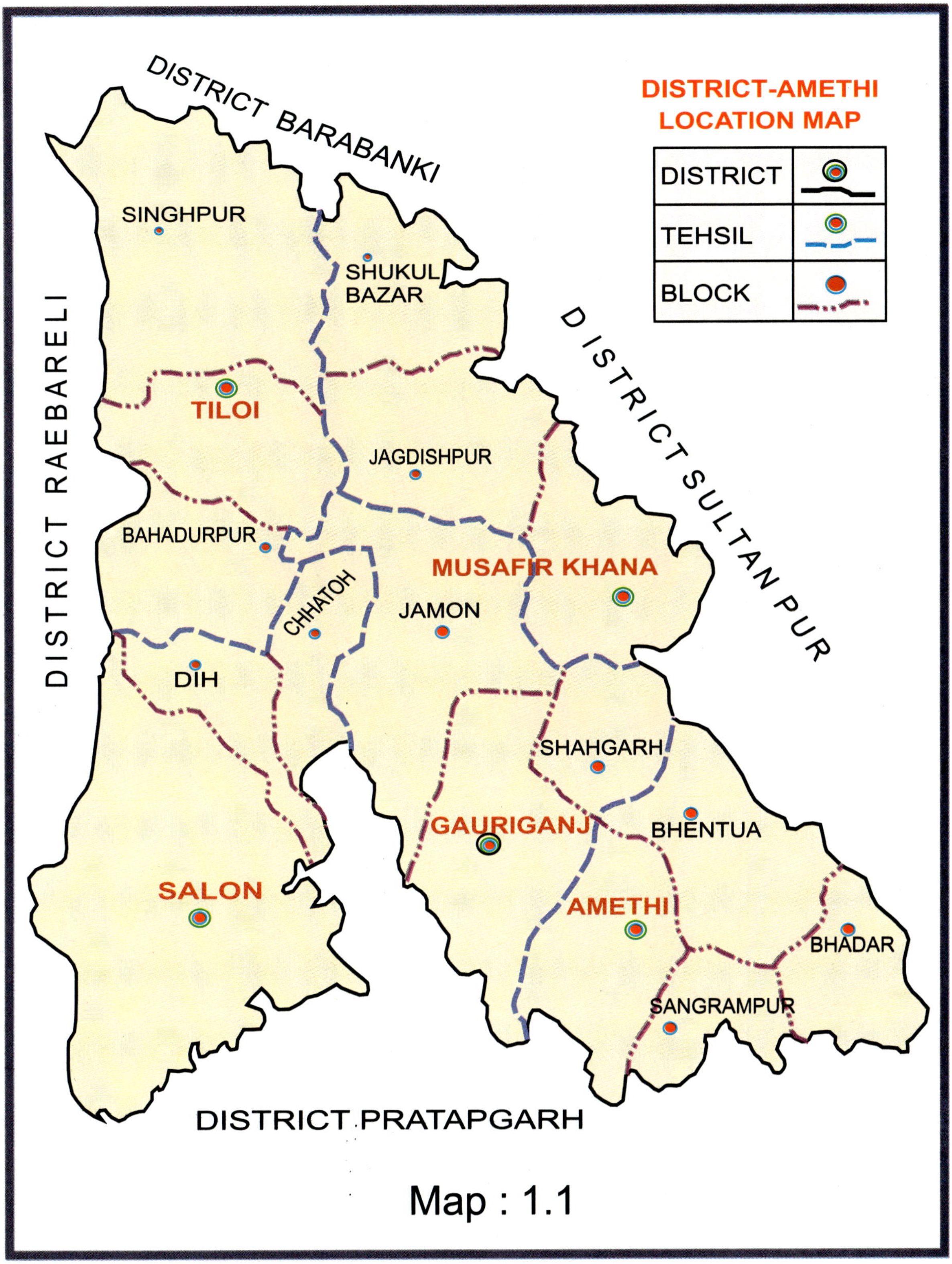

Map 1.1: Blocks and Tehsils, Amethi Districts

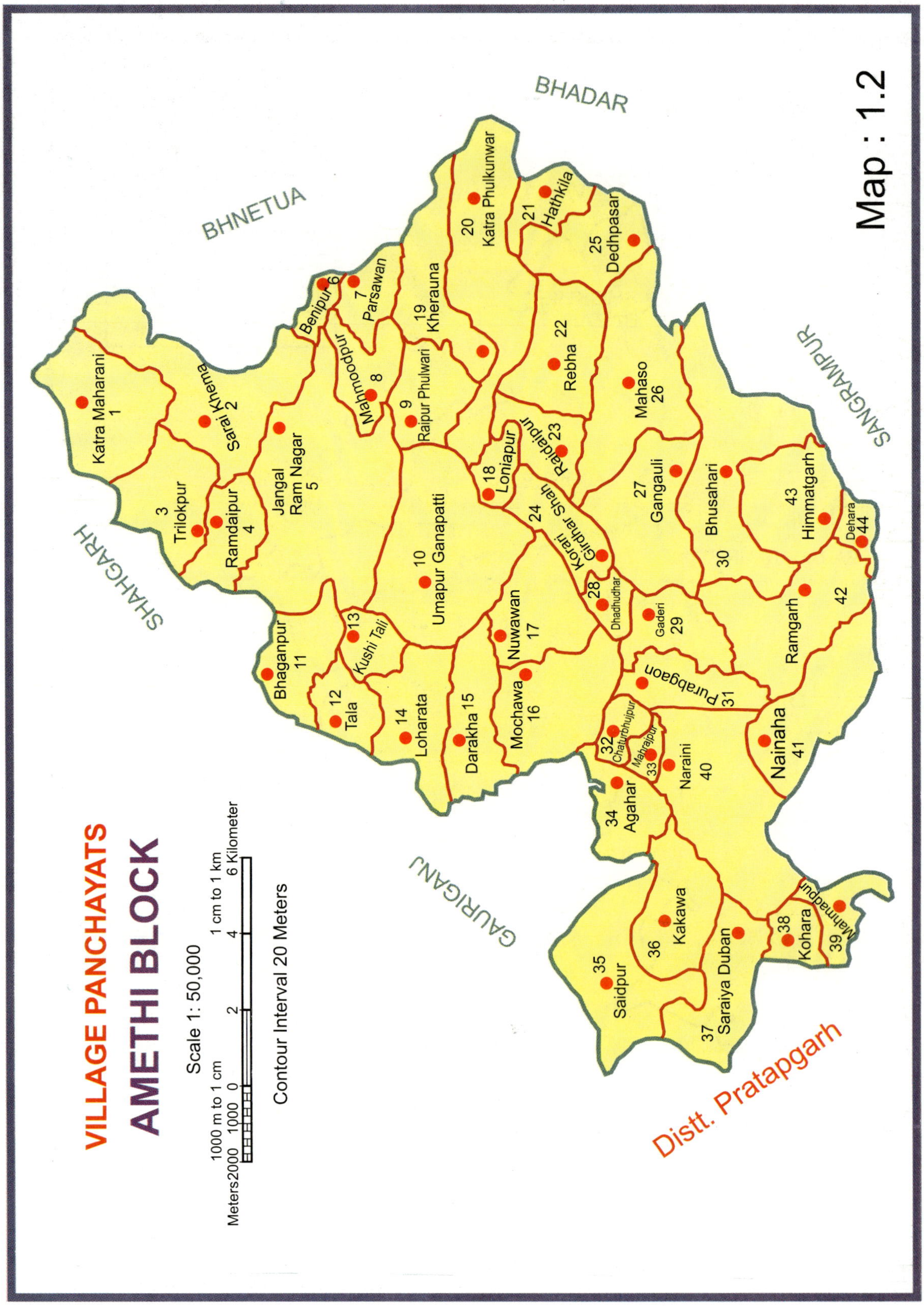

Map 1.2: Village Panchayats, Amethi Block

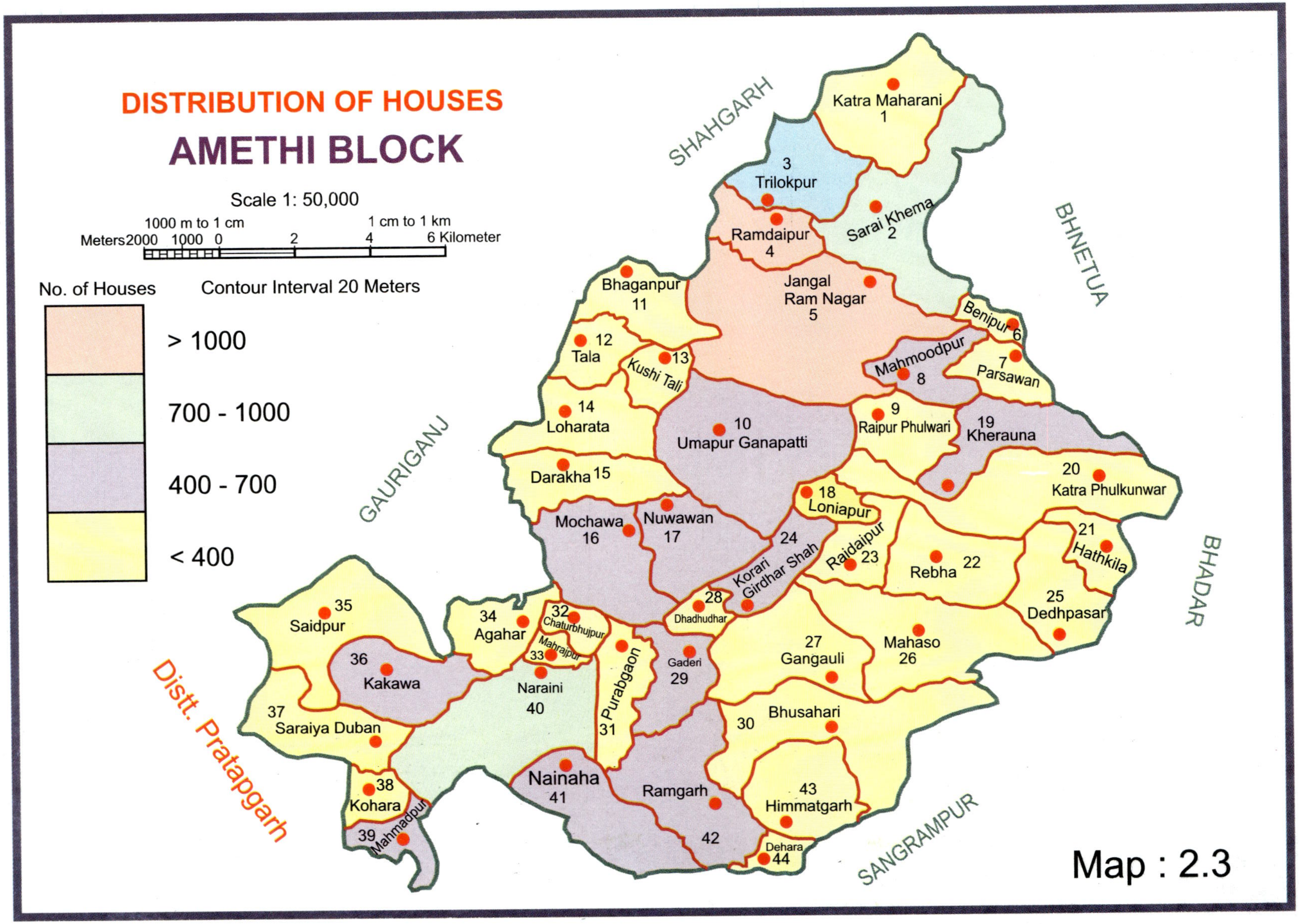

Map 2.3: Houses, Amethi Block

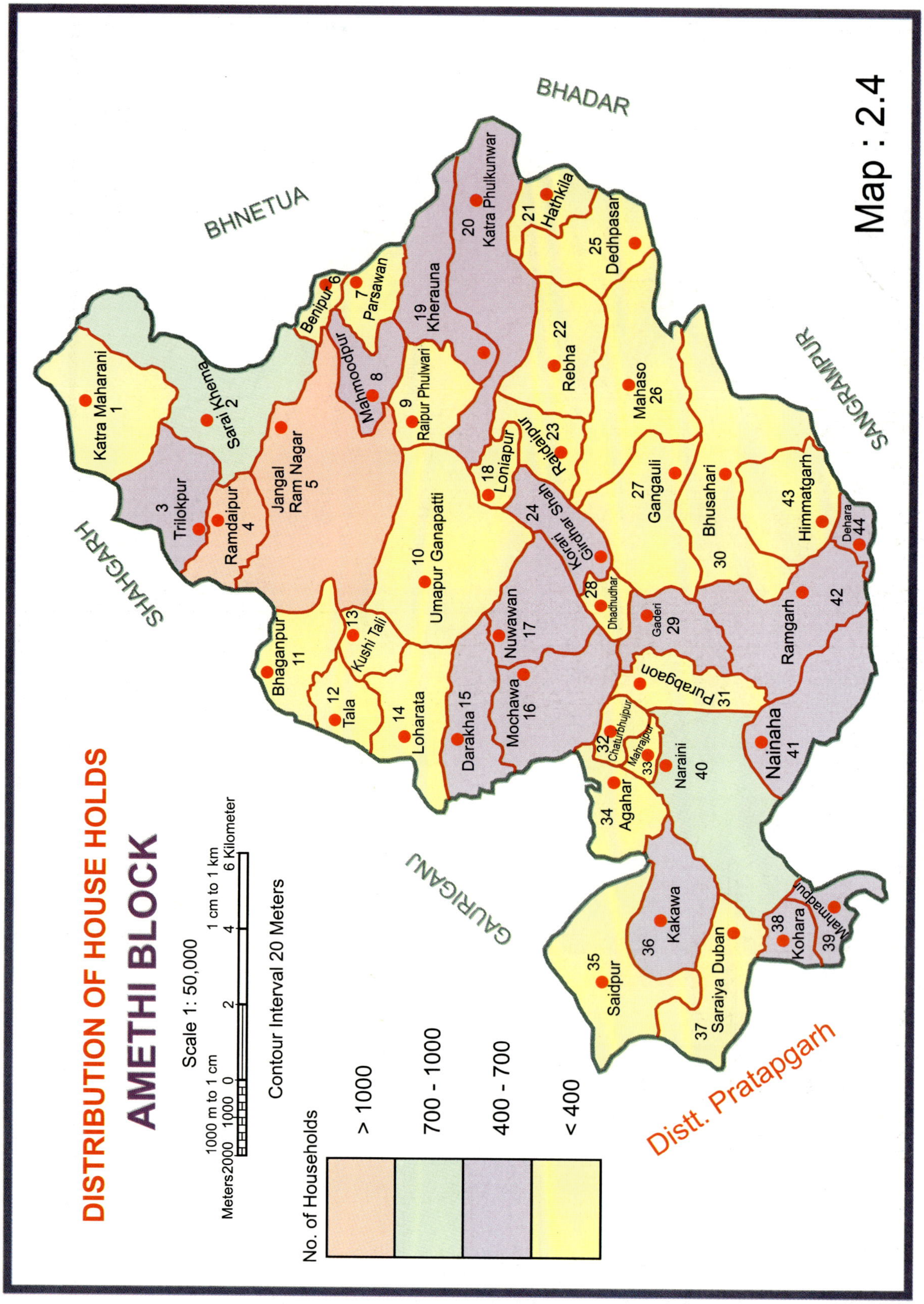

Map 2.4: Households, Amethi Block

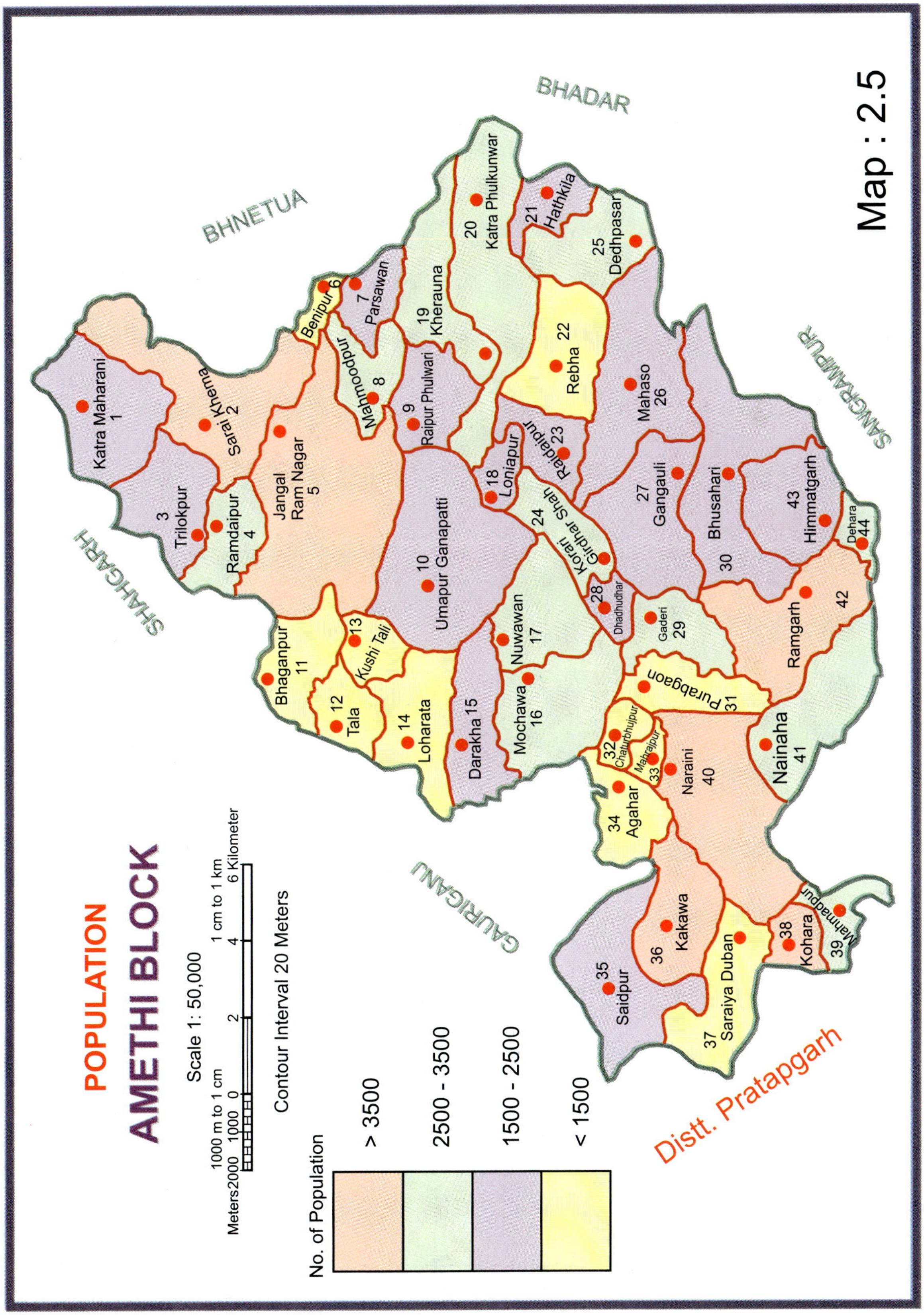

Map 2.5: Population, Amethi Block

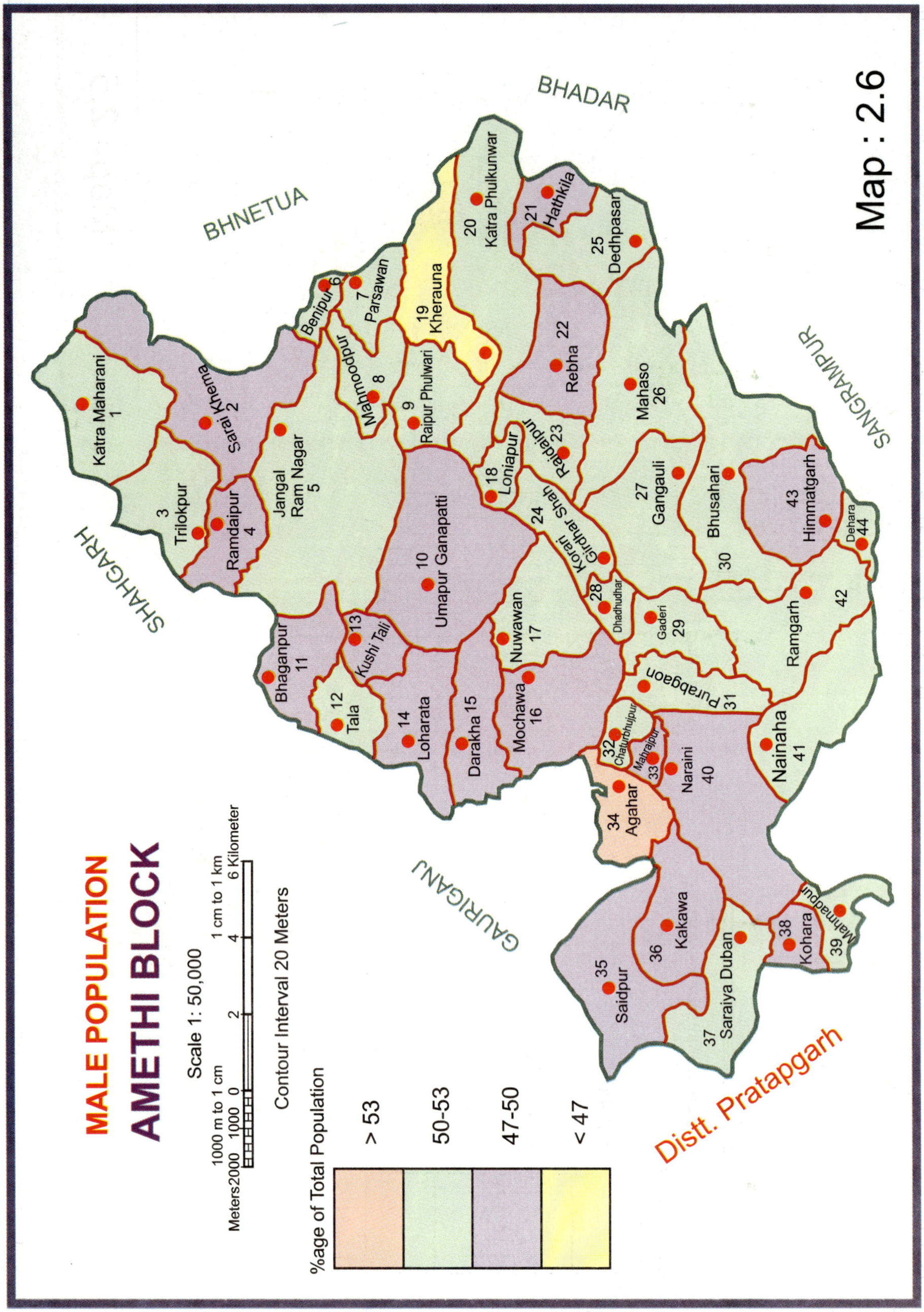

Map 2.6: Male Population, Amethi Block

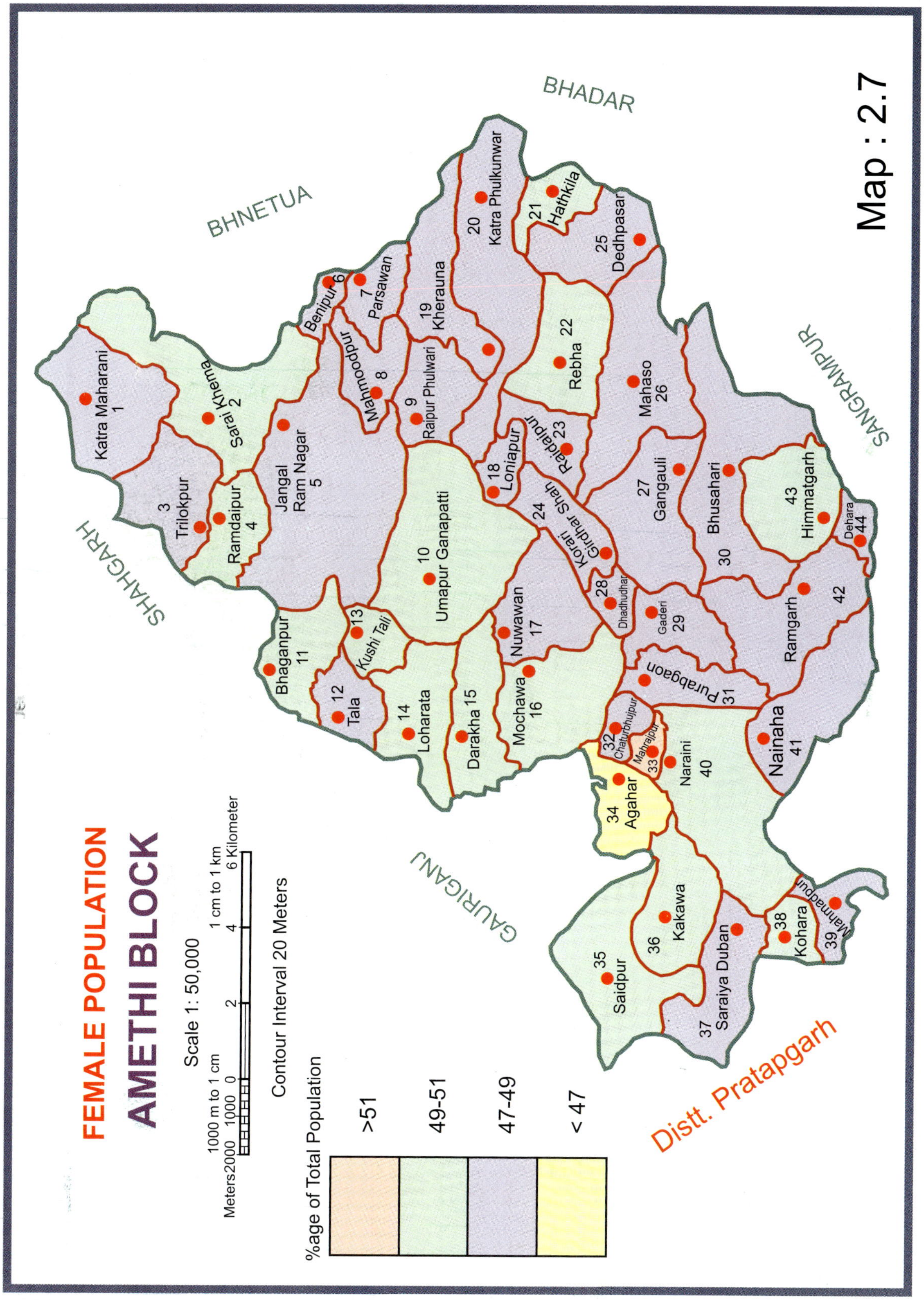

Map 2.7 Female Population, Amethi Block

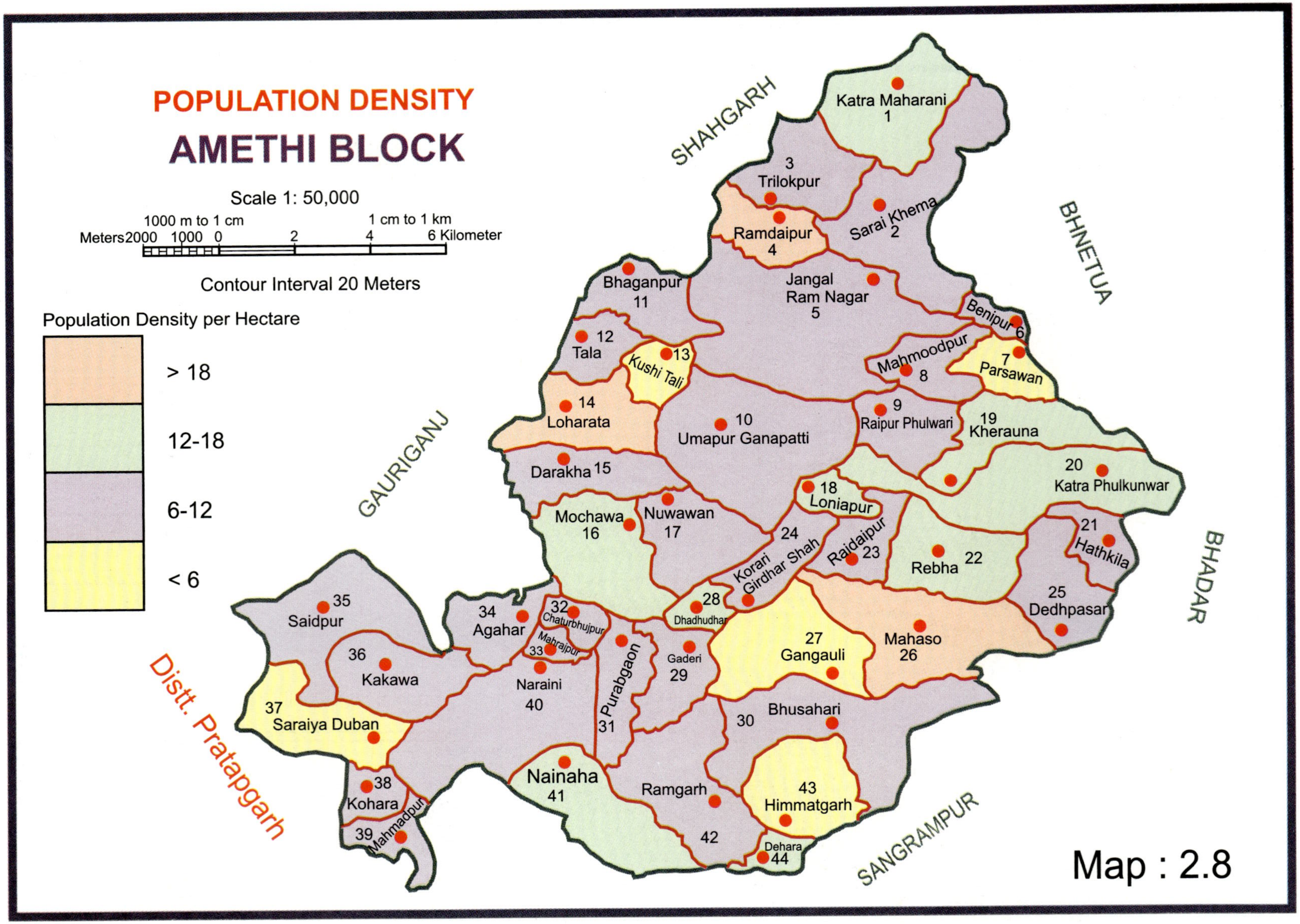

Map 2.8 Population Density, Amethi Block

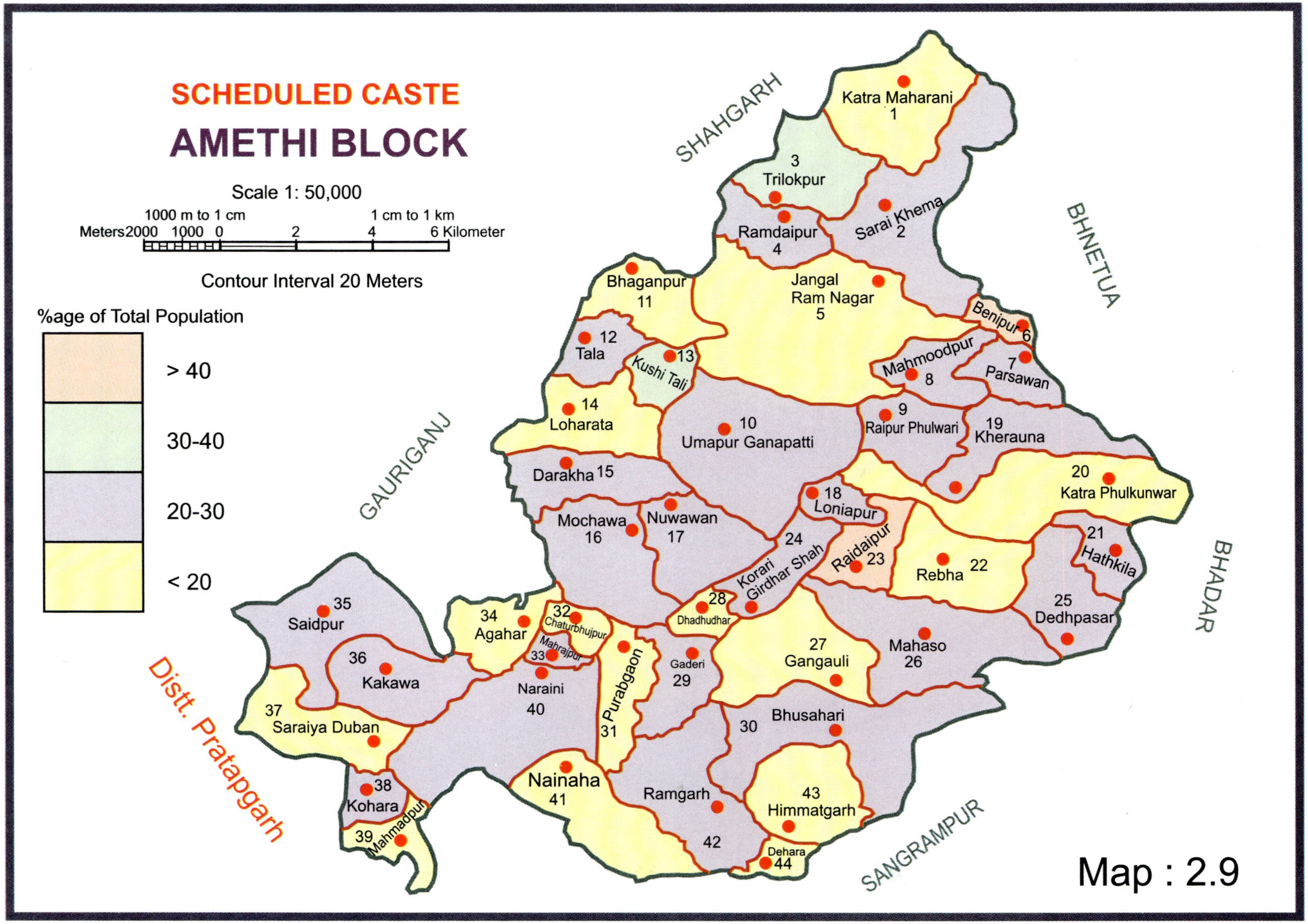

Map 2.9: Scheduled Caste, Amethi Block

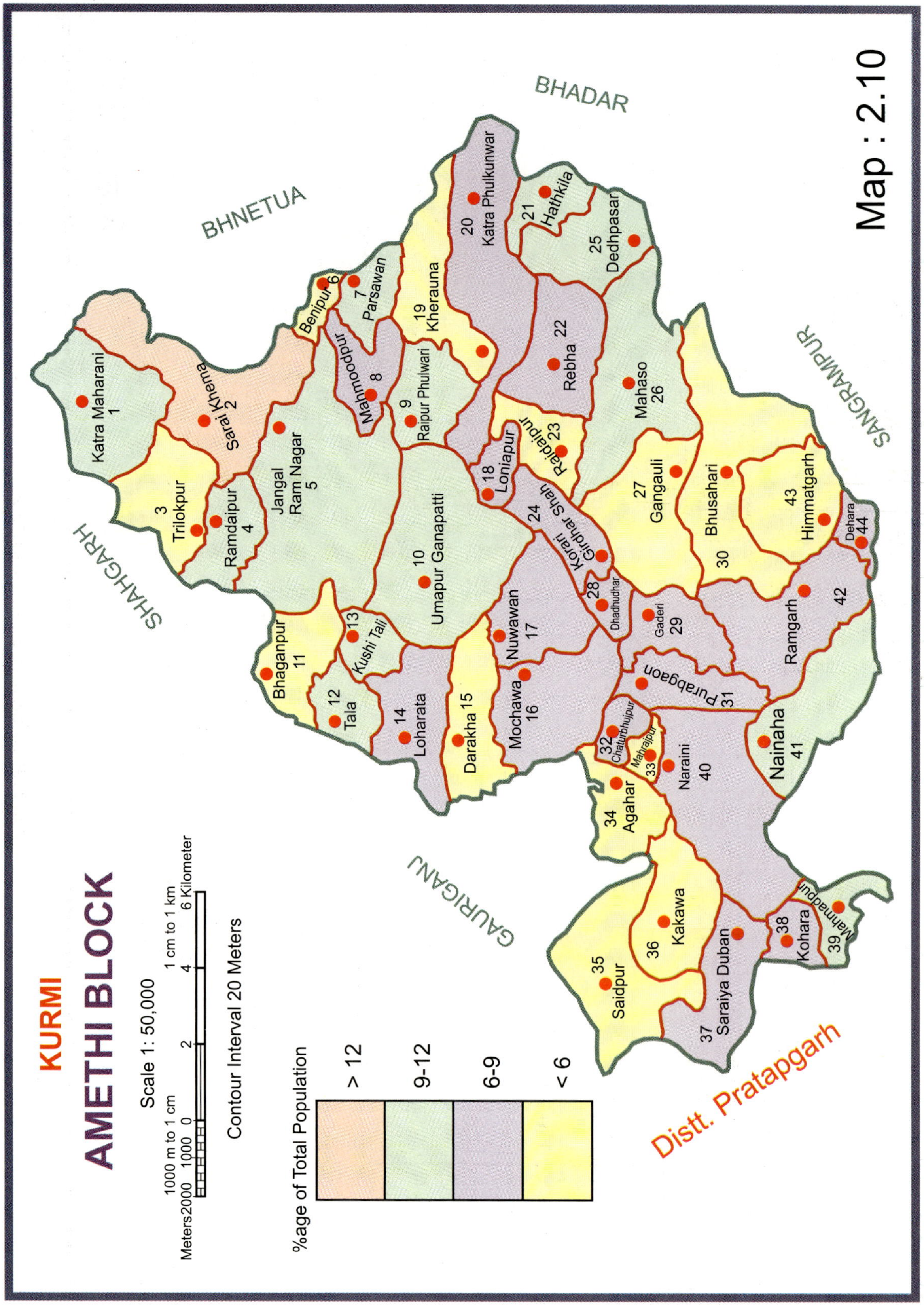

Map 2.10: Kurmi, Amethi Block

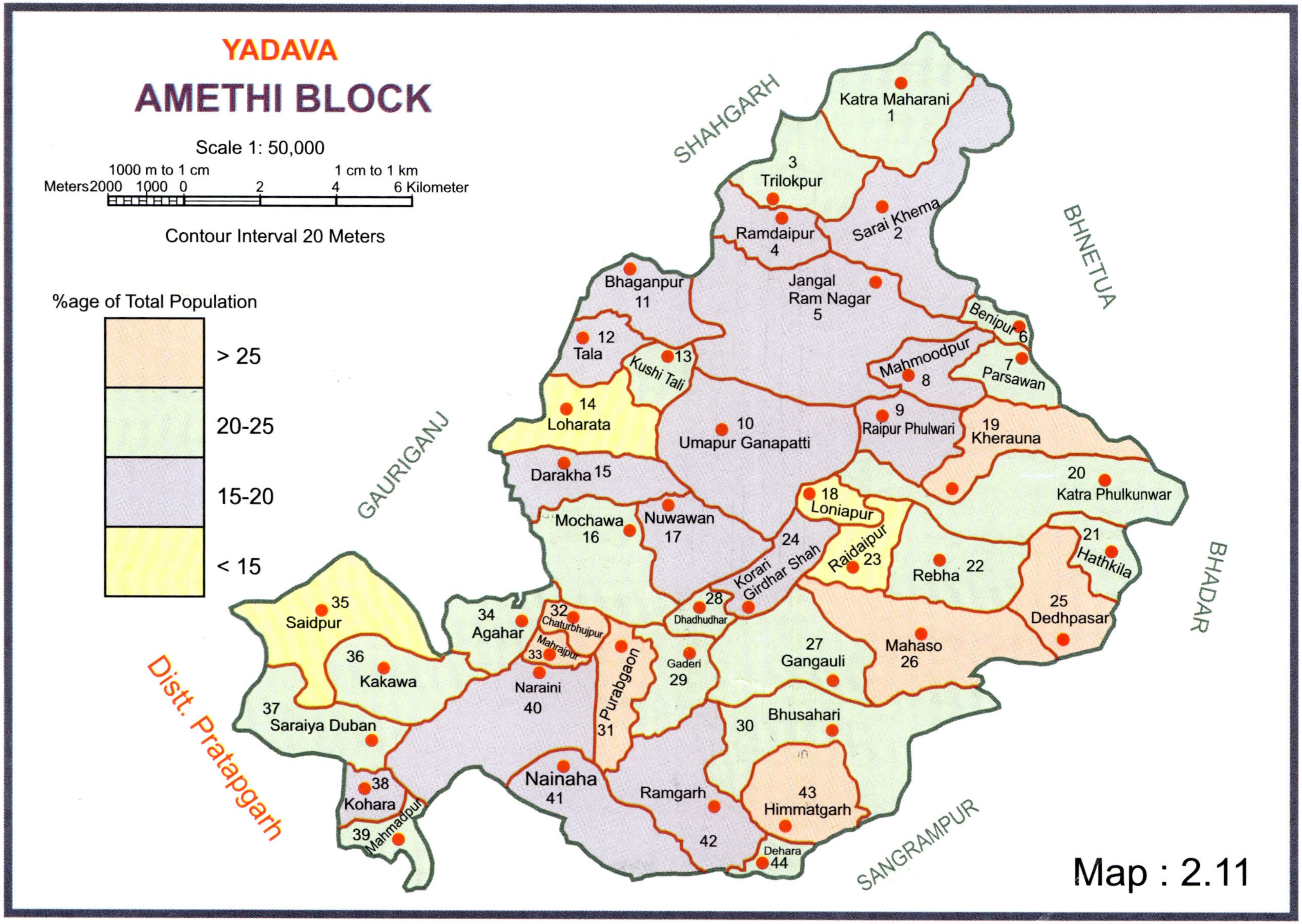

Map 2.11: Yadav, Amethi Block

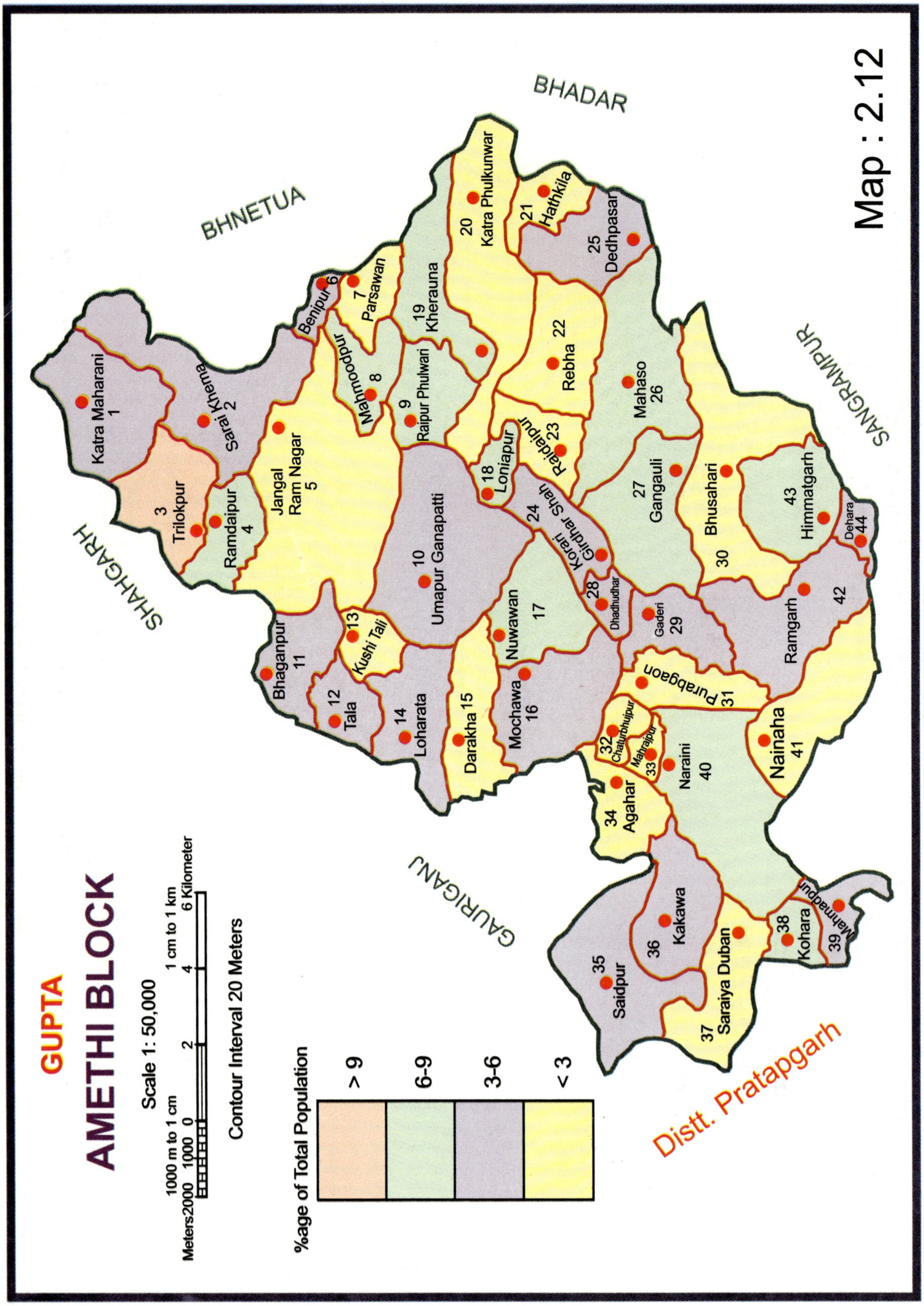

Map 2.12: Guptas Population, Amethi Block

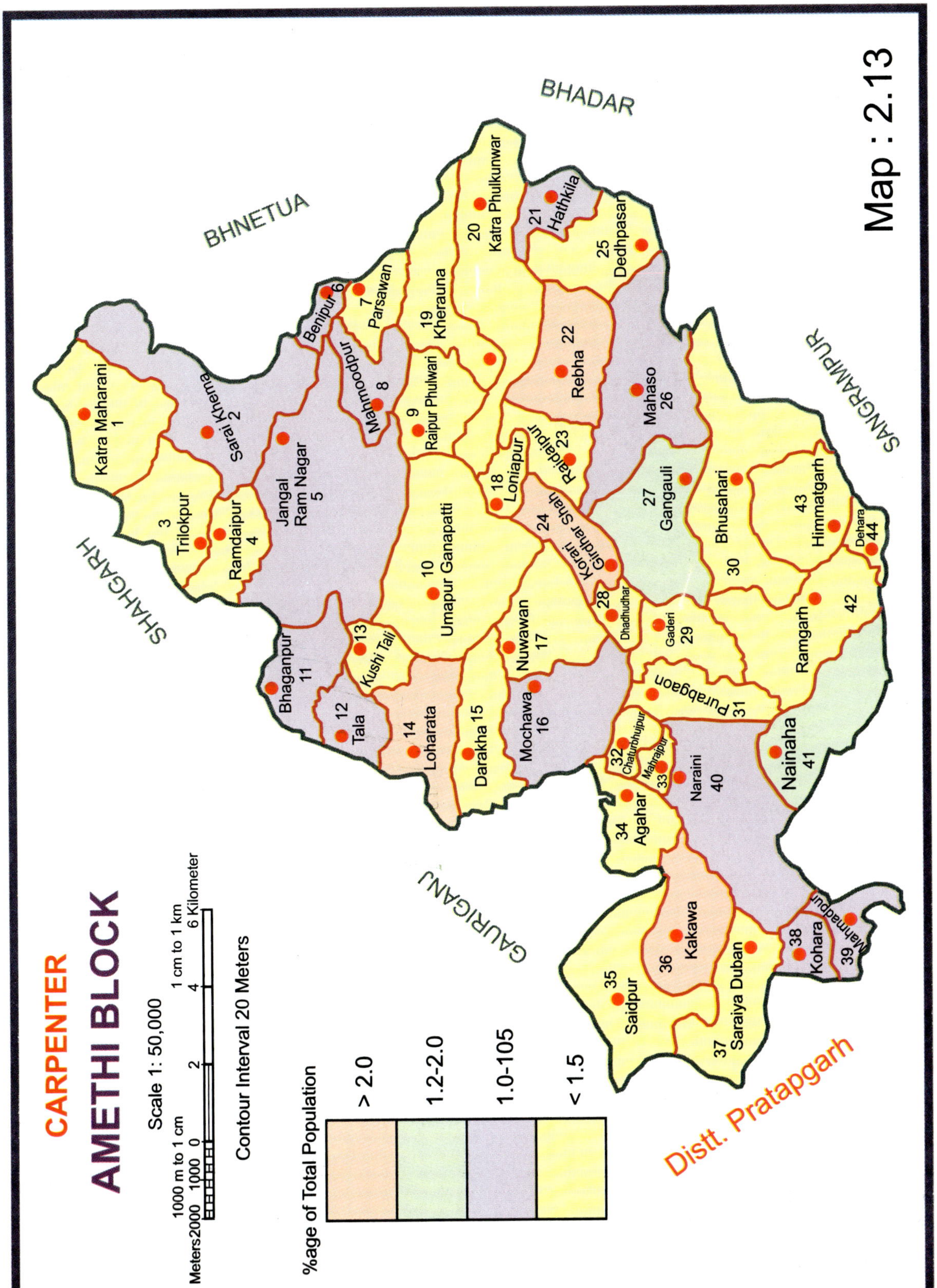

Map 2.13: Carpenter, Amethi Block

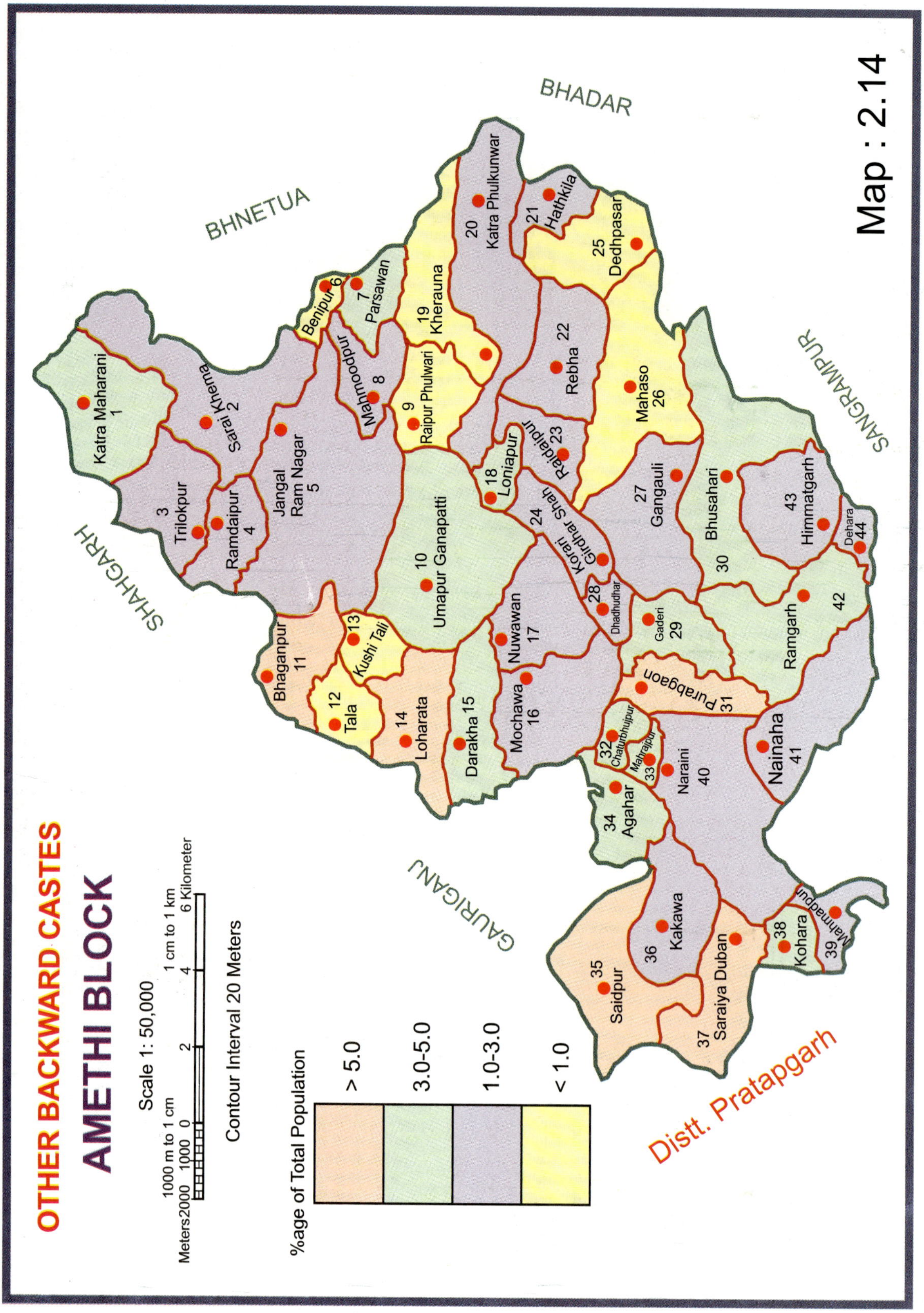

Map 2.14: Other Backward Castes, Amethi Block

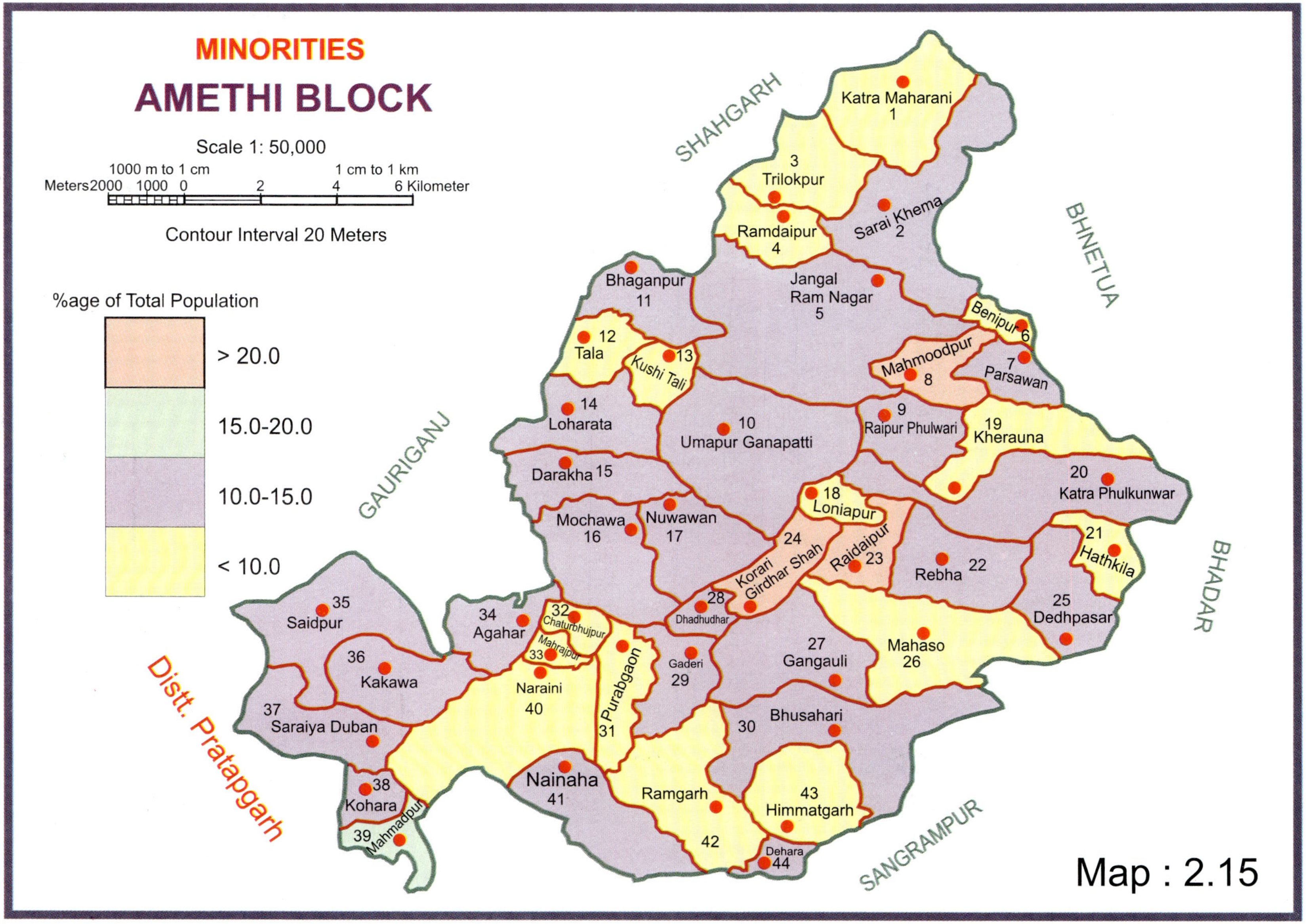

Map 2.15: Minorities, Amethi Block

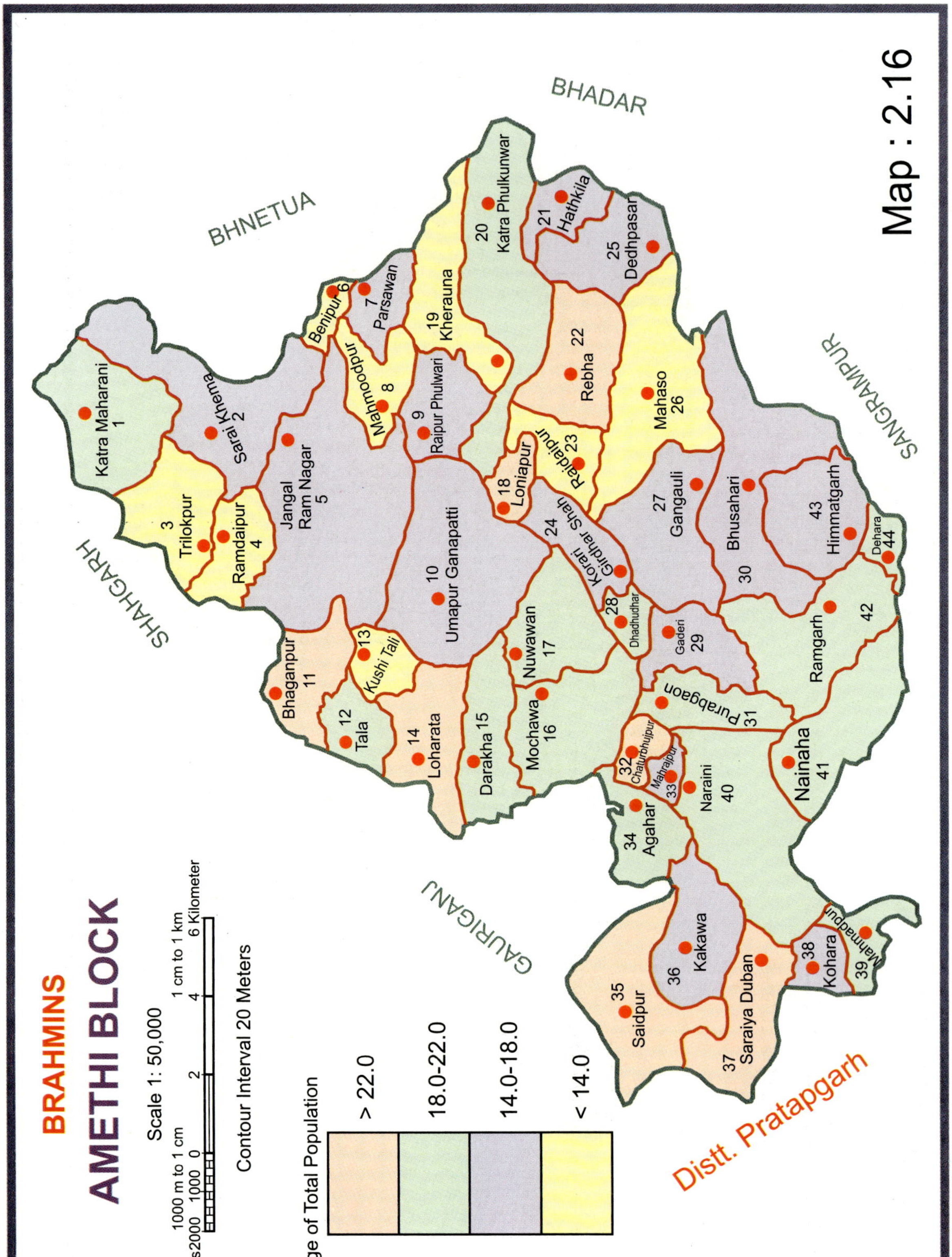

Map 2.16: Brahmins, Amethi Block

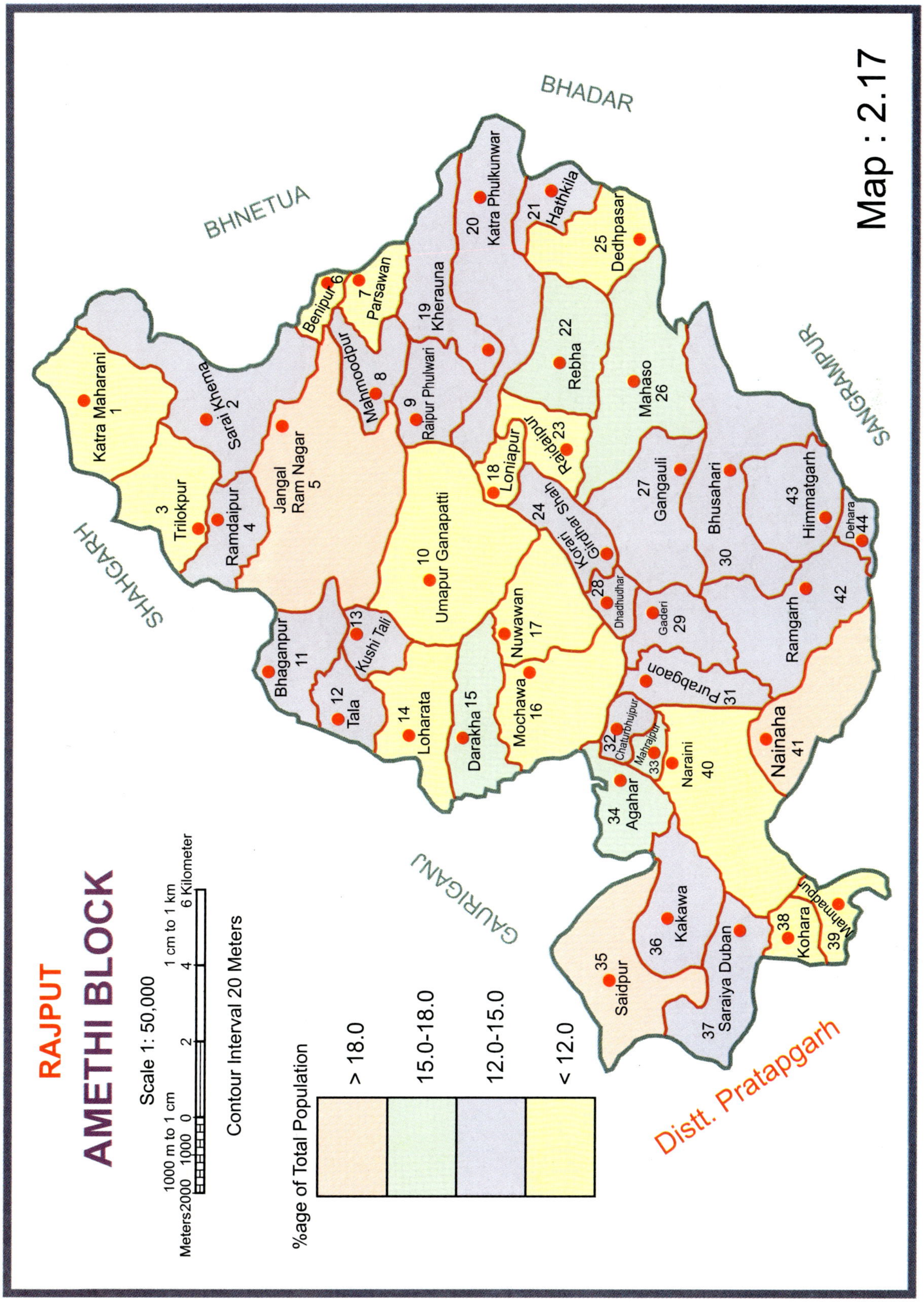

Map 2.17: Rajput, Amethi Block

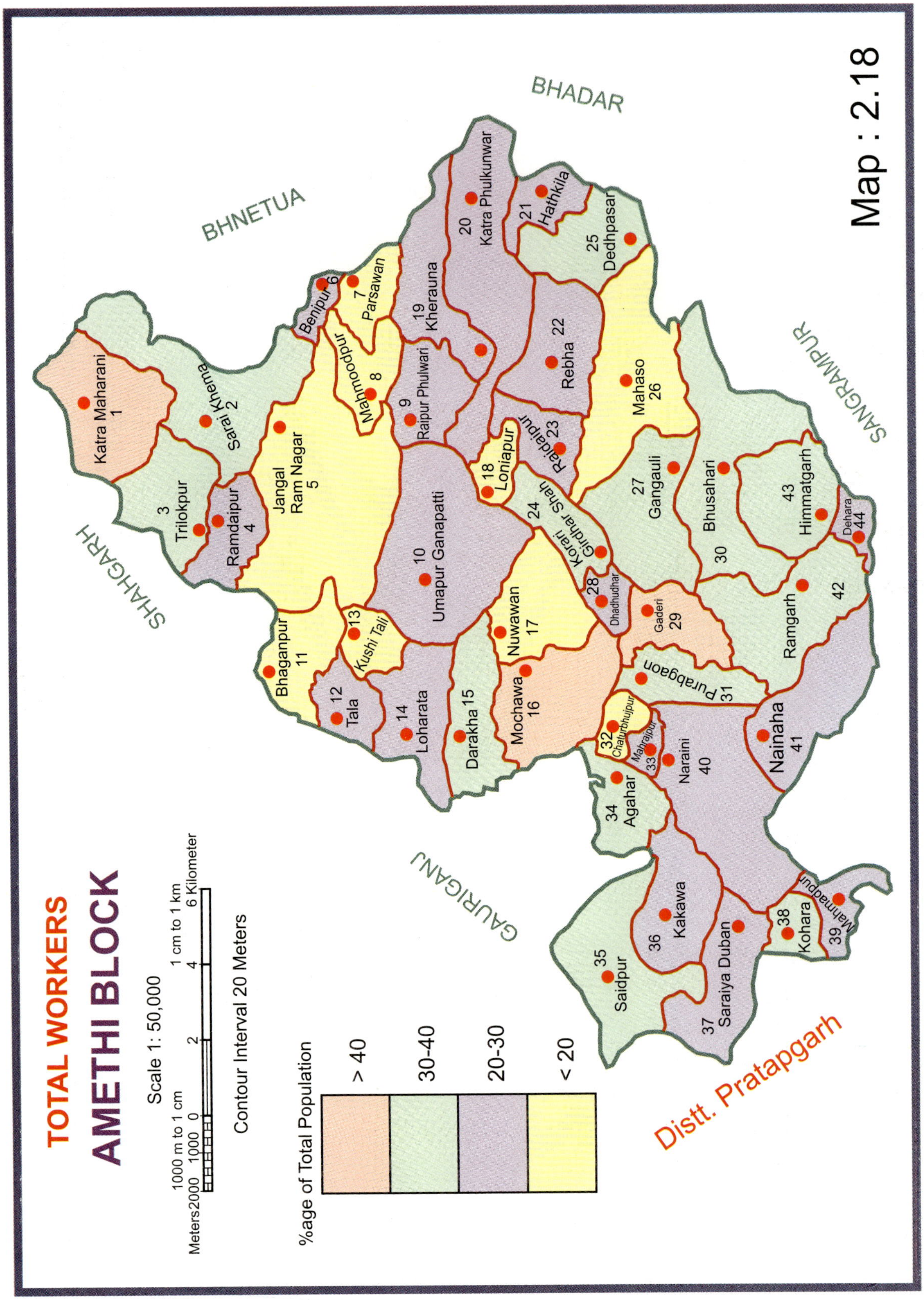

Map 2.18: Total Workers, Amethi Block

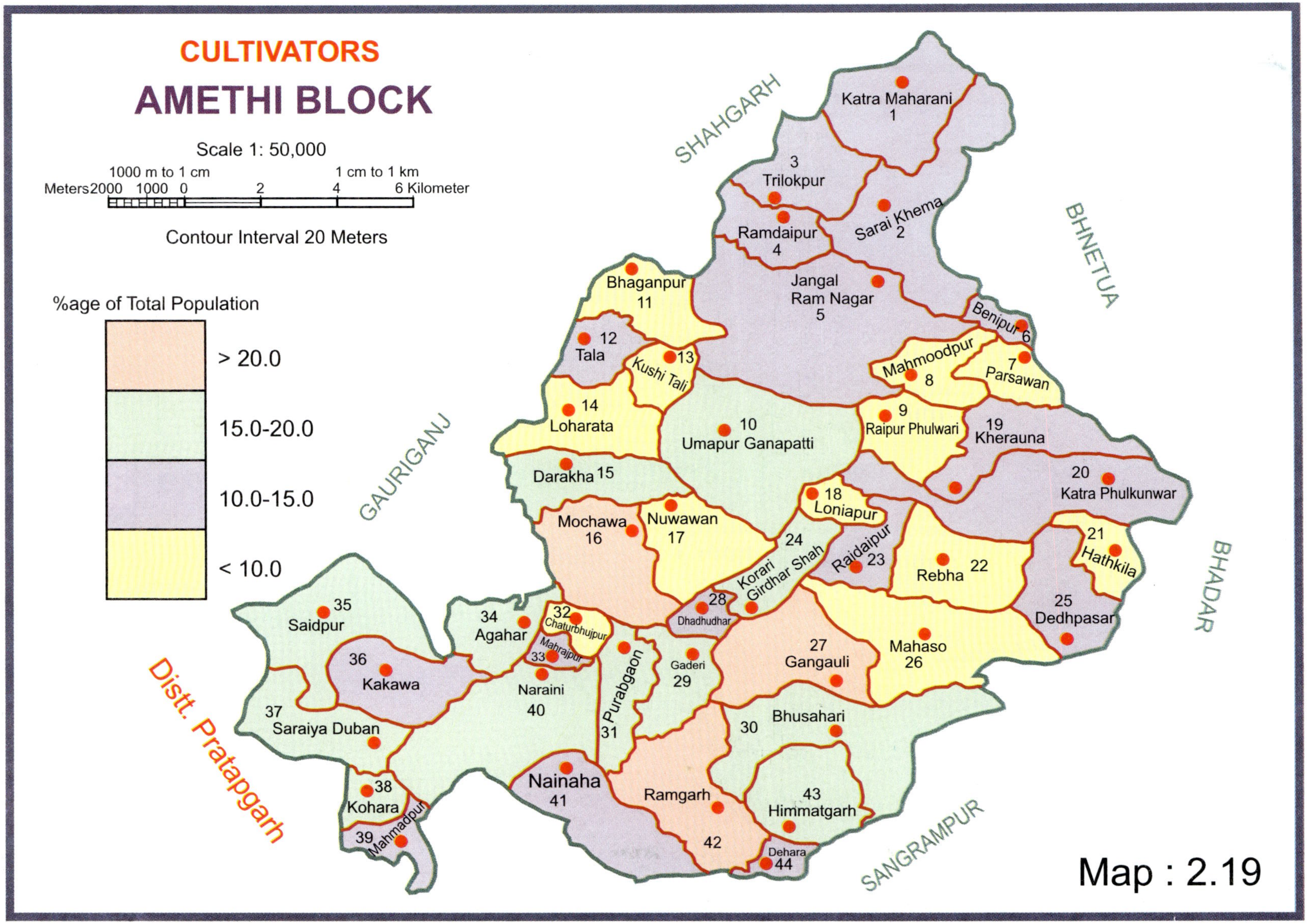

Map 2.19: Cultivators, Amethi Block

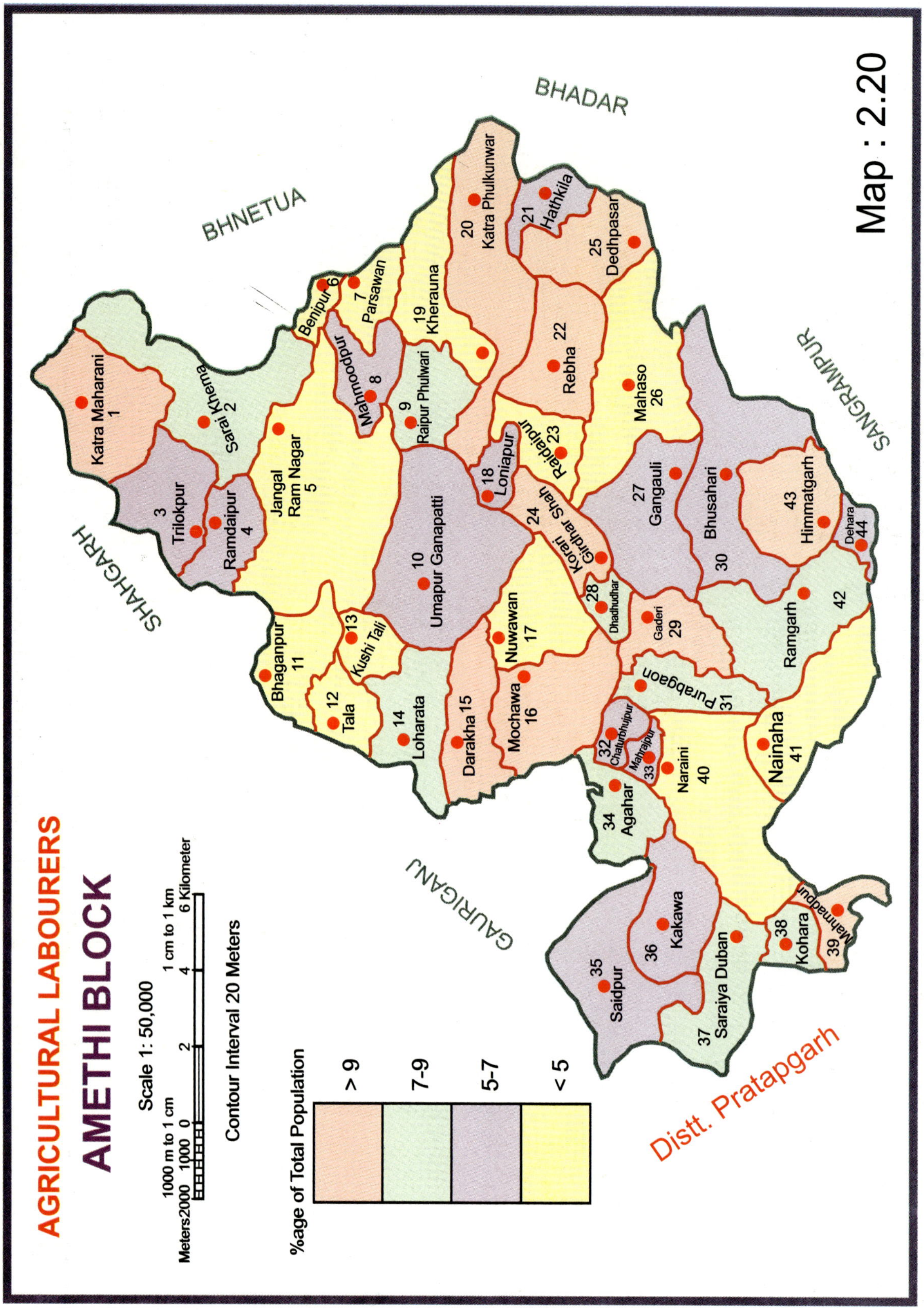

Map 2.20: Agricultural Labourers, Amethi Block

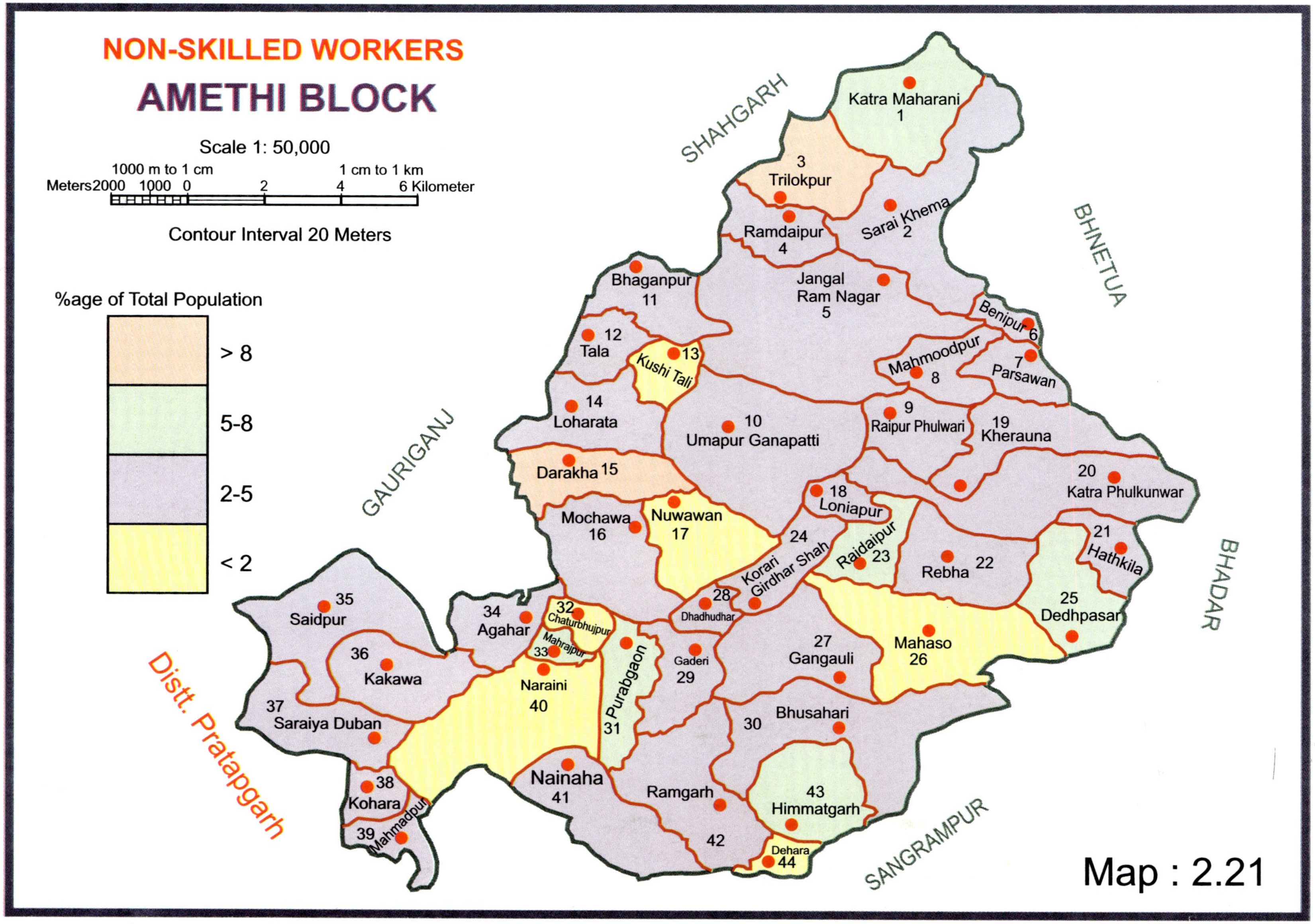

Map 2.21: Non-Skilled Workers, Amethi Block

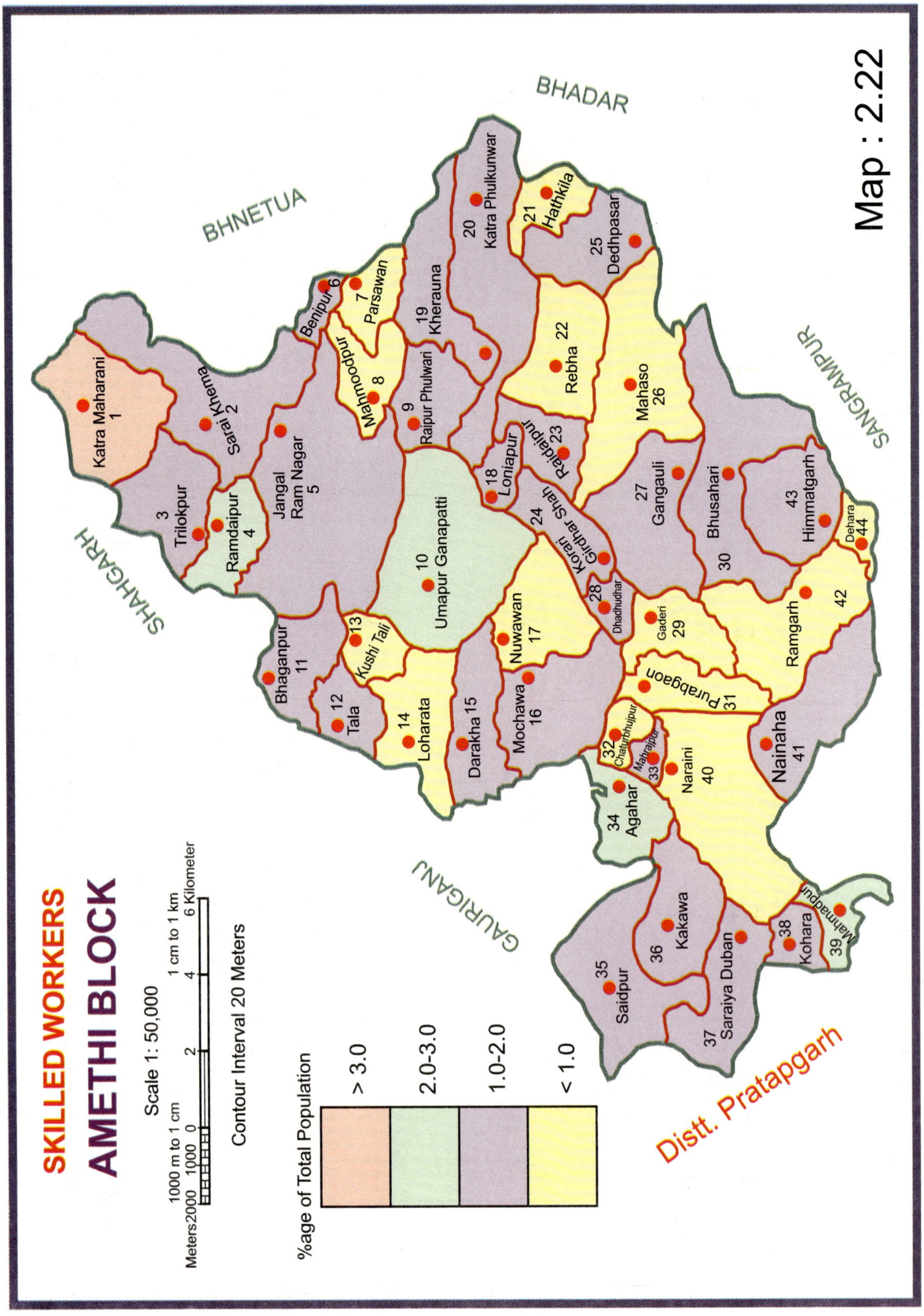

Map 2.22: Skilled Workers, Amethi Block

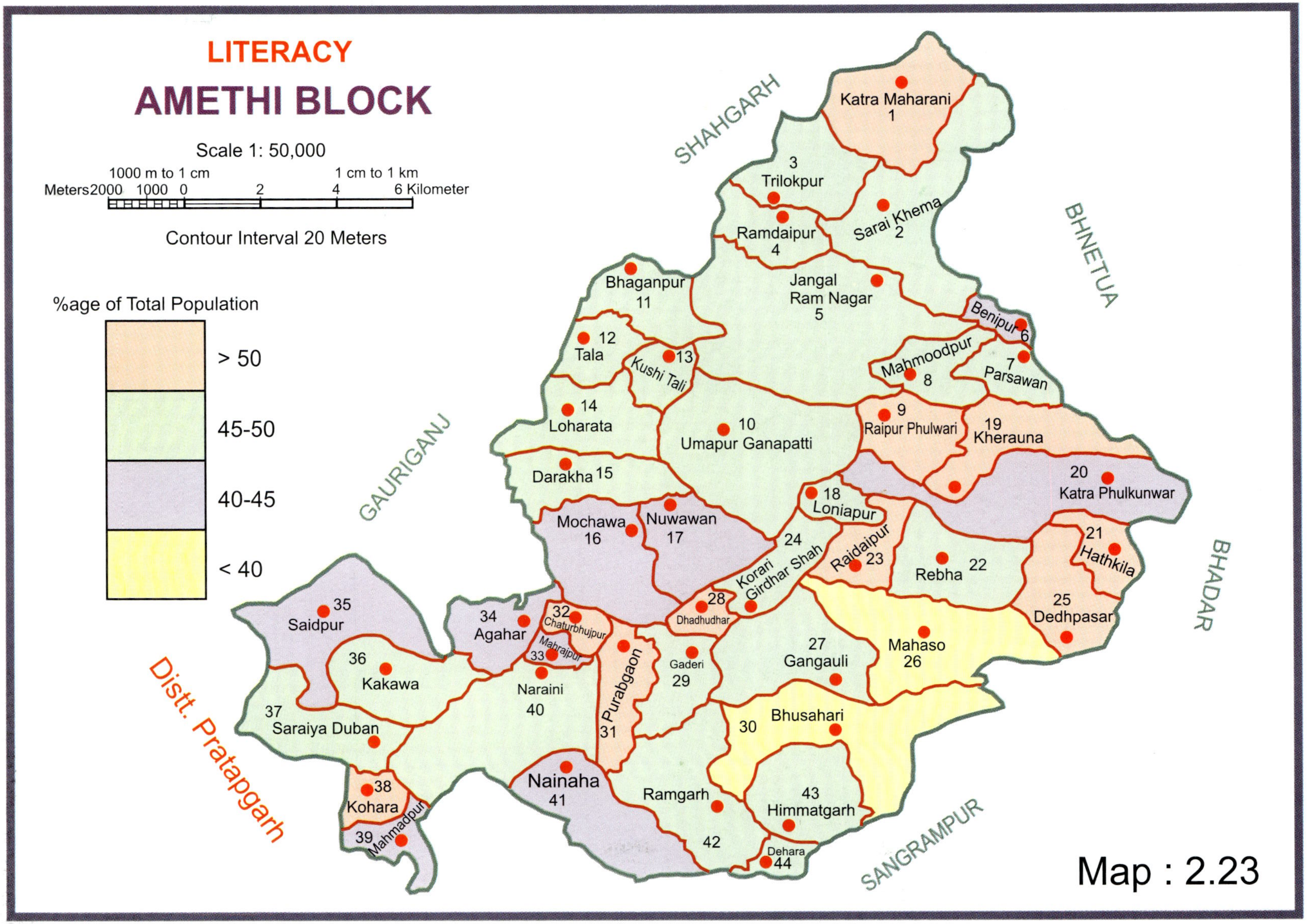

Map 2.23: Literacy, Amethi Block

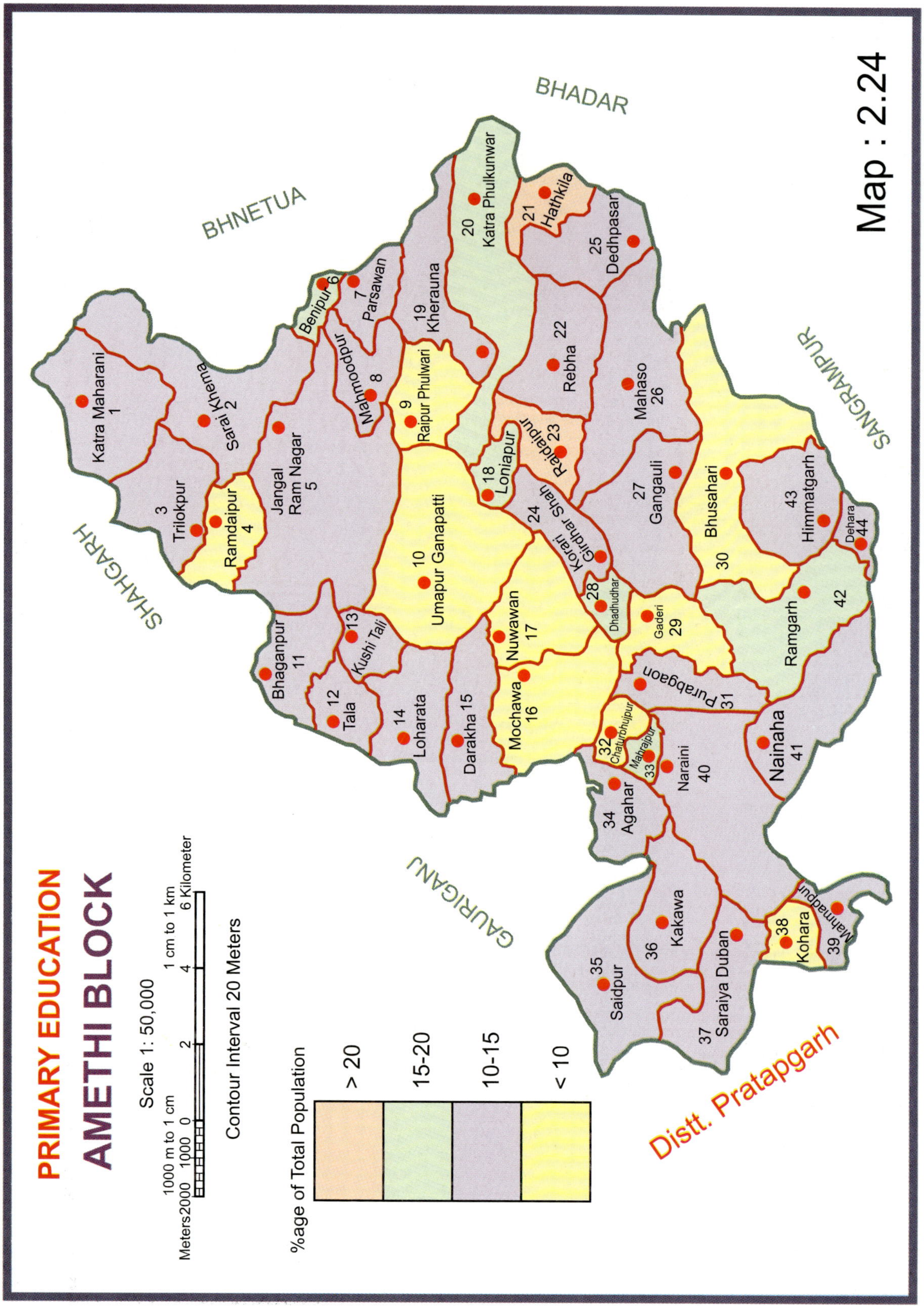

Map 2.24: Primary Education, Amethi Block

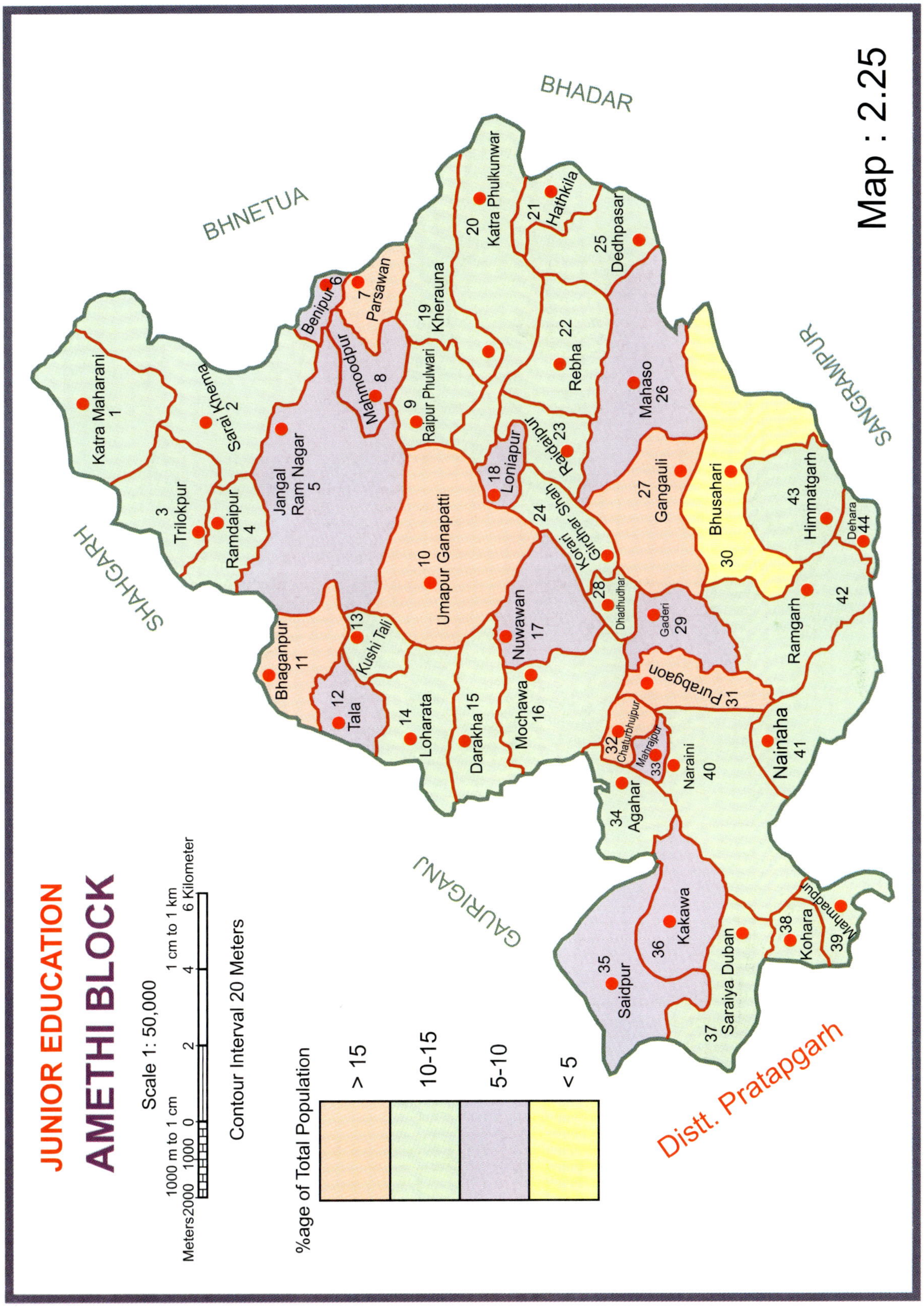

Map 2.25: Junior Education, Amethi Block

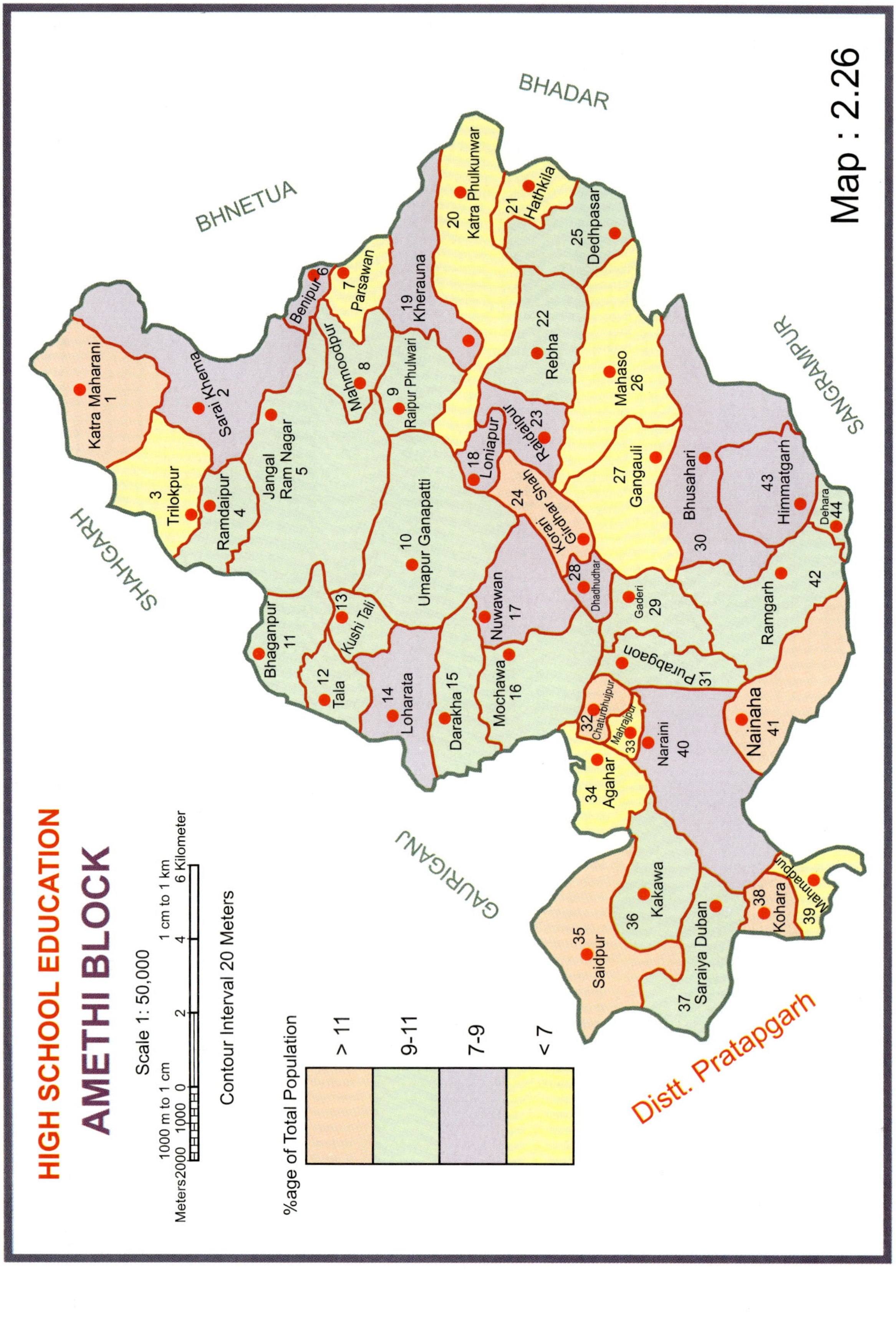

Map 2.26: High School Education, Amethi Block

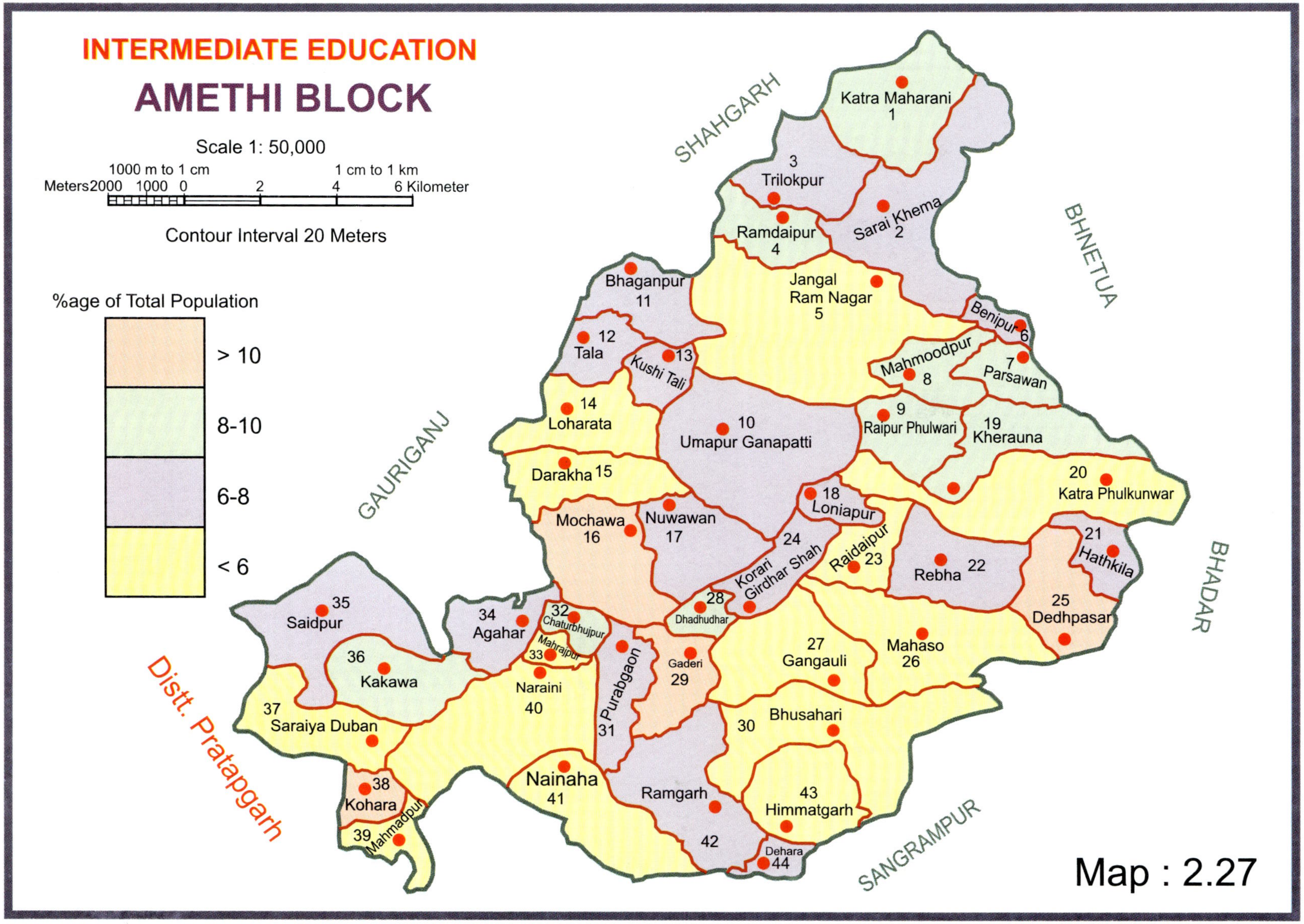

Map 2.27: Intermediate Education, Amethi Block

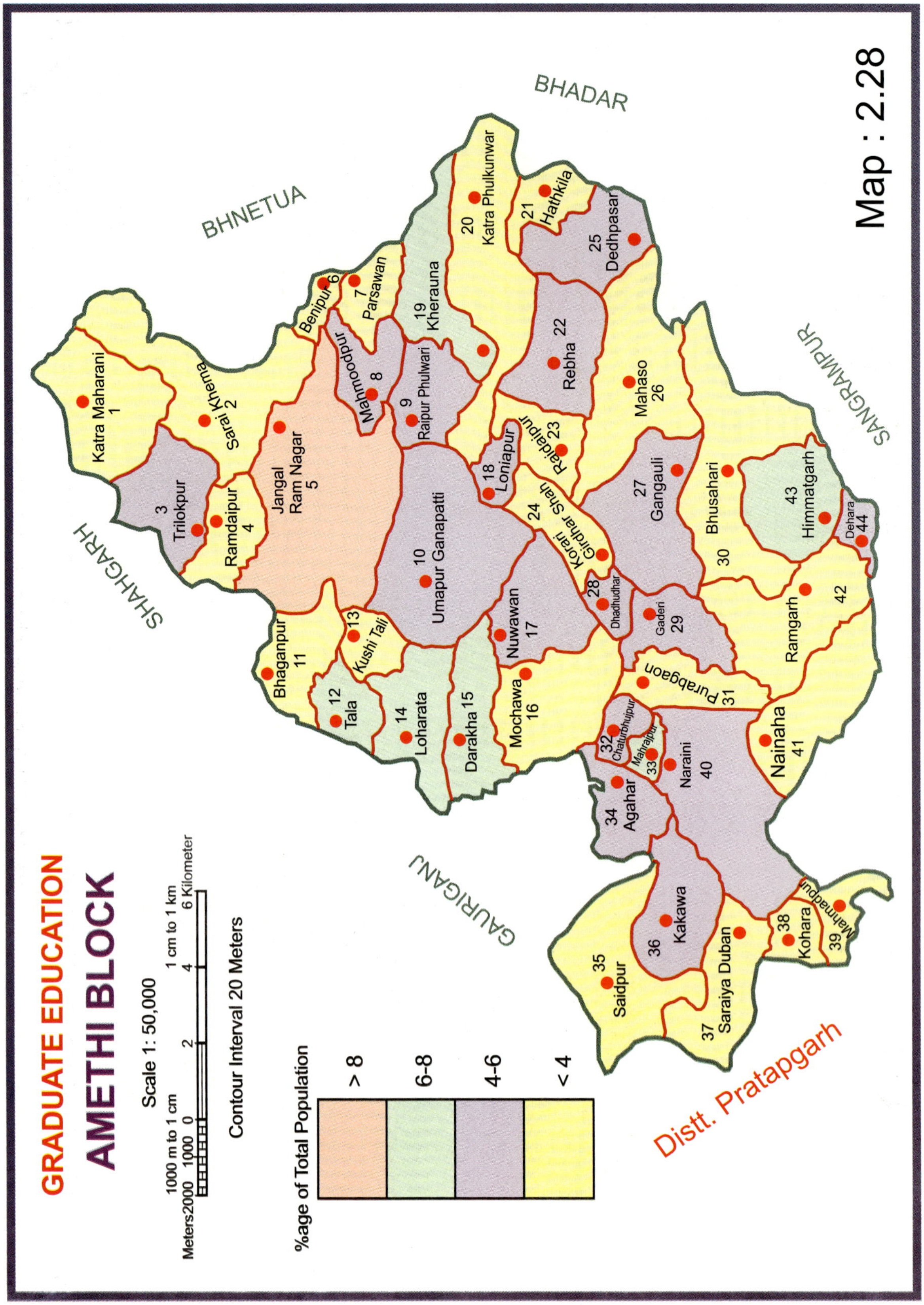

Map 2.28: Graduate Education, Amethi Block

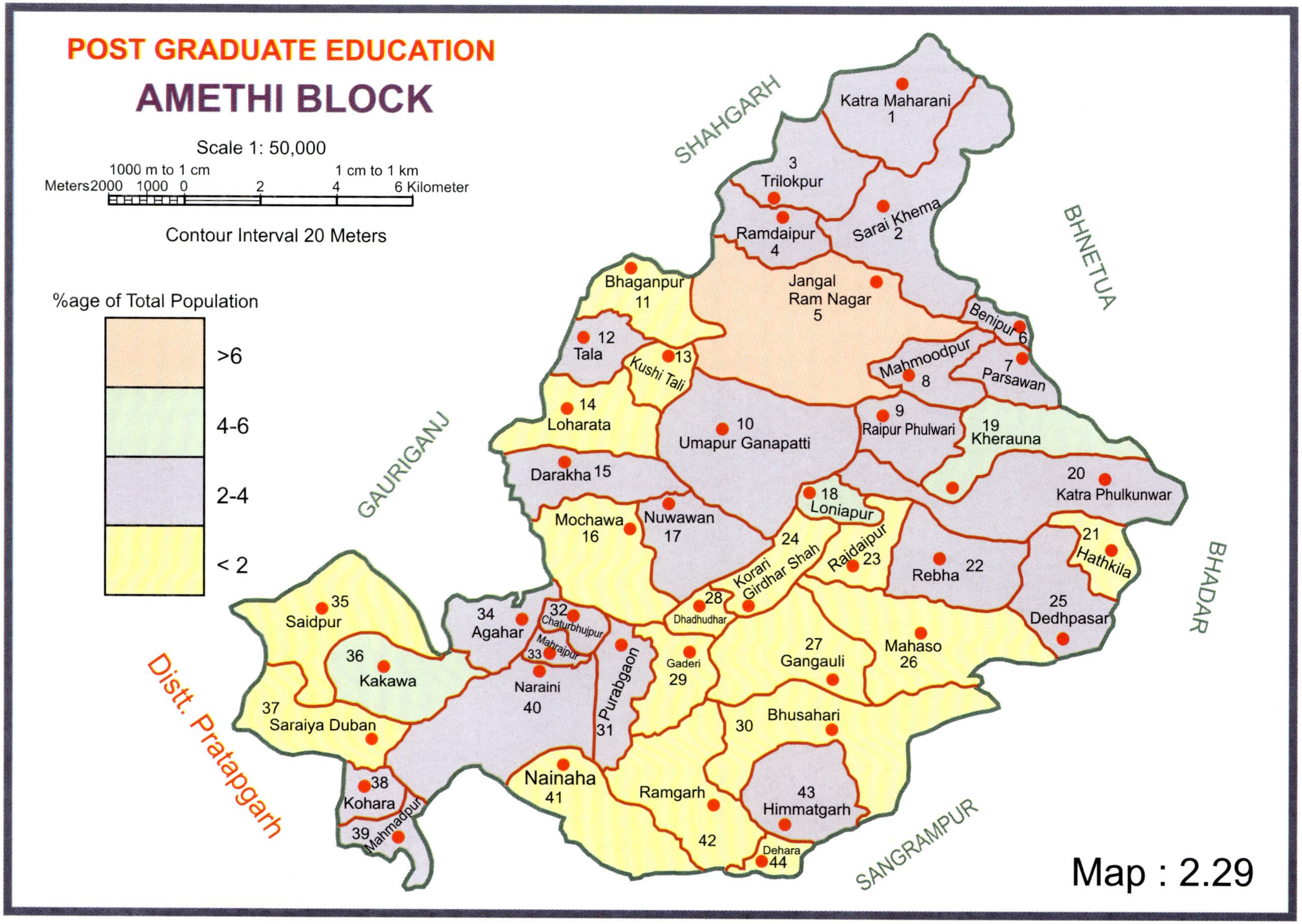

Map 2.29: Post Graduate Education, Amethi Block

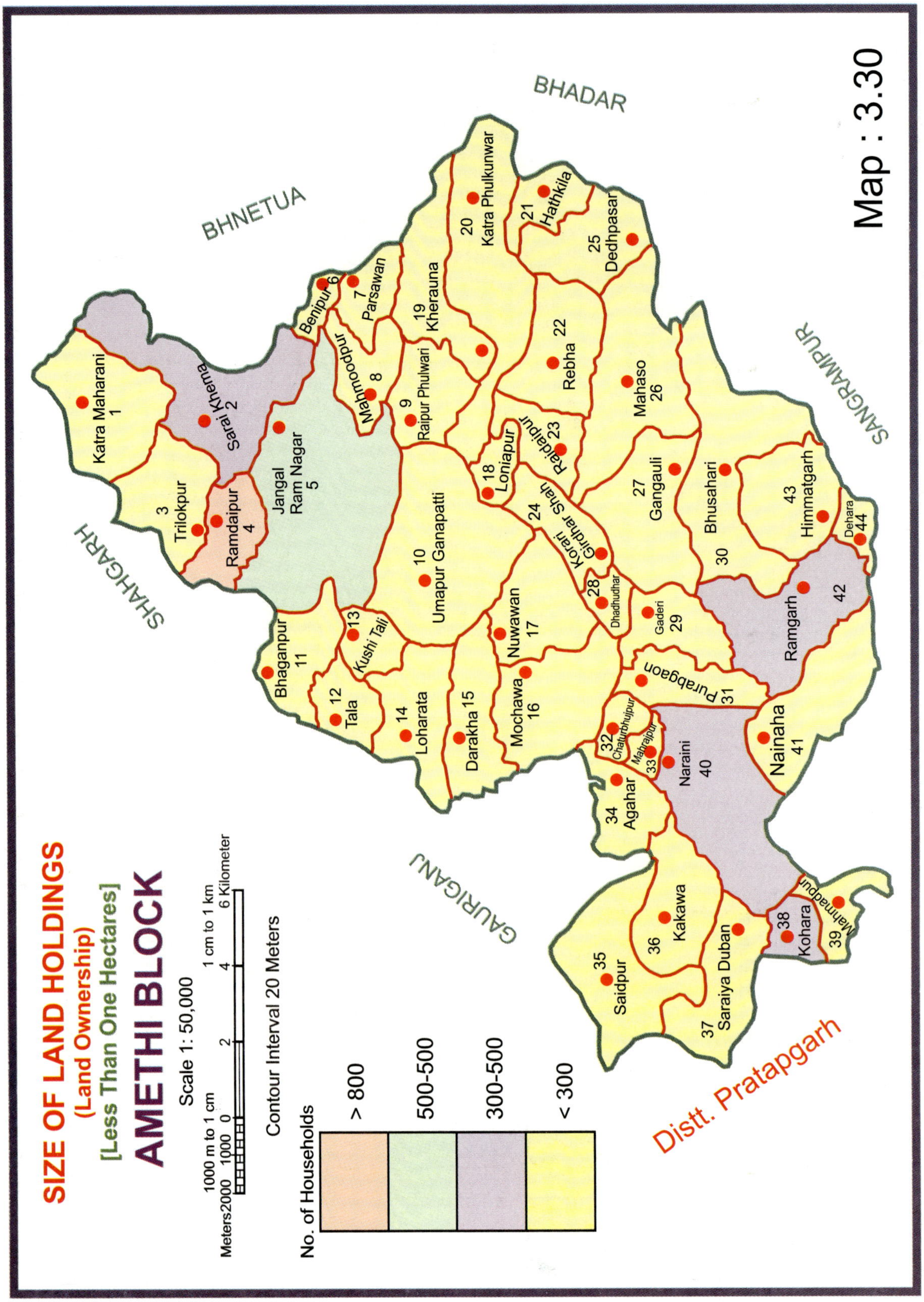

Map 3.30: Size of Land Holdings (Less than one hectare)

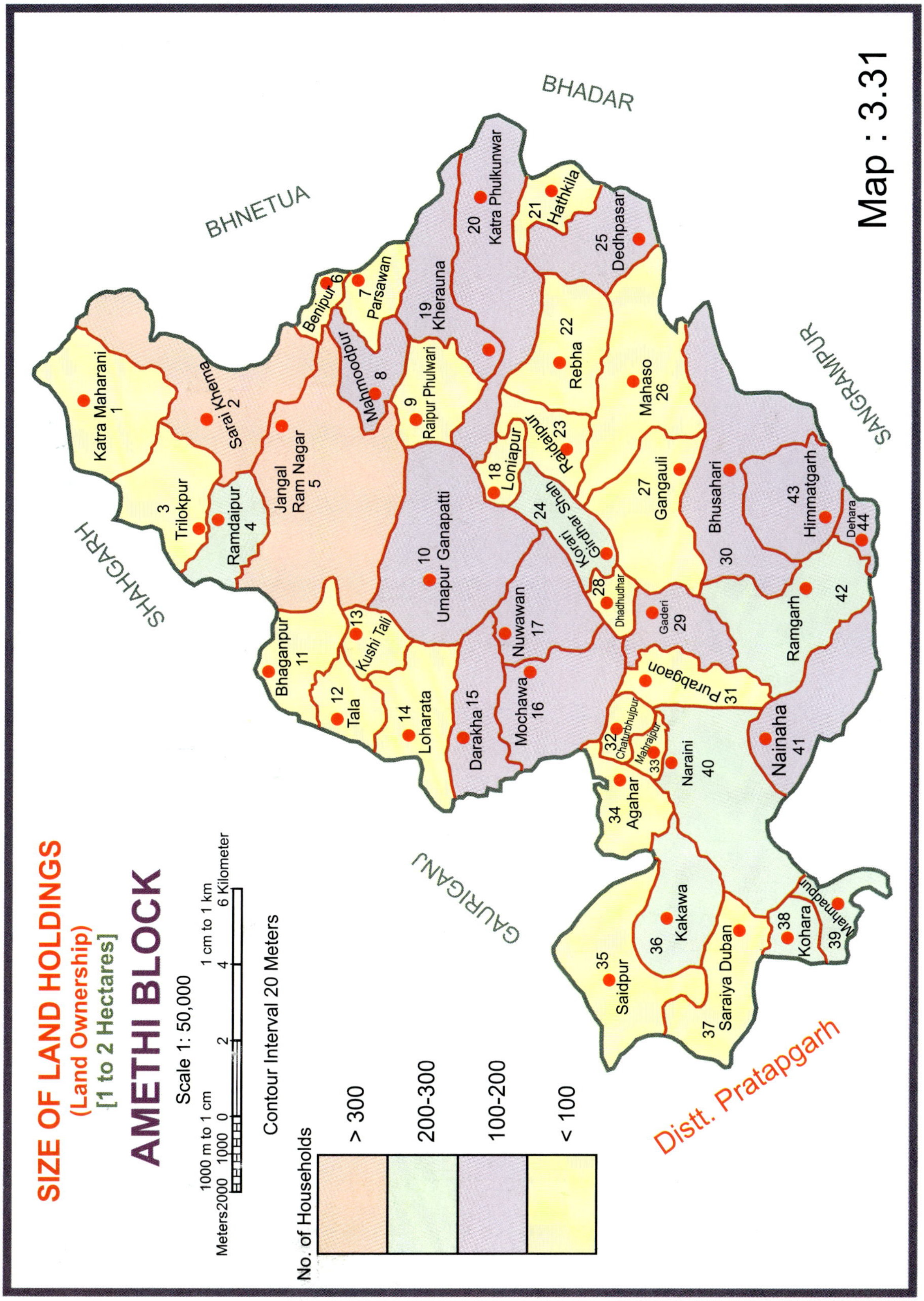

Map 3.31: Size of Land Holdings (1-2 hectares)

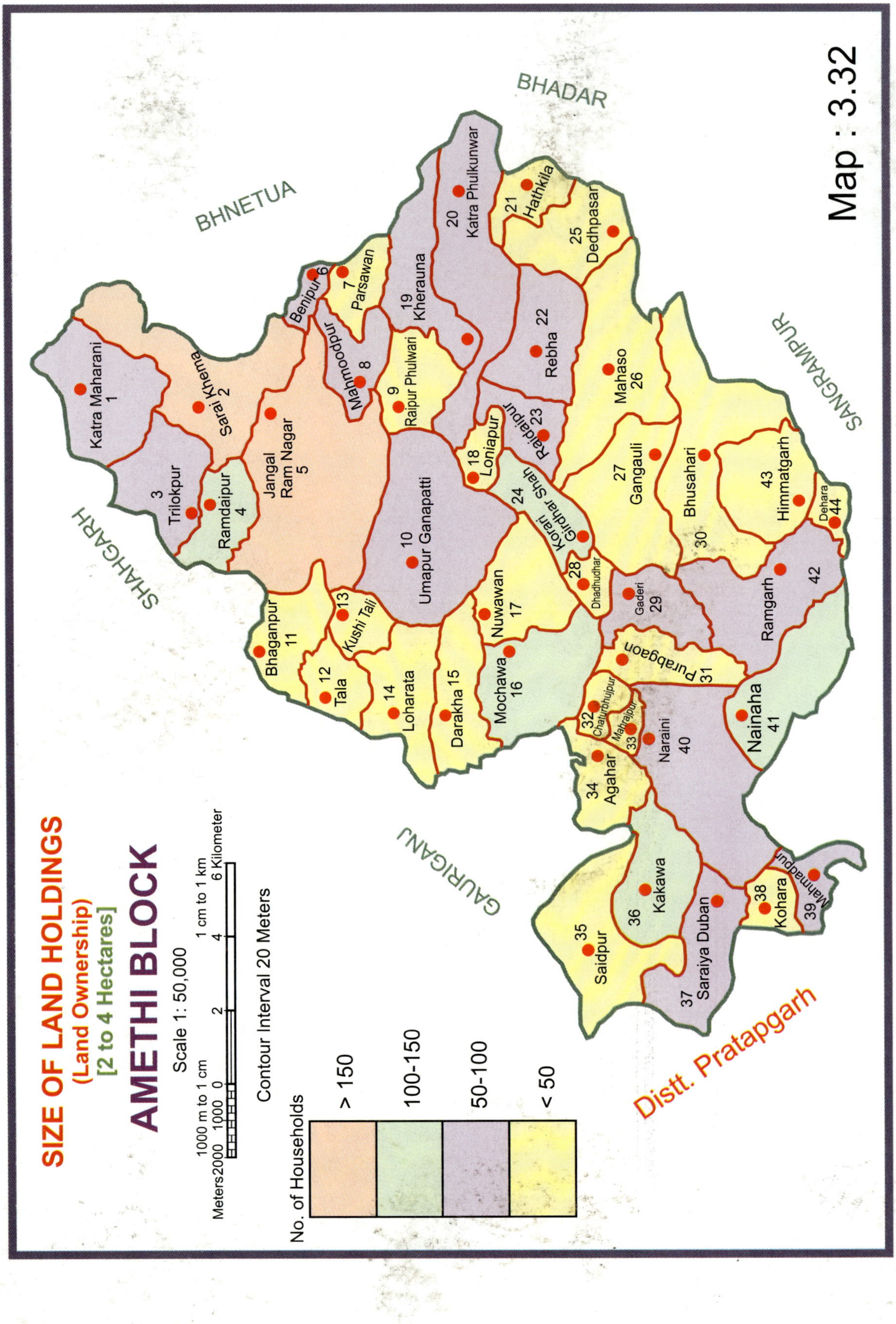

Map 3.32: Size of Land Holdings (2-4 hectares)

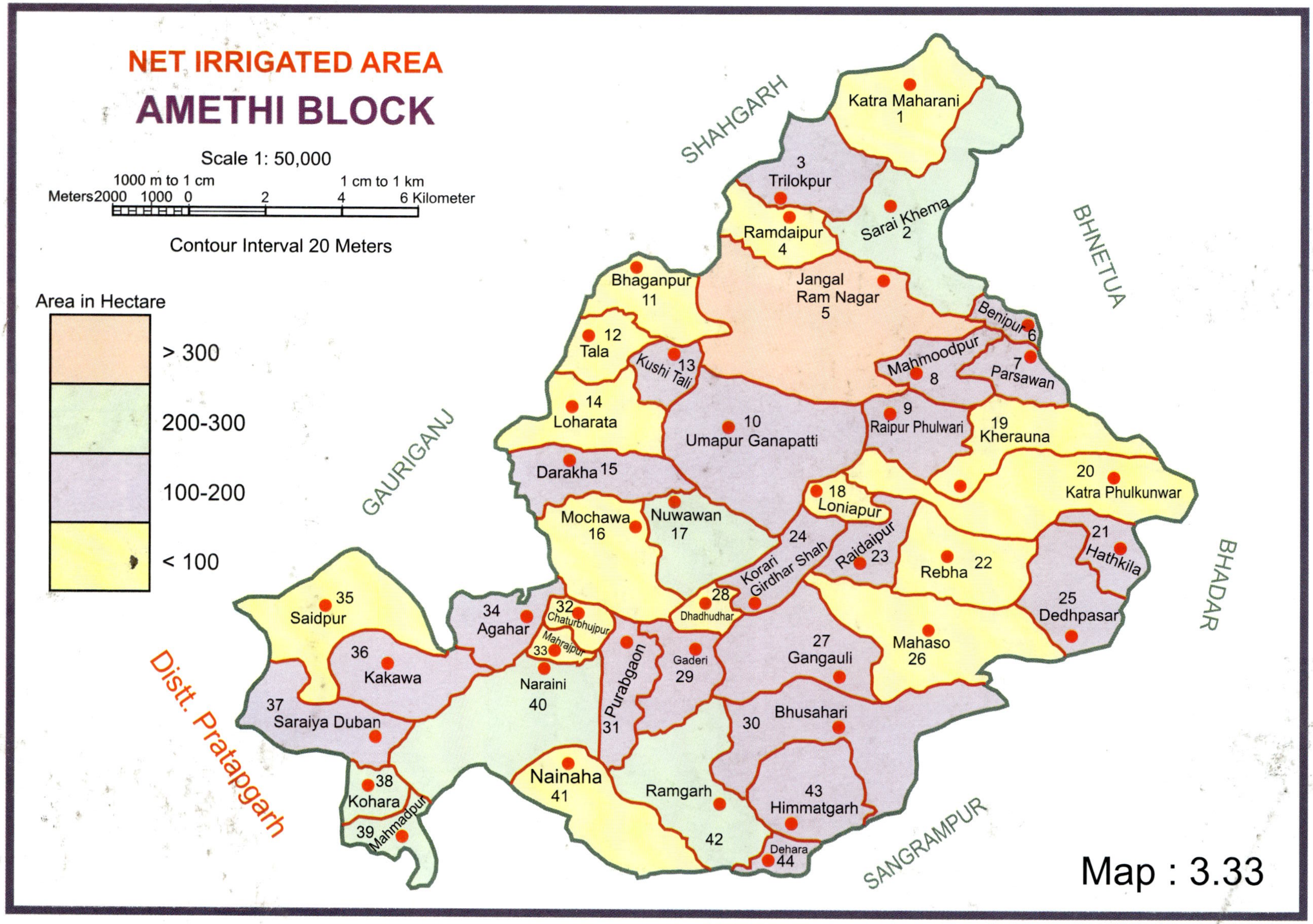

Map 3.33: Net Irrigated Area

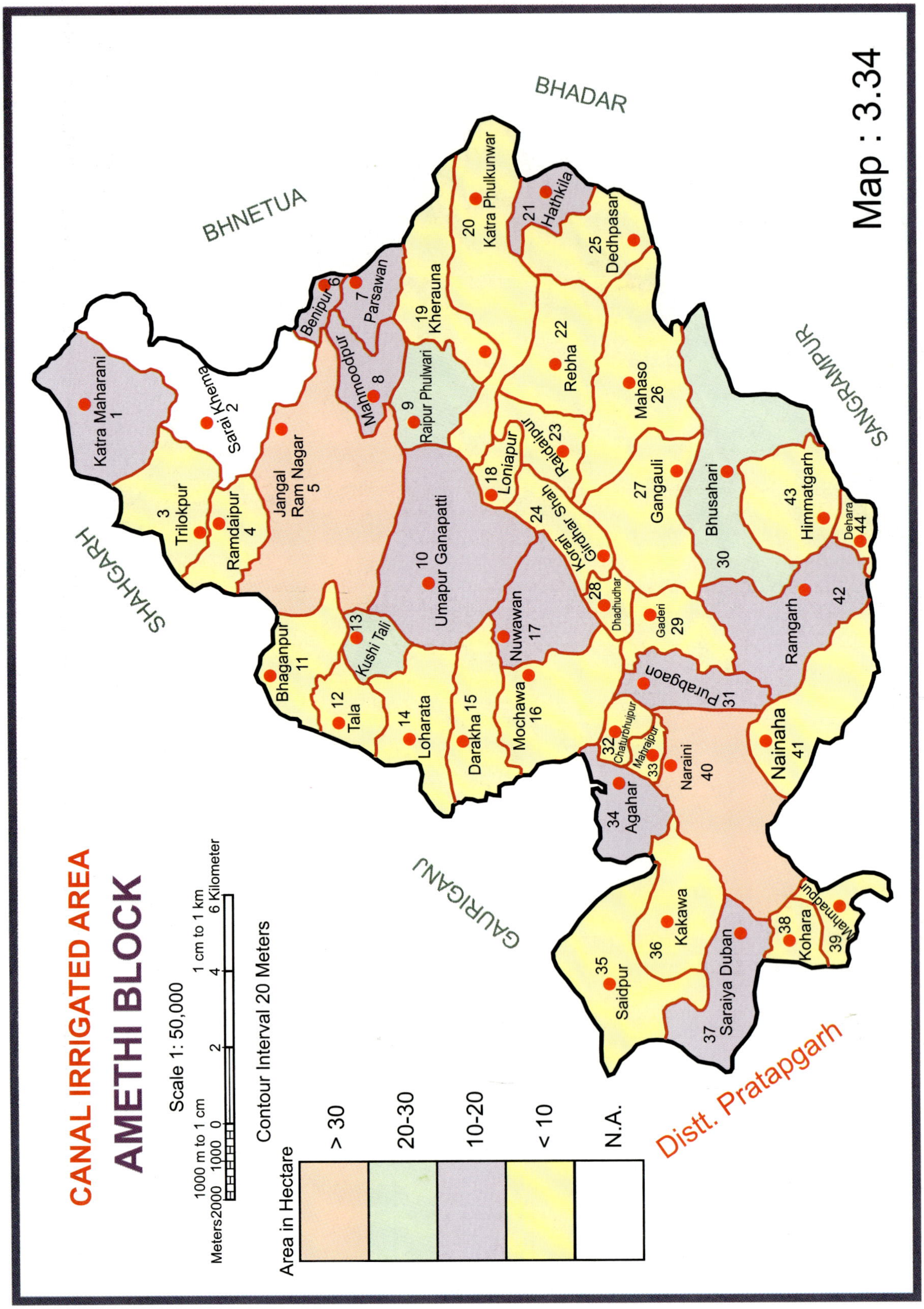

Map 3.34: Canal Irrigated Area

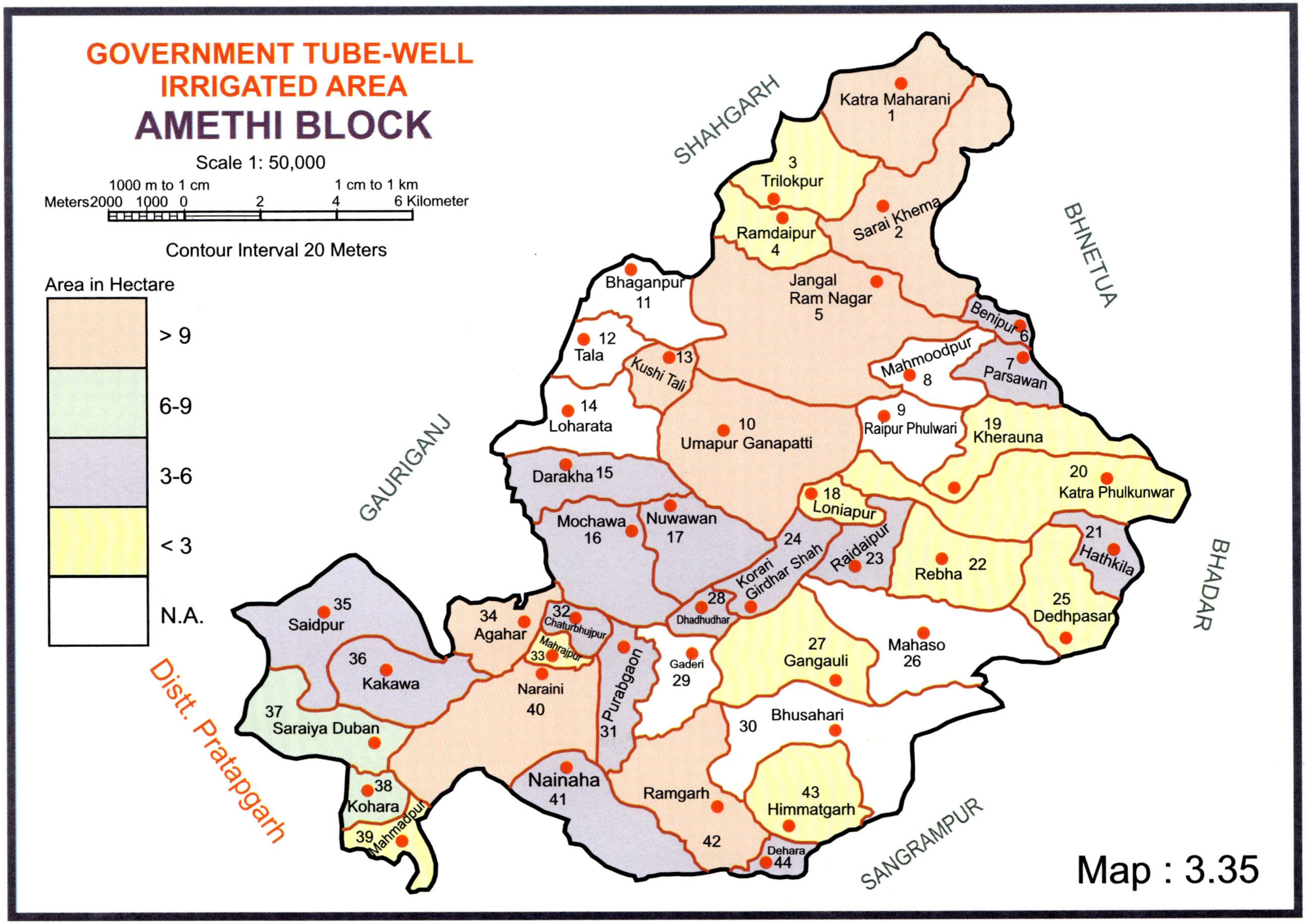

Map 3.35: Government Tube-well Irrigated Area

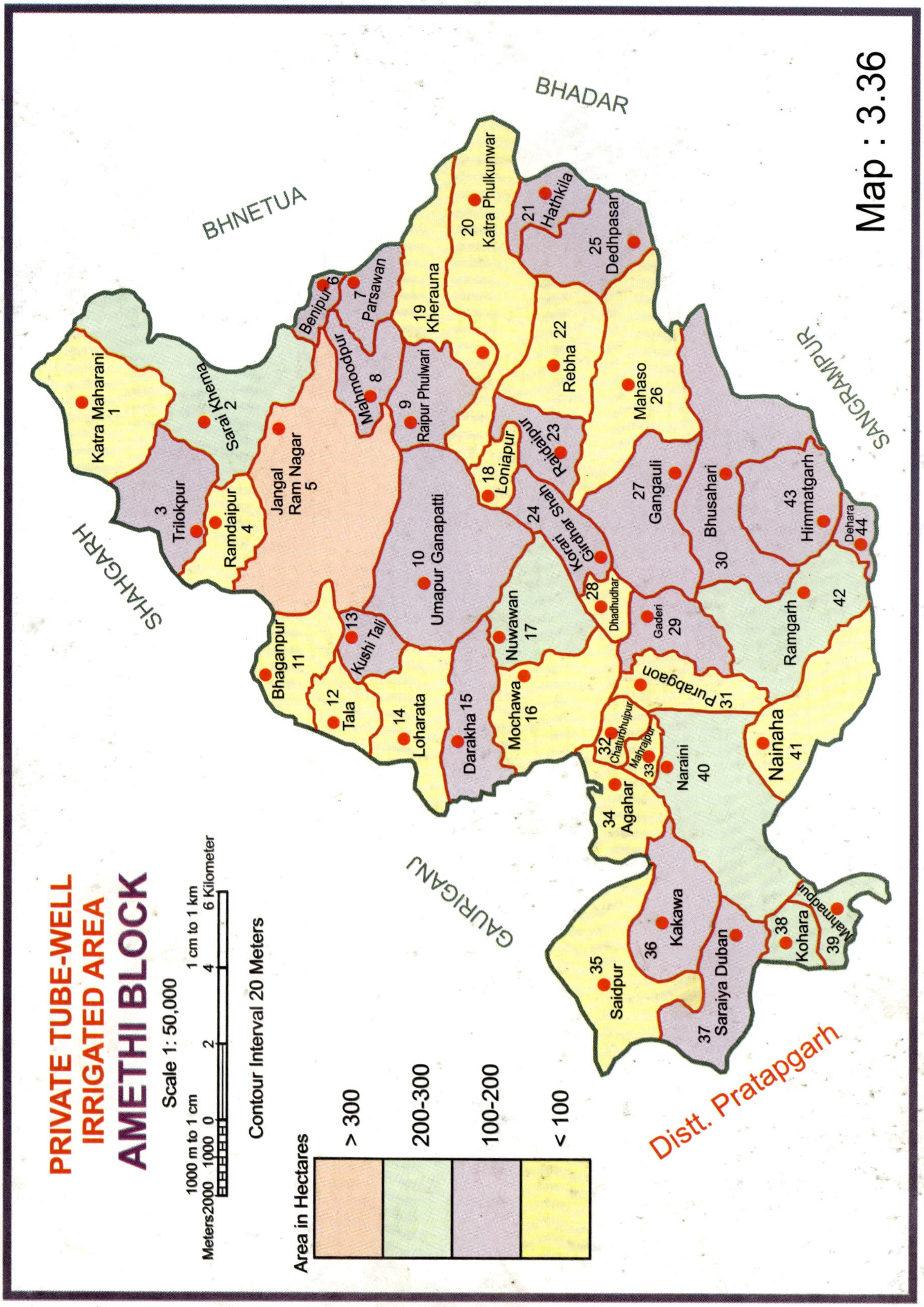

Map 3.36: Private Tube-well Irrigated Area

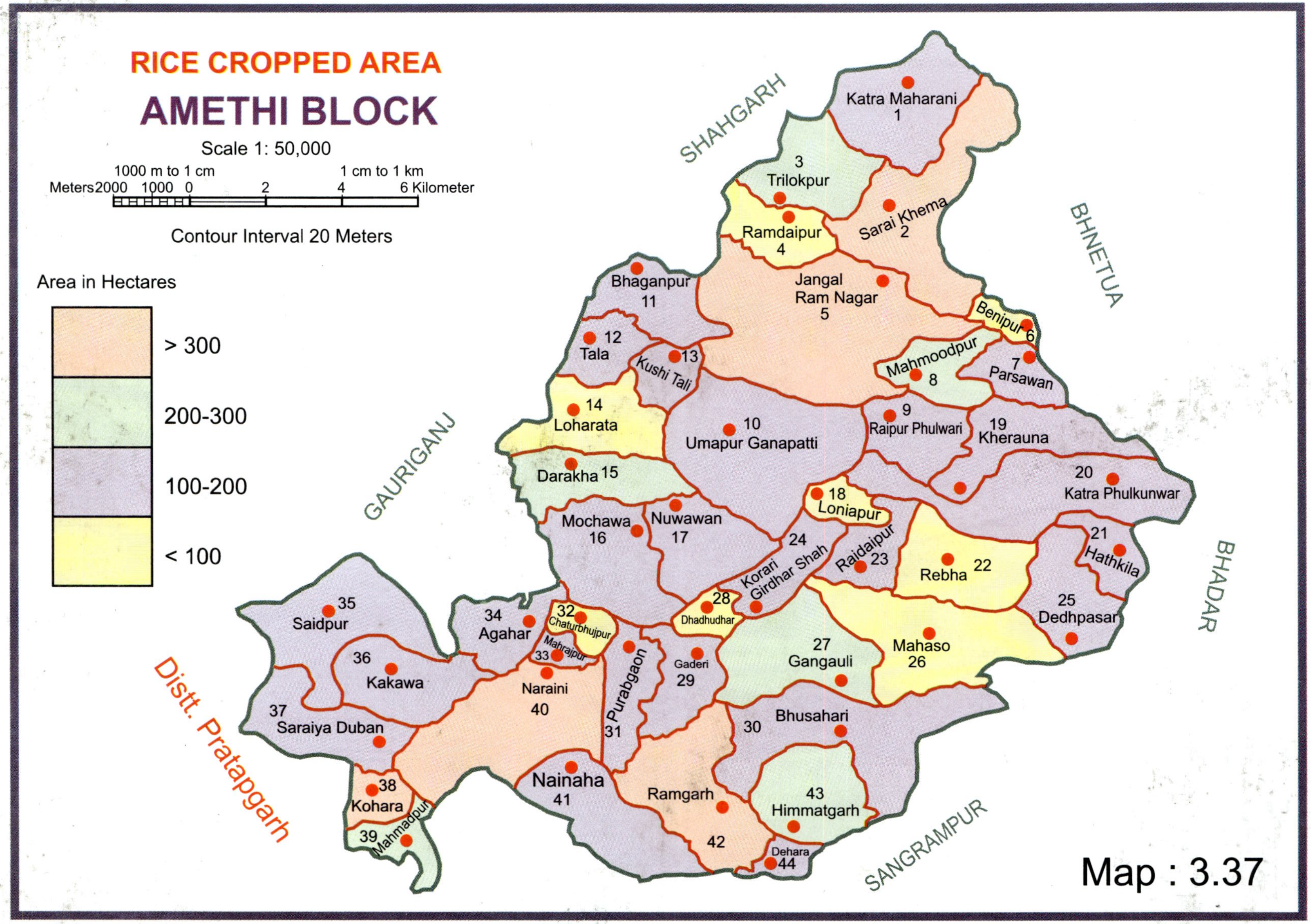

Map 3.37: Rice Cropped Area

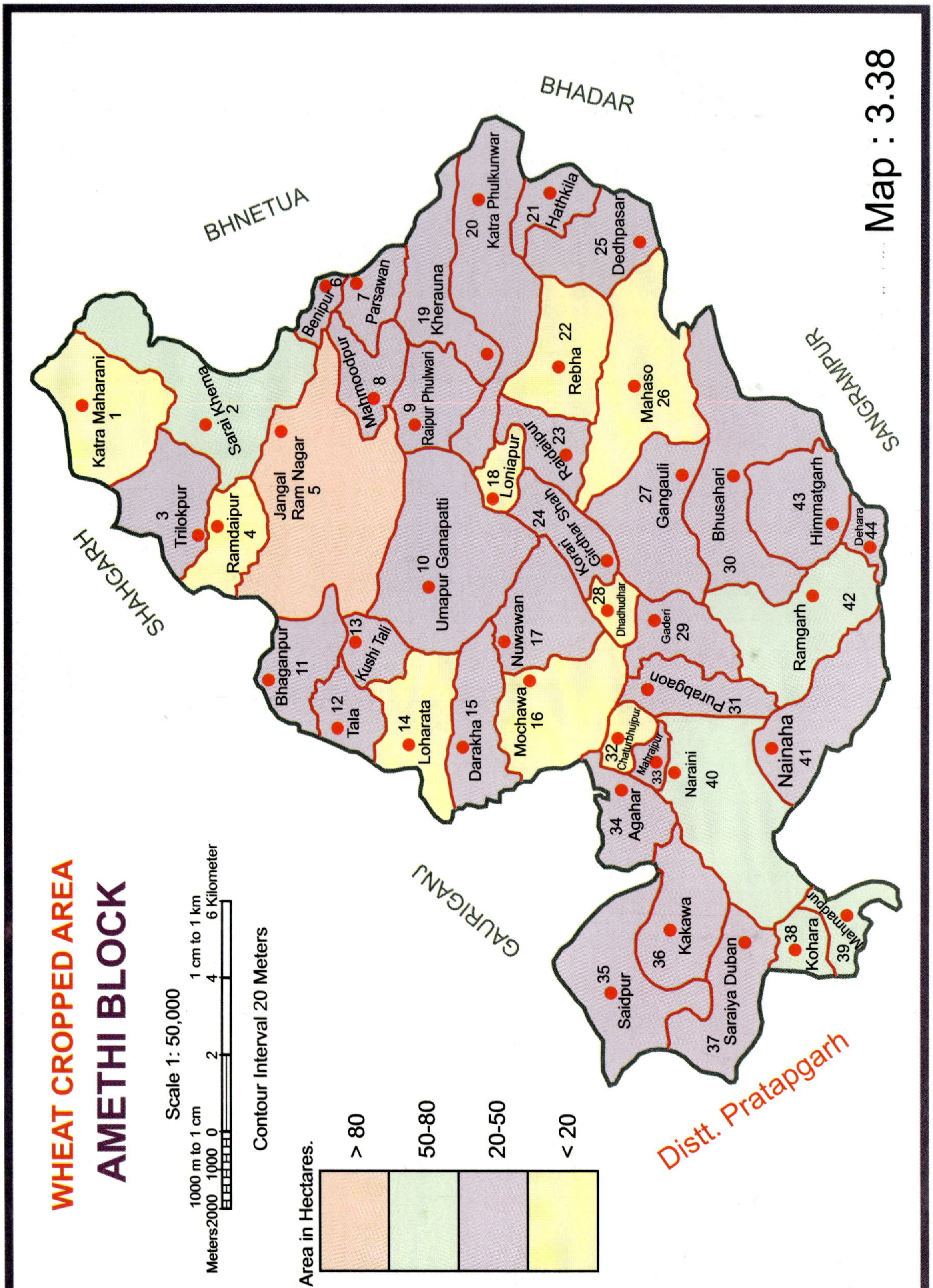

Map 3.38: Wheat Cropped Area

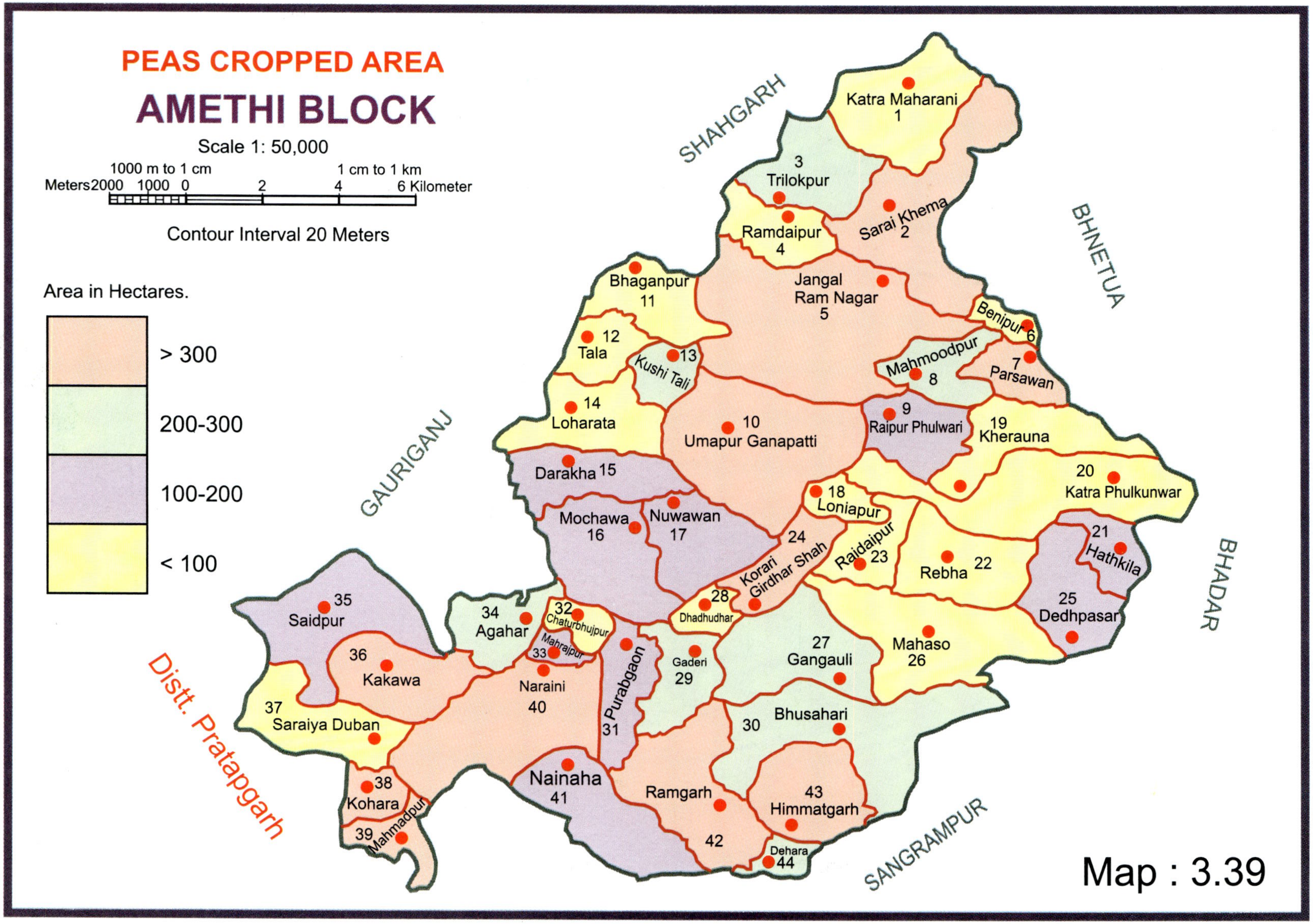

Map 3.39: Peas Cropped Area

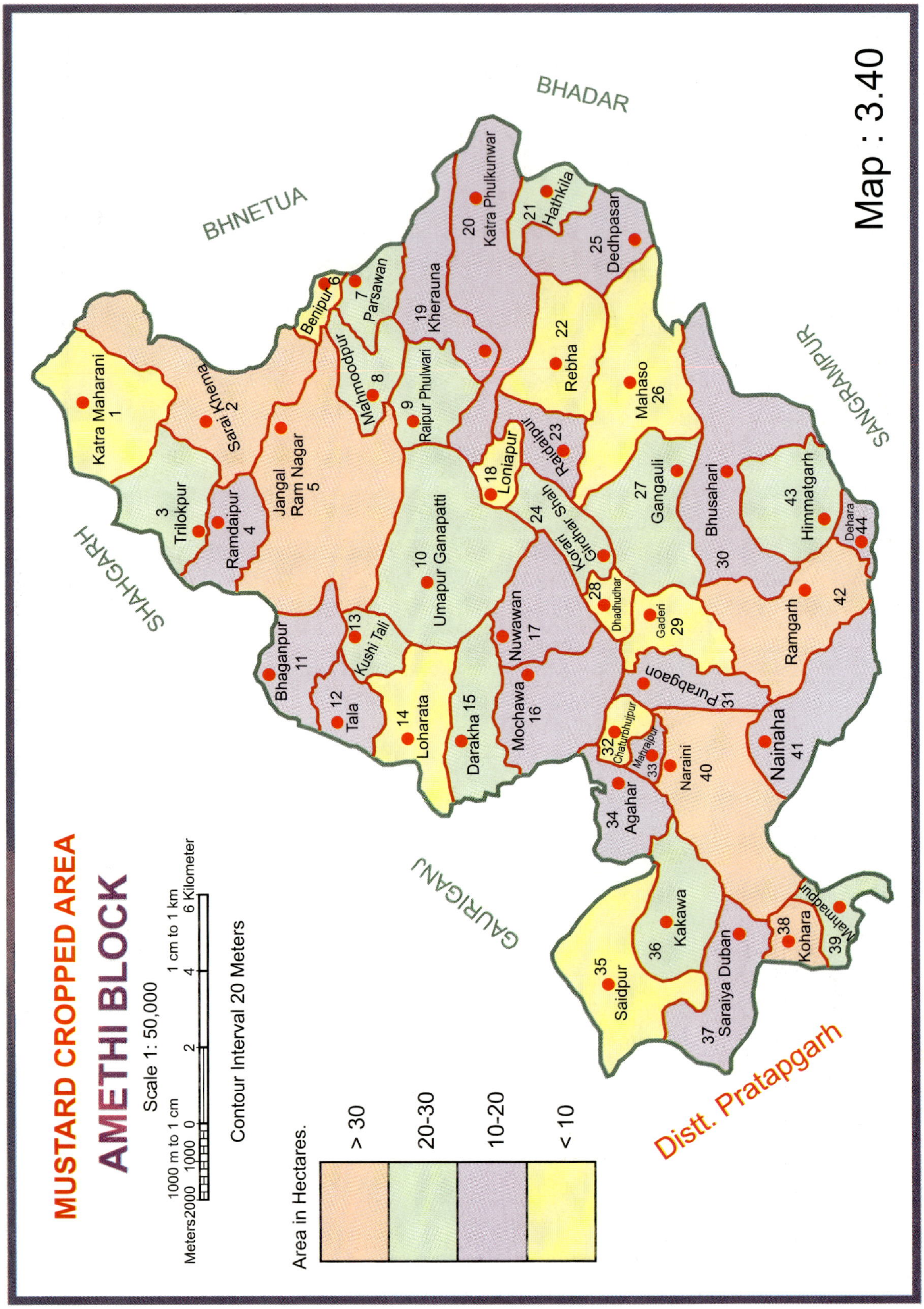

Map 3.40: Mustard Cropped Area

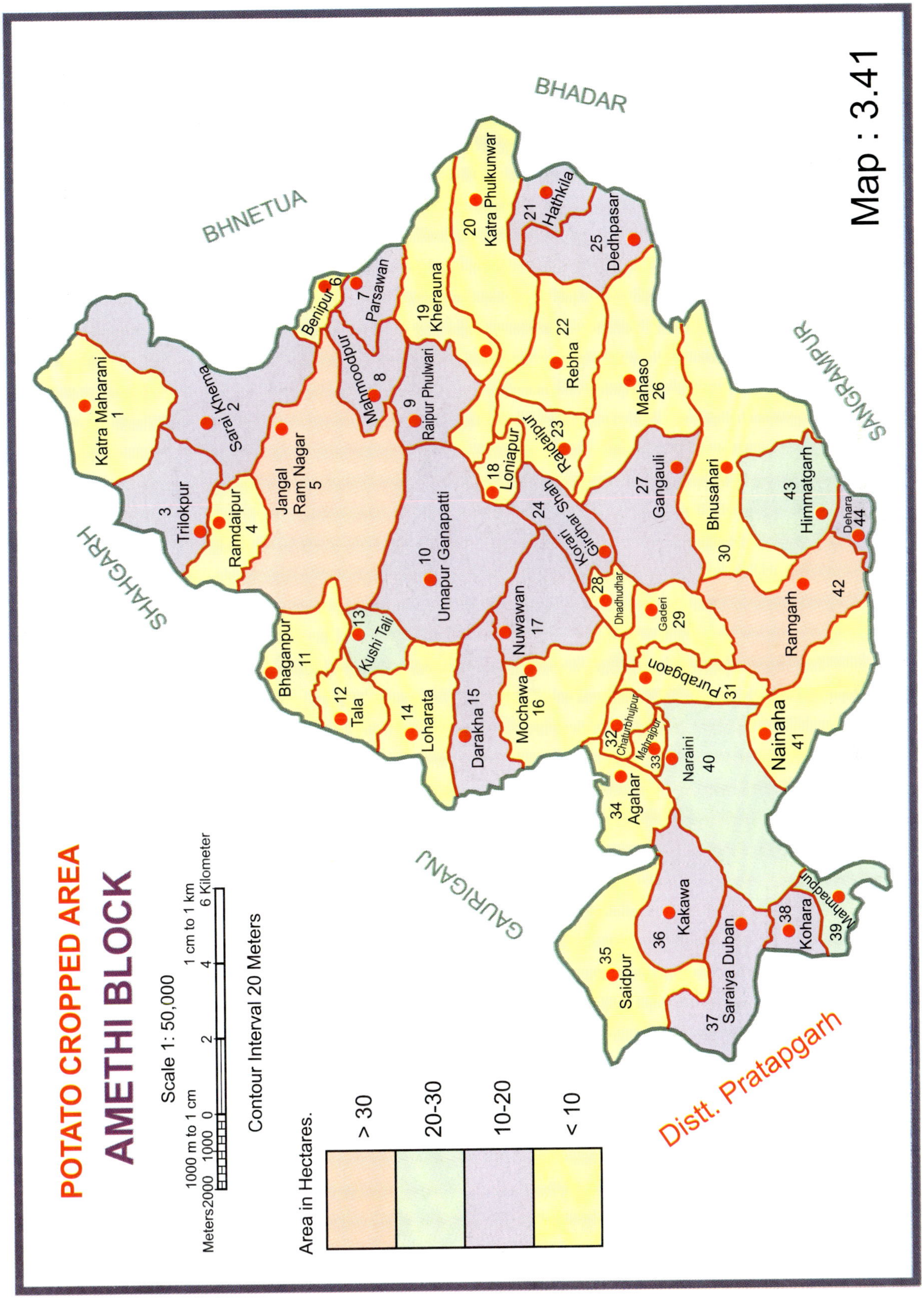

Map 3.41: Potato Cropped Area

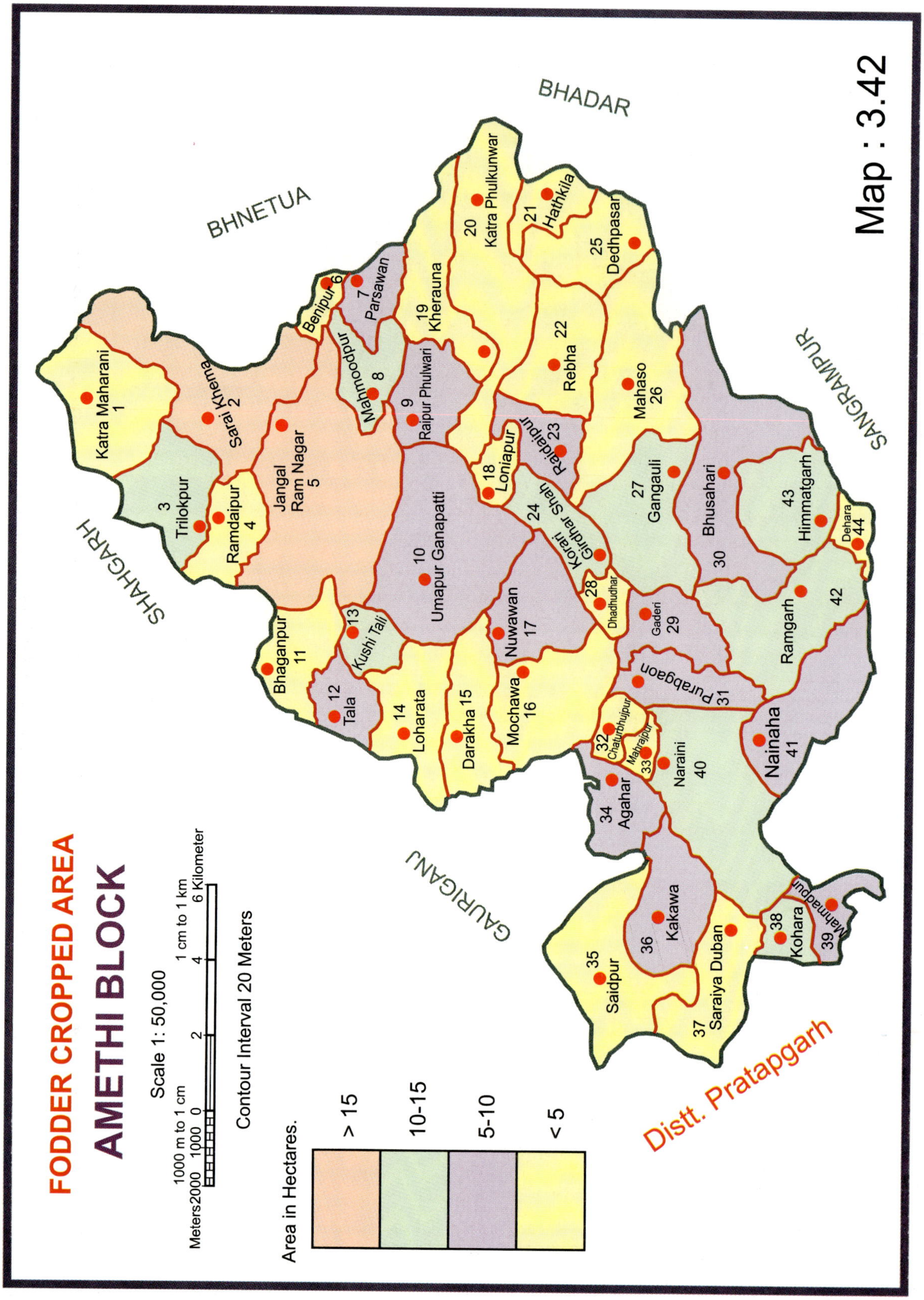

Map 3.42: Fodder Cropped Area

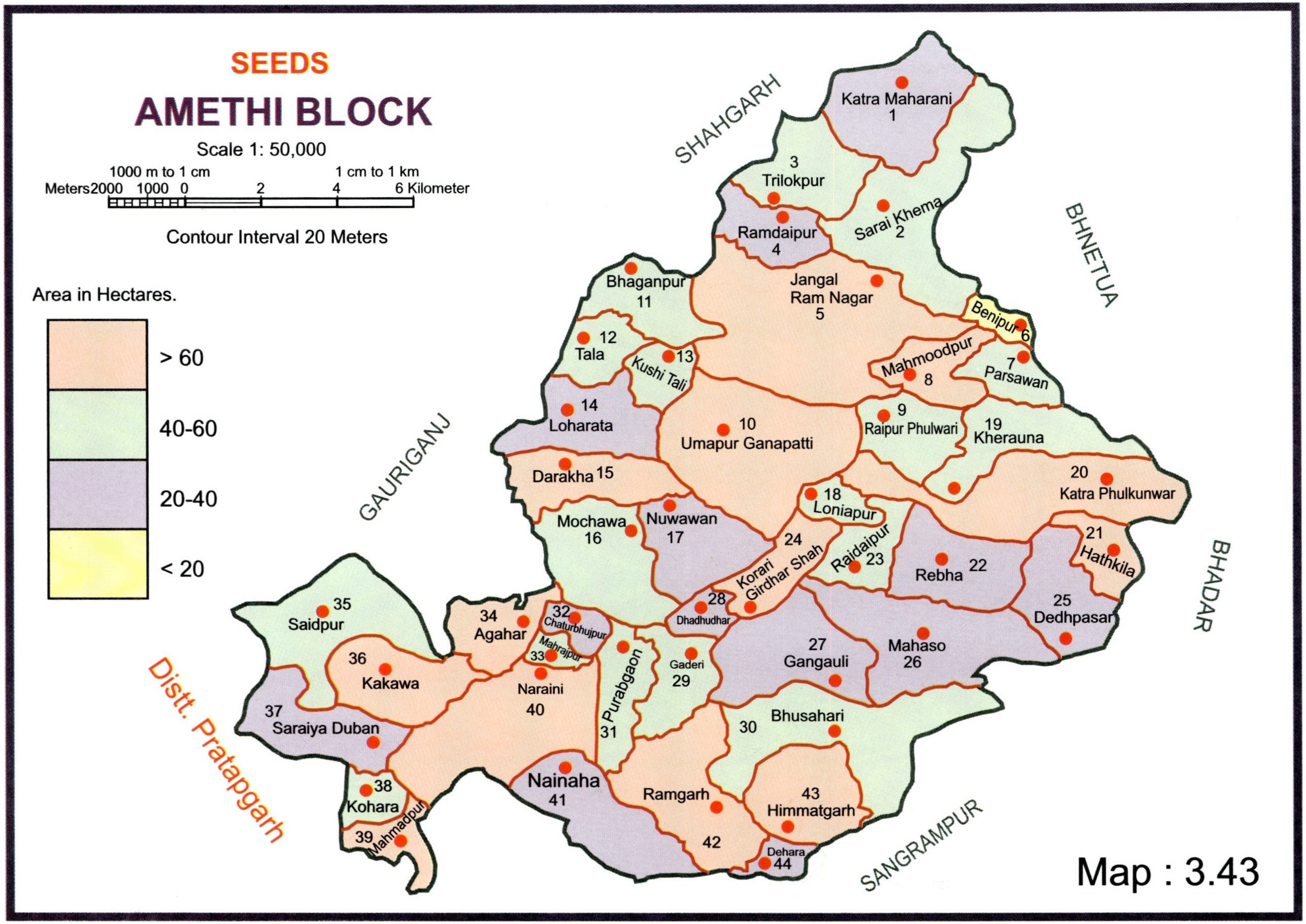

Map 3.43: Seeds

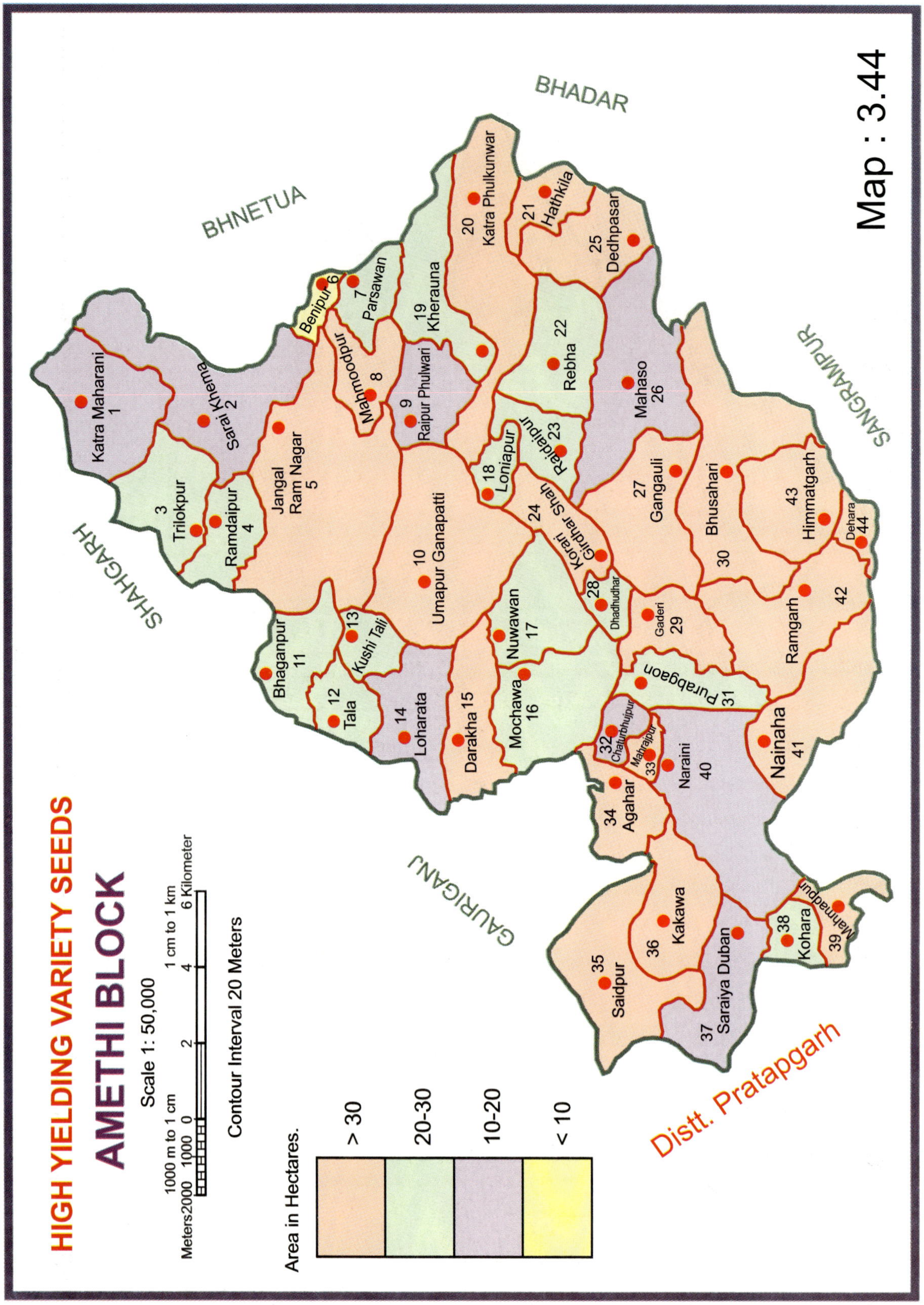

Map 3.44: High Yielding Variety Seeds

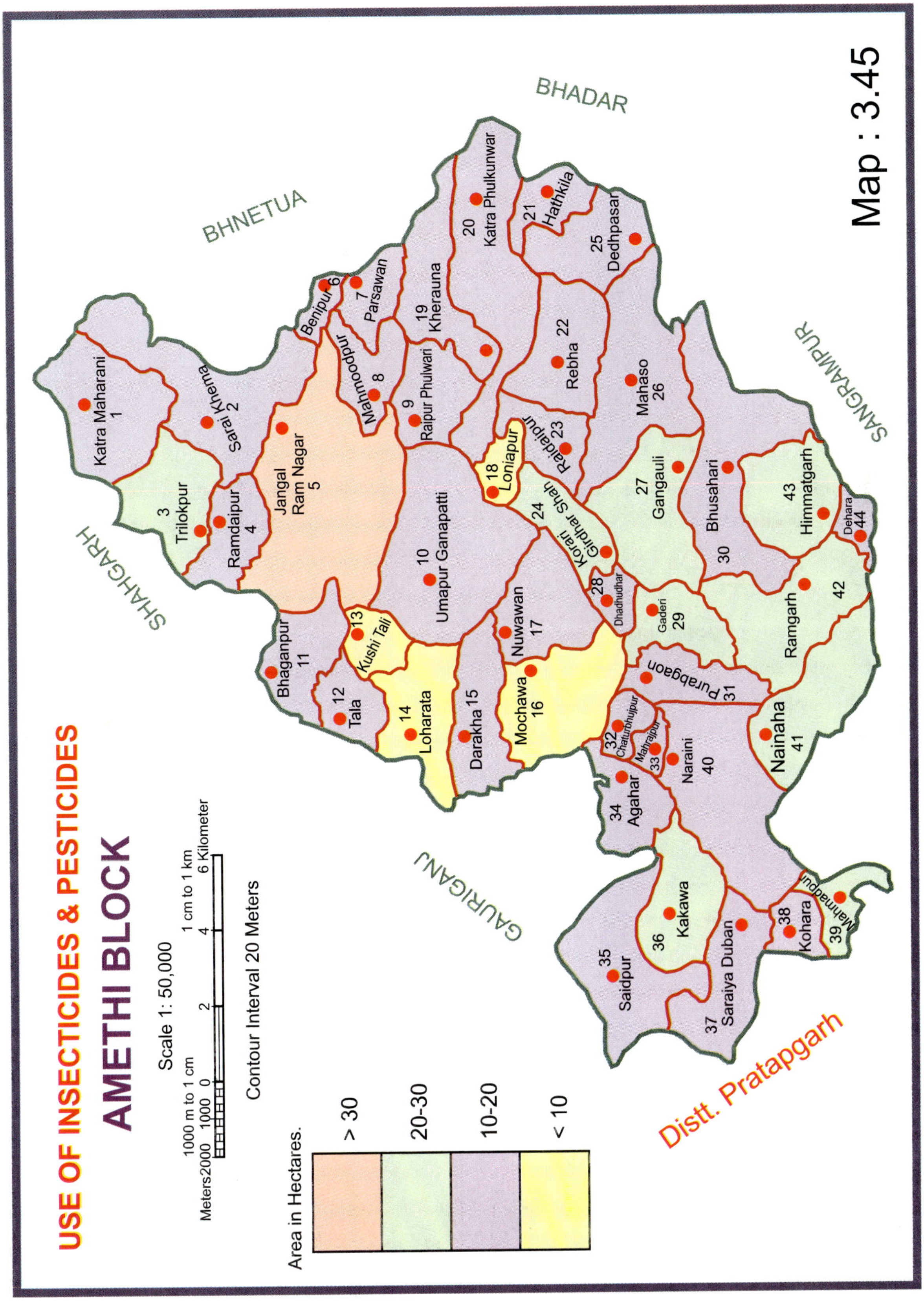

Map 3.45: Use of Insecticides and Pesticides

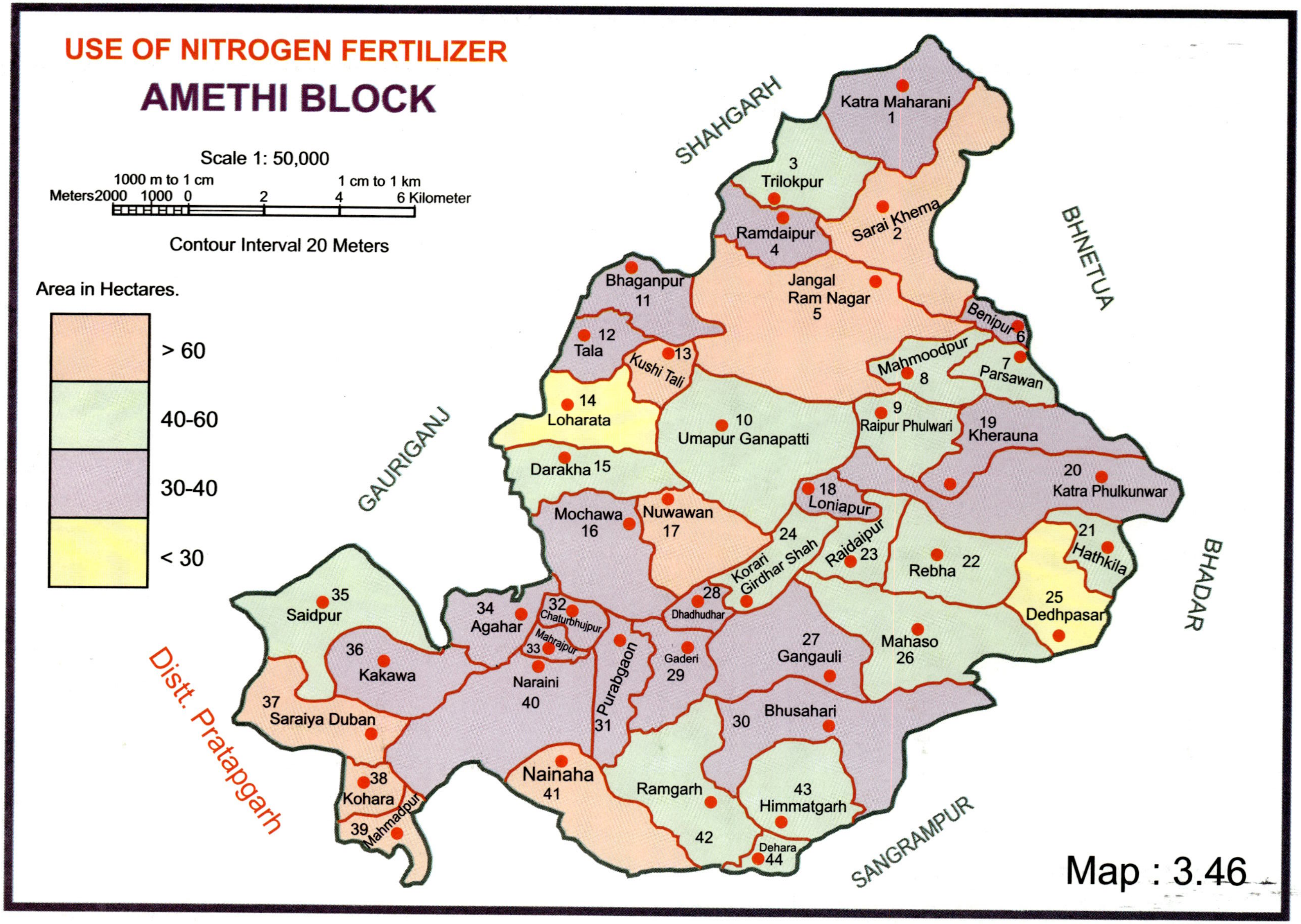

Map 3.46: Use of Nitrogen Fertilizer

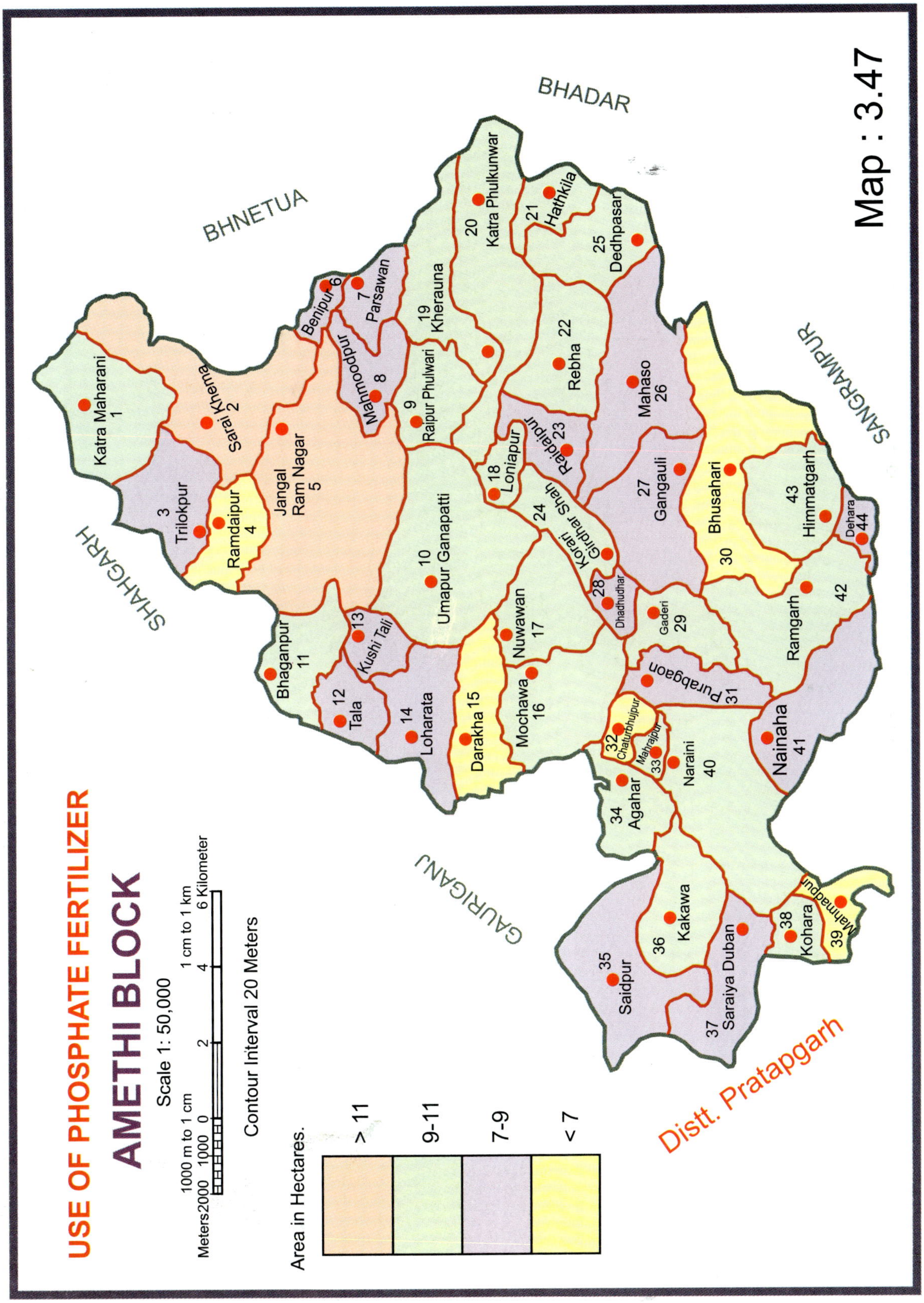

Map 3.47: Use of Phosphate Fertilizer

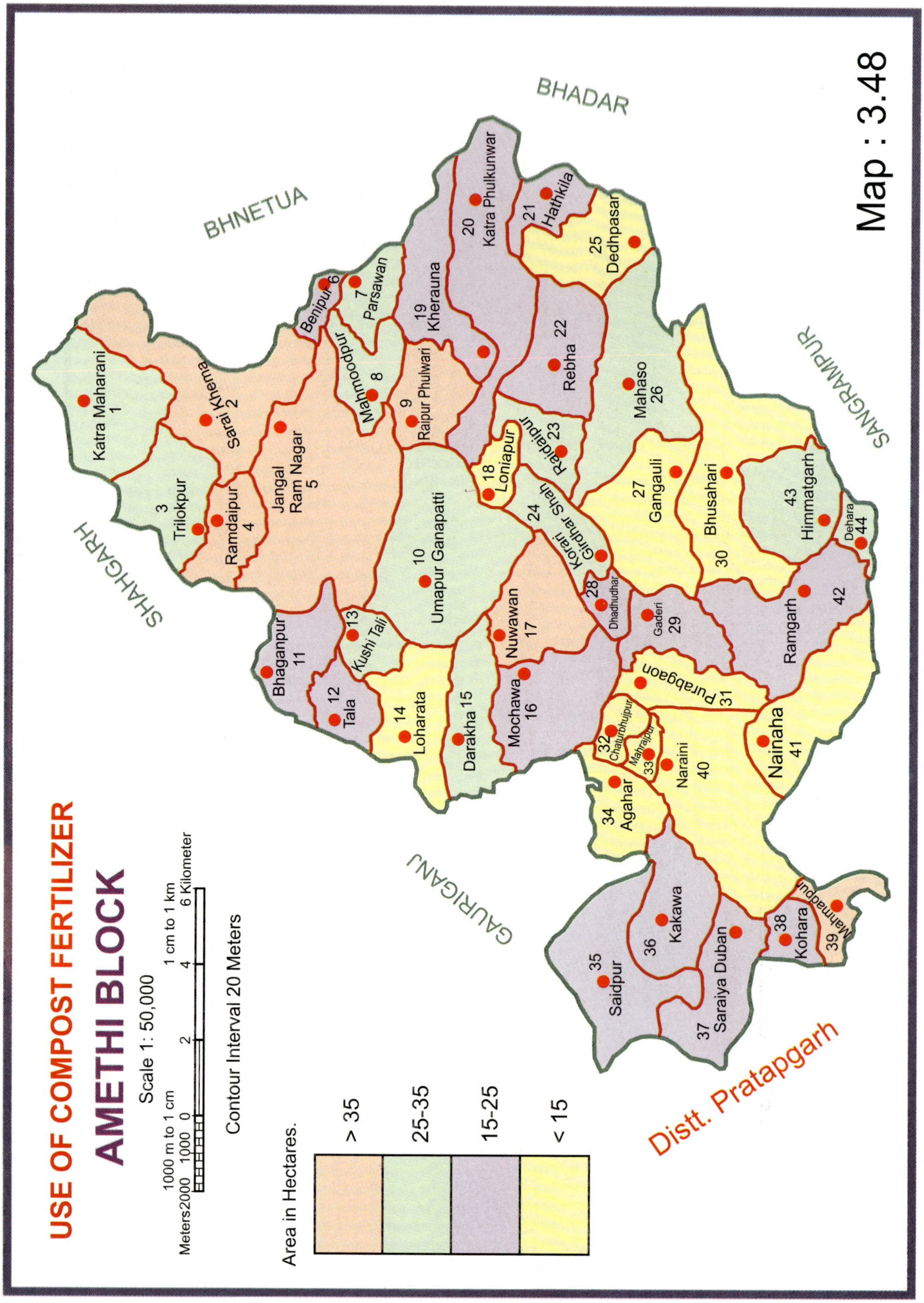

Map 3.48: Use of Compost Fertilizer

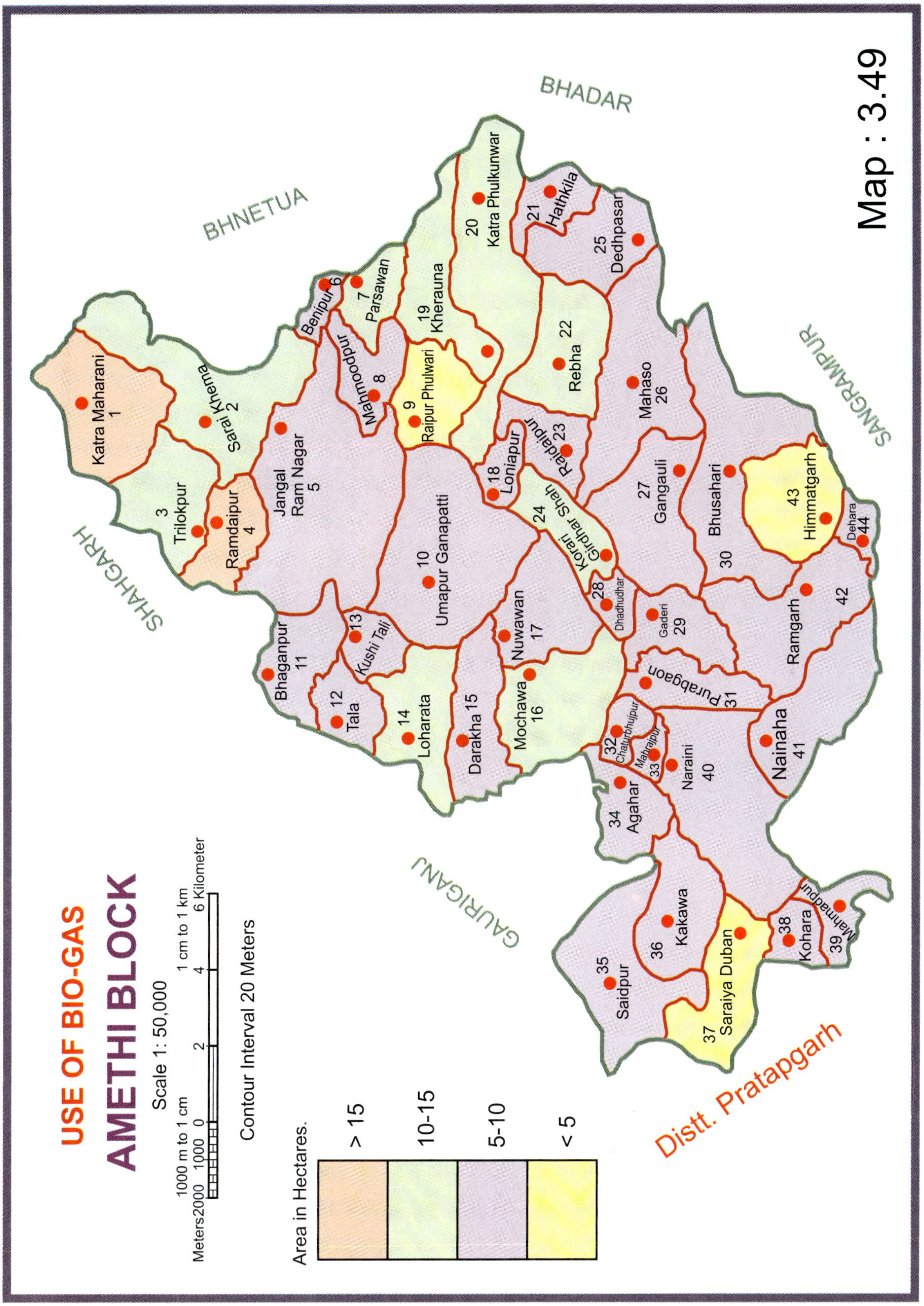

Map 3.49: Use of Bio-gas

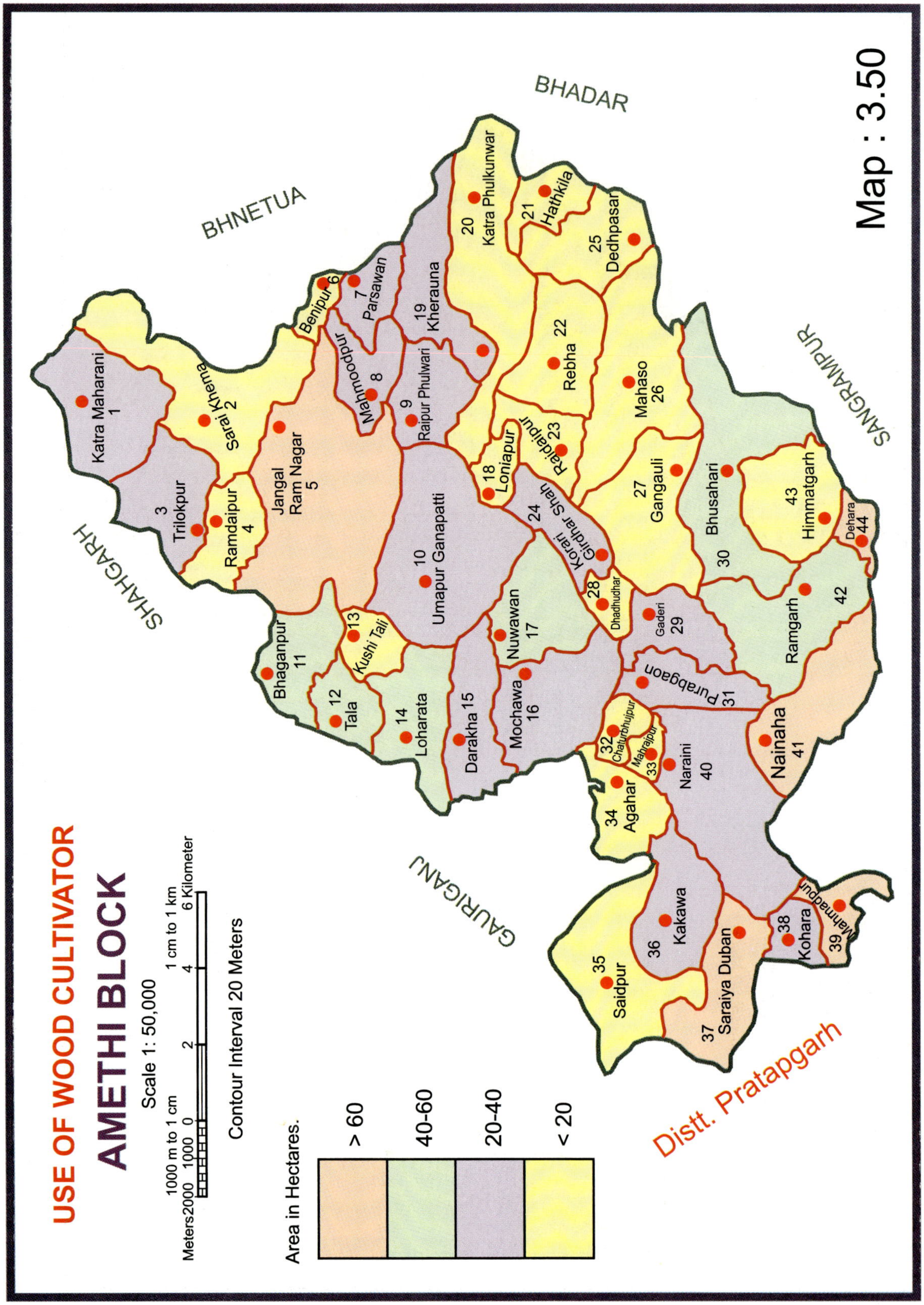

Map 3.50: Use of Wood Cultivator

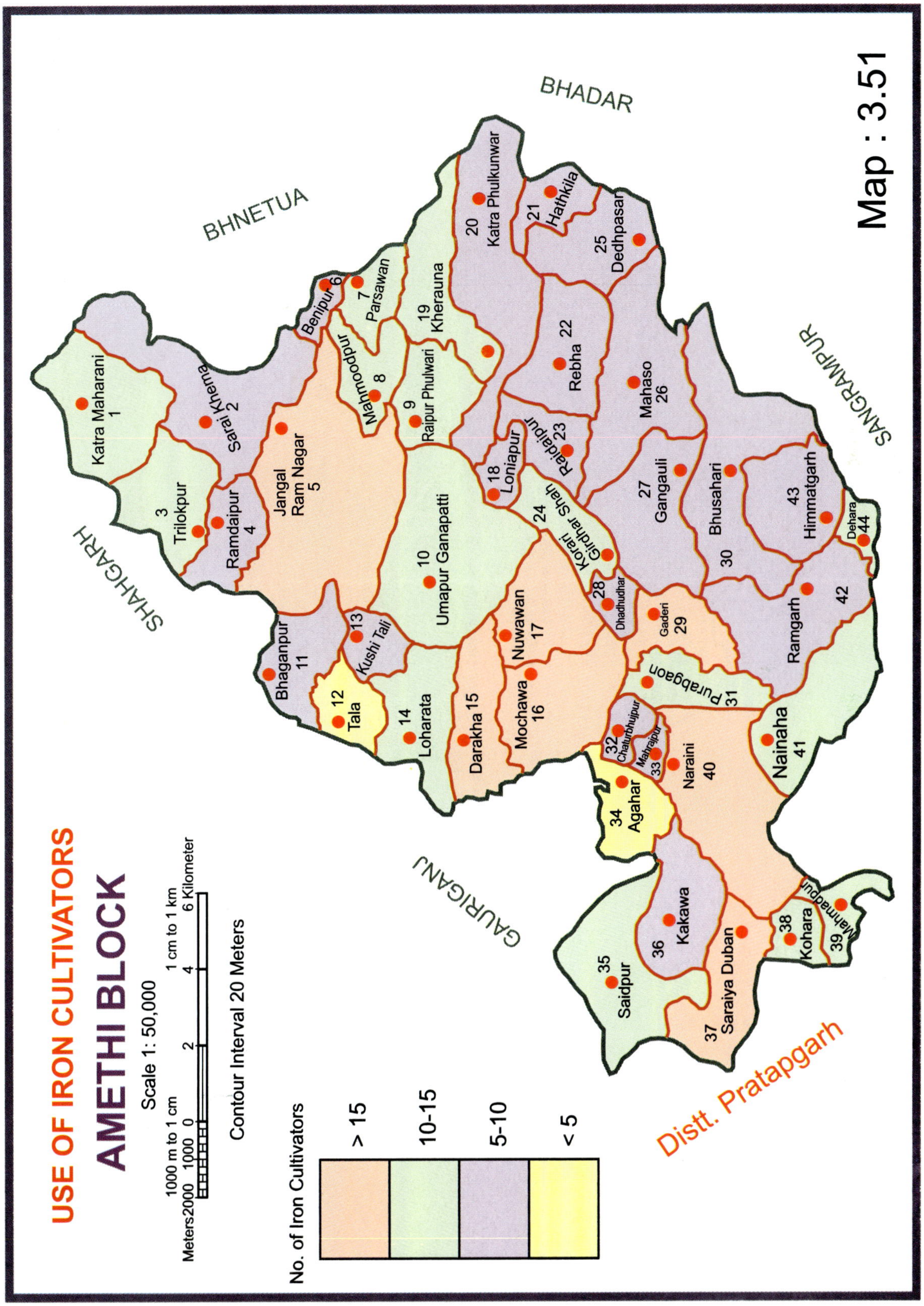

Map 3.51: Use of Iron Cultivator

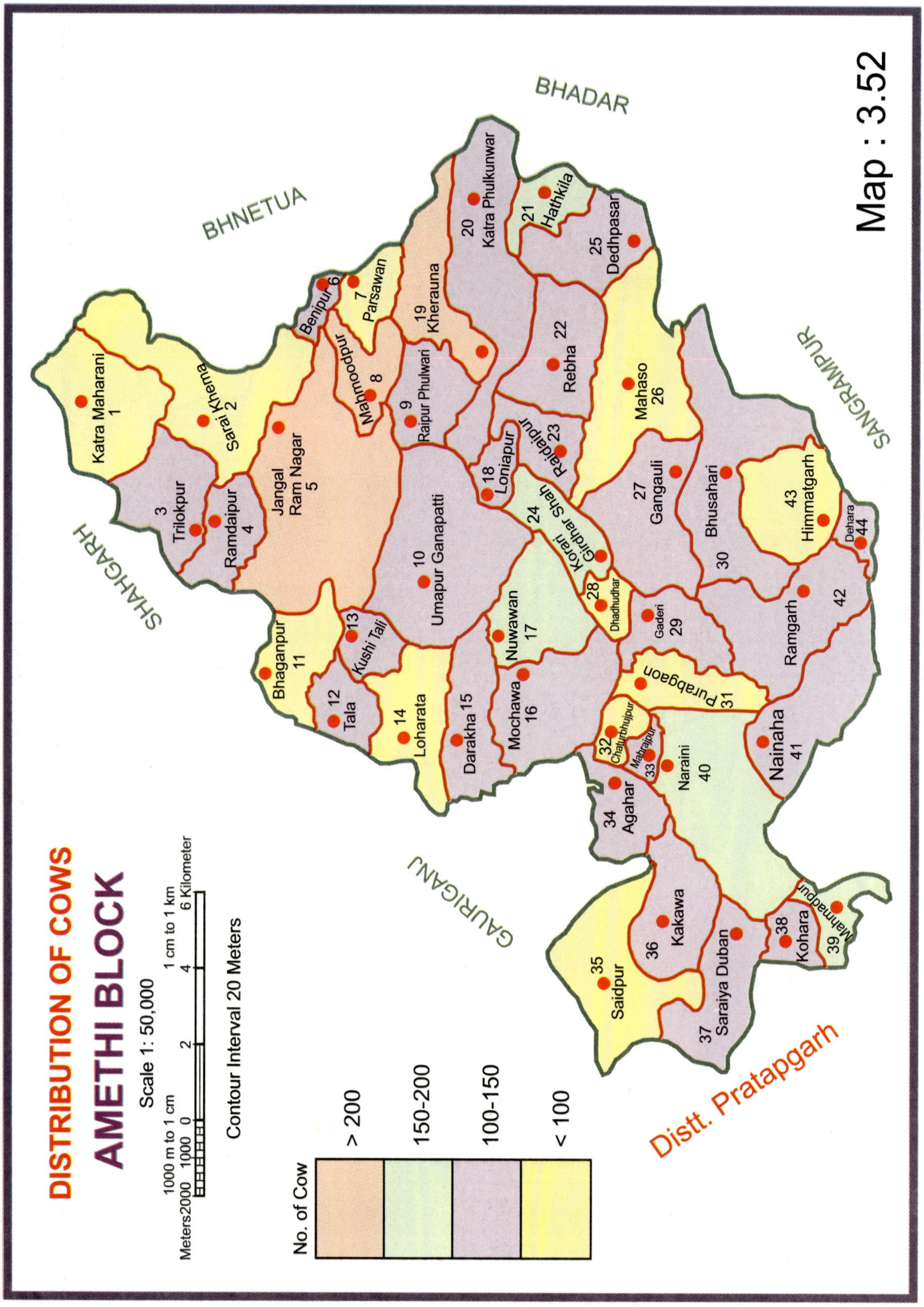

Map 3.52: Distribution of Cows

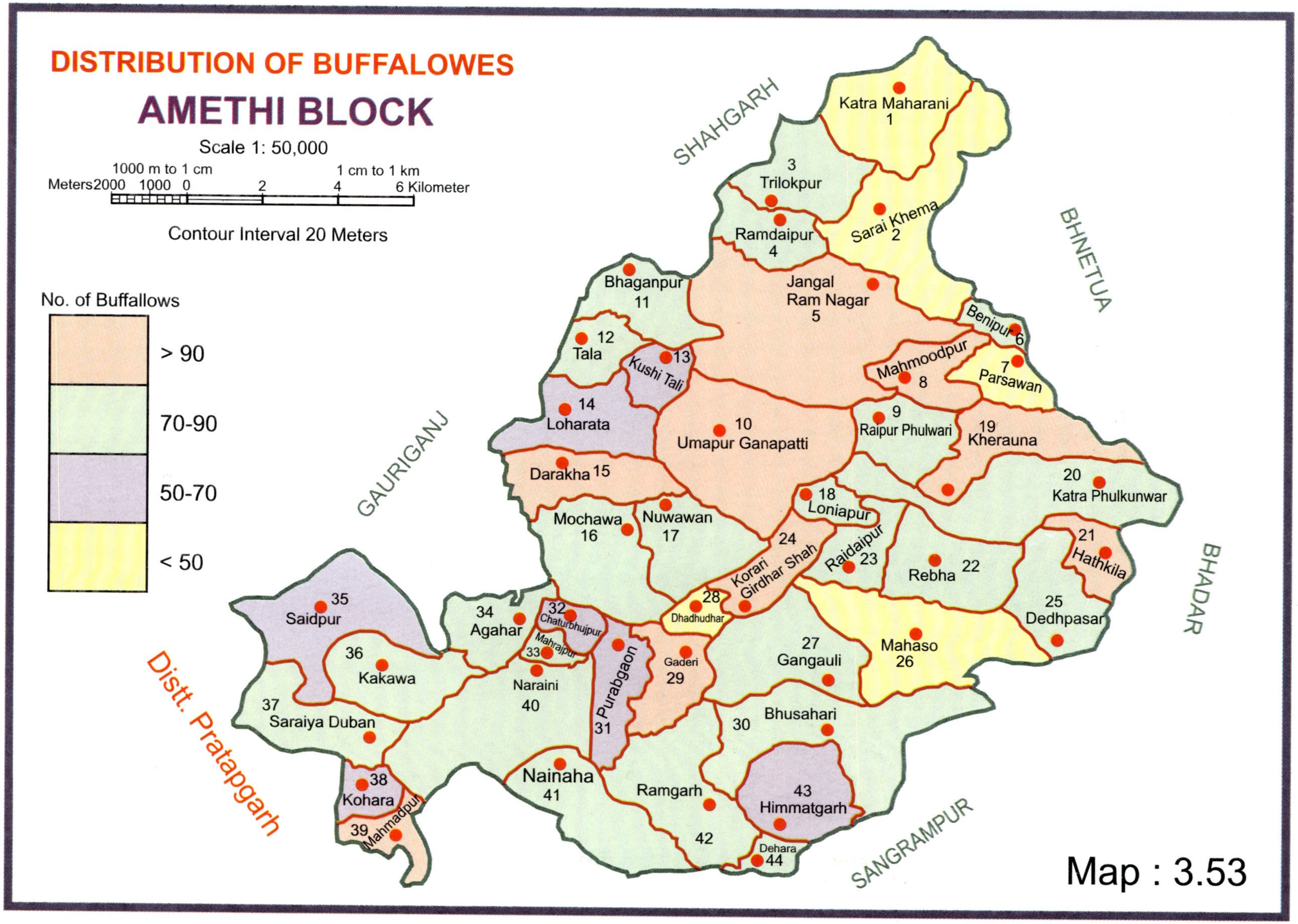

Map 3.53: Distribution of Buffalowes

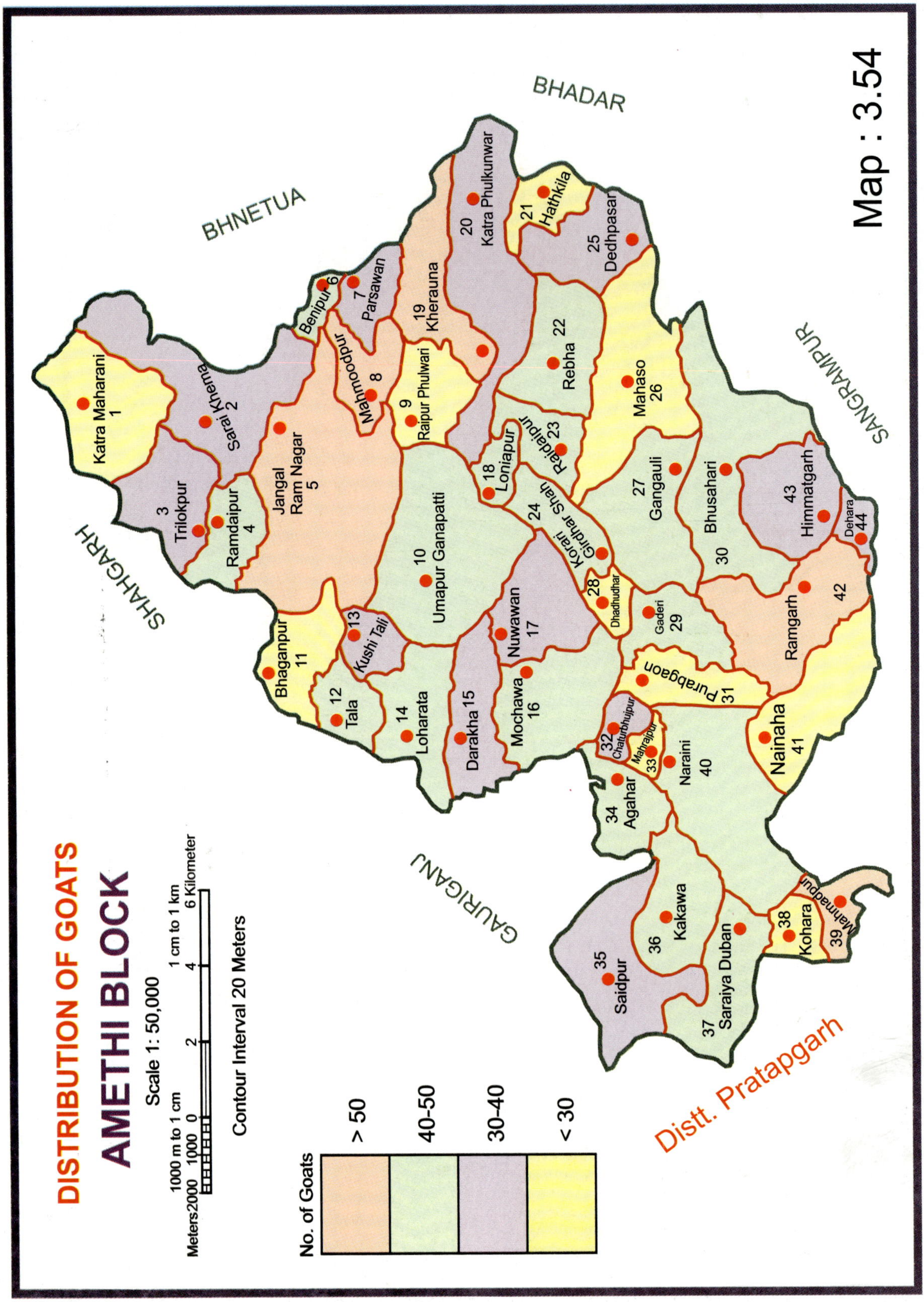

Map 3.54: Distribution of Goats

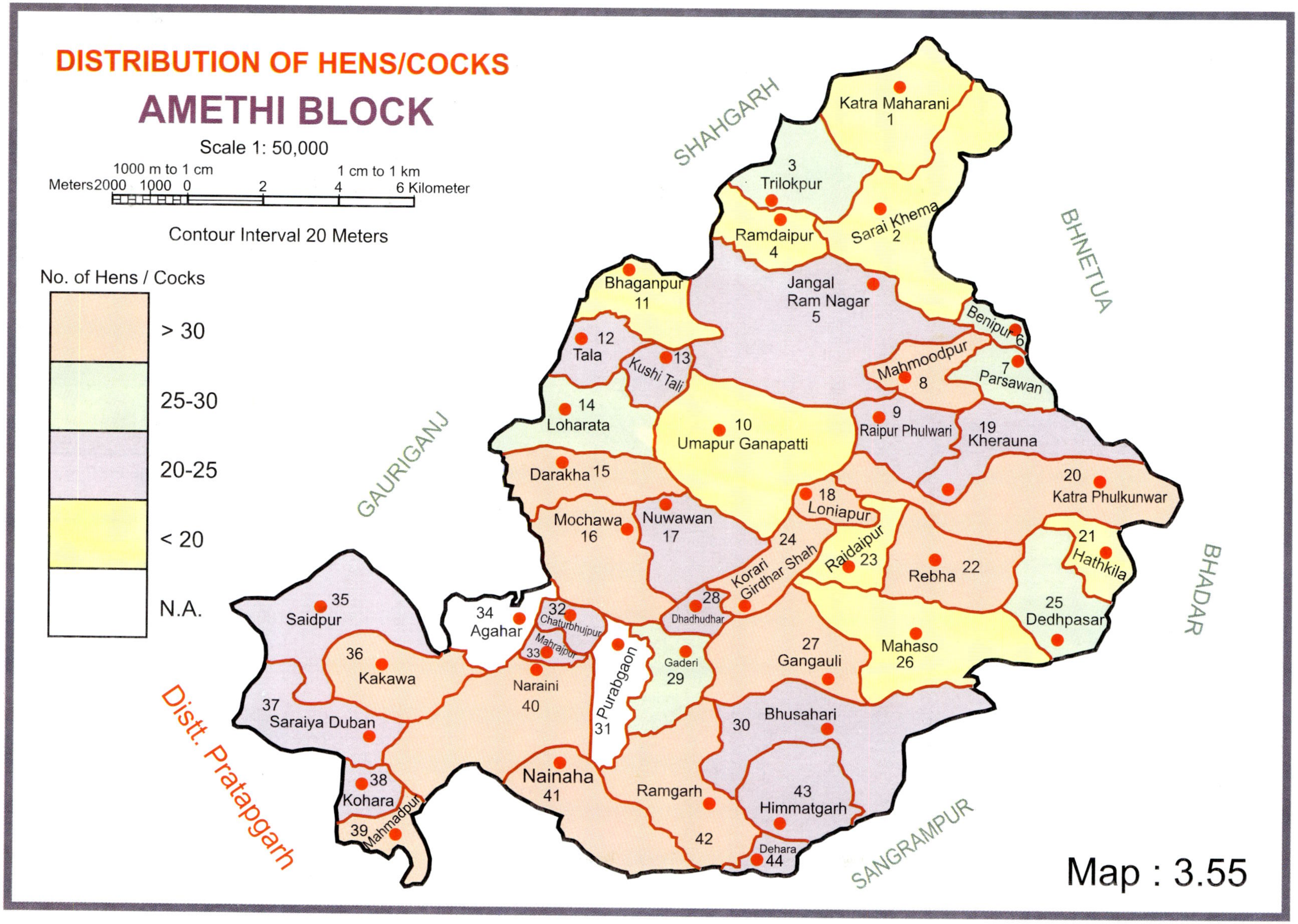

Map 3.55: Distribution of Hens/Cocks

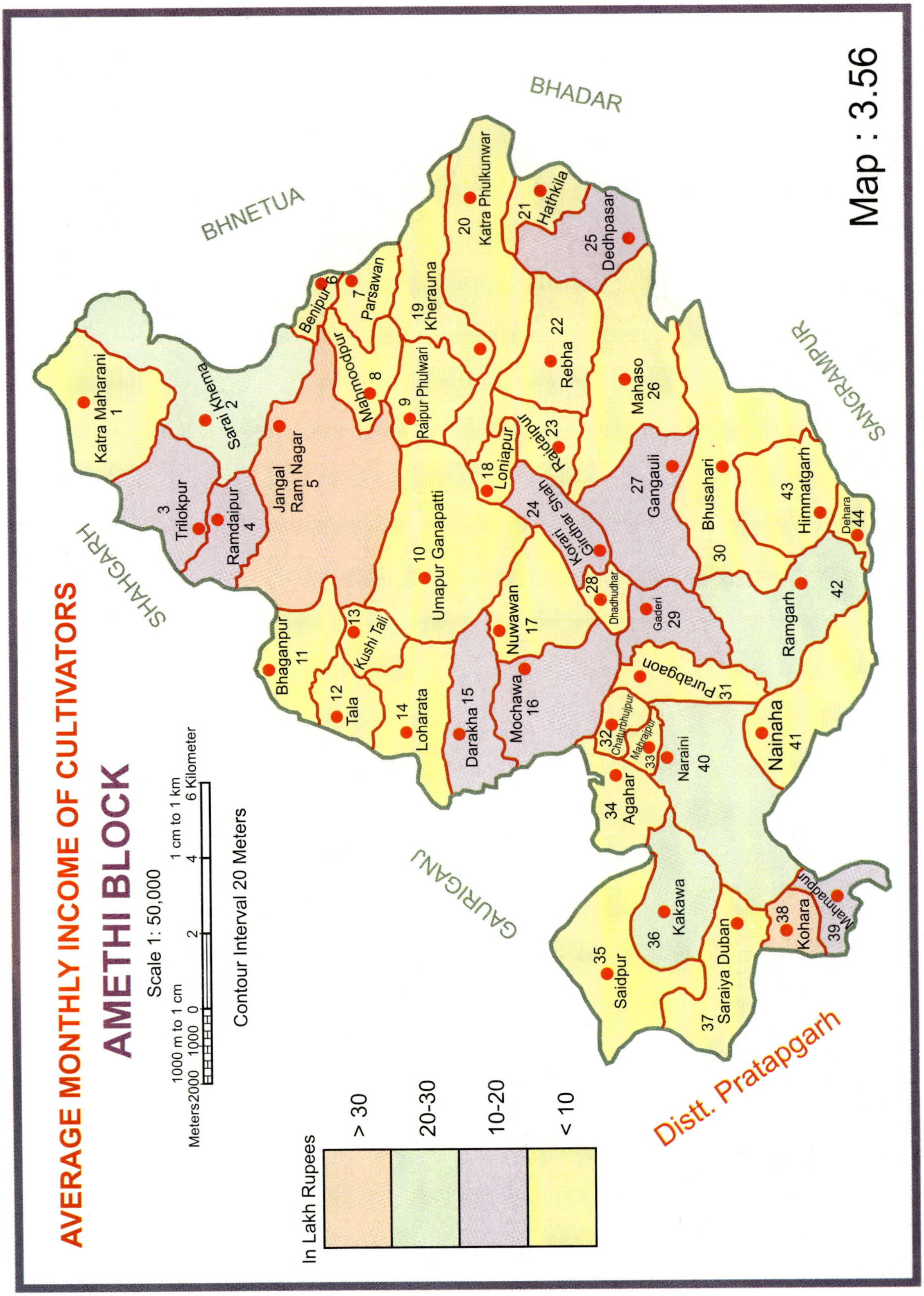

Map 3.56: Average Monthly Income of Cultivators

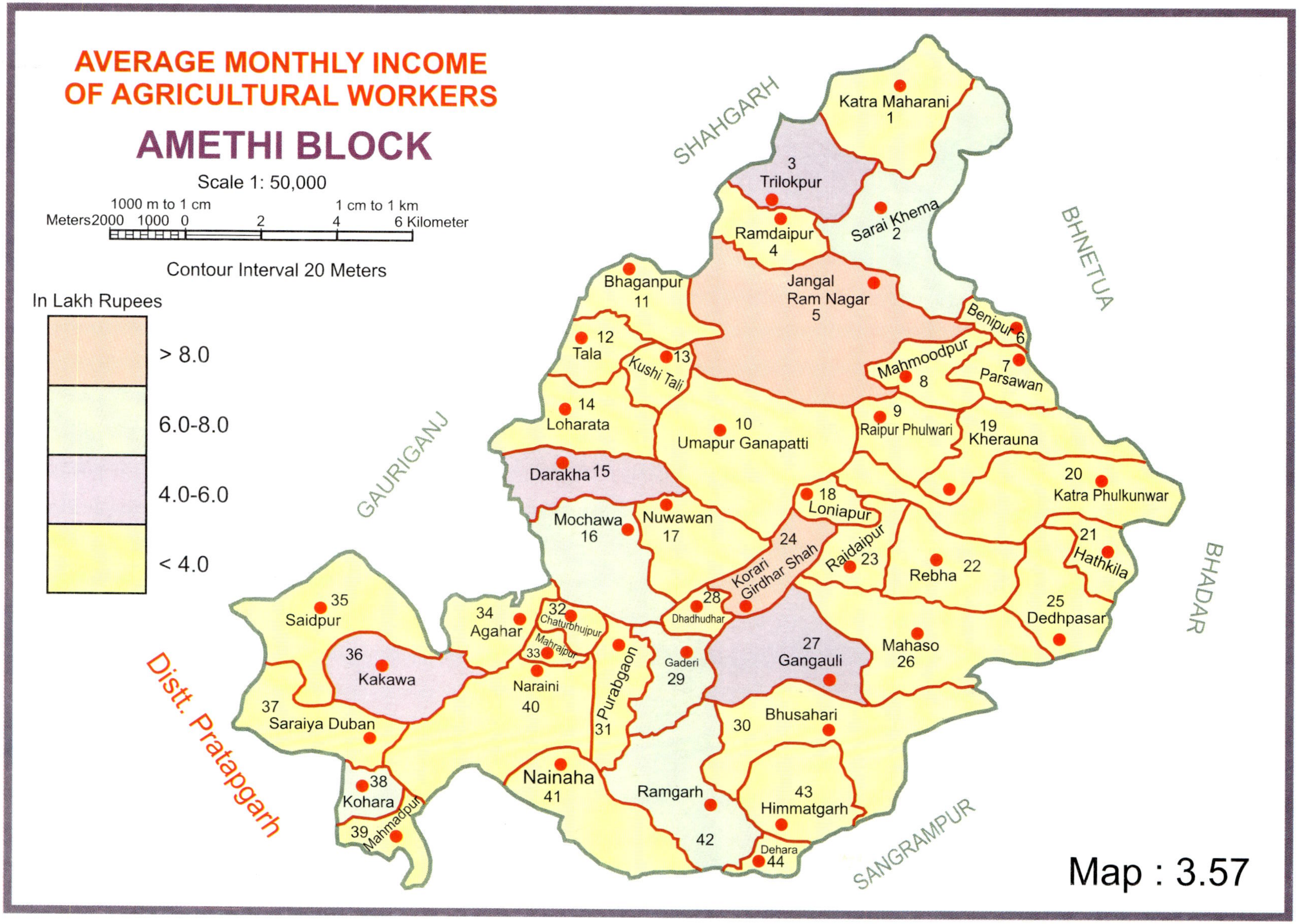

Map 3.57: Average Monthly Income of Agricultural Workers

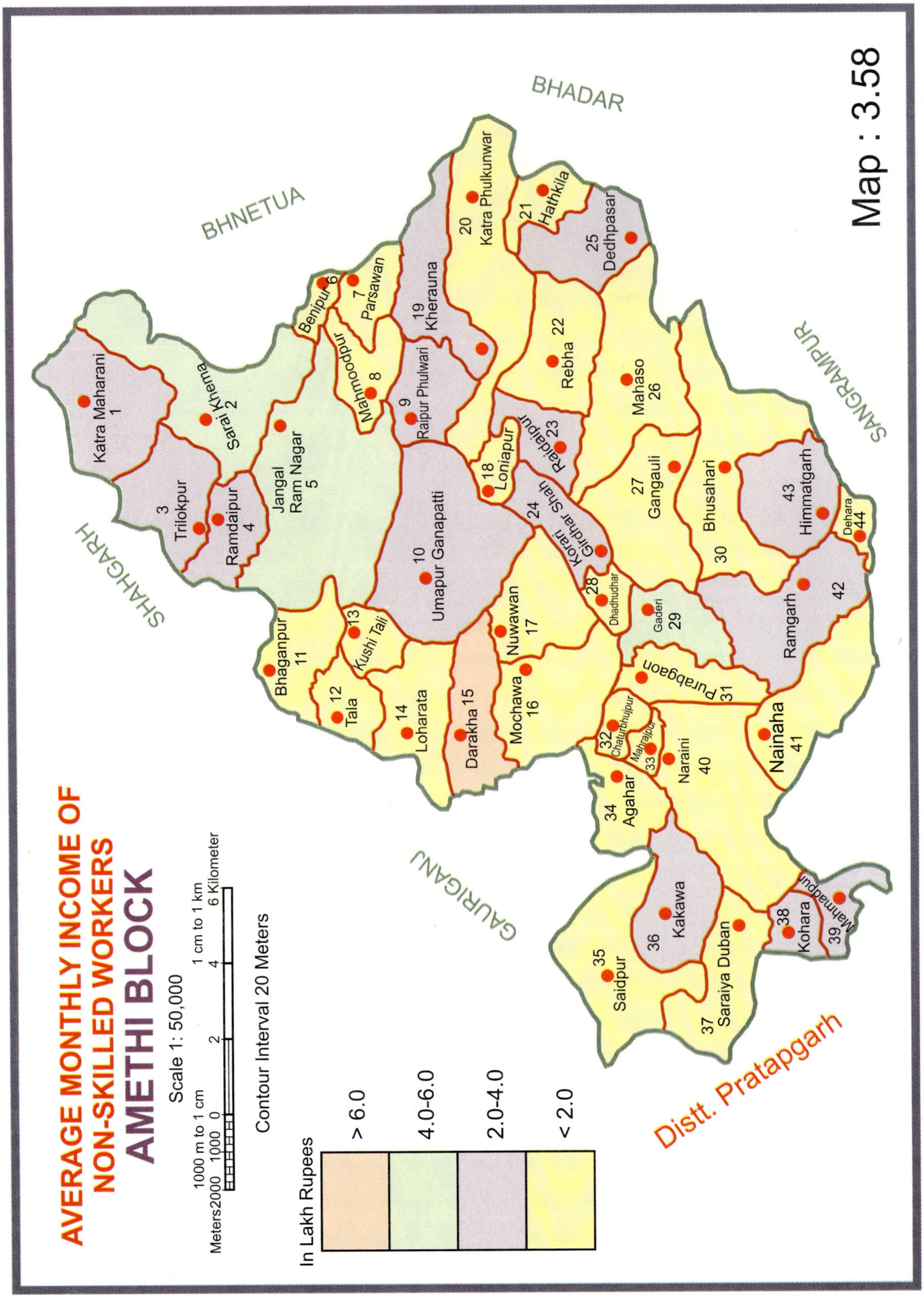

Map 3.58: Average Monthly Income of Non-Skilled Workers

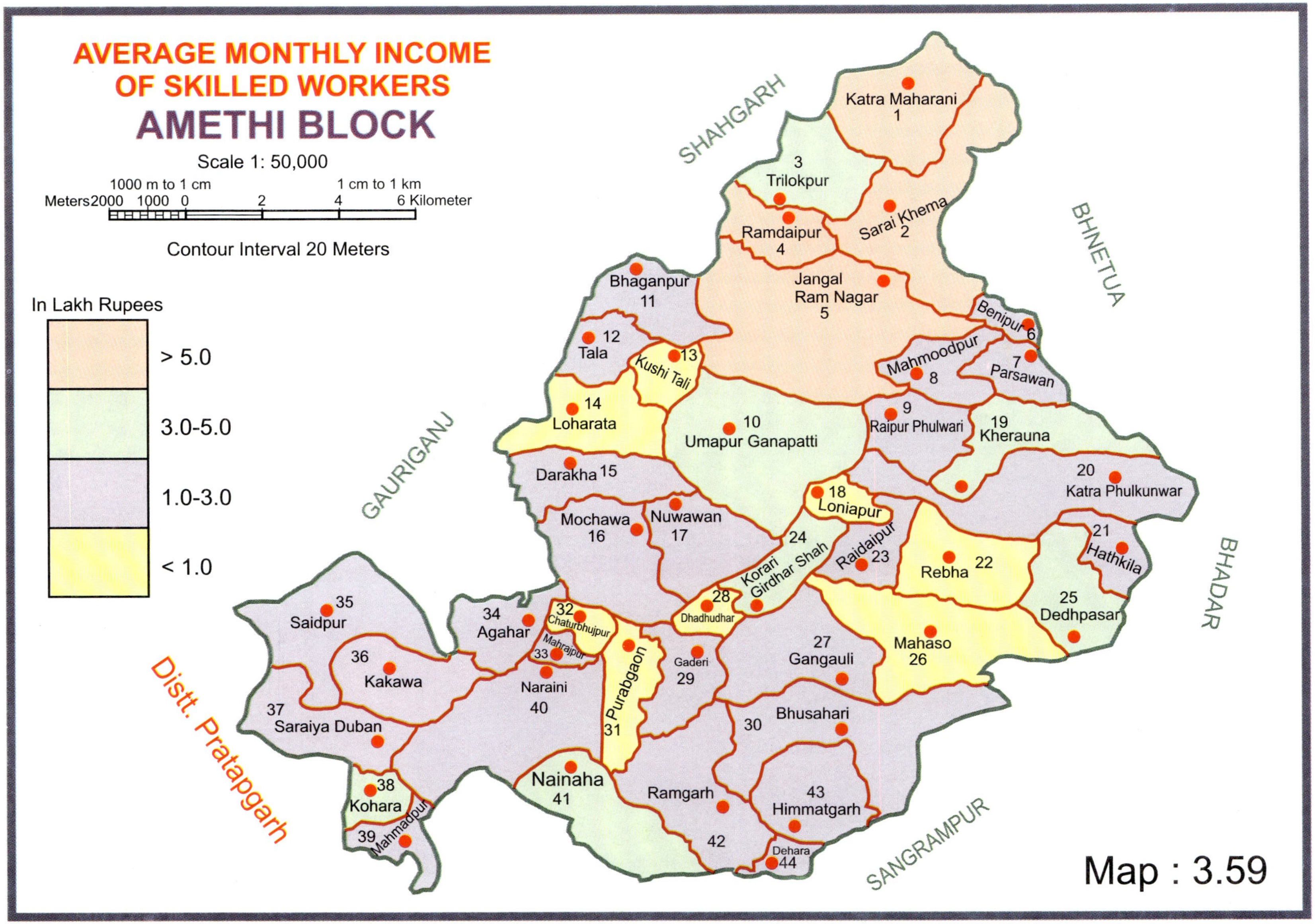

Map 3.59: Average Monthly Income of Skilled Workers

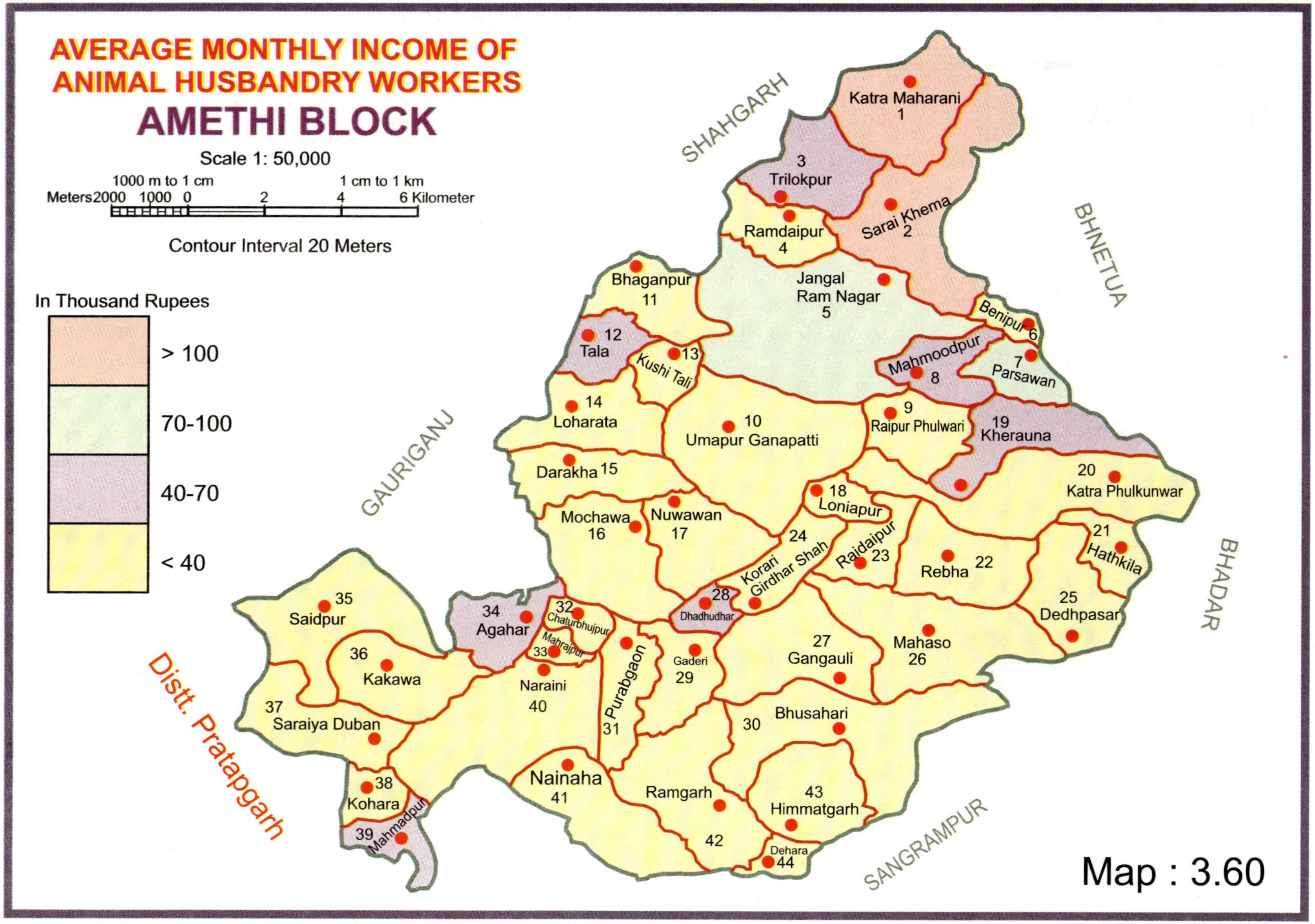

Map 3.60: Average Monthly Income of Husbandry Workers

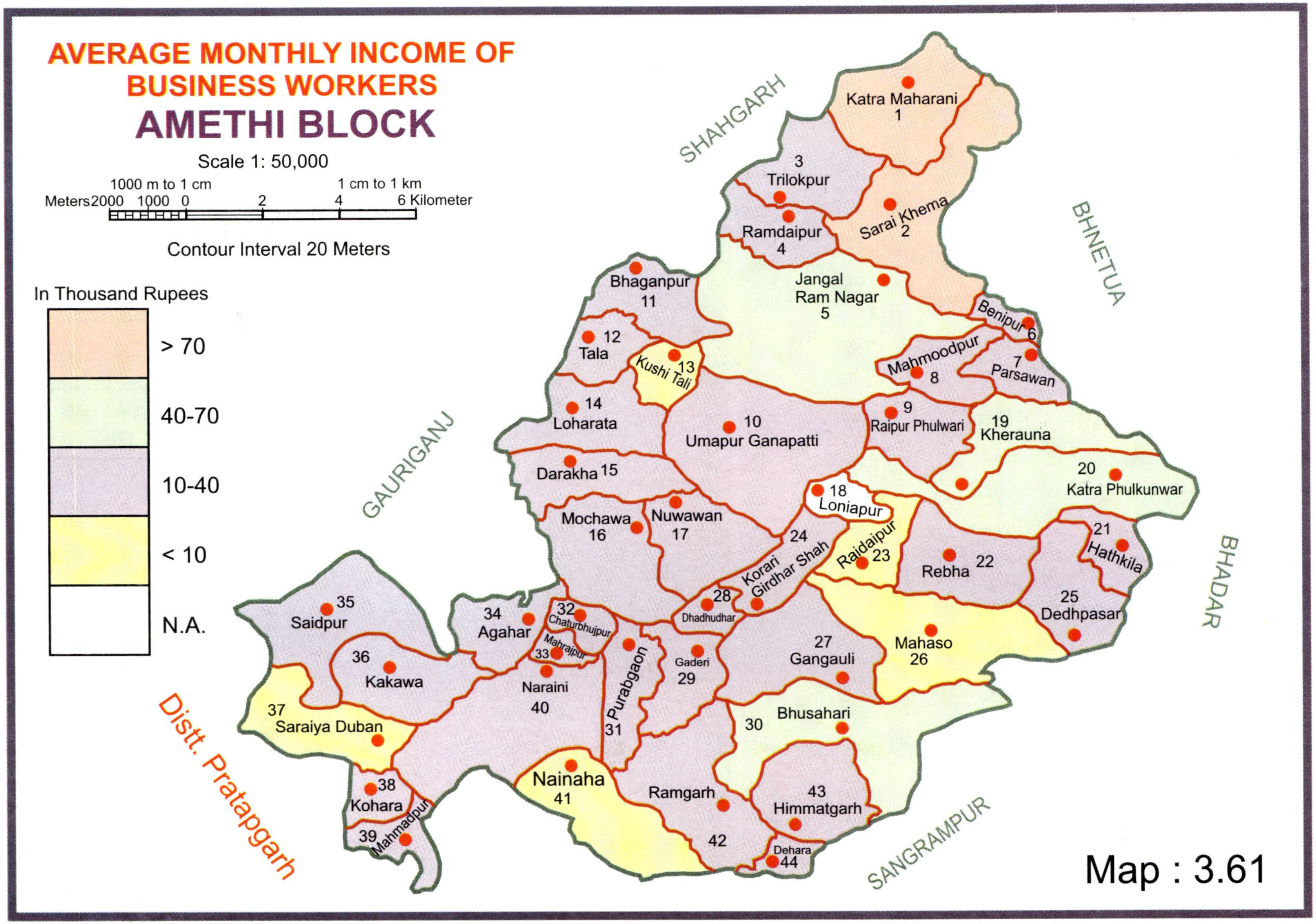

Map 3.61: Average Monthly Income of Business Workers

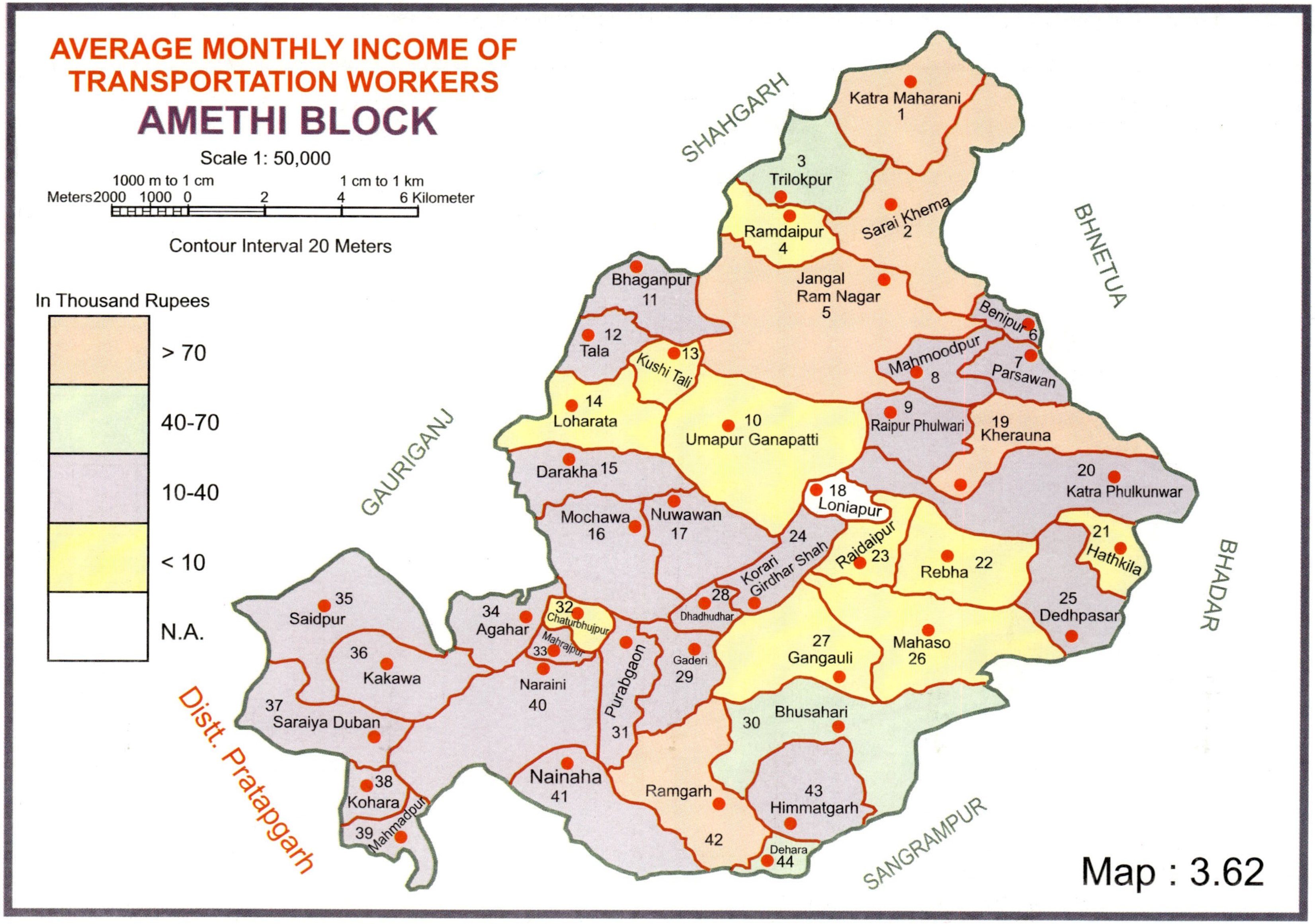

Map 3.62: Average Monthly Income of Transportation Workers

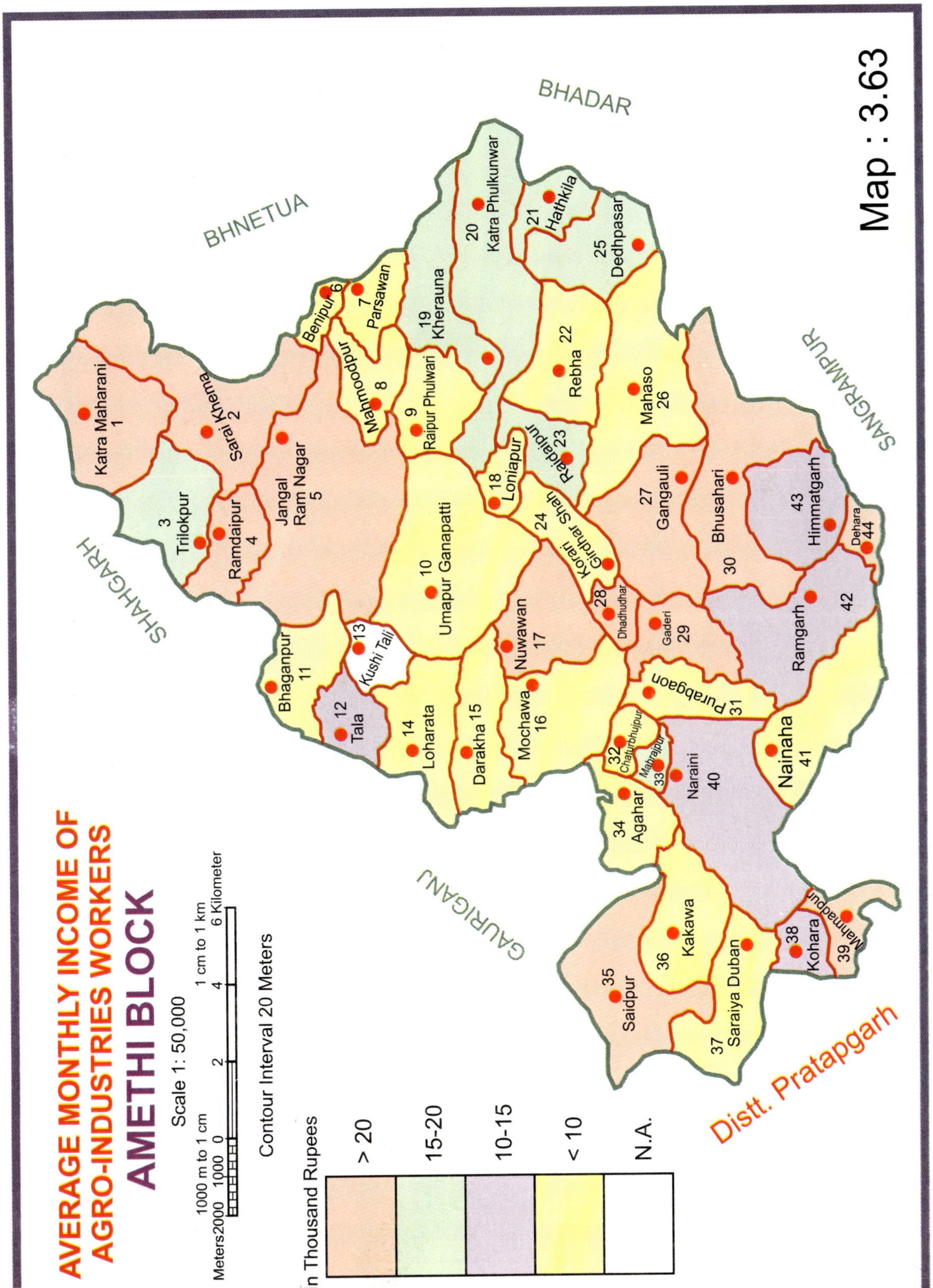

Map 3.63: Average Monthly Income of Agro-Industries Workers

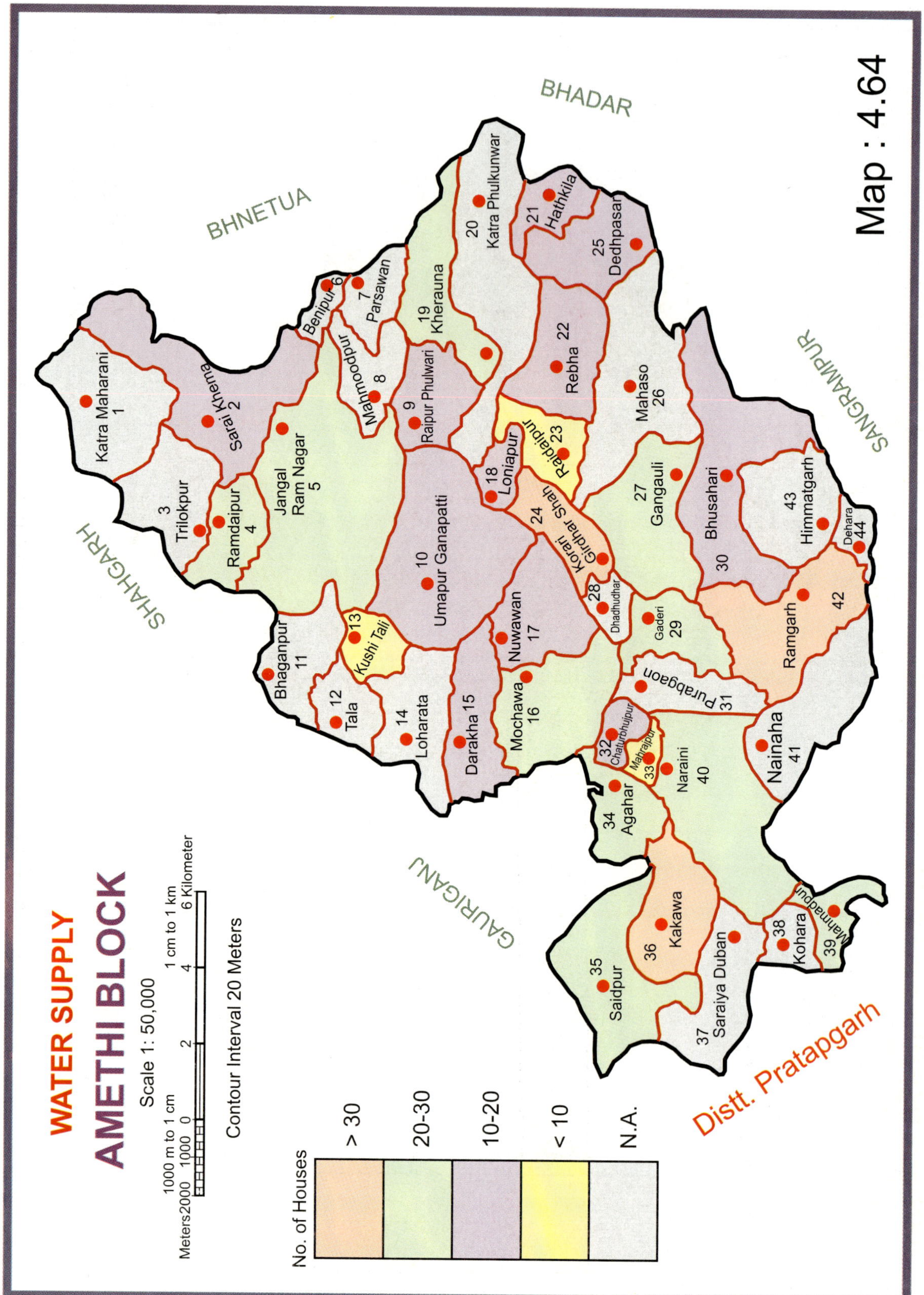

Map 4.64: Water Supply

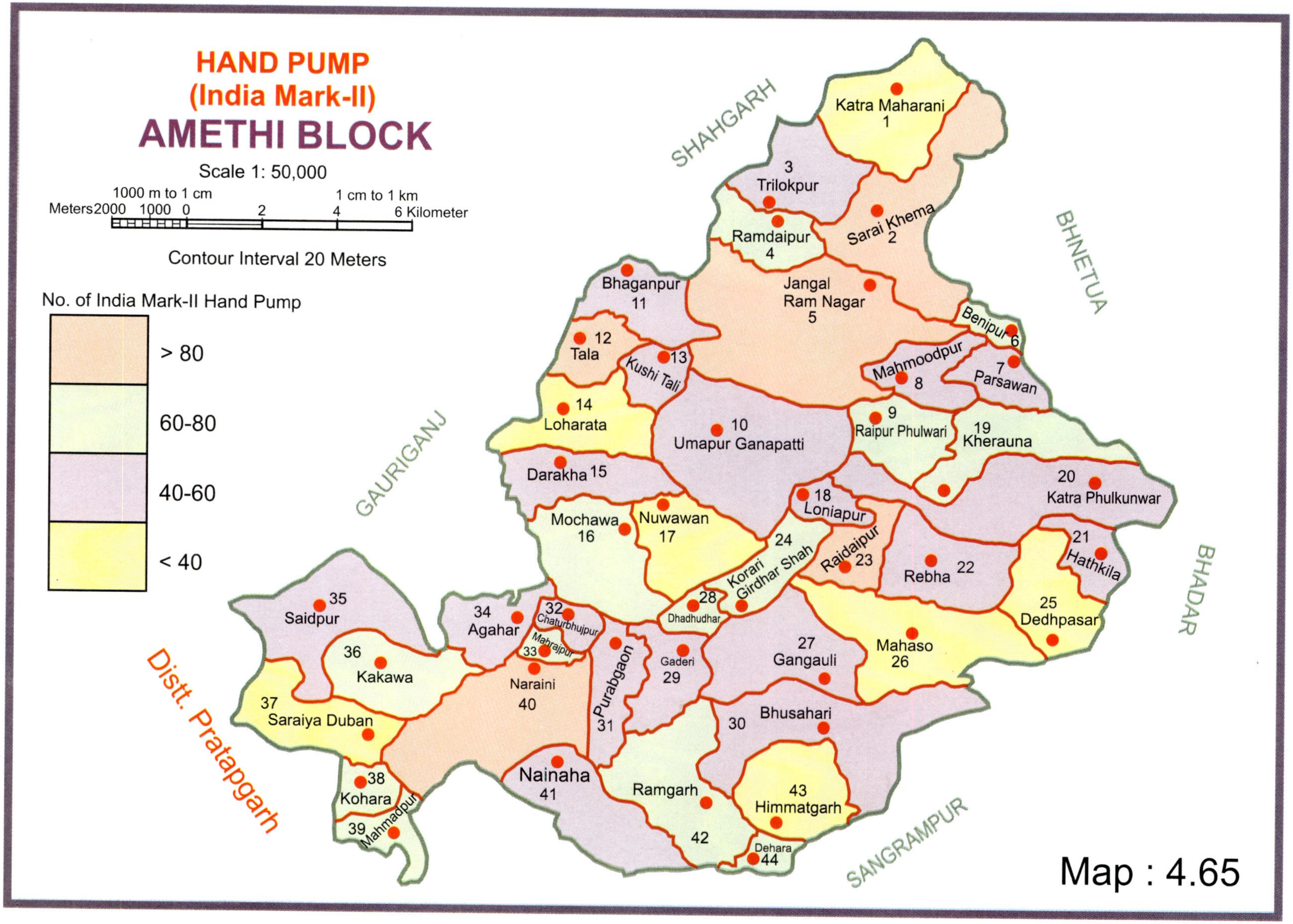

Map 4.65: Hand Pump (India Mark-II)

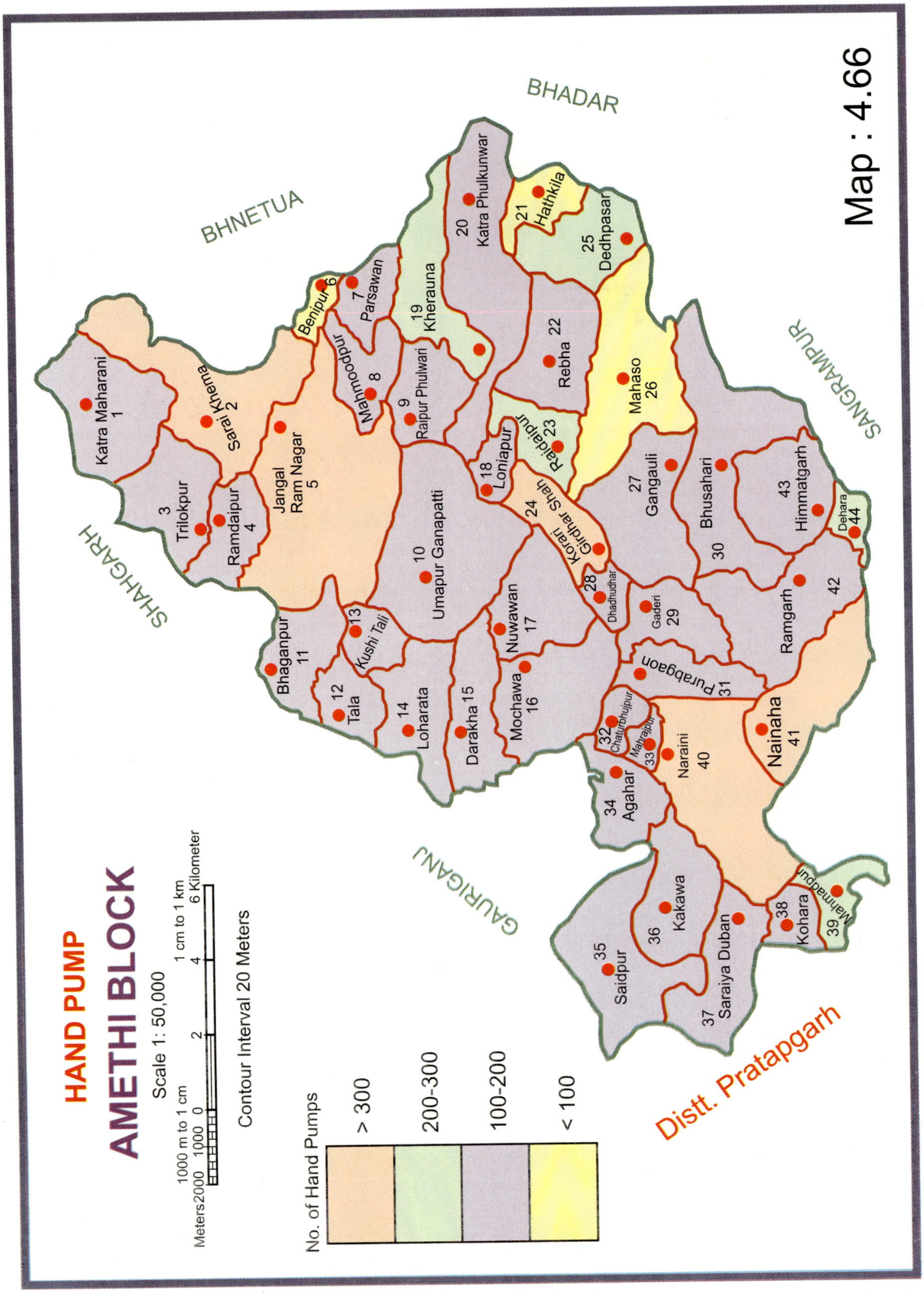

Map 4.66: Hand Pump

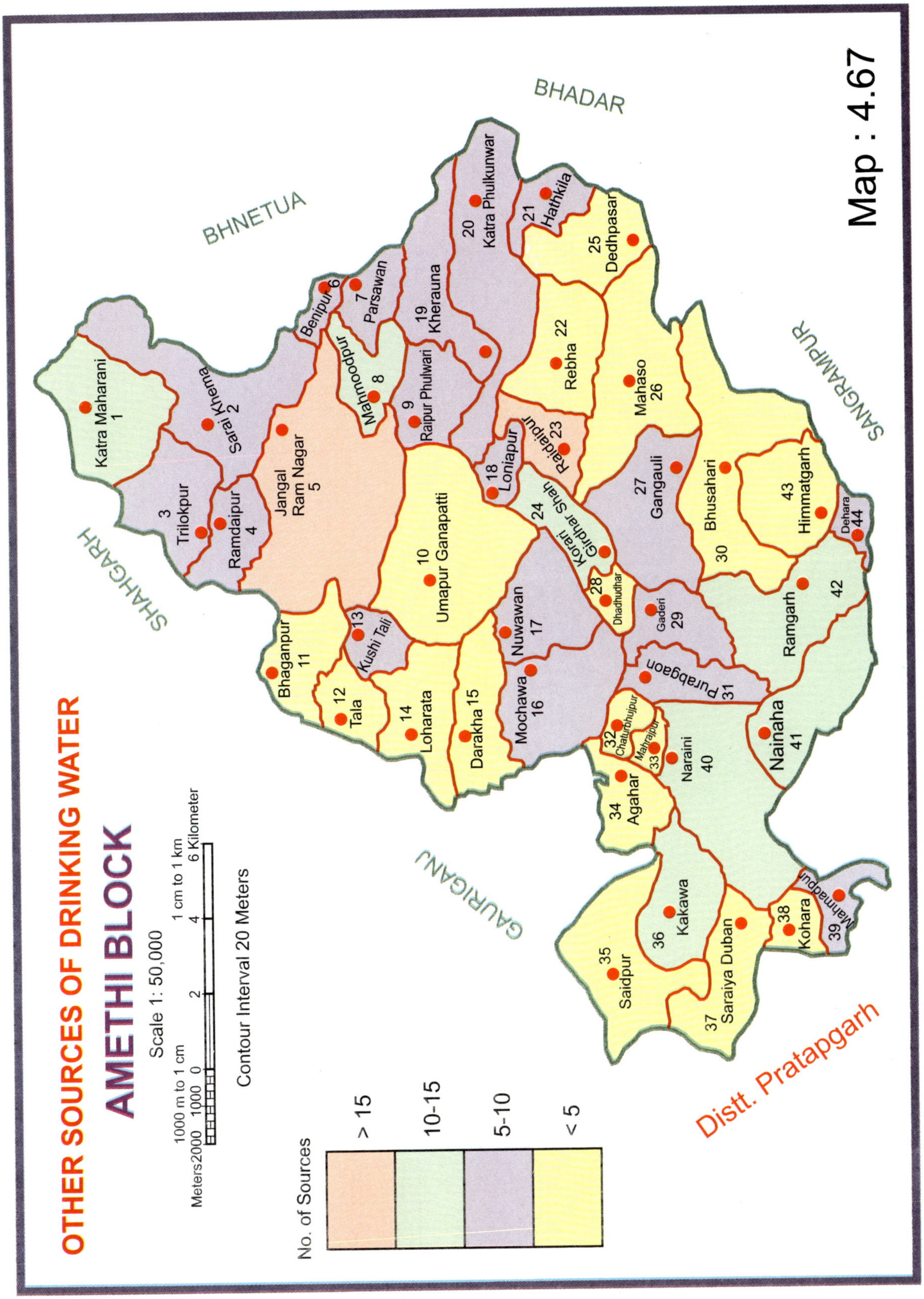

Map 4.67: Other Sources of Drinking Water

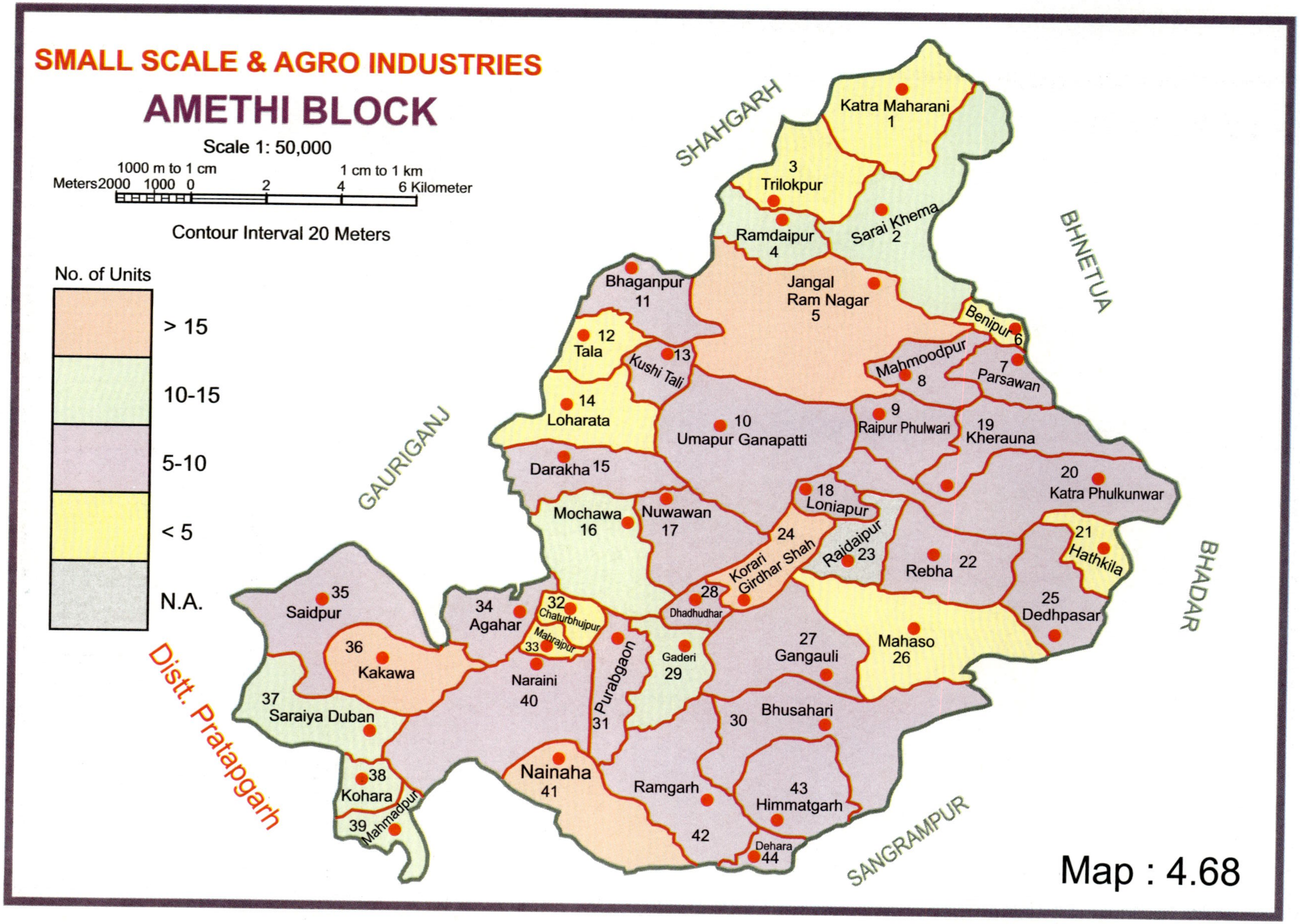

Map 4.68: Small Scale and Agro Industries

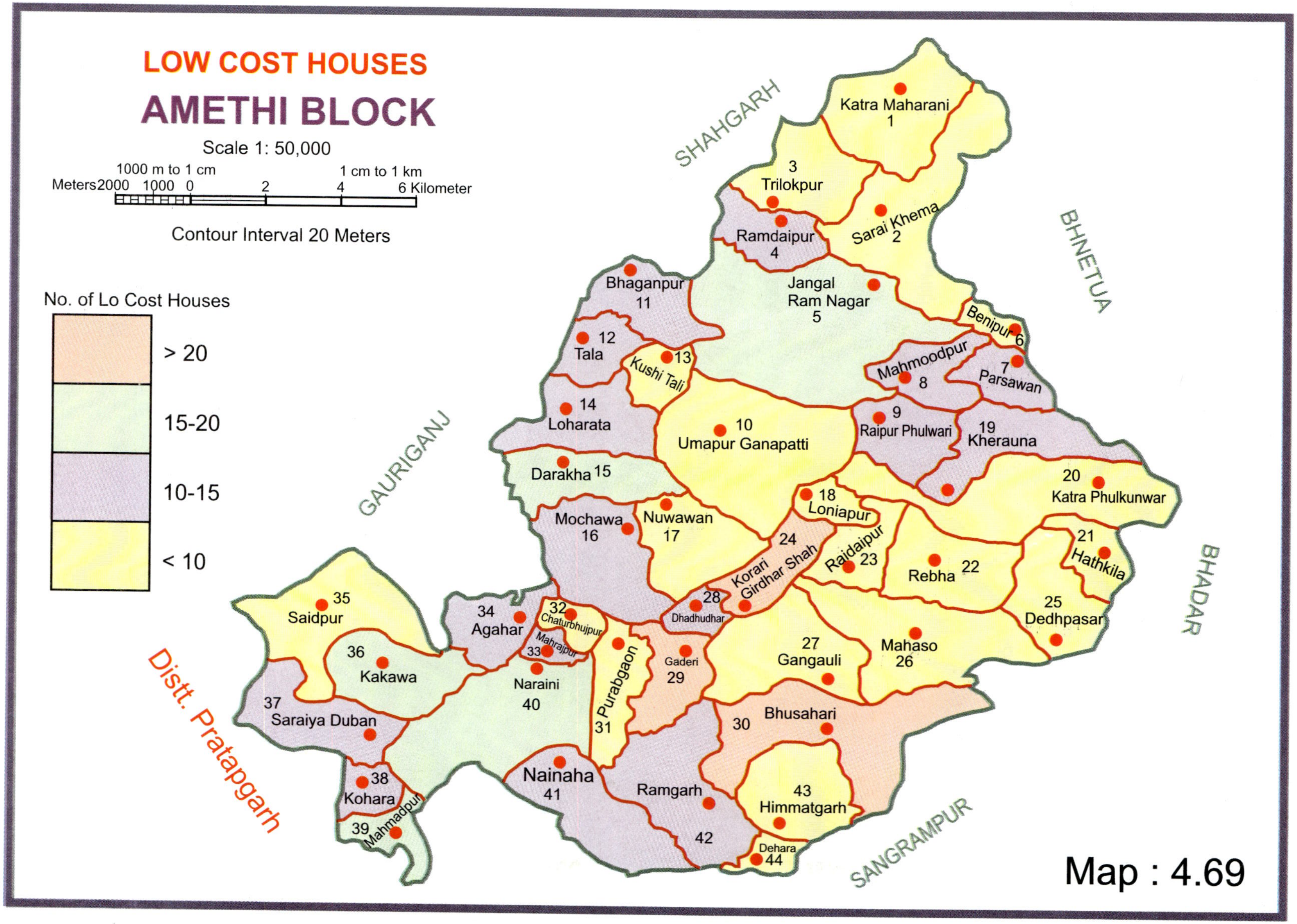

Map 4.69: Low Cost Houses

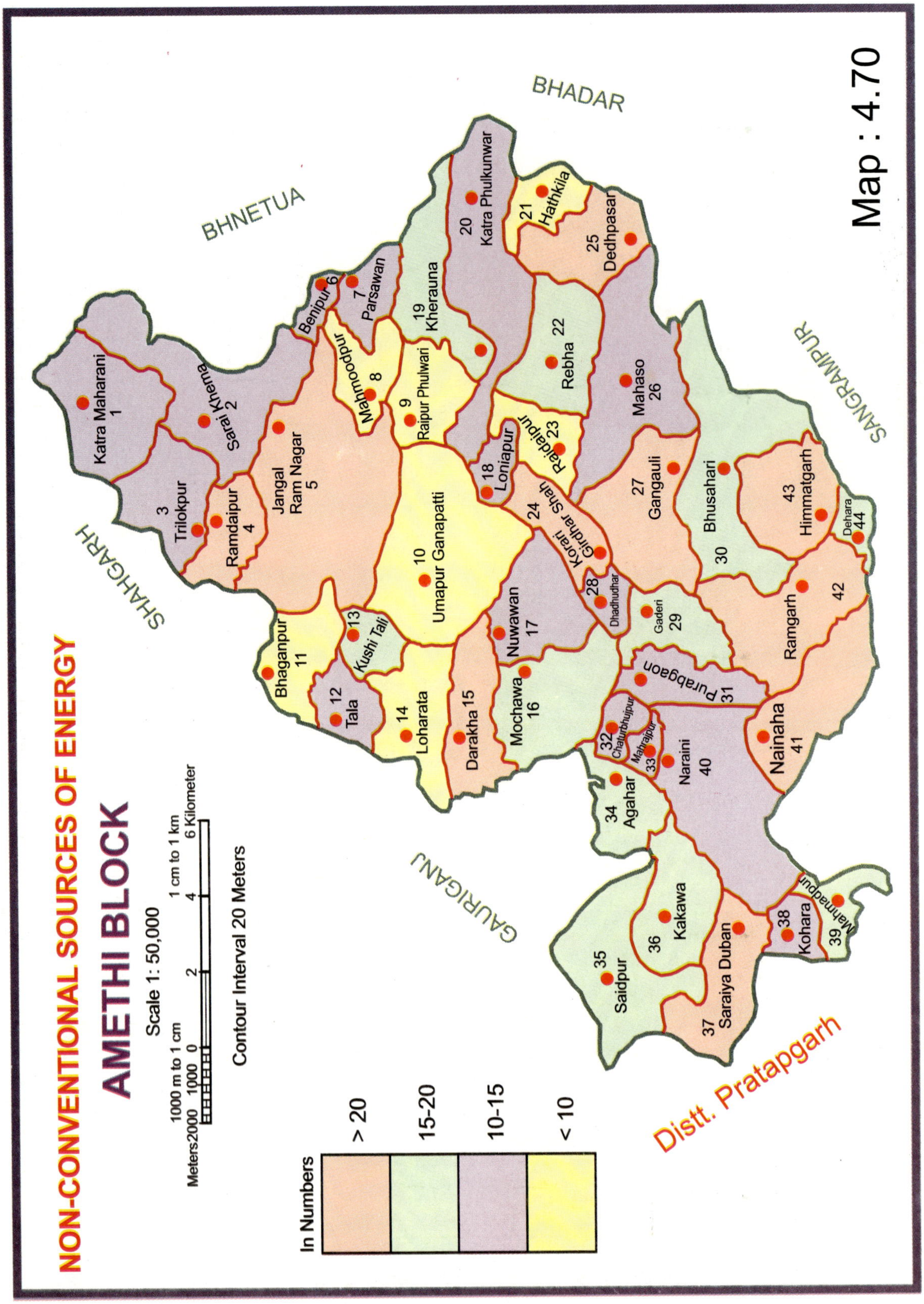

Map 4.70: Non-Conventional Sources of Energy

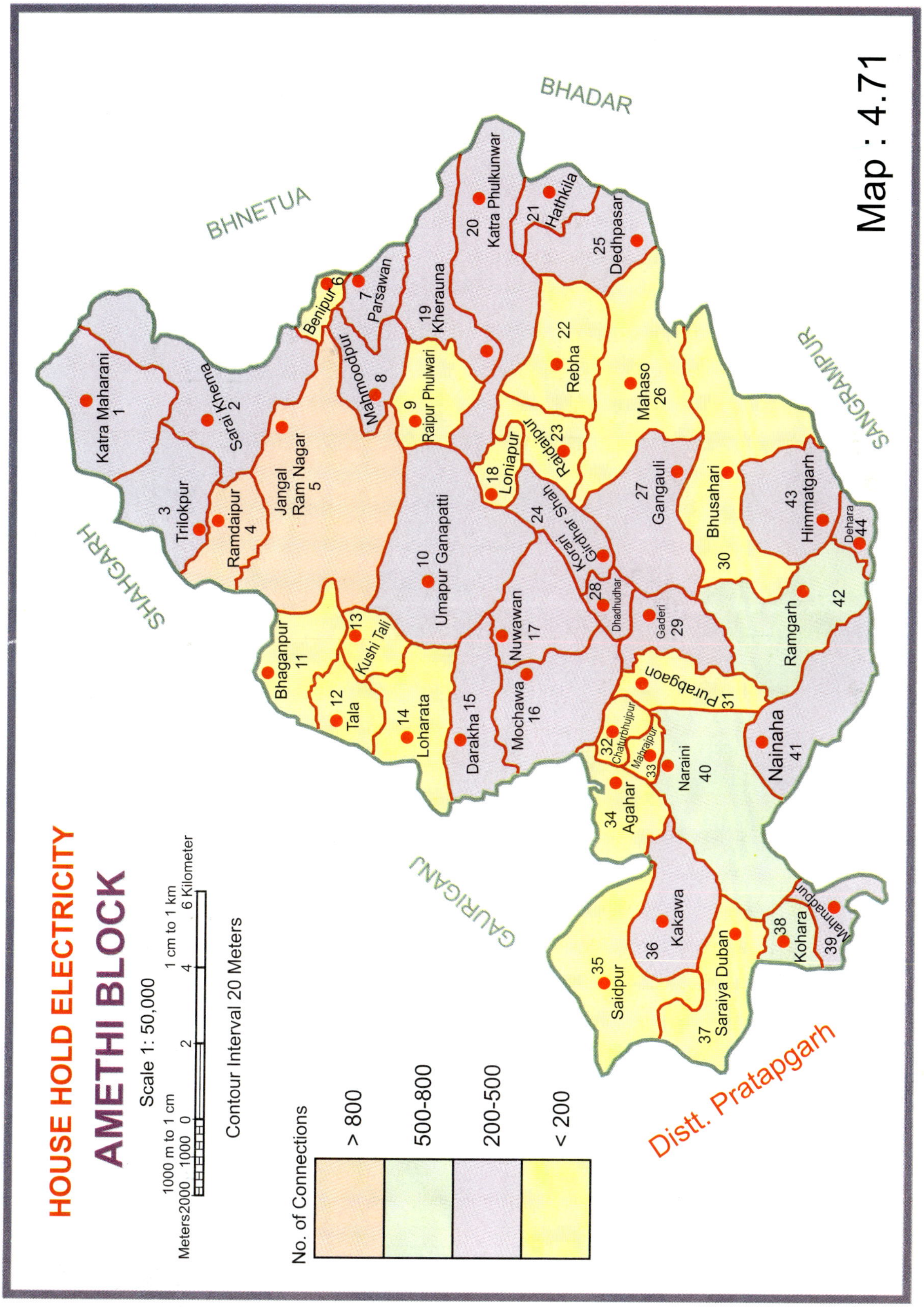

Map 4.71: Household Electricity

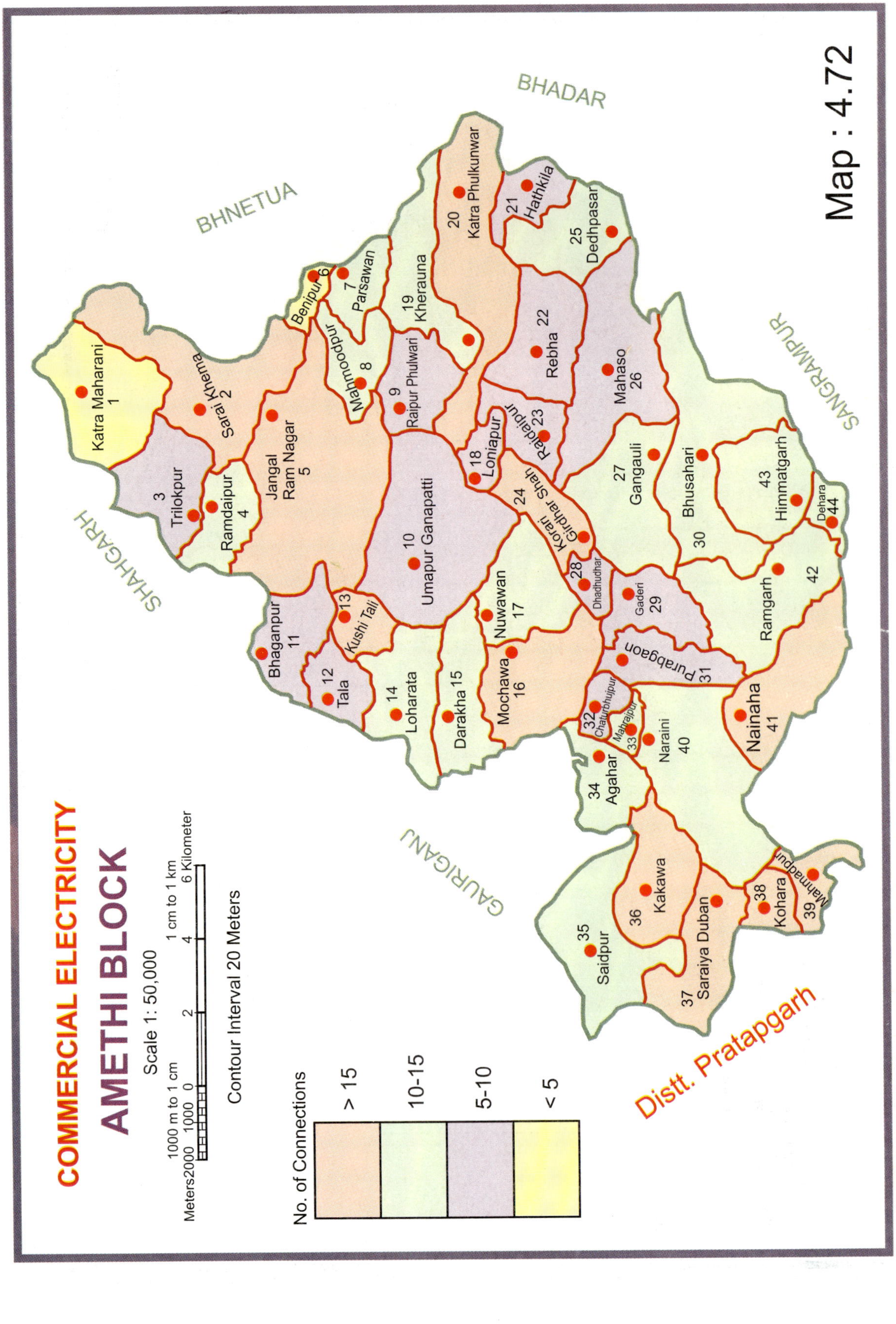

Map 4.72: Commercial Electricity

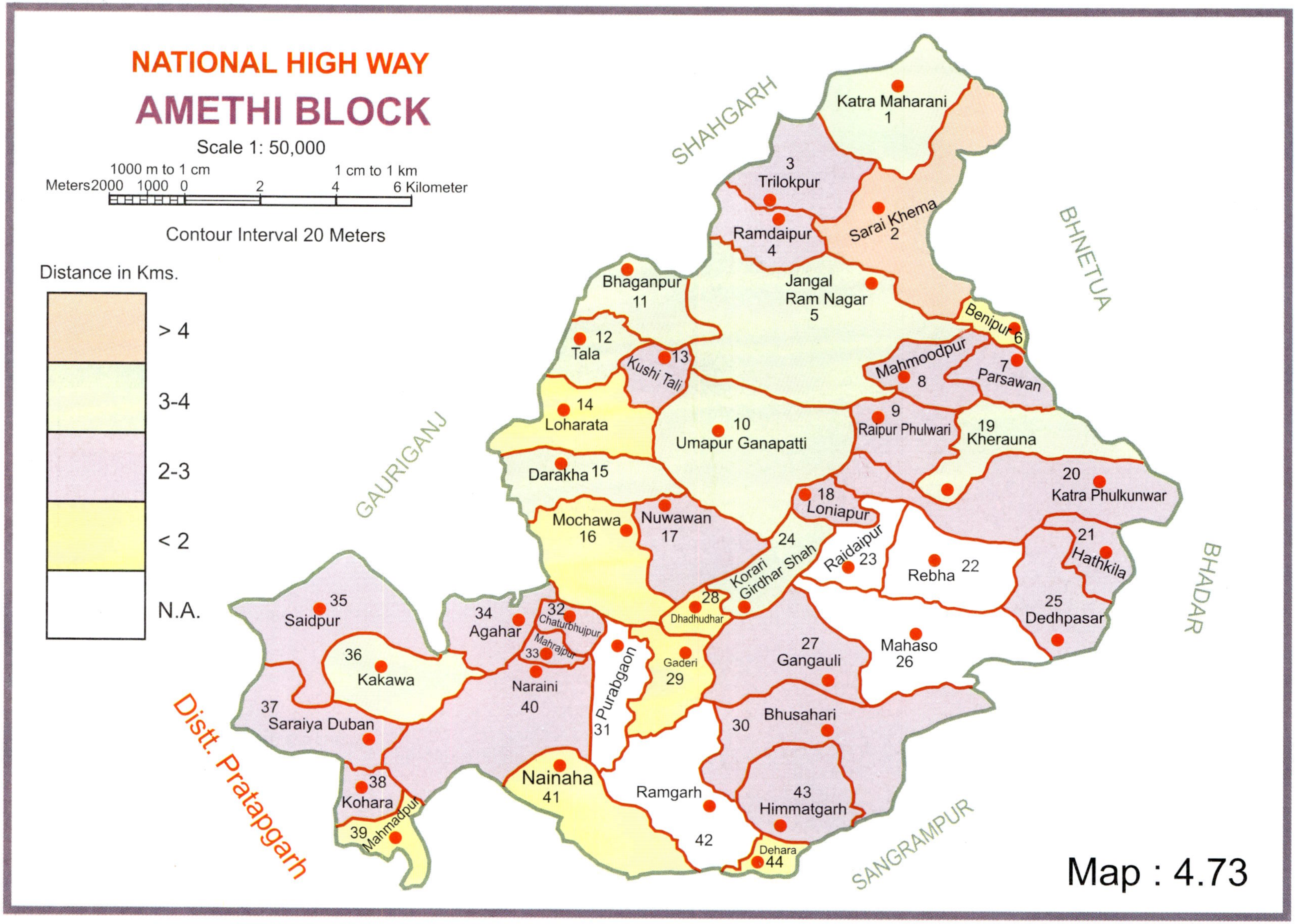

Map 4.73: National Highway

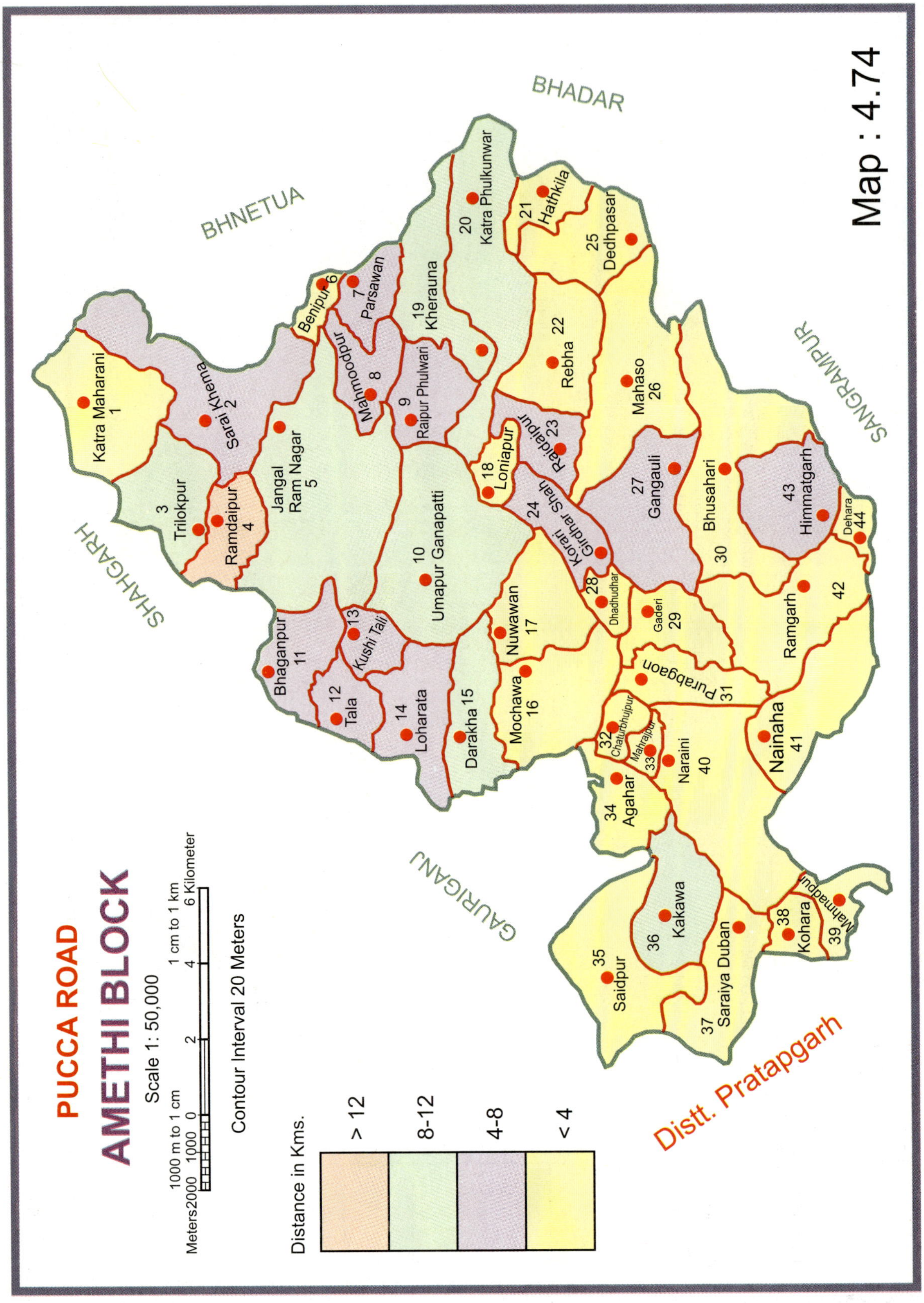

Map 4.74: Pucca Road

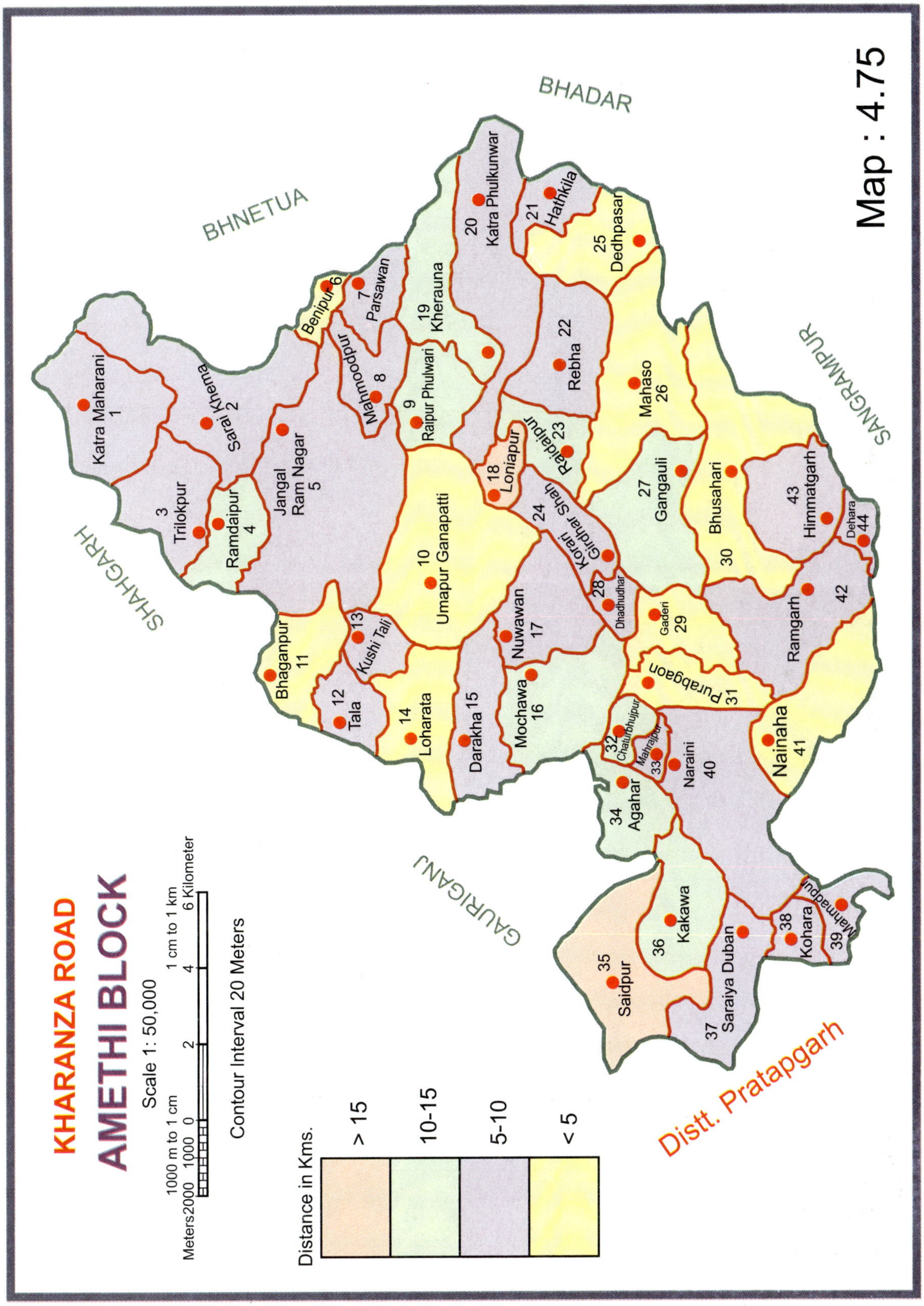

Map 4.75: Kharanza Road

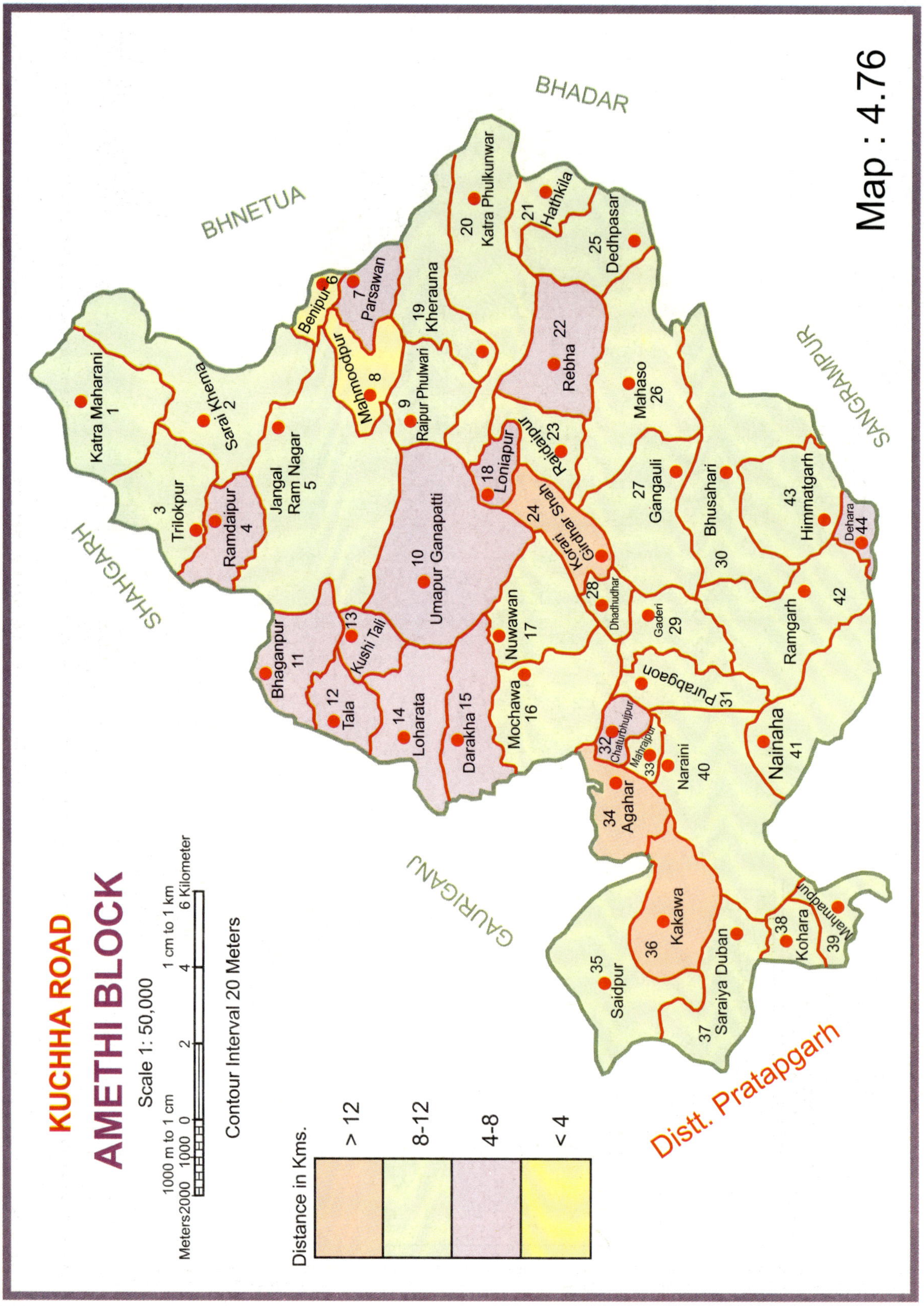

Map 4.76: Kuchha Road

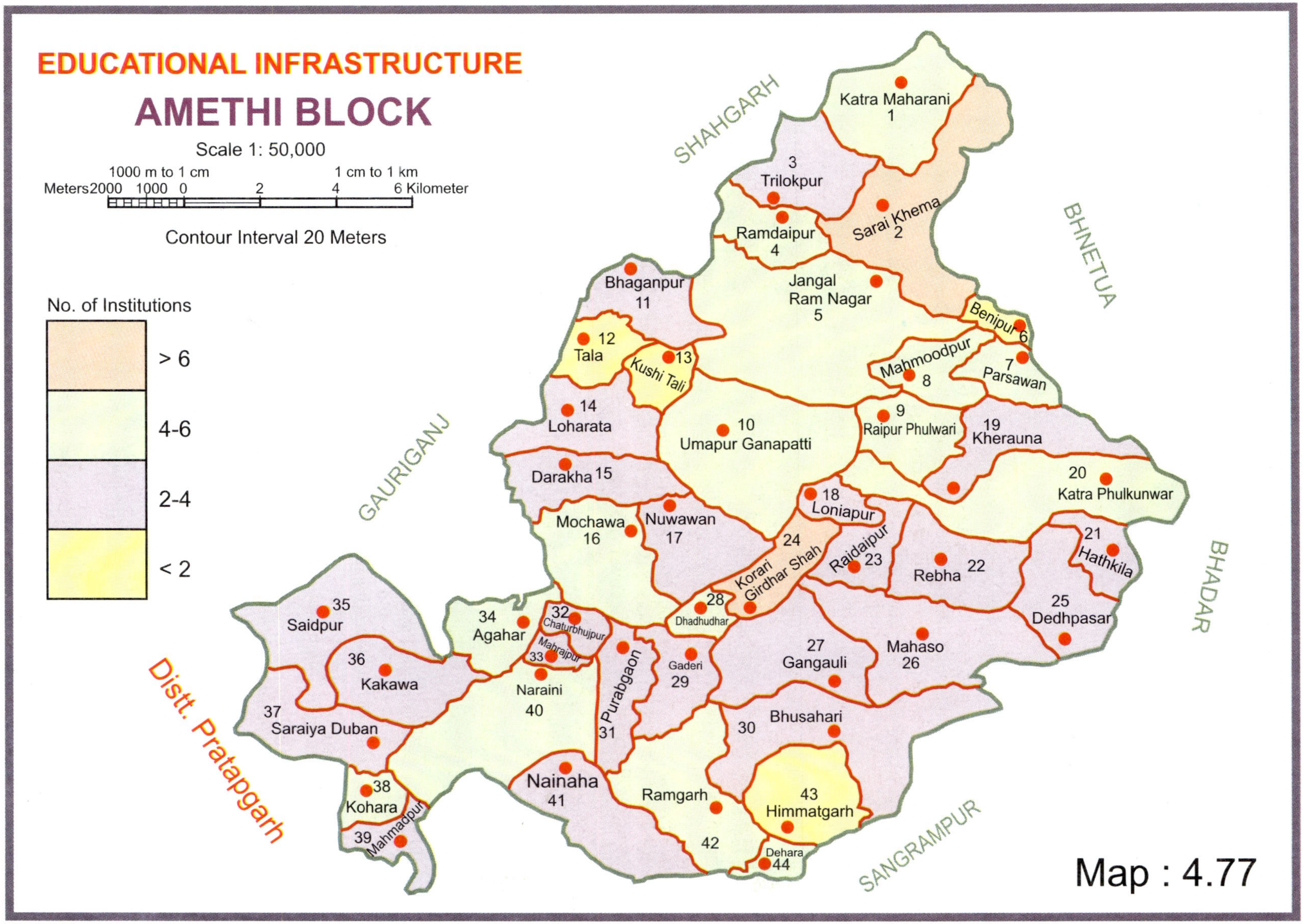

Map 4.77: Educational Infrastructure

Index

Advanced technology applications, 25, 108
Agricultural activities, 2, 13, 46, 69, 71, 105, 122–123, 144, 147–148
Agricultural cropping, 13, 71, 75, 77, 79, 83–84
  barley cropped area, 80
  fodder cropped area, 83
  mustard cropped area, 82
  pattern, 81
  peas cropped area, 82
  potato cropped area, 83
  rice cropped area, 79
  sugarcane cropped area, 83
  wheat cropped area, 80
Agricultural crops, 14, 79, 87, 89, 104, 146–147
Agricultural implements
  agricultural implements/tools, 92
  high-tech cultivators, 92
  iron cultivators, 90
  other high-tech implement, 93
  tractors, 93
  wood cultivator, 90
Agricultural inputs, 3, 19, 102–103, 145–146, 153
Agricultural labourers, 12, 14, 55, 68, 71–72, 98, 143
Agricultural land, 73, 89–90, 93–94, 104, 146–147
Agricultural productivity, 3, 13–14, 32, 42, 55, 72, 77, 79, 84–85, 87, 89–90, 103–105, 146–147, 153
Agriculture and Horticulture Department, 111
Agro-forestry, 13, 72
Agro-industries workers, 59–60, 69, 98, 102–103, 106, 144–145, 148
Agro-industries, 4, 15, 28, 113, 119, 122–123, 136, 138, 141, 150, 152
Ahirs and Gadaria caste, 56
Angan Badi Kendra, 129
Animal Hospital Institutional Infrastructures, 137, 152
Animal Hospitals and Medical Health Centres, 138, 152
Animal husbandry activities, 69, 97, 105, 144, 148
Animal husbandry, 2–3, 14, 28, 48, 56, 94–95, 105, 132, 141, 148, 153
  buffalos, 94
  cows, 94
  goats, 96
  hens/cocks, 97
  horses, 96
  pigs, 97
Animal husbandry workers, 12, 56, 60, 68, 94, 98–100, 103, 106, 143, 145, 148
  deprived, 105, 148
Aspirations, 20–22, 25, 29, 108, 120, 141
Assistant Nursing Midwife Centres, 130

Backward castes ranging, 51
Backward castes, 45–46, 48–49, 51, 53, 68–69, 94, 143–144
Backwardness, socio-educational, 69, 143
Banking infrastructure, 133
Barley, 13, 79–82
Below Poverty Line (BPL), 11, 119–120, 122, 125, 127, 130
Benipur Village Panchayats, 48
Better quality of life, 1, 22, 29, 120, 141
Bharat Sanchar Nigam Ltd. (BSNL), 132, 137, 152
Bio-gas, 89, 105, 147
Block Development, 34, 129
Block Panchayat, 19, 37, 111, 124–125, 127
Buffalos, 14, 94–97, 105, 148
Business Administration, 66, 127

Capacity building, 23, 25, 109–110
Carpenters, 32, 46, 49–50, 69, 144
Cartographic Techniques, 20
Caste composition, 2–3, 12, 19, 28, 31–32, 37, 39, 44, 47, 52–53, 68, 70, 141, 143–144
  Brahmins, 45, 52
  Carpenter, 46, 49, 68
  Gupta, 46, 49, 68, 143
  Kshatriya, 45
  Kurmi, 46, 48, 68, 143
  minorities, 51
  occupational, 60
  other backward, 45–46, 51
  Pal/Gaderia, 14, 96
  professional, 153
  Rajput, 52–53
  Scheduled Caste, 46
  Shudras, 45
  upper, 52–53
  Vaisya, 45
  Yadav, 46, 48–49
Chemical fertilizers, 14, 87–89, 104, 115, 147
Chief Development Officer (CDO), 113
Child development, 111, 130
Collection of milk, 69, 144
Commercial agricultural system, 79
Commercial scale, 83
Compost fertilizers, 88–90, 104–105, 147
  use of, 89
Constitution of India, 3, 109, 135, 149
Constitutional Amendments Act, 25, 109
Construction of low cost houses, 120, 136, 150
Construction workers, 56–57, 60, 68–69, 143–144
Cows, 14, 94–95, 97, 105, 148
  distribution of, 94
Cropped area, 80, 82–84, 104, 146
  agricultural, 104, 147

Cropping system, 123
Cultivated area, 13, 85, 87–89, 103, 146

Darakha village panchayats, 66, 99, 129
Data management system, 24
Demography
female population, 43
households, 42
houses, 40
male population, 43
population density, 44
population, 42
Department of Science and Technology, 10, 24
Development
common people's, 60
rur-ban, 23
socio-economic, 40, 53, 60, 111
sustainable economic integrated, 72
urban, 32, 110
Development of appropriate tools, 108
Development of rural areas, 1
Development of spatial data technologies, 108
Development programmes, 2–3, 25–26, 29, 31, 107, 111, 134, 139, 142, 149
completed rural, 115
integrated, 23, 27, 109, 140
planned, 21
rural, 2, 27, 37, 139
Development schemes, 110
Developmental activities, 129
economic, 2
Developmental goals, 10, 20
Developmental planning, 2, 21
Developmental plans, 39
Developmental programmes, 23
implemented village, 31
integrated, 21
planned, 21
Distribution of cultivators, 55
District Development Committee, 109
District Fisheries Development Agency (DFDA), 112
District Planning Committee (DPC), 113
Drainage system, 104, 146
Drinking water, 15, 28, 113, 115–118, 135, 138, 141, 150, 152–153
contaminated, 115
good quality, 115, 118
hand pumps, 117
India Mark-II hand pumps, 116
mission, 115
other sources, 118
sources of, 118, 135, 150
water supply, 116

Economic backwardness, 12, 14, 71, 76, 84, 89, 92, 98, 102–103, 119, 146
Economic development, 11, 73, 103, 120, 127, 136, 146, 150
integrated, 1, 26, 120, 139
Economic growth, 2, 40, 72, 123, 127, 136, 150
Economic Infrastructure, 72
Economic Resources Data Base Management System (ERDBMS), 72, 103, 145
Economic sector, 72
Education
adult, 60
elementary, 130
Medical, 66
public school, 138, 152
technical, 66
Educational goals, 60
Educational infrastructure, 4, 15, 28, 60, 127, 136–138, 141, 151–152
Educational profile, 3, 12, 19, 28, 31–32, 38–39, 70, 141, 145
Educational programmes, 44
managerial, 66
various, 60
Electricity, 15, 28, 113, 121–123, 136, 141, 150
Energy
commercial electricity, 122
household electricity, 121
non-conventional sources of energy, 120
Explanation mechanism, 29, 141
Explanatory system, 19

Female population, 40, 43–44, 69, 144
Fertility status, 14, 71, 75, 79, 84, 88–90, 103–105, 146–147
Fertilizers
compost, 89
nitrogen, 88
phosphate, 88
use of, 87
Financial powers, 3, 36, 111, 135, 149
Fisheries and Animal Husbandary Programmes, 72
Fisheries Department, 112
Fodder, 3, 79, 83, 104, 147, 153
Food Supply, 111–112

General seeds, 85, 87
Geo-Spatial Data Management, 24
Geographic Information System, 20, 24–25, 29, 141
Goats, 56, 94, 96–97, 105, 148
Government Tube-wells, 77
Grassroots level planning, 25
Grassroots level policy, 25
Green manuring, 88, 104–105, 147
Growing population, 3, 11, 15, 27, 104, 109, 118, 135, 138, 140, 147, 150, 152–153
Guptas, 45–46, 49, 69, 144

HAL Public School and Marketing Centre and Army Recruitment Centre, 133
Hamlet villages, 18, 40, 119, 121
Hand pumps, 111, 117–118
Hanumatha Rao Committee, 24
Health centres, primary Medical, 15
Hens/cocks, 94, 97, 105, 148
High Yielding Variety, 71, 73, 85, 87
application of, 71, 85
seeds, 72
High-tech cultivators, 92–93, 105, 148
Himmatgarh village panchayats, 49, 52
Hindu Temples, 113, 129
Historical period, 5, 11–12, 40, 45–46, 52–53, 60, 68, 70, 76, 89–90, 94, 143–144
Holistic analysis, 2, 24
Horses, 14, 94, 96–97, 105, 148
Horticulture Department, 111
Human Infrastructural Resources Data Management System (HIRDMS), 153
Human infrastructural resources, 10, 32
Human Infrastructure Economic Infrastructure, 12
Human Infrastructure Information System, 2
Human Infrastructure Institutional Infrastructure, 14
Human Infrastructure Social Infrastructure, 11
Human Resources Data Management System, 23–26, 29, 31–32, 68, 72–73, 142
Human resources data, 25–26, 29, 31, 141
Human resources information system, 25

Implementation process, 20, 29, 141
Implementing institutions, 12, 32, 66, 70, 108, 145
Income
of agricultural workers, 98
of agro-industries workers, 102
of animal husbandry workers, 99
of business workers, 101
of cultivators, 98
of non-skilled workers, 99
of skilled workers, 99
of transportation workers, 101

Indicators
  choice of the, 15
  economic infrastructures, 17
  institutional infrastructures, 18
  of social infrastructures, 16
  social sectoral, 31
Indira Awas Yojana (IAY), 15
Industrial Training Institute, 15, 65, 137, 151
Industrial Training, 65–66
Information and Communication Technology (ICT), 24
Information System, 36
Information Technology, 127
Infrastructural Resources Data Management System (IRDMS), 107–108, 134, 153
Infrastructural resources, 3, 6, 10, 19–20, 22, 24, 26, 28–29, 33, 37, 136, 140–142, 150
Infrastructural system, 122
Inorganic amendments, 14, 71–73, 89, 104–105, 147
Insecticides, 13–14, 19, 71–73, 87, 104, 115, 147
  use of, 87
Institutional capacity building, 10, 25, 108
Institutional capacity, 108
Institutional Infrastructural Indicators, 15
Institutional Infrastructural Resources Data Management System (IIRDMS), 107–108, 134, 149
Institutional infrastructural resources, 3, 107, 109, 115, 133–135, 138, 149, 152
Institutional infrastructure, 2–4, 11, 14–15, 18–19, 27–28, 107–109, 113–115, 119, 126–127, 130–135, 137, 139, 141, 148–149, 152
  basic, 15
  developed, 27, 139
  educational, 128–129, 136–138, 151–152
  historical, 129
  indicators of, 18
  maintained, 114
  professional educational, 137, 151
Institutions, 23, 127
  decision-making, 25
  educational, 44, 127–129, 137
  end-user, 25
  local level, 109
  multi-level, 23
  social, 38–39, 68, 143
Integrated Child Development Scheme (ICDS), 130
Integrated development, 2, 20, 22, 26–27, 29, 31–32, 37, 39, 70, 73, 103, 109–110, 123, 139, 145–146
Integrated Rural Development Programmes (IRDP), 2, 15, 24, 26, 29, 31, 103, 110, 146
Integrated rural development, 25–26, 29, 32, 73, 142
Integrated sustainable development, 1, 3
Integrated village development, 2, 12, 27, 34, 107–108, 113, 115, 125, 127, 133, 135–136, 139, 149–151, 153
Iron cultivators, 13, 90–93, 105, 147
  use of, 90
Irrigated area, sources of, 78–79
Irrigated land, 77
Irrigation, 3, 13, 32, 74, 77–80, 103–104, 115, 146, 153
  canal irrigated area, 77
  net irrigated area, 77
  other sources of irrigated area, 78
  private tube-well irrigated area, 78
  sources of, 13, 71–73, 77–79
  tube-well irrigated area, 78

Jeep, 113, 130–132, 137, 151
Job Card, 125

Kali Temple, 129, 137, 151
Kharanza road, 14, 113, 123, 125, 127, 136, 150
Kingship, 5, 11–12, 28, 45, 49, 53, 69, 73, 140, 144
Kohara Village Panchayats, 55, 63, 76, 93, 101, 127
Kuchcha road, 113, 125, 127
Kurmis, 32, 46, 48, 69, 144

Land concentration, 5, 12–13, 103, 146
Land development, 153
  integrated rural, 28, 141
Land holdings, 73, 75–76, 87, 92
Land owners, 71, 73, 75
Land ownership, 5, 11, 28, 45–46, 48–49, 60, 69, 73, 75–76, 140, 144, 153
  holdings between 2 and 4 hectares, 76
  holdings between one and two hectares, 75
  holdings less than one hectare, 75
  holdings more than 4 hectares, 76
Land records, 45
Land revenue records, 16, 45
Land revenue tax collection, 40, 45
Land rights, 5, 45–46, 48–49, 60, 68–69, 73, 143–144
Landless, 69, 73, 118–120, 127, 144
Legislative Assembly Local Area Development Fund, 115–116
Literacy
  business administration, 66
  graduate education, 63
  graduate engineers, 66
  high school education, 62
  industrial training, 65
  intermediate education, 63
  junior education, 62
  polytechnic, 66
  post graduate education, 65
  primary education, 62
  professional education, 65
Livelihood of weakers, 27, 73, 139
Local Area Development (LAD), 10, 25, 28, 36, 108, 115–116, 124, 140
Local Area Development Scheme, 36
Lohar, 46, 68–69, 90, 143–144
Low agricultural productivity, 13–14, 71, 85, 87–88, 92
Low cost housing, 119
Low size land, 92–94

Machinery, 93, 103, 106, 145, 148
Maharajpur and Kohara village panchayats, 51
Mahatma Gandhi National Rojgar Guarantee Act, 127
Male dominated society, 69, 144
Management and Medical and Health Educational institutions, 15
Management System, 25
Marketing centres, 57, 59, 69, 111, 127, 133, 144
Medical Health Centres, 113, 132–133
Micro level
  development unit, 110
  information system, 16
  policy planners, 108
Mid-day meal, 130
Milking programme, 56
Minorities population, 51–52
MNREGA programmes, 125
Multi-institutional
  framework, 25
  research, 25, 29, 134, 142, 149
Munshiganj Marketing Centre, 133
Musafirkhana, 11
Mustard, 13, 82, 84

Natioanl Highway Authority of India (NHAI), 127
National Atlas for Thematic Maps Organisation (NATMO), 18
National Resources Data Management System, 25
Natural and Human Resources Data Management System, 10
Natural Resources and Human Infrastructure Information System, 2
Natural Resources Data Management System (NRDMS), 25
Net Irrigated Area, 77
Nishad, 68–69, 143–144

Nitrogen Fertilizer, 88–89, 104, 147
Non-conventional sources of energy, 15, 28, 113, 120–123, 136, 141, 150
Non-scientific systems, 14
Non-skilled workers, 55–56, 68–69, 98–99, 102, 105, 143–144, 148
Non-spatial data, collection of, 24, 107
NPK, 13, 88

Operational implementation, 20
Operationalizing, 29, 107, 134, 142, 149
Optimum utilization, 3, 27, 29–30, 70, 79, 104, 108, 119, 140–142, 145, 147, 153
Organizational capacity, 25

Panchayat Institutional Infrastructure, 129
Panchayati Raj Institutions (PRIs), 3, 11, 15, 18–20, 24, 28, 37, 129, 141, 149
Participatory Planning Process (PPP), 3, 20, 27, 139–140
Participatory planning, 3, 109, 111
Pensions, 111
Pesticides, 13–14, 19, 71–73, 87, 104, 115, 147
Phosphate fertilizer, 88–89, 104, 147
Pigs, 94, 97, 105, 148
Planned programmes, 3, 20, 29, 110, 141
Planning process, 10–12, 19, 21–24, 28, 31, 68, 72–73, 107, 110, 133–134, 140, 142, 149
Planning programmes, 73
Policy planners, 21, 60, 84, 104, 117, 119, 121, 135, 138, 147, 150, 152
Policy planning, 2, 12, 18, 20–21, 27–28, 30–32, 73, 108, 113, 115, 129, 135, 139–140, 142, 149
Polytechnic institutions, 15
Poor agricultural productivity, 13–14, 71, 79, 102–104, 123, 145–147
Post harvest technology, 123
Potato, 13, 79, 83–84, 104, 147
Pradhan Mantri Gram Sadak Yojana (PMGSY), 124, 127
Primary education, 60, 62, 129, 138, 152
Primary field survey, 11, 26, 29, 31–33, 68, 141, 143
Primary Health Centres, 130, 133
Private hand pumps, 15, 115, 117–118, 135, 150
Professional education, 60, 65, 127
  business administration, 66
  graduate engineers, 66
  industrial training, 65
  polytechnic, 66
Programme implementation, 32
Public Call Centres, 132
Public Works Departments, 112
Pucca road, 14, 113, 123–124, 127

Rainwater harvesting, 78–79, 104, 146
Rajiv Gandhi Grameen Vidyutikaran Yojana, 120–122
Religious and Historical Infrastructure, 129
Remote rural areas, 1–2, 21, 27, 44, 103, 106, 109, 115, 117, 122–123, 136, 139–140, 146, 148, 150
Remote rural villages, 2, 27, 73, 122–123, 128, 140
Research community, 26, 109, 135, 149
Revenue villages, 6, 18, 29, 33–34, 40, 42, 110, 117, 119, 121, 127, 132, 141
  including, 6, 32, 40
Road
  kharanza road, 125
  kuchcha road, 125
  national highways, 124
  pucca road, 124
Rural areas, 1–3, 21, 23, 27, 109–110, 139
Rural development planners, 66
Rural development programmes, 2, 19, 21, 27, 30, 32, 109, 139, 142
Rural development schemes, 29, 142

Scholarships, 111
Scientific system, 104, 106, 147–148
Sectoral economy, 2
  primary, 2
  tertiary, 3
Sectoral indicators, 32, 34, 68, 143
Seeds and Fertilizers, Use of, 86
Seeds High Yielding Variety Seeds, 85
Seeds, 71–73, 84–87
Self-financing scheme, 15, 128
Service class providers, 11–12, 53, 69–70, 144–145
Service providers, 5, 12, 45–46, 49, 51, 53, 60, 69, 144
Settlement colonies, 117–118, 121, 124–125, 127
Shiva Temples, 129
Shudras, 45–46, 69, 144
Skill development, 103, 145
Skilled workers, 56, 60, 68–69, 98–99, 102, 105, 143–144, 148
Small scale industries, 4, 15, 28, 59, 119, 122–123, 136, 141, 150, 153
Social associations, 39, 68, 143
Social class system, 39
Social infrastructure, 2–3, 6, 11–12, 27–28, 31, 37–39, 41–42, 52, 59, 67–68, 139, 141–143
  integrated development of, 70, 145
Social Infrastructure, 37
  indicators of, 16
Social sectoral data, analysis of, 68, 142
Social system, 32, 38–40
Social upliftment, 69–70, 144–145
Social-economic-institutional data, 143
Social-forestry programmes, 13
Socio-economic planning, 20
Socio-economic-institutional infrastructures, 16, 20–21, 25, 27, 29, 32, 68, 139, 141, 143
Soil structure, 40
Soil, 12, 14, 71, 75–76, 79, 84, 88–90, 102–105, 145–147
  deteriorated fertility status of, 103, 146
  matiyar, 104, 146
Solar water pumps, 122, 136, 150
Spatial data management system, 108, 135, 149
Spatial data management technology, 25
Spatial data technologies, 25–26, 108
Special package, 119–120, 136, 150
Sub-Post Office, 130
Sugarcane, 13, 79, 83–84
Survey, intensive field, 16
Sustainable development, 29–30, 73, 107, 109, 141–142
Sustainable integrated development, 73

Taluqdars, 4–5, 11, 28, 73, 140
Tanga, 14, 131–132, 137, 151
Tap water, 116, 118
Tax collectors, 73
Technology development, 72
Technology inputs, 108
Techno-scientific methods, 84
Telecommunication, 132
Tertiary sectors, 2
Tractors, 13, 90, 93, 105, 148
Trade centre, 57
Traditional cultivation system, 93
Training programmes, special skill development, 106, 148
Transfer of technology, 108
Transport Communication, 130
Transportation workers, 12, 57, 60, 68, 98, 101, 103, 143, 145, 148
Trilokpur village panchayats, 49
Tube-wells, 111

Urban areas, 1–2, 27, 122, 139
Usarization, 12, 14, 71, 103–104, 146
Uttar Pradesh State Road Transport Corporation (UPSRTC), 138, 152

Vaisya, 45, 69, 144

Varna system, 39, 44–45
Vedic Period Society, 39
Village beneficiaries, 27, 138, 140, 152
Village development planners, 12, 103, 146
Village development, 21–22, 29, 34, 38, 110, 133, 135, 141, 149
sustainable, 22
Village Information System, 16, 32–35, 37, 72–73, 103, 109, 135, 145, 149, 152–153
Village Land Management Committee Members, 17
Village panchayats, 3, 14–15, 26–27, 34, 40, 56–57, 65–66, 72–73, 109–111, 115–116, 123–125, 127–133, 135–138, 140–141, 149–152
Village Patwari, 29, 141
Village Pradhan, 17, 116, 127, 129
Villages
developed, 48
dominant, 48
remote, 3, 27, 127, 130, 133, 139, 153
rural, 2

Water logging, 104, 146
Water resources, 22
Water supply, 15, 116
tap, 115–116, 118, 135, 150
Water
contaminated, 118
excess canal, 103, 146
irrigated, 104, 146
natural, 79
underground, 115
Waterlogged land, 13, 80, 84, 104
Waterlogging problems, 12, 14
Welfare programmes, 3, 27, 32, 110, 135, 139, 149
Wheat, 13, 79–80, 84, 104, 146
Women, 111, 130
Wood cultivators, 90, 93, 105, 147
Workers
agricultural labourers, 55
agro-industries workers, 59
animal husbandry workers, 56
business workers, 57
construction workers, 56
cultivators, 53
non-skilled workers, 55
office workers, 59
plantation , 56
skilled-workers, 56
small scale, 59
social-infrastructure, 54
transportation workers, 57
Worship programmes, 32, 45, 94

Yadavs, distribution of, 49

Zamindari/Taluqdari Abolition Act, 71, 73
Zila Panchayat, 34, 116
Zila Yojana, 16, 36
Zila Yojana Samiti, 113